MAKING READING REAL

SHARON M. SNYDERS, Ph.D.
Ivy Tech Community College

PEARSON

Boston Columbus Indianapolis New York San Francisco Upper Saddle River
Amsterdam Cape Town Dubai London Madrid Milan Munich Paris Montreal Toronto
Delhi Mexico City Sao Paulo Sydney Hong Kong Seoul Singapore Taipei Tokyo

Editor-in-Chief: Eric Stano
Senior Acquisitions Editor: Nancy Blaine
Development Editor: Paul Sarkis
Editorial Assistant: Jamie Fortner
Senior Marketing Manager: Kurt Massey
Project Manager: Anne Ricigliano
Project Coordination, Text Design, Art Rendering, and Electronic Page Makeup: Nesbitt Graphics, Inc.
Executive Digital Producer: Stefanie A. Snajder
Senior Digital Editor: Robert St. Laurent
Text Permissions: Warren Drabek, Express Permissions
Photo Permissions: Kerri Wilson, PreMediaGlobal
Cover Design Manager: John Callahan
Cover Designer: Kay Petronio
Cover Photos: yuyangc/Shutterstock and Gl0ck/Shutterstock
Manufacturing Buyer: Mary Ann Gloriande
Printer and Binder: Quebecor World Book Services/Taunton
Cover Printer: Lehigh-Phoenix Color/Hagerstown

Credits and acknowledgments borrowed from other sources and reproduced, with permission, in this textbook appear on the appropriate page within text [or on pages 498–501].

Lexile® is a trademark of MetaMetrics, Inc., and is registered in the United States and abroad.

Library of Congress Cataloging-in-Publication Data

Snyders, S. M.
  Making reading real / Sharon M. Snyders.
    p. cm.
  Includes bibliographical references and index.
  ISBN 978-0-13-242310-6
  1. Reading (Higher education)—Textbooks.   2. Study skills—Textbooks.   I.
Title.
  LB2395.3.S69 2012
  428.4071′1—dc23

1 2 3 4 5 6 7 8 9 10—QWT—14 13 12 11

PEARSON

www.pearsonhighered.com

ISBN-13: 978-0-13-242310-6 Student Edition
ISBN-10:   0-13-242310-3 Student Edition

ISBN-13: 978-0-13-242311-3   AIE
ISBN-10:   0-13-242311-1   AIE

DEDICATION

To my daughter Skye and my husband Mark.
Also to my students who make teaching and learning a joy!

Thanks for encouraging and blessing me every day!

—Sharon M. Snyders

Brief Contents

Detailed Contents

2 Main Ideas   63

3 Supporting Details   116

4 Implied Main Ideas 157

7 Facts and Opinions 288

10 Critical Thinking 415

A Note to Students

Welcome to a new way to read! You probably already know that reading is critical to your college and life success. When we need information or inspiration, we might look to sources such as books, magazines, newspapers, or the Internet for answers or ideas. We seek solutions from reliable sources when we care about issues. When we are interested, we read more, and when we read more, we improve our skills and become more confident and competent at reading.

Busy people are not usually willing to spend (or waste) time reading just anything. There is too much out there to read and not enough time to read it all. When we are gathering information, we may become overwhelmed with the amount of information available. We need to choose to read sources that are useful, relevant, and real. It is my hope that *Making Reading Real* helps you reach your goals and dreams.

I wish you the best!

Sharon Snyders

Preface

I was inspired to write this textbook when I looked at my students' faces and heard their complaints about how meaningless the material was in the reading textbooks I was assigning. When I heard them talk about how they just didn't like to read or express how hard it was, I knew there had to be a better way. Many of my students told me they had never read a complete book and rarely read anything at all! It was heartbreaking to see students who had decided they would never be someone who was good at reading. My students came from different life circumstances and were dealing with many difficult and sometimes dangerous issues in their lives. I knew that if I could just find a way to get them reading, they might find answers, inspiration, and hope to change their lives.

Unique Features of This Text

Making Reading Real is different from other reading textbooks because it includes three key features to keep students interested and help them to learn: relevant content, diverse sources, and engaging activities designed expressly for different learning styles.

This book includes the familiar structures of a reading textbook that we need for academic skills development: building vocabulary with word parts and in context, finding the main ideas and supporting details, finding implied main ideas, recognizing patterns of organization, detecting facts and opinions, recognizing inferences and an author's purpose and tone, and developing critical thinking.

While this book includes coverage of—and practice with—the necessary reading skills, it also includes content selected to be relevant to students. Unlike other books, many of which include unrelated excerpts from different disciplines, each chapter of *Making Reading Real* has engaging material from diverse sources—magazines, the Internet, literature, textbooks, and other media—all of which relate to a central theme. The themes were chosen to help engage students in the process of reading, and they include topics such as life relationships, money management, and health and wellness.

Each chapter in *Making Reading Real* also includes coverage and activities for students with different learning styles so that *all* students will improve their reading skills. At the beginning of every chapter there is a *Spotlight on Learning* box. This section highlights different learning styles and gives examples of ways the learning styles are used. Individual chapters also include collaborative projects, kinesthetic or hands-on activities, personal reflections, and ways to use the Web to enhance reading. Activities related to each lesson are grouped together within each chapter.

Each student will have the opportunity to access and understand his or her own learning style by going to an Internet Web site. Students will also learn an effective reading strategy, *SQ3R* (presented in context in Chapter 2, "Main Ideas"), and some note-taking strategies that will help them succeed in this course as well as in other college courses.

Making Reading Real incorporates many activities that reinforce knowledge so students can build confidence and competence with a particular skill. In addition, some activities involve new information using the latest technology and others may encourage students to get involved in current social issues.

Integrated throughout the book, students will also find the *Spotlight on Success Plan:*

Spotlight on Success Plan

PRACTICE *THE NEW SKILL* (3 practice questions)

REVIEW *WHAT YOU LEARNED* (5 review questions)

MASTER *THE LESSON* (10 section mastery questions)

The *Spotlight on Success Plan* works like this:

When a concept is first introduced, students are given an example and then three quick practice exercises. When students immediately practice the new skill, they build competence and confidence. After several concepts have been learned, students are then given a five-question review. The reviews may be more challenging as they cover more than one concept. Since the students have confidently been practicing each concept as it is presented throughout the chapter, the review will reinforce their learning. At the end of a chapter, but before the longer reading selections are presented, each chapter has two to three ten-question mastery tests. The mastery tests are more challenging and comprehensive for the skills presented in the chapter.

Students who have used the *Spotlight on Success Plan* have indicated they are comfortable when they know what to expect in each chapter. They can rely on the rhythm of building up to the more difficult material. They like the quick exercises when they are first learning and are more willing to tackle the challenges as the chapter progresses.

Instructors can adapt the Spotlight on Success Plan to fit the needs of students. When students need immediate practice to learn a new skill, they can turn to the "Practice the New Skill" exercises following the topic. If students understand the concept with just the example in class or by doing one of the three practice exercises, instructors can either skip the other exercises or assign them as homework.

The "Review What You Learned" exercises can be used as quick quizzes in class or as out-of-class assignments. The exercises in Review are more challenging than those in Practice. Assessing the student at this level will help the instructor know if more instruction and/or practice are needed.

The "Master the Lesson" assessment is more challenging than the Practice and Review. Instructors may choose to assign one of the Mastery tests as homework or as an in-class quiz. If more practice is needed, the second Mastery test can be done.

As mentioned earlier, each chapter also includes in-depth readings related to the chapter theme, so students can pull together the skills and practice using them on more challenging texts. The readings at the end of each chapter come from (1) the Internet, (2) textbooks, (3) literature, (4) magazines/periodicals, and (5) visual images.

Making Reading Real was written to give students real choices about what they read. Each chapter contains more readings than most students and professors will cover in a week or two of class. Most of the readings are only excerpts of longer, richer, and more in-depth material. All of the material has been cited to give students the reference if they'd like to read more. I carefully chose materials for this book hoping they will spark curiosity and encourage students to read more. The intent of this book is to present opportunities to become a better reader while using practical, useful, thought-provoking, entertaining, and uplifting material. It is my greatest hope as a teacher and author that students will improve their skills, confidence, and enjoyment of reading through *Making Reading Real*.

Organization

Each chapter presents reading skills and concepts while adhering to a theme. We start Chapter 1, Vocabulary, with the theme of Adjusting to College. This offer tips about getting used to college and at the same time, teaches vocabulary through context clues and word parts such as prefixes, roots, and suffixes.

Chapter 2, Main Ideas, helps students to focus on an author's main point in paragraphs related to the theme of Life Relationships. This chapter includes reading about accepting others who are different from us and improving the relationships important in our lives. After developing the skills of finding the topic and the main idea, students can practice their skills with several longer readings at the end of the chapter. This chapter also introduces students to the SQ3R strategy for reading.

In Chapter 3, the text will guide students to better understand Supporting Details. This chapter uses reading material related to the theme of Time Management. Material in this chapter is related to managing time at school, at work, and in personal life.

Once students have mastered finding the main idea and supporting details, they learn how to find Implied Main Ideas in text in Chapter 4. This chapter uses the theme of Global Issues to develop reading skills while thinking more deeply about issues affecting our world.

In Chapters 5 and 6, students will learn to determine an author's Patterns of Organization. Paying attention to an author's organizational pattern helps students to read more effectively and efficiently. In these chapters, the readings relate to the theme of Money Management.

Chapter 7 helps students begin to develop the skills for critical thinking, starting with separating Facts from Opinions. Using the theme of Current Social Issues, exercises and activities are used to develop students' ability to distinguish opinions from facts, while also exposing them to issues related to politics, populations, and poverty.

Once students can tell the difference between facts and opinions, they learn to make Inferences. Chapter 8 helps students to read between the lines and begin to draw important conclusions in reading. In this chapter, the theme of Goal Setting and Achievement offers true stories and articles about people who have achieved their personal, academic, and career goals.

Chapter 9 will enable students to determine the Author's Purpose and Tone. Using the theme of Entertainment, students will read selections related to movies, music, food, sports, and hobbies while learning to understand how authors use different words to convey meaning. They will also learn how writers often intertwine more than one purpose to persuade, inform, and/or entertain their audiences/readers.

Making Reading Real enables students to incorporate everything they have learned in a chapter on Critical Thinking. In Chapter 10, they will synthesize their reading skills and apply them to reading text from timely and engaging sources. The theme of Health and Wellness is useful since we are bombarded every day with how-to articles, Internet sites, and televisions shows about self-improvement. Critical Thinking is crucial when we are sorting through the volumes of material available on this topic today. This chapter incorporates different perspectives and teaches students how to determine the validity and intention of authors' words.

With the help of *Making Reading Real*, my hope is that students will develop the ability to examine written materials, explore diverse sources, and determine their usefulness for real decisions that need to be made in life.

Supplements to Accompany *Making Reading Real*

Instructor's Manual and Test Bank (ISBN 013242312X). The Instructor's Manual features lecture hints, in-class activities, handouts, and quizzes to accompany each chapter, as well as sample course outlines and other helpful resources for structuring and managing a developmental reading course. The Test Bank consists of 30 multiple-choice questions per chapter. The Instructor's Manual and Test Bank is available both in print and for download from Pearson's Instructor Resource Center (www.pearsonhighered.com/irc). Written by Rochelle Favale of College of DuPage and Mary Jeffery of College of Dupage and Waubonsee Community College.

MyTest Test Bank (ISBN 0205222560). Pearson MyTest is a powerful assessment generation program that helps instructors easily create and print quizzes, study guides, and exams. Select questions are drawn from the Instructor's Manual and Test Bank to accompany *Making Reading Real* and from other developmental reading test banks. Unique questions may be added. Save the finished test as a Word document or PDF to export it to WebCT or BlackBoard. Available at www.pearsonmytest.com.

PowerPoint Presentation (ISBN 0205210740). PowerPoint presentations to accompany each chapter consist of classroom-ready lecture outline slides, lecture tips and classroom activities, and review questions. Available for download from Pearson's Instructor Resource Center. Written by Diane Schellack of Burlington County College.

Answer Key (ISBN 020511895X). The Answer Key contains the solutions to the exercises in the student edition of the text. Available for download from Pearson's Instructor Resource Center.

Annotated Instructor's Edition (ISBN 0132423111). An annotated instructor's edition is available for this text. It provides answers to the activities and exercises in the text printed on the write-on lines that follow each exercise.

Acknowledgments

Thank you to the following reviewers who took your time to read various versions of the manuscript and provide valuable suggestions to improve *Making Reading Real*:

Karin Alderfer, *Miami Dade College*

Angela Barber, *Pearl River Community College*

Kathy Barker, *Grays Harbor College*

Marie Barnes, *Wayne Community College*

Gary Bergstrom, *College of the Desert*

Meredith Bohne, *Quinsigamond Community College*

Beth Conomos, *Erie Community College*

Mike Costello, *New Mexico College*

Beverly Dile, *Elizabethtown Technical & Community College*

Julia Erben, *Gulf Coast Community College*

Dr. Xiwu Feng, *LaGuardia Community College*

Teresa Fugate, *Lindsey Wilson College*

Carol Hagan, *Jefferson College*

Kayla Gardner Harding, *Tulsa Community College*

Elaine Herrick, *Temple College*

Dr. Mary Huffer, *Lake Sumter Community College*

Debbie Lee, *Nash Community College*

Peter M. Marcoux, *El Camino College*

Diana Mareth, *Del Mar College*

Linda Mininger, *Harrisburg Area Community College*

Juliann Myers, *Vincennes University*

Cindy Ortega, *Phoenix College*

Cynthia Ross, *State College of Florida*

Diane Schellak, *Burlington County College*

Miriam Simon, *Montgomery College*

Majorie Sussman, *Miami Dade College*

Michelle Van de Sande, *Arapahoe Community College*

Sonja Yturralde, *Imperial Valley College*

I appreciate your honest constructive criticism as well as your encouragement throughout the development process. Hearing what you and your students need kept me motivated to work hard to improve the book!

In addition, I want to thank Nancy Blaine from Pearson for pulling all the pieces together in the last few months of the process. I thank my editor, Paul Sarkis, for his ideas and support along the way as the text was being developed. Thanks to Kathy Smith for her careful editing. Thank you to Pearson's Production, Marketing, Permissions, and Supplements departments for all their hard work to take care of the details. I also want to thank Pearson's sales team, especially Ted Krischak, Nicole, and Amy, for encouraging me and for working so hard to make sure everyone gets the books and materials they need for successful learning.

Sincere thanks to my colleagues at Ivy Tech Community College, Purdue University, the Indiana Association for Developmental Educators (INADE), the National Association for Developmental Educators (NADE), and the College Reading and Learning Association (CRLA) for their great discussions and ideas, for sending me articles and books their students like, for trying out many of my exercises and readings with their own students, and for giving me honest feedback over the past several years.

Thanks to my students for letting me know what they like and don't like and for telling me when the exercises are engaging and when I need to change them. I also thank my students for being excited to try new activities and ways of learning—you continue to make teaching and writing a joy!

Deepest thanks to my family, neighbors, and friends who often heard much more about the book than they probably needed or wanted to know. Special thanks to our dear friends Pastor Stacy and Kim Littlefield and my wonderful sisters, Lorrie Tracy, Donna Nevin, Debbi Pelligrini, and Marybeth Chappell who have read to me and shared inspirational words all my life—thanks for being so encouraging and supportive. Thanks as well to Doug and Kristy Griffin for your constant and meaningful encouragement.

Thanks so much to my very loving daughter Skye and husband Mark for all the times you patiently listened as I brainstormed or shared material and for the many creative ideas you shared!

Finally, I want to thank the readers, non-readers, and soon-to-be-discovered readers, who have inspired me and kept me motivated during the times I didn't think I could do all the work required to bring this book to life. I know what knowledge and joy are in store for you as you discover your abilities! My hope is for every person to experience liberation through reading and understanding any type of material life presents. Thanks for giving me this opportunity to share the empowerment and joy of reading with you!

—Sharon M. Snyders

Introduction: Get Ready to Learn

Spotlight on Learning Styles

One of the best things you can do for yourself and for your success as a student is to discover your learning preference. The VARK Questionnaire is one of many different assessment tools available. You may take the questionnaire online by logging onto the website www.vark-learn .com and by following the directions.

Now that you know your learning preferences, you can choose strategies and techniques that will work best for you. Throughout *Making Reading Real* there are several activities to accompany each skill. Consider trying the activities which best match your learning style preference.

In *Making Reading Real* we will be referring to the different learning styles as

 Look (seeing)

 Listen (hearing)

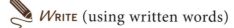 Write (using written words)

 Do (hands-on, experiencing)

Think about how you can use your strengths and preferences to maximize your learning.

Reading Techniques (SQ3R)

SQ3R is simply an organized strategy for reading. The letters in the acronym represent the steps in the strategy: S is for Survey; Q is for Question; and 3R is for Read, Recite, and Review. It may seem strange at first, but once you've practiced it a few times, SQ3R will become a useful technique for you to use when you read. You'll be able to stay focused on the material and retain the important information.

Survey	Skim over the material. Read the title, subtitle, subheadings, first and last paragraphs, pictures, charts, and graphics. Note italics and bold print.
Question	Ask yourself questions before you read. What do you want to know? Turn headings and subheadings into questions and/or read questions if provided.
Read	Read the material in manageable chunks. This may be one or two paragraphs at a time or under one subheading at a time.
Recite	Recite the answer to each question in your own words. This is a good time to write notes as you read each section. Repeat the question-read-recite cycle.
Review	Look over your notes at the end of the chapter, article, or material. Review what you learned and write a summary in your own words.

The SQ3R strategy is discussed in detail in Chapter 2. You will have the opportunity to learn about it more in depth and practice using it in a structured way.

Note-taking Strategies

Active Reading

Before you do anything else—get out a pencil and maybe highlighters. Now, as you read, write things down.

Circle ideas you want to remember.

Jot down notes in the margin of the text   *NOTES,*
                                                            NOTES,
                                                            NOTES

Underline important concepts.

Write abbreviations for important definitions (def.) and examples (ex.).

If you like color, and are a visual learner, use highlighters.

Have paper nearby so you can write additional notes as you read.

Also, as you use the SQ3R strategy, you are doing more than letting your eyes move across the paper from left to right. You are now thinking about the text before you read, while you are reading, and when you are finished. You are asking questions and finding answers. You are processing what you read more than once, which will lead to better comprehension and deeper understanding of the material.

1 Vocabulary

LEARNING OUTCOMES

LO1 Examine how educated guessing and shortcuts can improve reading efficiency.

LO2 Use context clues to determine the meaning of unfamiliar words.

LO3 Use word parts to understand the meaning of words.

LO4 Apply new vocabulary strategies to your reading.

THEME Adjusting to College

1

SPOTLIGHT ON LEARNING STYLES 👁 Look 👆 Do

Discovering the meaning of unfamiliar words is like playing a game or working a puzzle. When we use word parts and sentence clues to figure out the meaning of a word, our brains provide us with a burst of the chemical *dopamine* as the reward for solving the puzzle. I learn best by **looking** and **doing**. This means I learn best by seeing and experiencing things. When I try to figure out a new word I check to see if any part of it looks familiar. I also pay attention to how the word is used in the sentence to see if it reminds me of something else I've encountered in my life. For instance, look at the sentence above with the word *dopamine*. I see the word part *dop* and think about the "reward" mentioned in the sentence. I also remember learning something about dopamine in the brain in a biology class and from a police officer who visited my class to discuss the effects of drugs on the brain. I also think about the slang word *dope* used for illegal drugs such as marijuana. When I use my *looking* and *doing* learning styles, I guess that the meaning of *dopamine* is "a chemical released in the brain that makes you feel good when you solve a puzzle."

Attending college means dealing with change in your life. You may:

- have just graduated, or you may be coming back to school after several years.
- be raising a family, living with your parents, roommates, or on your own.
- live five minutes from your campus or have a long commute.
- have worked for years and your company just laid you off.
- have had a medical or personal situation and needed to find a new career.
- be just looking to make a change to do something different.
- be tired of living paycheck to paycheck and want something better for yourself and your family.
- not yet know what you want to do, but think that getting a college degree is a good way to start.

No matter what your background or your situation is, all students have this in common: Succeeding in college requires taking the unique skills you've already developed in your life and applying those skills to new situations. Many things may seem strange, frustrating, or maybe even overwhelming when you first start college. But you will do fine if you keep a positive attitude and try to apply your previous knowledge to your new situation. An open mind will help you to learn new strategies, skills, and ideas, and to adjust to these new expectations.

You have the opportunity today to move forward and create the life you desire. You will select your major and many of the courses you wish to take. You will also choose where and how you will spend your energy and your time. And even when the to-do list gets longer, you still have a choice! Managing your time and using it wisely may be the most important skill you develop as you adjust to the demands of college.

Shortcuts, Time-savers, and Educated Guessing

Reading college level textbooks, professional journals, and research articles may involve a significant amount of your time while you are in college. Learning new vocabulary for specific majors may also require more effort as you progress in your studies.

> **LO1**
> Examine how educated guessing and shortcuts can improve reading efficiency.

Reading without knowing vocabulary words can be frustrating. You can be going along at a decent pace and then get stuck. Unsure of what the author means, you have to figure out what to do. What are your choices?

- Ask someone or maybe skip over the word?
- Get out a dictionary or look up the word online?

But, even if you choose one of these options, it can still feel irritating or discouraging to not know the words. You may even want to quit reading.

There are two important strategies you'll learn in this chapter that will help you make educated guesses when you encounter unknown words while reading. These suggestions may reduce the distraction of looking up words in the dictionary.

- Use context clues to determine new words.
- Use word parts (prefixes, roots, and suffixes) to figure out new words.

This chapter will enable you to build on what you may already know and help you refine that knowledge so you can use it with college level reading.

Using Vocabulary in Context (What clues can help me figure out the word?)

Context clues give the listener or reader some hints about the meaning of the unknown word by using the surrounding text (or context). You probably have already successfully used this technique throughout your life as you encountered unfamiliar words. The strategy requires paying attention to the surrounding text for hints about the unknown word.

> **LO2**
> Use context clues to determine the meaning of unfamiliar words.

For example, if you were asked to state the meaning of *conifer*, it might be difficult to figure out without some background knowledge. But, the better context clues you were given, the easier it would become to guess the meaning.

Try to guess the meaning of the word *conifer* with the clues given in the sentences below.

Fifty conifers were delivered to the front door.

_____

There aren't enough clues because many things could be delivered to a front door.

She opened the package and then planted the 50 conifers.

_____

You might make a better guess that a conifer is a plant, but you would still not be sure what type of plant.

She planted the 50 conifers along the edge of her property, each about 15 feet apart, and hoped they would grow larger to eventually block the wind.

_____

Then you might guess a conifer is a large plant or a tree, but what kind?

When the conifers were about 6 feet tall, she planned to cut one down in December, bring it into her house, and decorate it with lights and ornaments.

_____

If you are familiar with the tradition of Christmas trees, then you would understand that a conifer is an evergreen tree. You could use your knowledge and the clues in the sentence to guess at the meaning of the word *conifer*.

If you are a forestry or horticulture major, it may seem more important for you to know the word *conifer* since it refers to a type of tree. However, this word may be found in many different texts and contexts including public policy, environmental concerns, business, or health affairs and involving discussions of the economics of cutting down forests, the medicinal values of certain trees, and many other situations. The strategies and exercises in this chapter will help you improve your ability to learn new words in various subjects, contexts, and majors.

Four Types of Context Clues

1. Synonyms and Definitions
2. Antonyms
3. Examples
4. Experience, Prior Knowledge, and Perception

Synonyms and Definitions

Synonym clues are words that mean the same as the unknown word. Sometimes the clue is in the sentence before or after the one with the unknown word. Sometimes authors give the definitions of words very clearly within the sentence. In this case the meaning of the new word is obvious. Textbook authors frequently use this technique to help students learn new words.

EXAMPLE

Directions: Circle the word or phrase that best matches the italicized word.

1. Some students prefer a *pragmatic* approach to learning. They may learn better with practical assignments rather than theories.

   a. practical   c. creative

   b. inventive   d. interesting

2. If there is a question about your enrollment in a course, it may be important for you to visit your *registrar*, or college records officer, to ensure your student records and registration are correct.

   a. financial aid officer   c. bookstore

   b. advisor   d. records officer

In question 1, the word *pragmatic* means (a) practical, and for question 2, the *registrar* is defined as (d) the college records officer.

PRACTICE THE NEW SKILL

Directions: Circle the word or phrase that best matches the italicized word.

1. Bob's first week of college seemed *formidable*. He thought it might be impossible to complete the assignments that were due in every class.

   a. interesting   c. boring

   b. annoying   d. difficult to accomplish

2. Your college *transcript* is a listing of your courses, credit hours, and grades for past semesters.

   a. course schedule   c. list of past courses and grades

   b. dean's list

3. College offers an opportunity to enrich your cultural understanding by giving you the chance to get to know people from *diverse*, or different, backgrounds from your own.

   a. opportunity   c. different

   b. cultural   d. background

Antonyms

Antonym clues are words that mean the opposite of the unknown word. In this case you will need to look for clues that contrast with the unknown word. One hint is to look for signal words such as *in contrast to*, *as opposed to*, *while*, *on the other hand*, or *but*.

EXAMPLE ———————————————————————————————

Directions: Circle the word that best matches the italicized word.

1. Fred keeps to himself most of the time but Enrique, on the other hand, is quite *gregarious*.

 a. aloof   **b.** insecure   **c.** hot-tempered   **d.** sociable

2. The poor grade on my test indicates *insufficient* preparation on my part. Next time, I'll know to study more.

 a. enough   **b.** more   **c.** too little   **d.** adequate

In question 1, Enrique is the opposite of Fred, who "keeps to himself." Therefore, Enrique's *gregarious* personality means (d) sociable. In question 2, studying "more" is the opposite of *insufficient* so the opposite of "more" is (c) too little.

PRACTICE THE NEW SKILL

Directions: Circle the word that best matches the italicized word.

1. Maria will do well in our class since she is *receptive* to new ideas, unlike Kelsey, who thinks she knows it all.

 a. open   **b.** adjusted   **c.** opposed   **d.** hostile

2. Getting enough sleep helps you concentrate. However, lack of sleep can be *detrimental* to your ability to think.

 a. harmful   **b.** developmental   **c.** beneficial   **d.** determined

3. Many students prefer professors who *intersperse* activities into their lectures as opposed to those who put the activities at the end of the lesson.

 a. gather   **b.** shake   **c.** limit   **d.** sprinkle

Examples

Authors also may give examples of a concept to help the reader understand the meaning of a word. When looking for examples it is important to think about what the author is trying to explain and make a picture or a movie in your mind.

EXAMPLE

Directions: Circle the word that best matches the italicized word.

1. Academic *integrity* can be demonstrated by doing your own assignments, using appropriate citations in research papers, and keeping your eyes on your own exams.

   a. interest   **b.** manipulation   **c.** honesty   **d.** plagiarism

2. Students may not realize they are *plagiarizing* if they paraphrase something from an author and do not cite the source of the information.

   a. copying   **b.** stealing   **c.** hiding   **d.** citing

In question 1 above, doing your own assignments, using appropriate citations, and keeping your eyes on your own exam are examples of (c) honesty. Question 2 gives an example of *plagiarizing* as paraphrasing without citing. Answer (a), copying, would not make sense since the example discusses paraphrasing. Answer (d) is not correct because the sentence states the student does not cite. If you replace the italicized word, *plagiarizing,* in place of the word *hiding,* the sentence does not make sense. Therefore, answer (b), stealing, would be the best choice.

PRACTICE THE NEW SKILL

Directions: Circle the word that best matches the italicized word.

1. Good ways to become *acclimated* to a new college might include attending the new student orientation, finding your classrooms before the first day, and looking over the college Web site for information.

   a. adjusted   **b.** involved   **c.** excited   **d.** disoriented

2. Joining student organizations, attending college activities, and getting to know classmates contribute to a student's *socialization* in their school.

   a. prioritization   **b.** isolation   **c.** belonging   **d.** avoidance

3. Building *rapport* with your instructors can be done by asking questions during class or visiting with them during their office hours.

   a. a relationship   **b.** bridges   **c.** respect   **d.** an idea

Experience, Prior Knowledge, and Perception

You may also use your own experiences, prior knowledge, and perception of the text to help you determine the meaning of unknown words. Think about situations at work, home, or activities in your life. You might also think about stories you've heard or read and people you've known. Overall, use all of your senses and insights to make an educated guess about the meaning of the unknown word.

EXAMPLE ————————————————————————————————

Directions: Circle the word that best matches the italicized word.

1. Being *frugal* is necessary when living on a tight budget.

    a. thrifty   **b.** sensitive   **c.** obsessive   **d.** carefree

2. It is *imperative* that he find a parking spot if he expects to get to class on time.

    a. demanding   **b.** unlikely   **c.** important   **d.** irrelevant

In question 1, *frugal* means (a) thrifty, and in question 2, *imperative* means (c) important. If you imagine living on a tight budget, then thrifty makes sense. If you have ever tried to find a space to park your car in a crowded parking lot, then you'd remember from your own experience how important it would be.

PRACTICE **THE NEW SKILL**

Directions: Circle the word that best matches the italicized word.

1. Following a map and asking directions are ways to prevent *disorientation* on an unfamiliar campus.

    a. financial loss   **c.** catching a cold

    b. fearing crowds   **d.** getting lost

2. Knowing your professors' grading *criteria* will help you meet their expectations throughout the semester.

   a. applications

   b. requirements

   c. considerations

   d. transcripts

3. Making new friends will be easier if you make a point to *mingle* with new people throughout the day.

   a. attend class

   b. watch

   c. socialize

   d. walk

REVIEW *WHAT YOU LEARNED*

Vocabulary in Context

Directions: Circle the word or phrase that best matches the meaning of the italicized word in each sentence.

1. Talking to someone who has taken a course before may be useful. A student who has *preceded* you may know what it takes to succeed.

   a. prepared   b. left   c. gone before   d. invited

2. It is important to deal with *hindrances* to your success early in the semester. Rather than prevent you from reaching your goals, good study skills and time management will help you achieve them.

   a. aggravations   b. questions   c. obstacles   d. hints

3. Frank seemed to be looking for a fight. His *contentious* attitude interfered with the learning process.

   a. argumentative   b. bored   c. confused   d. focused

4. Studying is *imperative* to college success. It is necessary to study several hours per week for each hour you are in class.

   a. optional   b. time consuming   c. suggested   d. necessary

5. Getting to know some of your classmates will be *advantageous* later if you have questions about an assignment or need to go over the lecture notes.

   a. helpful   b. tricky   c. skillful   d. honest

REVIEW **WHAT YOU LEARNED**

Vocabulary in Context

Directions: Circle the word that best matches the meaning of the italicized word in each sentence.

1. Students who are *sanguine* when they begin college may have a better time adjusting. Being hopeful, confident, and cheerful may make it easier to deal with the stresses of a new situation.

   a. sad   **b.** optimistic   **c.** melancholy   **d.** stressed

2. We told him that he should talk to a counselor and not bring his *adversarial* attitude to the classroom. He was having a bad day and just looking to pick a fight.

   a. cooperative   **b.** quarrelsome   **c.** reflective   **d.** finicky

3. Due to the increased pressure and stress with which students must cope, it is *crucial* to develop a support system of family, friends, and college staff.

   a. important   **b.** minor   **c.** a problem   **d.** difficult

4. Students who know their learning style can find ways to make their studying more *constructive*.

   a. essential   **b.** productive   **c.** destructive   **d.** important

5. Jennifer knew that going to college was going to be *arduous,* unlike high school, where she never had to open a book and still earned decent grades.

   a. easy   (b. difficult)   c. confusing   d. fun

Recognizing Word Parts (Where have I heard this before?)

At this point in your life, you have probably already acquired thousands of words in your vocabulary. Many of these words are built with the same word parts. When you see word parts you already know in an unfamiliar word, it will help you guess the meaning of the new word.

> **LO3**
> Use word parts to understand the meaning of words.

In college you will encounter new subjects that contain unfamiliar vocabulary words. In order to succeed, you should use what you already know and work from there. Building on the known word parts and memorizing more will help increase your vocabulary exponentially.

Let's see how the word parts work together to form words. First, think about a familiar word such as *thermometer.* It is made up of two parts: *therm* and *meter.* When you see the word *thermometer* you might think about other words with *therm* such as *thermos, thermal* underwear, or *thermostat.* What do those words have in common? A *therm*ometer measures the temperature; a *therm*os controls the heat of a liquid; *therm*al underwear keeps me warm while I'm sledding; and a *therm*ostat controls the temperature in my house. So, perhaps, the word part *therm* has something to do with temperature or heat.

Therm o **meter** (measures *temperature*)

Therm os (controls *temperature* of a liquid such as coffee or hot chocolate)

Therm al underwear (keeps the heat or *temperature* in)

Therm o stat (controls the *temperature* in a room)

You might also think about words with *meter* such as the metric measurements: *meter, centimeter, millimeter, kilometer,* etc. If you know that *thermometer* measures temperature, and *therm* is temperature, then *meter* must mean to measure.

Meter (metric measurement of approximately one yard)

Centi **meter** (1/100 of a meter)

Milli **meter** (1/1000 of a meter)

Kilo **meter** (1000 meters)

So, if you see the word <u>*micrometer,*</u> you can think about how *meter* means "measure" and then see if the word part *micro* looks familiar. You might ask yourself where else you've seen the word part *micro.* How about *microscope, micro-organism, microwave ovens,* or *micro machines?* Then ask what these words have in common. Well, a *microscope* zooms in to view very small particles and *micro organisms* are very small life forms or organisms. *Microwave* ovens use small waves to conduct heat and *micro machines* are tiny toys. Going back to *micrometer,* you just put *micro* (meaning "very small") with *meter* (meaning "measure") and you will understand that a *micrometer* measures very small items with precision.

Microscope (views very small organisms)

Micro-organism (very small organisms or life forms)

Microwave oven (uses small waves to conduct heat)

Micro machines (tiny toys)

Micrometer = Small + measure = Measures small items

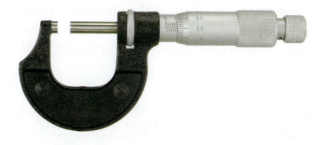

Then, if you have an opportunity to enroll in a *microeconomics* class or a *microbiology* class, you will have a better idea of what to expect. Remember to think about what you already know. If you know *micro*, then think about what looks familiar in *economics*. Do you see the word *economy* is similar to *economics*? Then you can make an educated guess. With *microbiology* you know that *micro* is small, but what about *biology*? The word part *bio* means "life" and the word part *logy* means "study of." So, if you enroll in microbiology, you will study small life forms. Thinking about what you already know will allow you to quickly figure out the meanings of new words in college.

Microeconomics = **Micro** + **economics** =

Small-scale economics

Microbiology = Micro + biology =

Small + biology =

Small + bio + logy =

Small + life + study of = **Study of small life forms**

Word parts may be more easily remembered if you study them in related groups. Similar to remembering names, dates, or directions, it may help to have a clear pattern or relationship between words. It also helps to use the word parts repeatedly to reinforce them in your memory. Like learning the alphabet or your basic math facts, mastering word parts can serve as a critical foundation for building the rest of your vocabulary. Once you've learned to recognize the patterns and memorized the unfamiliar word parts, you should notice a dramatic increase in your word knowledge.

Prefixes, Roots, and Suffixes

Words in the English language are primarily made up of Latin and Greek word parts. The root of the word will reveal the basic meaning. Prefixes then may be added to the beginning of the word and suffixes may be added to the end of the word to create more specific meanings. In the next few pages of this chapter, you will have the opportunity to learn many word parts and to use them to improve your reading. The lists of prefixes, roots, and suffixes below include word parts you may use to build your vocabulary.

Prefixes

A *prefix* is a word part located at the beginning of a word. A prefix changes the meaning of the word and it cannot stand alone. The prefix *pre* in the word *prefix* means "before." In college you may encounter many prefixes even before the first day of classes. For instance, you may have been required to take this reading course as a _prerequisite_ to other courses that entail a significant amount of college level reading. In this case, you might be *required* to pass the reading course *before* other courses can be taken. You may also have _prepared_ for college by completing a placement exam and an admissions application.

Prefix = word part that comes <u>before</u> the word and changes the meaning

Prerequisite = required <u>before</u> you take another course

Prepared = ready or equipped <u>before</u> you do something else

It may be easier to learn prefixes by grouping them in related categories. It will also be beneficial if you connect the word parts you are learning in this course to words you see in your other college classes. For example, the list of prefixes representing numbers below may also be used in your math or music classes.

Prefixes Representing Quantities

Prefix	Meaning	Example	Definition
semi	half, partly	semicircle	half circle
mono	one	monotone	one tone
uni	one	uniform	the same as others
multi	more than one	multiply	more than one addition
poly	many	polygon	many sides
du, duo	two	duet	two singing together

EXAMPLE ──────────────────────────────

Directions: Fill in the blank with either the prefix or the meaning from the list above.

_____ precious = <u>less than or partly</u> precious gem

If you wrote *semi* in the blank above, you are correct.

PRACTICE THE NEW SKILL

Directions: Fill in the blank with either the prefix or the meaning from the list above.

1. <u>mono</u>nucleosis = an infectious disease with an abnormal increase in the number of white blood cells with _____<u>one</u>_____ nucleus in the bloodstream

2. _____<u>du</u>_____al purpose tools = <u>two</u> uses for one tool

3. _____<u>multi</u>_____tasks = does <u>many</u> tasks at the same time

Prefixes Representing Quantities (continued)

Prefix	Meaning	Example	Definition
bi	two	bisect	cut in two
tri	three	triangle	three angles
dec	ten	decade	ten years
cent	hundred	century	one hundred years
kil	thousand	kilogram	one thousand grams
mil	thousand	millimeter	1/1000 of a meter

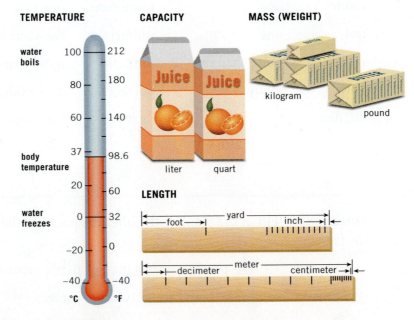

PRACTICE THE NEW SKILL

Directions: Fill in the blank with either the prefix or the meaning from the list above.

1. <u>bi</u> cycle = _____two_____ wheels

2. <u>bi</u> <u>cent</u> ennial = _____two_____ _____hundred_____ years

3. _____tri_____ athlon = an athletic event involving <u>three</u> events: swimming, bicycling, and running

Prefixes Representing Time

Prefix	Meaning	Example	Definition
ante	before	anterior	toward the front or head
post	after	postpone	delay until later
pre	before	prerequisite	required before something else
re	again	reapply	apply again
retro	backward	retroactive	applicable to the past (laws, pay)

PRACTICE THE NEW SKILL

Directions: Fill in the blank with either the prefix or the meaning from the list above.

1. <u>ante</u> date = precede in time or date _____before_____ the actual time

2. <u>pre</u> meditate = plan _____before_____

3. _____retro_____ spect = looking backward or thinking about the past

Prefixes Showing Direction/Relationship

Prefix	Meaning	Example	Definition
ab, a	away from	asymmetrical	not symmetrical
ac, ad, af, ag, as, at	to or toward	accredit	accept as true
co	jointly, together	cohabitate	live together

circum	around	circumference	distance around a circle
de	down	decline	bend or slant down
e, es, ex	out	exterior	outside

PRACTICE *THE NEW SKILL*

Directions: Fill in the blank with either the prefix or the meaning from the list above.

1. <u>ad</u>mission = to send _____to_____ (allow in, as to a school or movie)

2. _____co_____ operate = work <u>together</u> toward a common goal

3. _____ab_____ normal = <u>away from</u> normal (odd)

Prefixes Showing Direction/Relationship (continued)

Prefix	Meaning	Example	Definition
inter	between, among	interstate	between different states
intra	within	intravenous	within a vein
per	thoroughly, through	perspire	excrete through the skin
pro	for, forward	promote	to move forward
sub	below or under	submarine	under the water
sym, syn	together	symbiosis	living together of organisms
super	above or higher	superpower	leading country of the world
trans	across	transmit	send along

PRACTICE *THE NEW SKILL*

Directions: Fill in the blank with either the prefix or the meaning from the list above.

1. <u>inter</u> collegiate = _____between_____ the colleges (as in athletic leagues)

2. <u>intra</u> mural = _____within_____ the limits of a school (as in athletic teams)

3. _____per_____ ennial = lasting <u>through</u> several years as a plant

Prefixes Meaning *Not*

Prefix	Meaning	Example	Definition
a, an	not, without	asymmetrical	not symmetrical
anti	opposite or against	antiterrorism	against terrorism
dis	opposite or not	disrespect	not respect
il (before l)	not	illiterate	not literate
im (before b, p, or m)	not	immature	not mature
in	not	insecure	not secure
ir (before "r")	not	irresponsible	not responsible
mis	wrong	misplace	wrong place
non	not	non-profit	not for profit
un	not	unpredictable	not predictable

PRACTICE *THE NEW SKILL*

Directions: Fill in the blank with either the prefix or the meaning from the list above.

1. _____<u>mis</u>_____ understanding = <u>not</u> understanding

2. <u>ir</u>replaceable = _____<u>not</u>_____ replaceable

3. _____<u>im</u>_____ possible = <u>not</u> possible

REVIEW *WHAT YOU LEARNED*

Vocabulary in Word Parts—Prefixes

Directions: Fill in the blank with the prefix.

1. _____kil_____ owatt = a <u>thousand</u> watts of electricity

2. _____re_____ align = align <u>again</u>

3. _____post_____ game = <u>after</u> the game

4. _____de_____ generate = going in a <u>downward</u> direction (as in conditions getting worse)

5. _____pro_____ motion = <u>forward</u> move in one's career

REVIEW *WHAT YOU LEARNED*

Vocabulary in Word Parts—Prefixes

Directions: Fill in the blank with the meaning.

1. <u>syn</u>ergy =_____together_____ action or operation (as of muscles, drugs, etc.)

2. <u>in</u>complete =_____not_____ complete

3. <u>poly</u>linguist = speaks _____many_____ languages

4. <u>e</u>gress = way _____out_____ (as a door or outlet)

5. <u>pro</u>gress = steps _____forward_____(as a movement forward)

Roots

A root is the base of a word or the place a word's meaning originates. Greek and Latin language roots make up much of the English language. Becoming familiar with roots will help you expand your vocabulary. When you encounter a new word, you can think about what looks familiar and then make an educated guess about its meaning.

Roots Representing Feelings or Emotions

Root	Meaning	Example	Definition
cred	believe	incredible	not believable
path	feeling or suffering	empathy	understanding of another

patho	disease	pathologist	one who studies diseases
phobia	fear	xenophobia	fear of strangers

PRACTICE *THE NEW SKILL*

Directions: Fill in the root or the meaning that makes the most sense.

1. Psycho ___patho/y___ = mental disease

2. <u>cred</u>ible = ___believe___ able

3. biblio<u>phobia</u> = ___fear___ of books

Roots Representing Motion or Action

Root	Meaning	Example	Definition
cap, capt	to seize or take	captive	a prisoner
duc, duct	to lead	educate	to lead to knowledge
fac	to do or make	manufacture	to make
port	to carry	export	to carry out of a country
spec	to look	speculate	to look into the future
tract	to pull	tractor	farm machine for pulling
tort	to twist	contort	to twist out of shape
vers, vert	to turn	reverse	turn backwards

PRACTICE *THE NEW SKILL*

Directions: Fill in the root or the meaning that makes the most sense.

1. in<u>spect</u> = ___see___ in or into

2. con<u>duct</u> = ___lead to guide___ through

3. trans___port___ = to <u>carry</u> across

Roots Representing Communication

Root	Meaning	Example	Definition
audi	to hear	audition	to hear one's performance
dic, dict	to speak or tell	diction	how words are pronounced
graph, gram	write	telegraph	send across a distance
miss, mitt	to send	remit	to send again
phono	sound	phonograph	record the sound
scrib, script	to write	prescription	to write before
voc, voke	to call or voice	vocation	one's calling or ministry

PRACTICE THE NEW SKILL

Directions: Fill in the root or the meaning that makes the most sense.

1. <u>audi</u>torium = a hall where people gather to _____<u>hear</u>_____ a lecture or performance

2. auto_____<u>graph</u>_____ = one's own <u>written</u> signature

3. pre_____<u>dict</u>_____ = <u>to tell</u> something before it happens

Other Roots

Root	Meaning	Example	Definition
cide	to kill	homicide	kill a person
fer	to bear	transfer	to bear across
luc, lum	to shine or light	luminaria	lights
logy, ology	study of	psychology	study of the mind
spir	breathe	inspiration	breathe (idea) into
tele	distance	telephone	sounds across distance
vita, viv	life	vitality	full of life

PRACTICE THE NEW SKILL

Directions: Fill in the root or the meaning that makes the most sense.

1. _____tele_____phone = hear across a <u>distance</u>

2. <u>vit</u>al signs = signs of _____life_____ (as in pulse, blood pressure, temperature)

3. _____fer_____ tile = able <u>to bear</u> offspring (as in animals, people, or plants)

REVIEW WHAT YOU LEARNED

Vocabulary in Word Parts–Roots

Directions: Fill in the blank with the meaning that matches the root.

1. pesti<u>cide</u> = _____kill_____ insects or pests

2. trans<u>luc</u>ent = to _____see_____ across the material (clear; see-through)

3. con<u>tort</u>ion = _____twisted_____ expression (frown or scowl)

4. <u>scrip</u>ture = _____written_____ word of God (the Bible)

5. <u>fact</u>ory = a place where items are _____made_____

REVIEW WHAT YOU LEARNED

Vocabulary in Word Parts–Roots

Directions: Fill in the blank with root that matches the meaning.

1. con_____duct_____or = one who <u>leads</u> (such as a train engineer or for a musical orchestra)

2. _____tort_____ion = a different <u>twist</u> or perspective

3. in_____voke_____ = to <u>call</u> in (or appeal to)

4. re_____tract_____ = to <u>pull</u> back

5. _____spir_____itual = <u>breathe</u> life into (religious, holy, divine)

Suffixes

Suffixes are word parts found at the end of words. A suffix changes the meaning of the word by changing the form of the word but still keeping the basic meaning (or root) the same.

Suffixes That Form Nouns

ance	resist	resistance
cy	advocate	advocacy
ence	differ	difference
ion	impose	imposition
ism	patriot	patriotism
ite	graph	graphite
ity, ty	mature	maturity
ment	move	movement
ness	well	wellness

PRACTICE THE NEW SKILL

Directions: Add the appropriate suffix in the blank.

1. The results were important. The import_____ance_____was obvious to all involved.

2. He was a skeptic about the new rules. His skeptic _____ism_____ created trouble for him.

3. She was so happy when she was singing. Her happi_____ness_____was contagious to those around her.

Suffixes That Form Nouns Related to a Person

ee	refer	referee
er	teach	teacher
or	act	actor
ian	library	librarian
ist	art	artist

PRACTICE *THE NEW SKILL*

Directions: Add the appropriate suffix in the blank.

1. She liked to paint. She was a paint _____er_____.

2. He was nominated for the award. He was a nomin_____ee_____.

3. They liked to study history. They were known as histor_____ian_____s.

Suffixes That Form Verbs

ate	luxury	luxuriate
ize	character	characterize
ify	simple	simplify

PRACTICE *THE NEW SKILL*

Directions: Add the appropriate suffix in the blank.

1. I had to put all the numbers on the list in order. In other words, I had to numer_____ate_____ the list.

2. She said we needed to earn the certificate of completion. To do so, we had to cert _____ify_____ the books.

3. He had a theory about the goat parasites. He began to theor _____ize_____ about how to make the goats healthier.

Suffixes that Form			Adjectives	Adverbs (add "ly")
able	capable of	respect	respectable	respectably
ible	capable of	cred	credible	credibly
ful	full of	success	successful	successfully
ous	full of	courage	courageous	courageously
less	without	hope	hopeless	hopelessly

PRACTICE THE NEW SKILL

Directions: Add the appropriate suffix in the blank.

1. The student could predict the professor's behavior. The professor's behavior was predict _____able_____.

2. The students felt outrage over their classmate's behavior. The classmate's behavior was outrage_____ous_____.

3. She had hope about her future. She was hope_____ful_____.

REVIEW WHAT YOU LEARNED

Vocabulary in Word Parts—Suffixes

Directions: Change the form of the word to complete the sentence.

1. The professor needed a transparent copy of the diagram to show the class. She needed a transparen_____cy_____.

2. He was ready to indulge in the chocolate. He was looking forward to his indulg _____ence_____.

3. The way he preached inspired them. They said the preach _____er_____ was awesome!

4. She always tried to be perfect. Some called her a perfection _____ist_____.

5. They were not afraid of the test. They were fear_____less_____.

REVIEW WHAT YOU LEARNED

Vocabulary in Word Parts—Suffixes

Directions: Change the form of the word to complete the sentence.

1. They strived for equal rights. They worked for equal_____ity_____.

2. The students composed their music. They created musical composit_____ion_____s.

3. The club had a call-out to recruit new members. Their recruit_____ment_____ strategy included offering pizza and pop for the first meeting.

4. She made sure to dress so others would respect her. She dressed in a respect_____able_____ manner.

5. He cared about her feelings. He care_____fully_____ considered what she said.

"BRB" (Be Right Back) Vocabulary Skills

> **LO4**
> Apply new vocabulary strategies to your reading.

When you are reading and come across a new word, you might need to take some time to figure it out. The *"BRB"* or *Be Right Back* skills let you get away from the reading passage for a short time, and then return to it as soon as possible. Just like when talking, texting, or chatting on Facebook, you might have to leave a conversation for a little while, but you plan to *be right back*.

Your new vocabulary skills of using word parts and context clues to figure out meaning are very helpful as you encounter unknown words. There will be times, however, when you will need to consult an outside source, such as the dictionary, to determine the correct meaning of a word. Readers who know when to use one or more of the three methods (word parts, context clues, and dictionary) to decide the meaning of unknown words will have better results in less time. The sooner you can figure out the word meaning and get back to your reading, the easier it will be to comprehend the text.

"BRB" Using Context Clues and the Dictionary

What clues in this sentence can help you figure out the meaning of *formidable*?

Bob's first week of college seemed *formidable*. He thought it might be impossible to complete the assignments that were due in every class.

| Bob was worried that he might be facing an impossible task. | Bob had to complete a number of assignments. | Bob's assignments were all due that week. |

Together, these facts let you infer that ***formidable*** means *difficult.*

Now look up the word ***formidable*** in the dictionary or on an Internet site, just to be sure. If you use a dictionary Web site, type your word into the search box. Online dictionaries also offer you the option of hearing the word pronounced when you press on a megaphone symbol after the word. Here is one result from an online dictionary:

for-mi-da-ble (each hyphen indicates a syllable or sound separation)

fawr-mi-duh-buh l (The pronunciation guide for the first entry shows how the word sounds; The emphasis is on the first syllable in bold print "for" sounds like "fawr"; "mi" uses the *I* sound like *mitten*; "da" uses the *uh* sound as in *under*; and the "ble" sounds like *bull*.)

fôr'mĭ-də-bəl, fôr-mĭd'- (The pronunciation guide for the second entry is quite different. It uses symbols you will probably also see at the bottom of the page or in a guide in a printed dictionary. This entry gives two ways to pronounce *formidable* and it uses different symbols to indicate the sounds. In this style, the syllable that is emphasized when you say the word has a diacritical mark (`) at the end. The first pronunciation puts the emphasis on the first syllable. The second pronunciation puts the stress on the second syllable. The second pronunciation puts the stress on the second syllable).

–adjective (this is the part of speech)
1. causing fear, apprehension, or dread: *a formidable opponent.*

2. of discouraging or awesome strength, size, difficulty, etc. intimidating: *a formidbable problem.*

3. arousing feelings of awe or admiration because of grandeur, strength, etc.

4. of great strength; forceful; powerful: *formidable opposition to the proposal.*

–Synonyms
1. dreadful, appalling, threatening, menacing, fearful, frightful, horrible.

–Antonyms
1. pleasant.

The dictionary entry has multiple definitions. But based on the context of the sentence, meaning number 2 confirms what we already discovered—*formidable* means difficult.

"BRB" Using Word Parts and Context Clues and the Dictionary

If you see a new word, such as *prestidigitation,* first you might recognize a word part or two and it may give you an idea about the meaning. Sometimes you can figure out words without using your list of memorized word parts. You can use words you already know to decode the new word.

The magician used ***prestidigitation*** to impress us with his card trick. He moved his hands so quickly that we didn't see how he switched the cards.

Presti	digita	tion
Sounds like *press* or *impress* or "presto chango" in magic.	Sounds like *digit* or another term for fingers.	Suffix that changes the word to a noun.

Next, examine how the word is used in the sentence or paragraph to see if there are any context clues to the meaning.

The magician used ***prestidigitation*** to impress us with the card trick. He moved his hands so quickly that we didn't see how he switched the cards.

The magician moved his hands.	The magician moved quickly.	We didn't see how he switched the cards.

Together, these facts let you infer that ***prestidigitation*** means *performing magic through quick hands.*

Checking our answer with an online dictionary we find:

pres·ti·dig·i·ta·tion (prĕs'tĭ-dĭj'ĭ-tā'shən) *n.*
1. Performance of or skill in performing magic or conjuring tricks with the hands; sleight of hand.

2. A show of skill or deceitful cleverness.

[French (influenced by prestigiateur, *juggler, conjurer,* from prestige, *illusion*), from prestidigitateur, *conjurer* : preste, *nimble* (from Italian presto; see **presto**) + Latin digitus, *finger*; see **digit**.]

When you go to a dictionary source, as in the example above, there may be multiple meanings for a word. Then you must use the context clues to help you decide which meaning makes the most sense. For example, in the sentence, *"The magician used prestidigitation to impress us with the card trick,"* we know that definition #1 is the better choice since it is specifically about a magician.

The dictionary also gives the origin of the word or word parts. Prestidigitation has French, Italian, and Latin origins. The study of word origins is called *etymology*. Reading the origins of words in a dictionary is a great way to expand your vocabulary and could also be a fun way to spend a rainy day if the electricity goes off.

PRACTICE THE NEW SKILL

Directions: Complete the word part chart, the context clues chart, and use the dictionary entries to infer the correct meaning of each word.

1. prerequisite

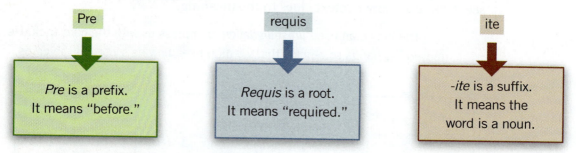

Pre

Pre is a prefix.
It means "before."

requis

Requis is a root.
It means "required."

ite

-ite is a suffix.
It means the
word is a noun.

From the word parts above, what can you infer is the meaning of *prerequisite*?

something that is required before something else

Directions: Using the context clues in the sentence, infer the meaning of *prerequisite*.

Reading class is a **prerequisite** or a class you must take before Psychology and English Composition.

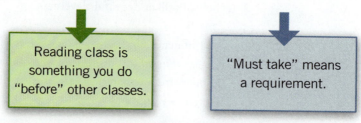

Reading class is
something you do
"before" other classes.

"Must take" means
a requirement.

Using the facts from the sentence, what can you infer is the meaning of *prerequisite*?

something you must take before something else

According to an online dictionary:

> **pre·req·ui·site**
> prē'rek wə zət,pri-[pri-**rek**-w*uh*-zit, pree-]
> *–adjective*
> 1.
> required beforehand: *a prerequisite fund of knowledge.*
> *–noun*
> 2.
> something prerequisite: *A visa is still a prerequisite for travel in many countries.*
>
> *—Synonyms*
> 2. requirement, requisite, essential, precondition.

Using the dictionary entry, which definition is best for *prerequisite* as it is used in the sentence?

something required before something else

2. **spectator**

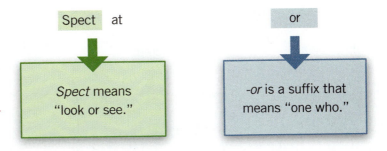

College is <u>not</u> a *spectator* sport. For learning to occur, a student must actively participate in class, not just sit and observe.

Students should not just sit and observe.	Learning requires active participation.	"Not" indicates an antonym clue or opposite meaning.

According to an online dictionary:

> [**spek**-tey-ter, spek-**tey**-]
> –*noun*
> 1.
> a person who looks on or watches; onlooker; observer.
> 2.
> a person who is present at and views a spectacle, display, or the like; member of an audience.
> 3.
> Also called **spectator shoe**. a white shoe with a perforated wing tip and back trim, traditionally of dark brown, dark blue, or black but sometimes of a lighter color.

Using word parts, context clues, and the dictionary, which definition of *spectator* is best?

1 – a person who looks on or watches; onlooker; observer

3. incredible

in	cred	ible
Means "not."	Means "believe."	Means "able to."

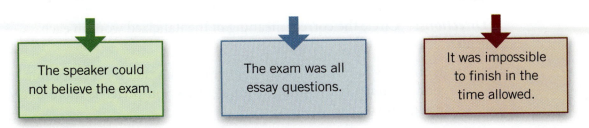

That exam was ***incredible***! It was impossible to finish in just 50 minutes. I could not believe the test had all essay questions!

The speaker could not believe the exam.

The exam was all essay questions.

It was impossible to finish in the time allowed.

According to an online dictionary:

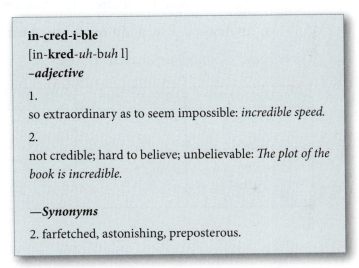

in-cred-i-ble
[in-**kred**-*uh*-*buh* l]
–*adjective*

1.
so extraordinary as to seem impossible: *incredible speed.*

2.
not credible; hard to believe; unbelievable: *The plot of the book is incredible.*

—*Synonyms*
2. farfetched, astonishing, preposterous.

Using word parts, context clues, and the dictionary, which definition of *incredible* is best?

1 – so extraordinary as to seem impossible

MASTER THE LESSON

Vocabulary

Directions: Circle the correct meaning of the italicized word in each sentence.

1. In college you can choose a variety of classes that meet according to your *inclinations*. Getting classes at times you prefer is more likely, though, if you enroll early.

   (a. preferences)   **b.** aptitudes   **c.** registrations   **d.** preparations

2. College students should get involved in activities outside of the classroom. They should participate in *extracurricular* activities.

   a. homework   **(b. additional)**   **c.** theatrical   **d.** work

Directions: Complete the chart below.

WORD/MEANING	PART/MEANING	PART/MEANING	PART/MEANING
3. biographer = One who writes of another person's life	4. bio = life	5. graph = write	6. er = one who
7. subscription = Payment in advance – under written	8. sub = under	9. script = written	10. ion = noun

MASTER THE LESSON

Vocabulary

Directions: Circle the correct meaning of the italicized word in each sentence.

1. Being *proactive* in college means to take the initiative on things you need to do.

   (**a.** taking initiative)   **c.** cautious

   b. prepared   **d.** active

2. A *commonality*, or common feature, of community colleges and four-year schools is that both expect students to be self-directed.

   a. self-directed   **c.** expectation

   (**b.** common feature)   **d.** commune

Directions: Complete the chart below.

WORD/MEANING	PART/MEANING	PART/MEANING	PART/MEANING
3. audiologist = One who studies hearing issues	4. audi = hear	5. olog = study	6. ist = one who
7. revitalize = Restore or bring back to life	8. re = again	9. vital = life	10. ize = verb

MASTER *THE LESSON*

Vocabulary

Directions: Fill in the blank with the meaning that matches the underlined word part.

1. <u>circum</u>vent = go _____around_____ the issue or situation (like when avoiding)

2. <u>ex</u>it = to go _____out_____

3. <u>super</u>natural = _____above_____ the normal or natural

4. <u>il</u>logical = _____not_____ logical

5–7. <u>incredible</u> = _____not_____ _____believe_____ _____able to_____
_____(not able to be believed)_____

Directions: Fill in the blank with the word part that matches the underlined meaning.

8. _____anti_____ smoking = <u>against</u> smoking

9–10. _____dis_____ respect_____ful_____ = <u>not</u> <u>full</u> of respect

LEARNING STYLE ACTIVITIES

Look, Listen, Write, Do

Look   Work with a small group or alone. Sketch a bare tree. Write one root word at the base of the trunk.

Think of all the words you know that use the root (for example, the root *cred* is found in *incredible*, *credit*, *credulous*, etc.). Write the words on the branches.

Repeat this looking activity with several different root words.

Listen   Say several words out loud that use more than one word part (prefixes, roots, and suffixes). Share your words with the class and see if they can guess the meaning of each word using their knowledge of word parts. (See example.) Answers will vary.

WORD/MEANING	PART/MEANING	PART/MEANING	PART/MEANING
Bibliophile = (one who loves books)	Biblio = book	Phile = love	

✎ **W**RITE   Generate a list of five words you might use specifically in your career. For example, people working in medical careers will use different techni-cal words than those in the business or computer fields. You may refer to your textbooks, professional journals, or the Internet for ideas. Use each word in a sentence and create context clues that clarify the meaning of the word. Circle the career-specific word in each sentence.

Sentences Using Context Clues Answers will vary.

1. _____

    _____

2. _____

    _____

3. _____

    _____

4. _____

    _____

5. _____

    _____

👆 **D**o   Using index cards create a set of flashcards with a word part printed on the front (i.e., word part is *super*) and the meaning and several examples printed on the back of each card (i.e., meaning of *super* is "above"; examples of *super* are *superman, supernova,* and *supermarket*).

(front of one index card)   (back of the same index card)

Word part	Meaning – ABOVE
SUPER	Examples – superman supernova supermarket

Read through the flashcards several times a day to help learn and remember the word parts. If your learning style is to look, you might draw pictures on the flashcards to remind yourself of what the prefixes mean. If your learning style is to listen, recite the cards out loud. If you prefer doing and like hands-on games and competition, challenge a classmate to see who can remember the most word parts in the shortest amount of time.

Reading Practice

The next section of the chapter will help you build your vocabulary skills as you read a variety of materials from diverse sources. All five of the readings address topics that will improve your success in adjusting to college.

The first reading is from an Internet site, www.college.gov. The readings for college students are titled *Boost Your Earnings* and *Find Your Passion*.

In the next reading, from a textbook called *Higher Learning*, the author discusses what she learned during her first year of college as a commuter student.

The third reading selection, a literature excerpt from the book *The Lakota Way*, talks about the character trait *perseverance*, which is much needed in college.

In the fourth reading selection from *U.S. News and World Report*, the article, "For Many Jobless, It's Back to School: Reversing Course: Learn How to Get in—and Pay for—a Good Retraining Program," discusses how to be optimistic about the way we perceive our situations and talk to ourselves.

The final reading is a set of photographs depicting students in different college situations.

Internet

READING 1

Boost Your Earnings

MORE EDUCATION = MORE OPPORTUNITY

"The moment I first realized that I could go to college was in middle school when I saw how hard my mother had to work to support three children."

—Jamal,
Louisiana State University

HIGHER SALARIES: EARN MORE DURING YOUR CAREER

- 4-Year Degree: $53,000/yr
- 2-Year Degree: $39,000/yr
- High School: $32,000/yr
- No High School: $24,000/yr

Studies prove it: continue your education after high school and you're likely to **make more money than people who stop at high school**. As an example, a college graduate can afford to buy a large, flat-screen TV in 1–2 months while a non-college graduate might have to work for 3–4 months to buy the same TV.

SKILLS FOR TODAY'S JOBS: HAVE MORE OPTIONS

Today, more jobs than ever before **require specialized** training or a two- or four-year college degree. More education means more choices, and that means more opportunities for you.

Fast Fact: Of the 20 fastest-growing occupations, more than half require an associate's degree or higher.

JOB SECURITY: KEEP WORKING

Your high school diploma is useful. But a college degree **increases your chance of employment by nearly 50%**. A two-year degree or even some college can have a positive impact on your ability to find and keep a job, too.

Fast Fact: The higher your education level, the higher your chances of finding and keeping a job.

MORE BENEFITS: GET THE IMPORTANT EXTRAS

There's more to a job than a paycheck. Jobs for college graduates typically offer more and better benefits than jobs requiring just a high school diploma. These can include health insurance and retirement plans you may not get at lower-skill jobs.

Find Your Passion

ENDLESS POSSIBILITIES

GOING TO WORK: CREATE A CAREER

Some people simply have "jobs," while others have "careers."

What's the difference? With a career, the kind of work you do is based on your interests. It's a path you've **chosen**. College can help you turn your passions and interests into a career you love.

Fast Fact: Choosing a college major does not limit you to one type of career.

CAREER POSSIBILITIES: WHAT COULD YOU DO?
DISCOVERING YOUR INTERESTS: LISTEN TO YOURSELF

What do you like to do? It's a tough question to answer, but spend some time considering it. Day to day, notice the things you do that interest you the most. During quiet times, where does your imagination lead you? Make note of these things as they come to you. Try these sites to match your interests to career possibilities.

WHAT'S A MAJOR: DECIDE WHAT TO STUDY

A college major provides a framework for your studies and the classes you'll need to take. Some majors, like engineering, prepare students for specific careers. Other majors, like liberal arts, can lead to many different career paths.

Not sure what to major in? Don't worry. Many schools don't require you to **declare** (choose) a major right away. And you can always change your major later on.

Fast Fact: Most college students change their majors at least once.

BE OPEN TO OPPORTUNITY: STAY CURIOUS

Over and over again, students say that college led them to career paths they never imagined for themselves, or weren't even aware of.

So, even if you know what courses you want to study, even if you already have a possible career in mind, stay open to new opportunities.

"There is no reason to have to know what you want to do when you come to college. College is a place and time for you to explore all those avenues and opportunities."

Adam,
Kansas State University

How did you choose your major? What is the best major?
Four students respond:

"I chose my major based on what subjects I enjoyed and excelled in during high school. Since writing for the school newspaper became my favorite class, I decided to major in journalism."

"Your choice of major depends on your interests and what you'd like to do after college. For example, I'm really interested in helping people, so I chose **psychology**."

"The best major is a completely personal decision. When you get to college you will have the chance to explore classes and subjects that will help you figure out the right major for you."

"There is not really a 'best' major. Remember to choose one that's interesting and enjoyable to YOU, not one that your friends and family think is best. After all, YOU will be taking the classes and doing the work!"

Source: www.college.gov Web site.

Directions: Use word parts and context clues to determine the meanings of the following words.

1. **require:** need, demand

2. **specialized:** particular, dedicated, expert

3. What is the difference between a "job" and a "career"? With a career, the kind of work you do is based on your interests. It's a path you've chosen. College can help you turn your passions and interests into a career you love.

4. **declare:** choose

5. **psychology:** study of the mind

Directions: Think about your college major. List words specific to your major, future career, or field of study. You may work with other students in your class to brainstorm ideas related to your major. *Hint:* You may want to use the Internet or your textbooks for ideas.

WORD	**DEFINITION**
6. _____	7. _____
8. _____	9. _____
10. _____	11. _____
12. _____	13. _____
14. _____	15. _____

READING 2

1040L   ## Outside In—The Life of a Commuter Student

Patti See (b. 1968) is a Senior Student Services Coordinator at the University of Wisconsin-Eau Claire, where she also teaches in the Women's Studies Program. Her poetry, fiction, and essays have been published in *Salon Magazine, HipMama, The Southeast Review, Women's Studies Quarterly*, and other magazines and anthologies.

How do you feel you fit in with the other students in your college? Are there others who may be experiencing some of the same feelings as you? Think about how you are adjusting to college and what you are learning about yourself as you read this passage.

1   It was long ago and far away, the way many of us think of our undergraduate years. I started college in the mid-'80s, a time when women my age defined themselves with big hair and a closet-full of stone-washed denim. There were few causes for college students then, just *Just Say No*, and abortion if you were into that sort of thing. I **pined** for a cause, for a purpose, for a normal life as a college student. I was a commuter, living in a community away from the university with roommates who spent winters in Florida.

2   I didn't know as a freshman that there are many ways to experience college and mine was just one of them. I didn't know that there were other students in my classes who weren't having the "traditional" college experience. I only focused on the fact that I wasn't living in a dorm with a stranger, **trying out different men like shoes,** joining a sorority or student organization, experimenting with lifestyles.

3   I was embarrassed that my parents didn't pay for me to go to college away from home. They gave me a place to eat, a car with insurance, every meal, everything that allowed me to commute the twenty minutes to school. At eighteen I didn't realize that putting myself through college, managing work and books, might be an experience in **self-reliance.** As the youngest of eight children, most of whom had gone to the university closest to home, I accepted that commuting was just what my family did. Like other teenagers, I thought my family was **abnormal.**

4   Though I was the last of their children to go to college, my parents still had no ideas what it was about. They saw college as extended high school, what people did these days, go to classes for another four years, get another diploma, get a job that pays more than factory work.

5   My father was a railroad man who worked his way up from switchman to yard master over forty years. My mother's career was built around children

and *rosary beads*. She was never without either of them for almost forty years and had no way nor need to retire from either. I didn't consider the **humble** beginnings of my peers, didn't know that half of the university population was made up of first-generation college students like me. I only focused on my own history. I didn't see myself as progress.

6   At new student **orientation**, the summer before my first semester, I watched the other first-years wander around campus with their parents, touring buildings, reading the course catalogue over lunch. I didn't even consider telling my parents about orientation. I recognized even then I was in it alone. One morning when I was suffering from something as **banal** as menstrual cramps or a hangover, my mother said into my pale face at breakfast, "If you feel sick at school, just go to the office and tell them you need to come home. You can do that, can't you?"

7   I didn't bother to explain there was no office, no one to tell, that the campus spans for miles. I nodded an "okay."

8   When I walked into my first class of 250 students, more bodies than my entire high school and its faculty combined, I had no point of reference. It was straight out of *The Paper Chase*. I thought then, without the sophistication. That was the first time in my life I was truly **anonymous**, a number, and I liked being in a flood of strangers. I graduated from a Catholic high school where everyone knew everyone else, and I was tired of it.

9   I learned early on that college freshman don't talk to one another in class, and I had no way outside of class to get to know any of them. My first semester, the closest I came to forming any sort of relationship with another person on campus was with janitors and professors. We swapped a familiar nod and hello in the hallways and nothing more. My first year of college evolved around my courses and working as a supermarket cashier and a nightclub waitress. I didn't give much thought to changing my situation, or even, in **retrospect,** outwardly disliking it. It was just what I did. I often felt so involved in the lecture and class discussions (though I didn't actually open my mouth in class till my sophomore year) that I felt as if I was going one on one with the professor.

10   Around midterm, my Psych. Professor wrote in the margin of a paper he returned, "Interesting insights. I'd like to talk about this sometime." My first reaction was, "Well-hadn't we?" Sure, 249 other students were in the class, but I knew he was talking to me. I just took his comments a step further. Leaving class, walking to my car, all the time I drove down Highway 53, **he was there in the passenger seat, conversing with me as I wrote my paper in my mind.** Students who live in the dorms or even in off-campus housing in clusters of men and women don't have the

---

Rosary beads—a Roman Catholic string of beads used for counting prayer
The Paper Chase—a movie and a television series about law school

opportunity to **bring their professors home with them.** Why would they? They've got clubs to join, games to attend, dorms to decorate, parties to go to. Poor things. That mentality sustained me throughout my undergraduate years. I relied solely on what went on in the classroom. I thought that was all there was to college: rigid professors who lectured to blank faces. I didn't have a blank face, and after taking my professors home with me, I no longer saw them as rigid.

11   **Intellectually,** I thrived. Socially, I didn't. I hung onto the three friends from high school who were still in the area. One was a commuter like me, engaged to a mechanic and simply looking for a piece of paper that allowed her to teach. She didn't seem to care that she had no connections, since she had already begun her real life by picking out china and flatware. Sometimes we had lunch together and talked about old friends who'd gone away to school. Once we went together to the bookstore to rent our textbooks, but it felt all wrong. Too high school for me. I had already adapted to the life of a loner on campus.

12   Another high school friend bounced from **menial** job to **menial** job and had enough money to celebrate with me at the end of the week. We spent weekends in *honky-tonk* bars, under-aged but dressed much older, and talked about the people we worked with, men and women twice our age, putting in their time at jobs they hated. We promised that wouldn't happen to us.

13   Another friend was a mother at nineteen, a woman who once wrote poetry like me. I loaned her my American Literature text books and visited her when her boyfriend was gone. We smoked cigarettes and watched movies when the baby was asleep, and sometimes I **coaxed** her into talking about what she read.

14   My life as a student was a balancing act between my old life as a "townie" and my new life as a "college girl," perfected by the twelve-mile difference between my childhood home and the university. I didn't get the do-over I always imagined students were given when they went away to school. I didn't get to **reinvent** myself, no longer a jock, a class clown, a stoner. I was just invisible. Looking back, I know that **becoming nobody was the seed of my reinvention of myself.** Time and distance help me recognize that without my experience I wouldn't be writing this now. But then, I was merely an outsider in both worlds. Friends and family teased me for staying home on Saturday night reading and becoming a *Beatnik*. I was anonymous to other first-year students in my courses because, I thought then, I didn't live in a dorm. The saddest part of my college career, I see now, was that there were no late night talks about Nietzsche or Anne Sexton or hot men in my gym class. Anything. Nothing. I had no one to tell what

---

Honky-tonk—slang for a cheap bar or saloon

Beatnik—a member of the Beat Generation, a youth culture of the 1940s–1960s characterized by rock music and the use of drugs

I was learning, no shared knowledge, so I made a game of sharing with myself on the way to and from school. I learned a lot in my twenty-minute commute.

15   I wouldn't have continued in school, would have quit to work in the plastics factory, the **allure** of a 401(K), if not for my passion for knowledge and desire to be somebody. I didn't know at eighteen who that somebody might be, but I had an **inclination** I'd find it in books, not a time card.

16   I started out as a journalism major because it was easy to explain to my parents. They understood what journalists do. My siblings chose "working" professions: nursing, dietetics, accounting. I was the only freak hooked on knowledge for learning's sake, not a job. Early in my sophomore year I declared English, though even months before I graduated my mother told relatives, "She's going to be a journalist." I never tried to explain what a liberal-arts degree meant. Even the phrase in my mother's mouth made me self-conscious. "English major," she said, like some people say in-surance with the emphasis on "in." It's like the way she still says someone "knows computer," something foreign and odd, too much for her mouth in one breath. I couldn't explain that I was a writer in training, taking in the world and its details until I was ready to write it. It's something I just knew, like having blue eyes. Even in high school after I bought a pair of sea-green Incredible Hulk-eyed contacts, I was still blue underneath, still a writer. It's something inside, like **serendipity** that works only if you know what you're looking for or where you've been.

17   That meant as a freshman I discovered Walt Whitman and e.e. cummings and Kate Chopin and still talked like a townie, a walking Ole and Leena joke who knew proper grammar. I could diagram a sentence and write a persuasive paper to save my soul, but I was still factory-worker potential. It's what I feared as a college freshman, and even after I graduated, finding myself someday dull at the machine. That fear made me drag myself out of bed every morning at 7 a.m., eat Wheaties, and drive to school. Mornings were for classes, afternoons and evenings for work. Late nights and weekend days were for homework. It wasn't ideal, but it was productive. I was never dull but sometimes led a dull life.

18   Throughout my four years, I had contact with other commuters, mostly former high school classmates. Though we had similar stories, tied to the area by families and not enough money for the dorms or off-campus housing, I believed my experience was somehow different. I avoided them and their offers to car pool. These were people I'd known for thirteen years, and they were beyond interesting to me then. We knew who wet her pants in second grade and who threw up at the senior class New Year's Eve party and who made out with whom on the forty yard line after the Homecoming game. These commuters represented where I came from and wanted desperately to forget, details **imbedded in my hometown DNA** that I thought, at eighteen, I needed to lose in order to make room for more important details.

19   Though I eventually had many **acquaintances,** I made only one friend throughout my college career, a woman who commuted her first year when she lived with her dying grandfather. We met in a five-hour-a-week French class after she transferred from a school in her hometown. The first year I knew her, she lived in an apartment with twelve other women. I often imagined myself in her place: what all of us might talk about as we made dinner or came home from the bars. Then I met some of her roommates and discovered business majors don't have intriguing late-night discussions or even intriguing discussions in daylight. I don't recall how we got to be more than passing acquaintances or the **circumstances** that led me to bring her home, only twenty minutes but a lifestyle away from the college town.

20   "You have *afghans,*" she said when she walked through my living room. She immediately sat in my mother's chair. What she meant was, *You live in a real home, with canned goods bursting from cupboards, no one screaming drunk upstairs at 2 a.m.*

21   "You have a lot of trophies," she said in my bedroom. Commuters often have no reason to pack their past lives away. I told her stories about before I was anonymous. She slept over when it was too late to drive home and we drank too much wine and ordered pizza at midnight, and I almost felt like a real college student.

22   Sometimes we'd get tipsy during some campus bar happy hour, and I'd tell her, "You're my only friend, man." So pathetically honest that she still teases me about it.

23   The first time she said, "You're so smart and nice, how can that be?" She didn't have many friends herself, and it comforted me as someone who always felt on the outside of campus life.

Afghans—knitted or crocheted blankets

24   "Commuter," I answered, and she understood.

25   Later as a graduate student I continued to commute, but by then it was no longer something to be embarrassed about. It was even exotic to the other 23-year olds too old to be slumming in student housing, while I was driving home to my rented house "in the suburbs." I was still on the outside, but I had good reason to be. I went home to see my husband and put my two-year-old to bed after class. My peers went to the bar, but **some of them traveled in the front seat with me as I imagined our conversations about the literature we discussed in class.**

26   When I was given the graduate student of the year award, my mother hinted about coming to the awards banquet. It would have been the first time either of my parents was on a college campus for something besides a **commencement** ceremony. Selfish or appropriate, I filled my table with professors who had influenced my life or at least my degree program.

27   I still commute the same route to and from school, though now I'm an instructor. When I landed my first job I considered moving nearer to campus, but — odd as it sounds—I knew I'd miss the time in my car. Even now, as I write this, the bulk of it I compose in my mind as I drive home from school, a conversation with a professor or peer or old friend, who has traveled with me a long time ago. ■

Source: See, Patti and Bruce Taylor. (2006). *Higher Learning Reading and Writing about College,* 2nd ed. Upper Saddle River, NJ: Pearson.

Directions: Using word parts, context clues, and/or a dictionary, determine the meaning of the following bold words.

1. I **pined** for a cause (see paragraph 1) _____
   longed, wished

2. an experience in **self-reliance** (see paragraph 3) _____
   depending on yourself

3. my family was **abnormal** (see paragraph 3) _____
   not normal, acting different from other families

4. the **humble** beginnings (see paragraph 5) _____
   simple

5. as **banal** as menstrual cramps or a hangover (see paragraph 6) _____
   commonplace, ordinary, trivial

6. I was truly **anonymous,** a number (see paragraph 8) _____
   unidentified, unnamed, unknown

7. in **retrospect** (see paragraph 9) _____
looking back
_____

8. menial job (see paragraph 12) _____
trivial, unimportant
_____

9. I **coaxed** her into talking (see paragraph 13) _____
persuaded, talked
_____

10. reinvent myself (see paragraph 14) _____
invent myself or my personality again
_____

11. the **allure** of a 401(K) (see paragraph 15) _____
attraction, appeal, charm
_____

12. I had an **inclination** I'd find it in books (see paragraph 15) _____
tendency to expect
_____

13. serendipity (see paragraph 16) _____
chance, fate, luck, destiny
_____

14. many **acquaintances** (see paragraph 19) _____
people you know, friends, connections
_____

15. circumstances (see paragraph 19) _____
situation, conditions
_____

Your Guess	**Dictionary**
16. orientation _____ Answers will vary. _____	point of reference
17. intellectually _____	rationally, academically
18. commencement_____	graduation

Critical Thinking

Directions: Write the meaning of the figurative phrases.

19. trying out different men like shoes (see paragraph 2)
She dated different types of men and saw the dating as very casual,

not too serious.

20. **he was there in the passenger seat, conversing with me as I wrote my paper in my mind . . . bring their professors home with them** (see paragraph 10)

    She imagined her professor was with her as she created her paper in her mind.

    She did not really bring her professor home.

21. **becoming nobody was the seed of my reinvention of myself** (see paragraph 14) When she started college, she wanted to start fresh with her personality. She didn't act like any type of person.

22. **imbedded in my hometown DNA** (see paragraph 18)

    The details of her life from her hometown were a part of her she

    didn't think would be easy to change.

23. **some of them traveled in the front seat with me as I imagined our conversations about the literature we discussed in class** (see paragraph 25)

    Since she was a commuter student she did not have the opportunity

    to stay on campus and talk with her classmates. So she imagined talking with

    them as she drove back and forth to college.

Literature

READING 3

1110L

The Meaning of Eight Miles

Joseph M. Marshall, III was born on the Rosebud Indian Reservation in what is now south-central South Dakota. Marshall was raised by his maternal grandparents and his first language is Lakota. He is a historian, educator, and speaker and he has been a technical advisor and actor in television movies, including *Return to Lonesome Dove*. A recipient of the Wyoming Humanities Award, he is the author of two collections of essays, *On Behalf of the Wolf and the First Peoples* and *The Dance House,* and a novel, *Winter of the Holy Iron.* He lives in Jackson Hole, Wyoming.

As you adjust to the expectations of college, think about how you might need to persevere in order to succeed. What lessons are you learning that you could pass on to the next generation?

Perseverance
Wowacintanka (wo-wah-chin-tan-gah)
To persist, to strive in spite of difficulties

1   Working for the Civilian Conservation Corps (CCC) in the 1930s, my grandfather Albert Two Hawk, then nearly fifty years old, was part of a construction crew building a dam. To get to work, he arose at four o'clock in the morning, walked eight miles to the job site, and then walked all day guiding (more like wrestling) a four-foot-wide dirt scoop pulled by a team of four horses. When the day's work was done, he **unharnessed** his horses; fed, watered, and put them in their pen; and walked eight miles home. This was his routine six days a week for several months. When I was about five and he was sixty-two, I watched him build a log house mostly on his own, with only hand tools. That was the first time I recall thinking my grandfather could do anything. Looking back on it now, anyone who can build a house while a five-year-old boy is underfoot in every **conceivable** manner is capable of miracles.

2   My grandfather was a man of many talents. He could **wield** an ax, a *bucksaw*, a hammer, or a butcher knife with **consummate** skill. He could skin and quarter a deer or a steer faster than anyone, and make skillet bread over a campfire. In such ways he was like many Lakota men of his generation, but there was something that set him apart. My grandfather had something that isn't dependent on a skill or strength. He knew how to **persevere**.

3   My grandfather certainly had the **requisite** skills to do the job for the CCC. He knew horses, for example, and wasn't afraid of hard work. The dollar or so he earned every day during the Depressions went a long way to support his family—my grandmother, my mother, my uncle. But walking eight miles to work, in addition

---

Bucksaw—a saw blade set in a large quadrangular frame

to many, many miles on the job, and then eight miles home—only to do it again the following day—required more than ability or physical strength.

4   I can't imagine the bone-weary **fatigue** he must have felt each night. My grandmother said he would arrive home, eat, and fall into bed. It's one thing to **succumb** to fatigue at the end of an exhausting day; it is quite another thing to wake up before dawn and persuade yourself to do it all over again. That is where perseverance kicks in.

5   Perseverance rises from the spirit—rather like a sleeping giant—when we've reached our physical limits or we've collided with a barrier that tells us we can't or shouldn't. It enhances strengths and capabilities, awakens our determination, and enables us to move beyond our limits, **coaxing** from us just enough effort to keep moving, to keep reaching and **striving** despite the weariness, or pain, or despair.

6   There were moments, I'm sure, when my grandfather felt as if he were battling with a giant that summer working for the CCC. He was at that time still in his physical prime and he was a very strong man. But it was more than physical strength that kept him going . . .

7   There have been moments in my life when Iya has come out of the darkness to overwhelm me and make me feel **insignificant** and not equal to the task, whether it was recovering from a broken hip or surviving the passing of my precious grandparents. Sometimes the giant has been so large and **menacing** that I have forgotten that within me is the means to defeat him. Within me, as within everyone, is the ability to persevere. Then I remind myself that darkness, despair, pain, and the absence of hope are what perseverance thrives on. When friends and **colleagues** seem to have deserted because you have made and stuck by an unpopular decision; when the **specter** of racial or gender bias has slammed a seemingly immovable obstacle in your path; when the weight of loneliness appears to have made you invisible to the world; when going to a job you don't like makes

you hate going through the front door; when facing a teacher whose only purpose is to make you so miserable even tying your shoe laces seems an impossible task; or when failure shakes your self-confidence, that's the time to pause and reach inside—and try again.

8   You can't truly succeed without perseverance. If you've easily accomplished many goals, you are indeed fortunate. But as my grandfather would often say, life isn't worth living unless you are forced to defend it now and then. Therefore you haven't truly tasted success unless you've picked yourself up after failure has knocked you down, as many times as it takes, until you accomplish what you've set out to do.

9   If I have within me one-tenth of my grandparents' ability to meet **adversity,** I can face anything. I'm reminded of that each time I see a stock dam anywhere, because it reminds me of one such dam called the Blue Rock Dam near White River, South Dakota, in what was the northern part of the Rosebud Reservation. The Blue Rock Dam is eight miles from where my parents now live, on the home site which Grandpa Albert and Grandma Nellie once lived. Eight miles is a long walk, but each is a lesson in perseverance. ■

Source: Marshall, Joseph M., III. (2001). *The Lakota Way, Stories and Lessons for Living, Native American Wisdom on Ethics and Character.* New York: Penguin Compass.

Directions: Use word parts, context clues, and/or a dictionary to define the following words.

1. unharnessed released from the harness
2. conceivable imaginable
3. wield use, carry
4. consummate expert, talented
5. persevere persist, keep trying
6. requisite required
7. fatigue tiredness, exhaustion
8. succumb give in, surrender
9. coaxing persuading
10. striving struggling, trying hard
11. insignificant not important
12. menacing threatening, frightening

13. colleagues _equals, social group_

14. specter _ghost, spirit_

15. adversity _hardship, difficulty_

Critical Thinking

16. Why did Marshall say his grandfather could do anything? _____
Answers will vary.

17. Marshall stated that his grandfather was "like many Lakota men of his generation." What did he say "set him apart"? _____
Answers will vary.

18. What were the "requisite skills" Marshall's grandfather demonstrated for working for the Civilian Conservation Corps? _____
Answers will vary.

19. Marshall stated that his grandfather walked eight miles to and from work each day. Why was this significant in the point Marshall was trying to make? _____
Answers will vary.

20. Marshall stated that his "grandfather felt as if he were battling with a giant." What did he mean? _____
Answers will vary.

21. Who do you think "Iya" is? _____
Answers will vary.

22. Describe a time when you have faced an "Iya." What did you do? _____
Answers will vary.

Activity

With a group, discuss what Marshall means by the statement "you can't truly succeed without perseverance." Share your group's interpretation with the class.
Answers will vary.

Magazine/Periodical   **READING 4**

For Many Jobless, It's Back to School: Reversing Course: Learn How to Get in–and Pay for–a Good Retraining Program

Do you know someone who lost their job? Or maybe you are returning to school after being in the work force. For many people, going back to school is the best option. Read the article below for more information about making the best of a bad situation.

1   At 47, Mike Christopher is considered a success of America's retraining system. After the Flint, Mich., car door panel factory where he worked shut in 2005, Christopher received federal grants and unemployment insurance to study computer-aided design at Mott Community College. That led to a good-paying job as a CAD designer at a medical instruments factory.

2   True, going without a paycheck during more than two years of schooling cost Christopher his house and car. But many buddies who *opted* for different retraining routes are still jobless. His retraining "actually worked better than I hoped," Christopher says. "I have no regrets."

3   Research shows that a substantial struggle followed by an eventual recovery is typical for the jobless who go back to school. Those who spend their downtime learning new skills typically earn less than their **non-retrained** counterparts initially, but they get more raises and generally earn more within three years. Much, however, depends on the type and quality of the retraining program.

FINDING THE RIGHT PROGRAM

4   Retraining programs that don't teach well or impress employers waste not only precious time but *scarce* dollars since federal education grants generally support only a first bachelor's degree. One exception: study for a teaching certificate.

5   Picking the right program can be a challenge since there are few job openings to train for these days, and it's hard to predict which industry will implode next. The demand for retraining is so great that many reputable and affordable programs are **swamped**. Community colleges, usually the first stop for anyone seeking retraining, are sometimes turning away students.

Opted—chosen
Scarce—limited

6   Some **charlatans** have sensed an opportunity in the *voracious* demand for retraining and have started programs that make too-good-to-be-true promises of certifications and *lucrative* jobs in just a few weeks. Experts and workers who have retooled themselves say there are three steps to choosing a good program.

7   **Focus on the future.** Basic 21st-century business skills such as accounting and technology are safe bets, says Anthony Carnevale, director of the Georgetown University Center on Education and the Workforce. And for now, the healthcare and elder-care fields seem to be on hiring binges despite the recession, he notes.

8   **Stick with accredited and reputable programs.** Mary Wright, project director for human capital at the Conference Board, suggests asking prospective employers which training programs and colleges they recruit from. Check colleges' accreditation with the U.S. Department of Education. The Department of Labor maintains a list of programs eligible for federal retraining funds.

9   **Beat the crowds.** Apply as early as possible. At Miami community colleges, students who registered months early got their classes, while last-minute applicants were shut out. Many late applicants who got in also had to take classes at odd hours or travel to out-of-the-way locations.

10   **Look for free programs.** Though not as impressive to employers as certificates or degrees, informal skills updates are often free. One-stop career centers and community organizations offer many free classes. Some prestigious universities, such as Carnegie Mellon, offer free online self-study courses. Even reading business books from the library can help sharpen your skills and employability, says Deb Cohen of the Society for Human Resource Management.

11   **Hunker down.** Lynn Welsh, a former Circuit City warehouse worker from Nazareth, Pa., **slashed** her budget to live on about 60 percent of her old income so she can survive on unemployment benefits while taking a two-semester, medical-office training course at Northampton Community College. The pay in her new field will probably be lower than the $17 an hour she previously earned. "It is going to be really, really tight," she says, but she hopes the new job will eventually lead to a better career. Odds are Welsh, too, will become another retraining success story. ■

Source: Clark, Kim. (Mar. 1, 2010). For Many Jobless, It's Back to School: Reversing Course: Learn How to Get in—and Pay for—a Good Retraining Program. *U.S. News & World Report. Vol. 147, Iss. 3, p. 66. Copyright 2009 U.S. News & World Report.*

Voracious—big
Lucrative—well-paid

Vocabulary

Directions: Use word parts and context clues to determine the meaning of the words.

Use word parts to determine the meaning of ***non-retrained*** from paragraph 3:

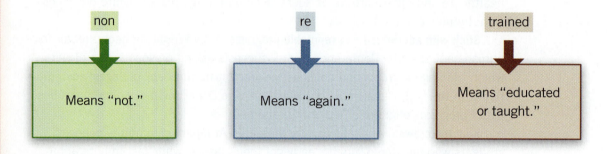

1. Based on the clues above what does ***non-retrained*** mean? _____

   not trained again

Use context clues to help you determine the meaning of ***swamped*** in paragraph 5.

The demand for retraining is so great that many reputable and afford-able programs are ***swamped***. Community colleges, usually the first stop for anyone seeking retraining, are sometimes turning away students.

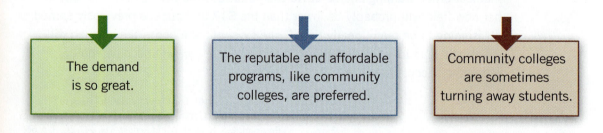

2. Based on the clues above, what is the meaning of ***swamped***? _____

   very busy

Use context clues to determine the meaning of **charlatans** in paragraph 6.

Some **charlatans** have sensed an opportunity in the voracious demand for retraining and have started programs that make too-good-to-be-true promises of certifications and lucrative jobs in just a few weeks.

They make too-good-to-be-true promises.	They promise certifications and high paid jobs in only a few weeks.	They've sensed an opportunity because demand for retraining is big.

3. Based on the clues above, what is the meaning of **charlatans**? _____
imposters, fakes, frauds

Use context clues to determine the meaning of the word **slashed** in paragraph 11.

Lynn Welsh, a former Circuit City warehouse worker from Nazareth, Pa., **slashed** her budget to live on about 60 percent of her old income so she can survive on unemployment benefits while taking a two-semester, medical-office training course at Northampton Community College.

She will need to live on 60 percent of her old income.	She must survive on unemployment benefits while going to college.	She needed to do something to her budget since she was no longer employed.

4. Based on the clues above, what is the meaning of **slashed**? _____
cut drastically

5–10. The author of the article offers several suggestions. Discuss your thoughts about the suggestions based on your experiences so far with college and/or retraining schools.
Answers will vary.

Visual Images   **READING 5**

Directions: Using context clues and/or word parts, circle the word that best matches the italicized word in the sentence.

1. The student in the photograph above seems *fatigued* as she tries to study.

    a. angry   **b. exhausted**   **c.** confident   **d.** eager

2. Her books are *strewn* all over her table.

    a. scattered   **b.** arranged   **c.** set   **d.** missing

3. The student's face shows that she is *exuberant* about her exam score.

    a. confused   **b. excited**   **c.** unsure   **d.** indifferent

4. Her reaction shows that she probably *surpassed* her own expectations for success.

   a. bypassed   **b.** surprised   **c.** doubted   **d. exceeded**

5. The professor is helping her students *ascertain* knowledge. She does not assume they already know the material in the course.

   a. forget   **b.** withhold   **c. learn**   **d.** connect

6. One could guess that the man in the front row is *unperturbed* based on his non-verbal clues.

   a. tired   **b.** unprepared   **c.** bored   **d. comfortable**

7. The student in the photograph is *deciphering* her textbook.

   a. reading   **b.** avoiding   **c.** carrying   **d.** showing

8. The pen in the student's hand in the photo on page 61 *implies* that she is also taking notes.

   a. dictates   b. indicates   c. replicates   d. eradicates

9. The students' *jovial* attitude is apparent by the smiles on their faces in the photograph above.

   a. concerned   b. unfriendly   c. fatigued   d. happy

10. The way they are sitting and laughing together shows their *camaraderie*.

    a. insecurity   b. friendship   c. weariness   d. fear

Additional Recommended Reading

Axelrod-Contrada, J. (2003, April). Finding Your Niche. *Career World, 31*(6), 25.

Light, R. J. (2001). *Making the Most of College: Students Speak Their Minds.* Cambridge, MA: Harvard University Press.

Prentice Hall Student Success SuperSite. http://www.prenhall.com/success/StudySkl/ld_current.html

See, P., and B. Taylor. (2006). *Higher Learning Reading and Writing about College*, 2nd ed. Upper Saddle River, NJ: Pearson.

Simon, C. (2002, February). You're There. Now What? *Campus Life, 60*(7), 30.

myreadinglab

For support in meeting this chapter's objectives, log on to www.myreadinglab.com and select Vocabulary and Vocabulary Development.

2 Main Ideas

LEARNING OUTCOMES

LO1 Employ the SQ3R technique for better reading comprehension.

LO2 Find the topic of a reading passage.

LO3 Use knowledge of the topic to lead you to the author's main idea.

THEME **Life Relationships**

SPOTLIGHT ON LEARNING STYLES 🔊)) *L*ISTEN

How many times have you heard someone say "I'm just not good with names"? Learning names is crucial in establishing positive relationships with people in academic, professional, and personal settings. So, if you think you are one of those people who is not good with names, how do you get better? I had a biology professor once who learned 1000 students' names each semester. He said we all have that ability in our brains but we don't use it. He took pictures of everyone and put names under the pictures and memorized the name-face connections. He would see us in lecture or in the hall and address us by name. I was impressed! I learn all of my students' names during the first class period, but I only have about 100 people to remember each semester. Here's what I do. I ask students to write their names on folded cards and place the cards in front of the table by their seats. Then as the class goes on, I look at their faces and say each name out loud. As I look at the person and the name, I repeat it out loud to hear myself say it. I try to learn three people at a time, then three or four more, kind of like a phone number. Once I've learned a group of three and then four names, I add three more. I repeat the names and look at their faces over and over. Eventually I have added the whole group in 3 to 4 student increments. I ask the students to join in and we all learn each others' names. When I see my students in the hall throughout the week I challenge myself to say their names out loud when I say hello. Forcing myself to say names when I see a person is a great way to reinforce the memory. Try it! You may surprise yourself!

Have you ever been reading and then realized you had turned several pages but did not remember what you just read? Maybe . . .

- Your mind wandered and you started thinking about something else (like your grocery list or your weekend plans), but your eyes kept moving along through the words.

- You concentrated on the text, but when you were finished reading you realized that you did not know for sure what you read.

To comprehend the text, it is important to:

- focus on the overall subject, or topic, of the passage.

- know what point the author is trying to convey.

This overall idea is called the *main idea.* In this chapter you will learn to recognize and use the author's topic and main idea when you read. You will also learn the SQ3R technique for reading. SQ3R is a system for reading that will help you focus on and retain relevant information. It is especially useful for reading college textbooks and journal articles.

While you are improving your skill at finding the main idea, you'll also be improving your understanding of the relationships in your life. The examples and practice in this chapter pertain to different types of life relationships including friends, co-workers, bosses, dates, partners, families, children, and even pets. So whether you are single or married, work outside the home or in, have children or pets, there should be information that will be useful to you in this chapter.

SQ3R (Survey, Question, Read, Recite, and Review for Better Comprehension)

If you've ever found yourself reading and then you couldn't remember what you just read, SQ3R will help. Or, if you read an assignment but then you didn't know what was important and what

LO1
Employ the SQ3R technique for better reading comprehension.

was not, SQ3R could be the answer. Another good reason to use SQ3R is to help you obtain and retain information you'll need for research papers and exams.

SQ3R is simply an organized strategy for reading. The letters in the acronym represent the steps in the strategy: S is for Survey; Q is for Question; and 3R is for Read, Recite, and Review. It may seem strange at first, but once you've practiced it a few times, SQ3R will become a useful technique to use when you read. You'll be able to stay focused on the material and retain the important information.

First, let's go over the five steps of SQ3R and then practice using them.

Survey	Skim over the material. Read the title, subtitle, subheadings, first and last paragraphs, pictures, charts, and graphics. Note italics and bold print.
Question	Ask yourself questions before you read. What do you want to know? Turn headings and subheadings into questions and/or read questions if provided.
Read	Read the material in manageable chunks. This may be one or two paragraphs at a time or the material under one subheading.
Recite	Recite the answer to each question in your own words. This is a good time to write notes as you read each section. Repeat the question-read-recite cycle.
Review	Look over your notes at the end of the chapter, article, or material. Review what you learned and write a summary in your own words.

S—Survey Look over the article or textbook assignment. Look at titles, subtitles, bold print, italics, pictures, charts, and graphs. Also, read the first and last paragraphs if you are reading an article, or the introduction and summary if it is a chapter in a textbook. Remember—you are just surveying, or skimming, the material to get an overview. For an article, it may only take a minute. For a textbook chapter, you may need 3–5 minutes. When you survey, ask yourself, "What are the overall topics that are included in the material I am about to read?"

Q—Question After you have done the survey, you can ask, "What do I want to learn from this material?" The survey revealed the major topics. Now you can ask questions you hope the material will answer. This step will help you stay focused because the material will have some real purpose for you. When you ask the questions and want to know the answers, it is easier to pay attention and keep your mind from wandering.

     With a textbook, you might use the chapter overview or summary questions. But don't stop there. Another good idea is to turn the bold print headings and subheadings in the chapter into questions by adding *who, what, where, when,* or *why* to the headings. For example, if the subheading is "Non-Verbal Expression of Emotion" you might ask "What are non-verbal expressions of emotions?" Asking yourself questions as you read will help you seek and find relevant information. This will improve your reading comprehension.

R—Read This step may seem obvious. But here is an important tip: Read manageable chunks of material, maybe a paragraph or two under just one subheading at a time. For example, once you have turned the subheading into a question, you can read and focus on just that one section. Then you can Recite the answer to your question before you go on to the next section.

R—Recite Remember, you should read in manageable chunks, such as a paragraph or two under one subheading. So, if you write the answer to a question just after you read that chunk of text, you will be able to record the important information in your own words. As you work your way through a longer article or chapter, you should repeat the Question–Read–Recite steps with each paragraph or two or with each subheading. This keeps you focused on one key idea at a time and allows you to stop and take a break without forgetting what you've already read.

     A suggestion that works well for many people is to read with a pencil in your hand. If you own the book or have a copy of the article, write your questions and answers on the page as you go through the material. If you don't own the book or don't want to write in it, then write in a notebook or on a sheet of paper. Either way, the practice of creating the questions and reciting the answers in your own words and writing them down for later review will help you etch the information into your memory.

R—Review Once you have finished reading the article or the chapter, look over all of your notes (your questions and answers). Read and reread all of the important information (not the entire article, just your notes). This is a good time to write a summary in your own words. Every time you process the reading material through your own mind, you enable yourself to better understand and remember it.

The amount of review you do will depend on the purpose of your reading. For example, if you read a newspaper article and you want to tell your friend about what you learned about the new non-smoking ordinance in your town, your purpose for reading will be different than if you need to retain and recall the information from your textbook for an exam in three weeks.

PRACTICE THE NEW SKILL

Survey	Skim over the material. Read the title, subtitle, subheadings, first and last paragraphs, pictures, charts, and graphics. Note italics and bold print.
Question	Ask yourself questions before you read. What do you want to know? Turn headings and subheadings into questions and/or read questions if provided.
Read	Read the material in manageable chunks. This may be one or two paragraphs at a time or the material under one subheading.
Recite	Recite the answer to each question in your own words. This is a good time to write notes as you read each section. Repeat the question-read-recite cycle.
Review	Look over your notes at the end of the chapter, article, or material. Review what you learned and write a summary in your own words.

Directions: Practice the SQ3R strategy as you read the article below.

S—Survey

What are you going to be focusing on when you read this article?
Ways to know you're dating a keeper

Q—Questions *(Turn the headings into questions and write them in the spaces provided.)*

R—Read *(Read one section at a time.)*

R—Recite *(Answer your questions as you read, and write them in your own words in the spaces provided.)*

5 Ways to Know You're Dating a Keeper

1   **Do they spend every waking moment focusing on you?** It may seem nice to have someone waiting on you hand and foot, but after a while all of the constant attention will get old fast. If they're too concerned with your life, they won't have time to live their own. On the other hand though, if they're sufficiently independent, then they will respect you and your time.

2   **Do you and your partner agree on everything?** Dating someone who has their own opinion is *much* more appealing than someone who's constantly taking your side. As long as they hear your position on an issue and defend their own (and aren't rude about it), your relationship will grow into a wonderful partnership.

3   **Do they answer texts/calls from other people when you're on a date?** Being on a cell phone when you're supposed to be spending time with your special someone is a way of saying "I don't care about you." If they ignore their calls and texts from other people, it's a sign that they are really interested in what you have to say.

4   **Are they nice to workers in restaurants and stores (and other people they don't *have* to be nice to)?** If your partner is polite and friendly to people they meet every day, especially people they don't know or people who will not help them get ahead, then they are genuinely nice. On the other hand, if they are rude or disrespectful to people they don't know or service workers, then you may want to think twice about them as a potential lifelong partner.

5   **Are they suspiciously perfect?** If they seem too perfect then they probably aren't as good as they appear. Anyone can put on an act and pretend to not have any flaws. A real keeper has imperfections, though; no one is perfect.

Directions: Using the SQ3R steps, write your questions and answers below. See Question 1 as an example.

Question 1: Do they spend every waking moment focusing on you?

Recite 1: Answers will vary.

Question 2: Do you and your partner agree on everything?

Recite 2: Answers will vary.

Question 3: Do they answer texts/calls from other people when you're on a date?

Recite 3: Answers will vary.

Question 4: Are they nice to workers in restaurants (and other people they don't have to be nice to)?

Recite 4: Answers will vary.

Question 5: Are they suspiciously perfect?

Recite 5: Answers will vary.

R—Review *(Review your notes and write a summary in your own words.)*
Answers will vary.

Finding the Topic (What is this about?)

The first step of SQ3R is to Survey the text. In surveying, you are trying to determine the **topic** of the material. How do you find the topic? Look for a word or phrase that the author uses several times throughout the paragraph or passage. For example, if you see the word *friends* three or four times in a paragraph, there is a good chance the topic is "friends." Another example is if you see the words *aunt, uncle, cousin, grandma,* and *grandpa,* the topic might be "relatives" since "relatives" is a general term that includes all of the individuals mentioned. The topic is the overall subject the paragraph or reading passage covers. It is also what you will be focusing on as you read.

> **LO2**
> Find the topic of a reading passage.

The first strategy to improve your comprehension is to make sure you know the topic or subject of the paragraph or reading passage. Writers must choose a general topic before they decide what details they are specifically going to include. Knowing this topic will help you stay focused.

First, let's practice finding the topic.

EXAMPLE ————————————————————————————————————

Directions: Circle the word that identifies the topic, or most general idea in the group of words.

aunt   uncle   extended family   grandparent

If you circled "extended family," you would be correct. Your "extended family" includes all of the other people listed: aunt, uncle, and grandparent.

PRACTICE THE NEW SKILL

Directions: Circle the general topic in each group of words.

1. texting   (communication)   Facebook   Skype

2. (lack of face to face)   long-distance relationships

   e-mails   telephone calls

3. amount of talking   offering solutions

   (gender communication differences)   ability to listen

Another way to practice finding the general topic of a group of ideas is to read several sentences and try to determine what they have in common.

EXAMPLE

Directions: Choose a topic for the group of sentences.

1. Topic _____ (friends   feeling down   support)

   a. True friends are people we can count on to be there for us.

   b. When you are feeling down, you call on a friend for support.

   c. Friends tell you when you are messing up.

If you chose *friends* as the topic, you are correct. All three sentences share the topic of *friends*.

PRACTICE THE NEW SKILL

Directions: Choose the topic for each group of sentences.

1. Topic _____ (cats   home   (pets))

   a. Pet owners deal with stress more effectively.

   b. When you come home from a hard day, a dog with a wagging tail can take away your irritability quickly.

   c. Petting a soft, purring cat lowers blood pressure.

2. Topic _____ (goals   relationships

      (college students' relationships)

    a. When a person goes to college, relationships with friends and family may change.

    b. Friends and family may treat you differently if they see you are moving ahead toward your life goals while in college.

    c. Support from family and friends is crucial to college students' success.

3. Topic _____ ((families)   neighbors   moving)

    a. Visiting relatives only once a year at family reunions is not sufficient for connecting in a meaningful way.

    b. It is hard to replicate special family bonds with neighbors and co-workers.

    c. Many people are glad to live close to their families during life crises.

Now that you can identify a general topic for a group of sentences, let's try this skill with a paragraph.

EXAMPLE ————————————————————————————————

Directions: Circle the topic of the paragraph below.

    You can't really know people from a distance. Reunions don't cut it. My extended family tries to get together at least once each year at a summer picnic or a holiday gathering. But what can I expect to happen in a few hours' time? There is a quick exchange about family events, but it's little more than headline news. I may know that my cousin got a new job, but it's unlikely she will take the time over a hot dog to relate how a recent cancer scare changed her entire outlook on life. If I lived nearby and shared some of her daily life, I would know and be able to offer my care and my prayers. But because she lives so far away, I'm not likely to be up-to-date on the meaningful events in her life. This is so terribly sad. And it's no way to live. But why are so many of us doing this?

Source: Miller, Dr. Will with Glenn Sparks, Ph.D. (2002). *Refrigerator Rights: Creating Connections and Restoring Relationships.* New York: Penguin Putnam, pp. 13–14.

a. knowing people   **c.** moving away from home

b. families   **d.** long-distance family relationships

In the paragraph above, knowing people (a) and families (b) are too broad to be the topic or focus of the paragraph. Moving away from home may be what some of the people did, but it is not the primary focus of the paragraph. The sentences are focused on the topic, (d) long-distance family relationships.

PRACTICE THE NEW SKILL

Directions: Circle the topic of each of the following paragraphs.

1.

When I remind myself, I can read some of my dogs' behavior. When their noses go to the ground, they've spotted something they might chase. When their bodies stiffen, they're expecting trouble. Panting, squinting, or cowering are symptoms of anxiety. Watching for such signals is both fascinating and helpful—if you know when your dog is about to bolt, it's much easier to teach him not to. Watching a dog's body language can also tell you if a child is upsetting him, or if another dog wants to play.

Source: Katz, Jon. (2005). *Katz on Dogs: A Commonsense Guide to Training and Living with Dogs.* New York: Villard Books, Random House p. 49.

a. playing with your pet   **c.** giving your dog attention

b. body language of dogs   **d.** panting behavior

2.

Another habit that gives women the impression men aren't listening is that they switch topics more often. Women tend to talk at length about one topic; men tend to jump from topic to topic. When a woman expresses her point of view, her female listener usually expresses agreement and support, whereas men point out the other side of the issue. Women see this as disloyalty and a refusal to offer support to their ideas. Women prefer other points of view expressed as suggestions and inquiries, rather than as direct challenges or arguments. Men are more comfortable with an oppositional style.

Source: Cava, Roberta. (2004). *Dealing with Difficult People: How to Deal with Nasty Customers, Demanding Bosses and Annoying Co-workers, Revised edition.* Buffalo, NY: Firefly, p. 44.

a. suggestions and inquiries

b. direct challenges or arguments

c. men's and women's communication styles

d. listening skills

3.

If we don't succeed, we yell the word "No" louder. We teach our children that if they don't respond the first time, we will say it louder. This teaches them that they don't have to mind until we reach a certain volume. I am much more impressed when a child responds to a normal tone of voice. Do I ever believe in yelling? If there is a loud noise like a truck that will make it harder for me to be heard I may yell, but in general I like using my normal voice.

Source: Hansen, Harold. (2000). *The Dog Trainer's Guide to Parenting: Rewarding Good Behavior, Practicing Patience and Other Positive Techniques That Work.* Naperville, IL: Sourcebooks, p. 81.

a. yelling

b. children

c. voice

d. voice volume and discipline

REVIEW WHAT YOU LEARNED

Finding the Topic

1. Circle the topic for the group of words.

competition   cooperation   support   interacting with co-workers

2. Circle the topic for the group of words.

awkwardness   first date feelings   insecurity   excitement

3. Choose the topic for the group of sentences.

Topic _____ (embarrassment   talking   (first date))

a. You may not know what to talk about with your date.

b. You may be afraid of spilling food or a drink on yourself in front of your date.

c. You have a unique laugh or mannerism and you're not sure how your date will respond to it.

4. Choose the topic for the group of sentences.

Topic _____ (medicine   (physicians)   technology)

a. Some physicians offer newer technology and procedures.

b. Some physicians use holistic or alternative medicine.

c. Not all physicians practice medicine the same way.

5. Circle the topic in the paragraph below.

Walking a pit bull is an interesting experience. No matter how happy-go-lucky and friendly that individual dog is, lots of people cross the street to steer clear. Some people are repelled by pit bulls, some by large dogs and others by all dogs. But those concerns go out the window if you happen to be walking a 14-week-old pit bull puppy, as I recently did. The little wiggly pup was a people magnet. It turns out that we can't help but love puppies, even pit bull puppies. There's just something about them.

Source: Dale, Steve. (Oct. 19–21, 2007). Why We Love Puppies. *USA Weekend.*

a. fear of pit bulls   **c.** loving puppies

b. walking your dog   **d.** fear of dogs

REVIEW *WHAT YOU LEARNED*

Finding the Topic

1. Circle the topic for the group of words.

   professor   lab assistant   instructor   (educators)

2. Circle the topic for the group of words.

   subordinate   (work relationships)   supervisor   co-worker

3. Choose the topic for the group of sentences.

   Topic _____ (my grandma)   visiting relatives
   listening to stories)

   a. When I visited my grandma she always offered me ice cream.

   b. My grandma always wore red lipstick.

   c. It was always fun to hear my grandma's stories about her past.

4. Choose the topic for the group of sentences.

   Topic _____ (customer service   wrong sized shirts
   (my experience at the mall)

   a. I went to the mall.

   b. I found a shirt that I liked, but the store didn't have it in my size.

   c. So I asked the customer service person for the shirt but she
   wasn't helpful.

5. Read the paragraph and choose the best topic from the choices below.

   Ed was filled with dread the next morning. He knew the news would
   not be good. Beattie started out by saying that he had never had a patient
   with whom he had become more emotionally involved than he had with
   Brian. "He is like a son to me and Joy is like my daughter." ("Which was
   a relief," Ed said later. "I noticed he had been hugging her a lot.") "But,"
   the doctor said, "Brian's left lung will have to come out." He felt that
   the cancer was confined to the chest, and if he could get the lung clean
   there was still a chance. He was planning to tell Brian his evaluation that
   afternoon.

   Source: Morris, Jeanne. (1974). *Brian Piccolo: A Short Season.*
   Chicago, IL: Rand McNally, pp. 127–128.

Brian Piccolo

a. medical evaluations

b. doctor and patient relationship

c. short football seasons

d. cancer

Determining the Main Idea (What does the author want me to know?)

Once you are focused on the author's general **topic**, then you can determine what specific message the author is trying to convey about that topic—the main idea. How do you find the main idea? As a reader, you should be looking for the **main idea** in the text by asking "What's the point of this paragraph?"

> **LO3**
> Use knowledge of the topic to lead you to the author's main idea.

For example, have you ever been listening to someone talk, and it seemed like the person was rambling on and on. Perhaps the person appeared to be telling totally unrelated stories or facts. You may have wondered, "What's the point?" When you asked that question, you were looking for the **main idea** the person was trying to communicate.

Let's use a visual aid to see the relationship of topic, main idea, and supporting details.

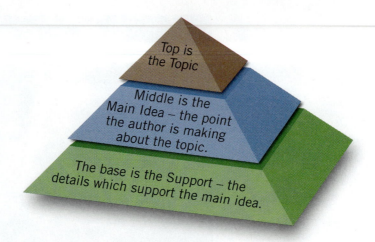

Think about the general topic "pets." If you were going to write about "pets," you'd need to decide what you want to say about pets. In other words, what point do you want to make? For instance, if you believe that "Living with pets has several positive effects on one's life," then you can discuss some of the advantages in the rest of the paragraph. See the diagram below.

T (Topic) = Pets

MI (Main Idea) = Living with pets has several positive effects on one's life.

SD (Supporting Details) = (See diagram for specific advantages for living with pets.)

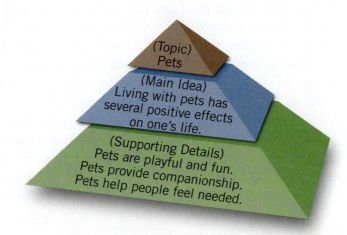

On the other hand, if you believe that "Owning pets is not worth the trouble," then you'd discuss the problems people have when they own pets. See the diagram below.

T (Topic) = Pets

MI (Main Idea) = Owning pets is not worth the trouble.

SD (Supporting Details) = (See diagram below for specific problems with pet ownership.)

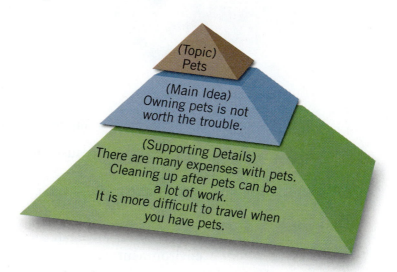

(Topic)
Pets

(Main Idea)
Owning pets is not worth the trouble.

(Supporting Details)
There are many expenses with pets.
Cleaning up after pets can be a lot of work.
It is more difficult to travel when you have pets.

PRACTICE THE NEW SKILL

Directions: Complete the pyramid using the information provided.

   1. (T = Topic; MI = Main Idea; SD = Supporting Detail)

_____T_____	My brother
_____MI_____	I could count on my older brother to be there for me when I needed him.
_____SD_____	I called my brother to pick me up from a party when people started drinking.
_____SD_____	My brother covered for me when Mom was really mad.
_____SD_____	My brother taught me how to play football so I could get an A in gym.

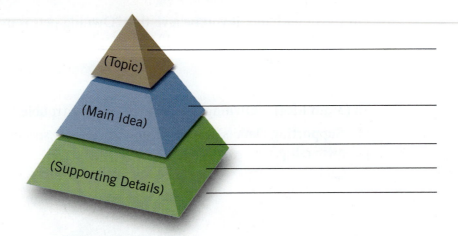

2. (T = Topic; MI = Main Idea; SD = Supporting Detail)

_____MI_____ A co-worker can cause much trouble for other employees.

_____SD_____ If a co-worker does not do her job, it can be more work for others.

_____SD_____ A co-worker can create an uncomfortable working environment.

_____SD_____ If co-workers behave unprofessionally, everyone suffers.

_____T_____ Co-workers

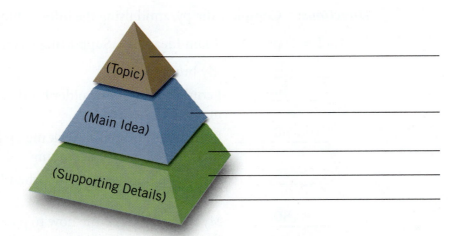

3. (T = Topic; MI = Main Idea; SD = Supporting Detail)

_____MI_____ I get along really well with my family.

_____SD_____ My family and I like to do similar activities for fun and relaxation.

_____T_____ Family

_____SD_____ When we travel, my family likes to explore many different things.

_____SD_____ My family members give each other space so we don't annoy one another.

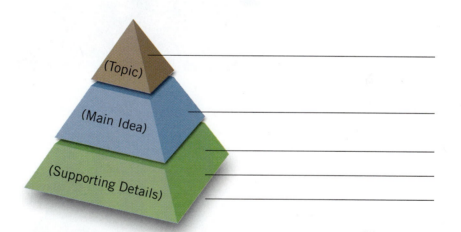

The main idea must be the author's main point about the topic. The main idea sentence (or sentences) is like an overview of the rest of the paragraph. It is also the idea the author is trying to convey about the topic. Remember: The **main idea** is not just a word or two—that is the **topic.** The **main idea** is a complete thought or sentence about the **topic.** The remaining sentences may be the **supporting details**; these are specific details that support the main idea.

EXAMPLE ——————————————————————————————————

Directions: Write **T** next to the general topic, **MI** next to the main idea, and **SD** next to the specific or supporting details in each group below.

_____ **a.** Watching older siblings can show you what works and what doesn't work with your parents.

_____ **b.** Siblings can teach each other about life.

_____ **c.** Younger siblings can help you learn to be compassionate and patient.

_____ **d.** Siblings

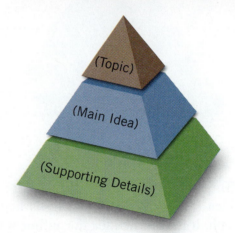

(Topic)

(Main Idea)

(Supporting Details)

In the example above, the topic is (d) siblings. The main idea is the point the author is trying to make about siblings, (b) siblings can teach each other about life. Then the supporting details are the other two sentences, (a) and (c). They are specific ideas that support the author's main idea.

PRACTICE *THE NEW SKILL*

Directions: Write **T** next to the topic, **MI** next to the main idea, and **SD** next to the supporting details in each group below. (You may also find it helpful to draw a pyramid diagram so you can see the relationships.)

1.

_____SD_____ **a.** Managers can show they care about their employees as people, not just their performance.

_____MI_____ **b.** There are many things managers can do to foster a good relationship with their subordinates.

_____T_____ **c.** Managers

_____SD_____ **d.** Good managers give praise when praise is due.

2.

_____T_____ **a.** Companions

_____SD_____ **b.** A companion may be someone you spend time with on a regular basis.

_____MI_____ **c.** The word *companion* can have different meanings to different people.

_____SD_____ **d.** A companion may signify someone to which a personal commitment has been made.

3.

_____SD_____ **a.** In a healthy relationship people do not insult each other.

_____SD_____ **b.** If someone pushes or shoves you, there is a problem with the relationship.

_____MI_____ **c.** There are signs to watch for to see if a relationship is healthy or unhealthy.

_____T_____ **d.** Relationships

Another way to improve your skill at finding the topic is to create your own specific details related to the main idea.

EXAMPLE ———————————————————————————————

Directions: Write your own specific details that support the main idea.

1. There are many ways to use technology to keep in touch with friends. What are three specific ways you might use technology to keep in touch with your friends?

a. _____

b. _____

c. _____

Some specific ways to keep in touch with friends using technology might include e-mail, text messages, IMing, voice mail, MySpace, or Facebook.

PRACTICE *THE NEW SKILL*

Directions: Write your own specific details that support the main idea.

1. Pressures of society may lead us away from our sense of right and wrong. This could affect many of our relationships. What are three specific examples of doing what is right versus doing what is wrong?

a. Answers will vary. _____

b. _____

c. _____

2. Volunteer work is a great way to strengthen relationships in the communities where we live. List three specific ways you might volunteer in your community.

a. Answers will vary. _____

b. _____

c. _____

3. Raising children while going to college can be challenging in many ways. What are three specific ways raising children while going to college might be challenging?

a. Answers will vary. _____

b. _____

c. _____

Now let's revisit the SQ3R reading process to help you find the topic and main idea.

When you read using the SQ3R process, in the Survey step you find the **topic**. Then you survey each subheading and create Questions. The answers to those questions will lead you to the **main idea** of each paragraph. So, for example, when you survey the material, you have an idea about what the overall subject or topic will be. Then you can look for the point the author is trying to make about the topic.

Survey	Skim over the material. Read the title, subtitle, subheadings, first and last paragraphs, pictures, charts, and graphics. Note italics and bold print.
Question	Ask yourself questions before you read. What do you want to know? Turn headings and subheadings into questions and/or read questions if provided.
Read	Read the material in manageable chunks. This may be one or two paragraphs at a time or the material under one subheading.
Recite	Recite the answer to each question in your own words. This is a good time to write notes as you read each section. Repeat the question-read-recite cycle.
Review	Look over your notes at the end of the chapter, article, or material. Review what you learned and write a summary in your own words.

Now you are ready to find the topic and main idea in a paragraph.

EXAMPLE

Directions: Circle the topic and underline the main idea in the paragraph below.

Even more important, the organizational principles that underlie McDonald's are coming to dominate our entire society. Our culture is becoming "McDonaldized," an awkward way of saying that many aspects of life are modeled on the famous restaurant chain. Parents buy toys at worldwide chain stores such as Toys 'R' Us; we drive in to Jiffy lube for a ten-minute oil change; face-to-face communication is being replaced more and more with voice mail, e-mail, and junk mail; more vacations take the form of resort and tour packages; television presents news in the form of ten-second sound bites; college admissions officers size up students they have never met by glancing at their GPA and SAT scores and professors assign ghostwritten textbooks and evaluate students by giving tests mass-produced for them by publishing companies. The list goes on and on.

Source: Macionis, John J. (2006). *Society: The Basics,* 8th ed. Upper Saddle River, NJ: Pearson Prentice Hall, p. 127.

The topic of this paragraph is "McDonaldization." The main idea is sentence 2, "Our culture is becoming 'McDonaldized,' an awkward way of saying that many aspects of life are modeled on the famous restaurant chain."

PRACTICE THE NEW SKILL

Directions: Circle the topic and underline the main idea in the paragraphs below.

1.

Are you an adult or still an adolescent? Does turning twenty-one make you a "grown-up"? According to the sociologist Tom Smith (2003), in our society, no one factor announces the onset of adulthood. In fact, the results of his survey—using a representative sample of 1,398 people over the age of eighteen—suggest that many factors play a part in our decision to consider a young person as "grown-up." According to the survey, the single most important transition in claiming adult status in the United States today is the completion of schooling, But other factors are also important: Smith's respondents linked adult standing to taking on a full-time job, gaining the ability to support a family financially, no longer living with parents, and finally, marrying and becoming a parent. In other words, almost everyone in the United States thinks a person who has done *all* of these things is fully "grown-up."

Source: Macionis, John. (2011). *Society: The Basics*, 11th ed. Upper Saddle River, NJ: Pearson, p. 77.

2.

When I remind myself, I can read some of my dogs' behavior. When their noses go to the ground, they've spotted something they might chase. When their bodies stiffen, they're expecting trouble. Panting, squinting, or cowering are symptoms of anxiety. Watching for such signals is both fascinating and helpful—if you know when your dog is about to bolt, it's much easier to teach him not to. Watching a dog's body language can also tell you if a child is upsetting him, or if another dog wants to play.

Source: Katz, Jon. (2005). *Katz on Dogs: A Commonsense Guide to Training and Living with Dogs*. New York: Villard Books, Random House, p. 49.

3.

Another habit that gives women the impression men aren't listening is that they switch topics more often. Women tend to talk at length about one topic; men tend to jump from topic to topic. When a woman expresses her point of view, her female listener usually expresses agreement and support,

whereas men point out the other side of the issue. Women see this as disloyalty and a refusal to offer support to their ideas. (Women) prefer other (points of view expressed) as suggestions and inquiries, rather than as direct challenges or arguments. (Men) are more comfortable with an oppositional (style).

Source: Cava, Roberta. (2004). *Dealing with Difficult People: How to Deal with Nasty Customers, Demanding Bosses and Annoying Co-workers, Revised edition.* Buffalo, NY: Firefly, p. 44.

REVIEW WHAT YOU LEARNED

Finding the Topic and Main Idea

1–2. Circle the topic and underline the main idea.

(Faith in God) was not a casual part of the lives of the (World War II generation). The men and women who went off to war, or stayed home, volunteer that their spiritual beliefs helped them cope with the constant presence of possible death, serious injury, or the other anxieties attendant to the disruptions brought on by war. Helen Van Gorder's faith helped her through the great strains of having a husband, and later a son, in the line of fire. Faith was the twin to love in the marriage of the Brodericks. On the front lines, chaplains were not incidental of the war effort. Some jumped with the Airborne troops on D-Day and others risked their own lives to administer last rites or other comforting words to dying and grievously wounded young men wherever the battle took them. The very nature of war prompted many who participated in it to think more deeply about God and their relationship to a higher being once they returned home.

Source: Brokaw, Tom. (1998). *The Greatest Generation.* New York: Random House, pp. 70–71.

3–5. List three ways faith helped people through the war.

Answers will vary.

_____

_____

_____

REVIEW WHAT YOU LEARNED

Finding the Main Idea

1–2. Circle the topic and underline the main idea.

We're simply hard-wired to be attracted to the little creatures. After all, their large foreheads and big round eyes are reminiscent of human babies. Clearly, we're predisposed to care for babies. "We're a nurturing species. We need to be," agrees animal behaviorist Patricia McConnell. "Our babies require a great deal of care for many years. When we see these cues, we can't help but respond with a rush of a hormone called oxytocin. We generalize our feelings to other species—including dogs."

Source: Dale, Steve. (October 19–21, 2007). Why We Love Puppies. *USA Weekend.*

3–5. List three reasons why humans are attracted to little creatures.

Their large foreheads and big round eyes are reminiscent of human babies.

We're predisposed to care for babies.

When we see these cues, we can't help but respond with a rush of a hormone called oxytocin. We generalize our feelings to other species—including dogs.

MASTER THE LESSON

Finding the Topic and Main Idea

Directions: Write **T** next to the topic, **MI** next to the main idea, and **SD** next to the supporting details.

1. _____MI_____ Getting to know your neighbors can be beneficial for several reasons.

2. _____T_____ Neighbors

3. _____SD_____ If you are away, your neighbors can watch over your home and report suspicious activity.

4. _____SD_____ In case of an emergency you can call on your neighbors for assistance.

5–8. Create a pyramid chart for the information above.

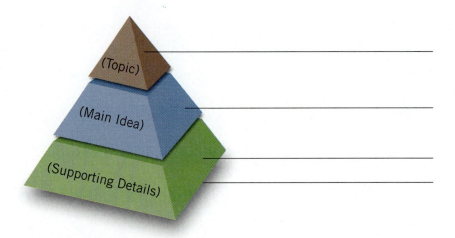

(Topic)

(Main Idea)

(Supporting Details)

9–10. Circle the topic and underline the main idea in the paragraph below.

Knowing that we are loved and respected by others is an essential ingredient in self-esteem, but ultimately (self-esteem) is an inside job. "Looking good" and putting a high polish on your self-presentation does *not* equal self-esteem. All the feel-good messages in the world can't give a child self-esteem if she does not experience herself as effective, competent, and true to herself. (The "do it myself" insistence of the toddler is a claim on self-esteem as well as on independence.) It's important that school-age girls be encouraged to develop areas of expertise and mastery that are recognized by the world beyond their immediate families. This sets up a positive self-esteem cycle. Each time she learns she can rely on herself, or relate effectively to others, or reach a personal goal, the more confidence she has for the next step in her development. And if she suffers a setback, the faster she is likely to recover and get moving forward again.

Source: Northrup, Christiane, M.D. (2005). *Mother-Daughter Wisdom: Creating a Legacy of Physical and Emotional Health.* New York: Bantam Dell, Random House, p. 319.

MASTER THE LESSON

Finding the Topic and Main Idea

Directions: Write **T** next to the topic, **MI** next to the main idea, and **SD** next to the supporting details.

1. _____SD_____ Women may try to give men advice even when they don't ask for it.

2. _____T_____ Men and women

3. _____MI_____ Men and women relate to each other in different ways.

4. _____SD_____ Men may try to solve a problem even when a woman only needs someone to listen.

5–8. Create a pyramid chart for the information above.

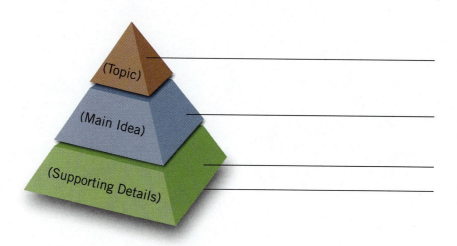

(Topic)

(Main Idea)

(Supporting Details)

9–10. Circle the topic and underline the main idea in the paragraph below.

If we don't succeed, we yell the word "No" louder. We teach our children that if they don't respond the first time, we will say it louder. This teaches them that they don't have to mind until we reach a certain volume. I am much more impressed when a child responds to a normal tone of voice. Do I ever believe in yelling? If there is a loud noise like a truck that will make it harder for me to be heard I may yell, but in general I like using my normal voice.

Source: Hansen, Harold. (2000). *The Dog Trainer's Guide to Parenting: Rewarding Good Behavior, Practicing Patience and Other Positive Techniques That Work.* Naperville, IL: Sourcebooks, p. 81.

LEARNING STYLE ACTIVITIES

Look, Listen, Write, Do

Use your college or local library to research "life relationships." First decide what type of relationship you'd like to study. For example, you may choose parent-child, significant other, spouse, grandparents, pets, etc. Then decide what you specifically want to know. You may work alone or collaboratively.

Write your topic:

_____

Write the main idea:

_____

Look   Look for pictures that exemplify special life relationships. Create a poster, PowerPoint, or collage with the pictures and summarize your findings in a visual format.

Listen   Listen to information from "talking books" (books on tape or CD) or podcasts. Prepare a verbal summary of your findings. You may record it or speak it to the class.

Write   Find written material such as books and magazines on your topic. Take notes and either write a summary or an outline of the important information.

Do   Search for movies (DVDs or videos) about your topic. Prepare a summary to demonstrate your findings to the class.

Reading Practice

The next section of the chapter will help refine your skills in finding the topic and main idea while you read a variety of materials. Remember to use SQ3R while you read. All five of the readings address topics related to life relationships.

The first reading is *The Five Love Languages* from an Internet Web site.

The second reading is a section, "Nonverbal Communication of Emotion," from an introductory psychology textbook.

The third reading is a short story, "With Help from a Friend" by Dorri Olds from *Chicken Soup for the College Soul: Inspiring and Humorous Stories about College.*

The fourth reading, "Work: When Personalities Clash," comes from *Psychology Today* magazine.

Finally, the fifth reading includes two visual images of couples relating in different manners.

In each of the reading selections, several vocabulary words are underlined. Use your knowledge of word parts and/or context clues to determine the meanings. Answering the questions following each reading will help you continue to develop your vocabulary and reading comprehension. In the visual reading you will need to find the main idea of the image.

Internet

READING 1

The Five Love Languages

Have you ever thought you were showing your loved one how much you care but he or she did not seem to receive it? Or perhaps you've experienced times when it seems that no matter what you did for someone they did not feel your love. Maybe you speak different love languages and don't know it. Read the Web site article below to learn about the different love languages people speak and how to speak in a language so they will feel loved.

Directions: Practice the SQ3R strategy as you read this Internet Web site excerpt.

Survey	Skim over the material. Read the title, subtitle, subheadings, first and last paragraphs, pictures, charts, and graphics. Note italics and bold print.
Question	Ask yourself questions before you read. What do you want to know? Turn headings and subheadings into questions and/or read questions if provided.
Read	Read the material in manageable chunks. This may be one or two paragraphs at a time or the material under one subheading.
Recite	Recite the answer to each question in your own words. This is a good time to write notes as you read each section. Repeat the question-read-recite cycle.
Review	Look over your notes at the end of the chapter, article, or material. Review what you learned and write a summary in your own words.

S—Survey

1. What are you going to be focusing on when you read this article? _____
   The Five Love Languages

2. What did you notice about the bold print subheadings? _____
   They list the five love languages.

Q—Question *(Hint: turn the five bold print subheadings into five questions—see below.)*

R—Read

R—Recite *(Write the answers to your five questions as you read each section—see below.)*

1   After many years of counseling, Dr. Chapman noticed a pattern: everyone he had ever counseled had a "love language," a primary way of expressing and interpreting love. He also discovered that, for whatever reason, people are usually drawn to those who speak a different love language than their own.

2   Of the countless ways we can show love to one another, five key categories, or five love languages, proved to be universal and comprehensive—everyone has a love language, and we all identify primarily with one of the five love languages: Words of Affirmation, Quality Time, Receiving Gifts, Acts of Service, and Physical Touch.

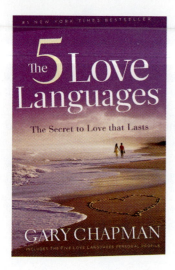

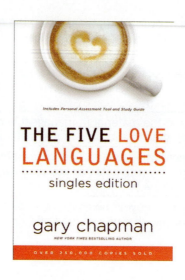

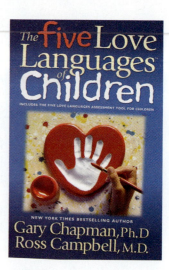

THE FIVE LOVE LANGUAGES

3   What if you could say or do just the right thing guaranteed to make that special someone feel loved? The secret is learning the right love language!

- **Words of Affirmation**
  Actions don't always speak louder than words. If this is your love language, unsolicited compliments mean the world to you. Hearing the words, "I love you," are important—hearing the reasons behind that love sends your spirits skyward. Insults can leave you shattered and are not easily forgotten.

- **Quality Time**
  In the *vernacular* of Quality Time, nothing says, "I love you," like full, undivided attention. Being there for this type of person is critical, but really being there— with the TV off, fork and knife down, and all chores and tasks on standby—makes your significant other feel truly special and loved. Distractions, postponed dates, or the failure to listen can be especially hurtful.

- **Receiving Gifts**
  Don't mistake this love language for materialism; the receiver of gifts thrives on the love, thoughtfulness, and effort behind the gift. If you speak this language, the perfect gift or gesture shows that you are known, you are cared for, and you are prized above whatever was sacrificed to bring the gift to you. A missed birthday, anniversary, or a hasty, thoughtless gift would be disastrous—so would the absence of everyday gestures.

Vernacular—language

- **Acts of Service**

  Can vacuuming the floors really be an expression of love? Absolutely! Anything you do to ease the burden of responsibilities weighing on an "Acts of Service" person will speak volumes. The words he or she most wants to hear: "Let me do that for you." Laziness, broken commitments, and making more work for them tell speakers of this language their feelings don't matter.

- **Physical Touch**

  A person whose primary language is Physical Touch is, not surprisingly, very touchy. Hugs, pats on the back, holding hands, and thoughtful touches on the arm, shoulder, or face—they can all be ways to show excitement, concern, care, and love. Physical presence and accessibility are crucial, while neglect or abuse can be unforgivable and destructive. ■

Source: Adapted from the Internet Web site *The 5 Love Languages*
http://www.5lovelanguages.com/learn-the-languages/the-five-love-languages/

3. *Question* What are words of affirmation? _____

4. *Answer* Answers will vary. _____

5. *Question* What is quality time? _____

6. *Answer* Answers will vary. _____

7. *Question* Why is receiving gifts important? _____

8. *Answer* Answers will vary. _____

9. *Question* What are acts of service? _____

10. *Answer* Answers will vary. _____

11. *Question* Why is physical touch important? _____

12. *Answer* Answers will vary. _____

13–15. Summarize the reading in your own words: Answers will vary. _____

_____

_____

_____

READING 2

Nonverbal Communication of Emotion

Communicating has as much to do with what we say as what we do not say. In the following reading from a psychology textbook you will learn about the importance of communicating your emotions non-verbally. As you read, think about how a sarcastic tone of voice, a sour facial expression, aggressive body language, close personal space and behaviors such as slamming doors often tell us more about how someone feels than the words they say.

Directions: Practice the SQ3R strategy as you read the textbook reading.

Survey	Skim over the material. Read the title, subtitle, subheadings, first and last paragraphs, pictures, charts, and graphics. Note italics and bold print.
Question	Ask yourself questions before you read. What do you want to know? Turn headings and subheadings into questions and/or read questions if provided.
Read	Read the material in manageable chunks. This may be one or two paragraphs at a time or the material under one subheading.
Recite	Recite the answer to each question in your own words. This is a good time to write notes as you read each section. Repeat the question-read-recite cycle.
Review	Look over your notes at the end of the chapter, article, or material. Review what you learned and write a summary in your own words.

What is the most obvious indicator of emotion?

1   Sometimes you are **vaguely** aware that a person makes you feel uncomfortable. When pressed to be more precise, you might say: "You never know what she is thinking." But you do not mean that you never know her opinion of a film or what she thought about the last election. It would probably be more accurate to say that you do not know what she is *feeling*. Almost all of us **conceal** our emotions to some extent, but usually people can tell what we are feeling. Although emotions can often be expressed in words, much of the time we communicate our feelings nonverbally. We do this through, among other things, voice quality, facial expression, body language, personal space, and **explicit** acts.

VOICE QUALITY

2   If your roommate is washing the dishes and says **acidly**, "I hope you're enjoying your novel," the literal meaning of his words is quite clear, but you probably

know very well that he is not expressing a concern about your reading pleasure. He is really saying, "I am furious that you are not helping to clean up after dinner." Other emotions can be expressed through voice quality as well. When Mae West, a once famous film star and master of sexual **innuendo**, asked, "Why don't you come up and see me sometime?" her voice oozed sensuality. Similarly, if you receive a phone call from someone who has had very good or very bad news, you will probably know how she feels before she has told you what happened. In the same way, we can literally hear fear in a person's voice, as we do when we listen to a nervous student give an oral report. Much of the information we convey is not contained in the words we use, but in the way those words are expressed.

FACIAL EXPRESSION

3   *Facial expressions* are perhaps the most obvious emotional **indicators**. We can tell a good deal about a person's emotional state by observing whether that person is laughing, crying, smiling, or frowning. Many facial expressions are innate, not learned (Ekman, 1994; Goldsmith, 2002). Children who are born deaf and blind use the same facial expressions as other children do to express the same emotions. Charles Darwin first advanced the idea that most animals share a common pattern of muscular facial movements. For example, dogs, tigers, and humans all bare their teeth in rage. Darwin also observed that expressive behaviors serve a basic biological as well as social function. Darwin's notion that emotions have an evolutionary history and can be traced across cultures as part of our biological heritage laid the groundwork for many modern investigations of emotional expression (Izard, 1992, 1994). Today, psychologists who take an evolutionary approach believe facial expressions serve an **adaptive** function, enabling our ancestors to compete successfully for status, to win mates, and to defend themselves (Ekman, 1992; Tooby & Cosmides, 1990).

BODY LANGUAGE

4   *Body language* is another way we communicate messages nonverbally. When we are relaxed, we tend to stretch back into a chair; when we are tense, we sit more stiffly with our feet together. Slumping and straightness of the back supply clues about which emotion someone is feeling. Beier (1974) videotaped people acting out six emotions: anger, fear, seductiveness, **indifference**, happiness, and sadness. Surprisingly, most people could communicate only two out of the six emotions. Indeed, one young woman appeared angry no matter which emotion she tried to project; another was **invariably** thought to be seductive.

PERSONAL SPACE

5   The distance that people maintain between themselves and others is called *personal space*. This distance varies depending on the nature of the activity

and the emotions felt. If someone stands closer to you than is **customary**, it may indicate either anger or affection; if farther away than usual, it may indicate fear or dislike. The normal **conversing** distance between people varies from culture to culture: Two Swedes conversing would ordinarily stand much farther apart than would two Arabs or Greeks.

EXPLICIT ACTS

6   *Explicit acts*, of course, can also serve as nonverbal clues to emotions. When we receive a telephone call at 2 a.m., we expect that the caller has something urgent to say. A slammed door may tell us that the person who just left the room is angry. If friends drop in for a visit and you invite them into your living room, you are probably less at ease with them than with friends who generally sit down with you at the kitchen table. **Gestures**, such as a slap on the back or an embrace, can also indicate feelings. Whether people shake your hand briefly or for a long time, firmly or limply, tells you something about how they feel about you.

7   You can see from this discussion that nonverbal communication of emotions is important. However, a word of caution is needed here. Although nonverbal behavior may offer a clue to a person's feelings, it is not an **infallible** clue. Laughing and crying sound alike, for example, and we bare our teeth in smiles as well as in snarls. Crying may signify sorrow, joy, anger, **nostalgia**—or that you are slicing an onion. Moreover, as with verbal reports, people sometimes "say" things nonverbally that they do not mean. We all have done something thoughtlessly—turned our backs, frowned when thinking about something else, laughed at the wrong

time—that has given offense because these acts were **interpreted** as an expression of an emotion that we were not, in fact, feeling.

8   Also, many of us overestimate our ability to interpret nonverbal cues. In one study of several hundred "professional lie catchers," including members of the Secret Service, government lie detector experts, judges, police officers, and psychiatrists, every group except the psychiatrists rated themselves above average in their ability to tell whether another person was lying. In fact, only one group, the Secret Service agents, managed to identify the liars at a better-than-chance rate (Ekman & O'Sullivan, 1991). Similar results have been obtained with other groups of people (e.g., DePaulo & Pfeifer, 1986). ∎

Source: Morris, Charles G. and Albert A. Maisto. (2005). *Psychology: An Introduction,*
12th ed. Upper Saddle River, NJ: Pearson Education, pp. 356–357.

Vocabulary

Directions: Use your knowledge of word parts and context clues to determine the meaning of the following words from the passage. If needed, you may look up the words in a dictionary, but be sure to select the correct meaning.

Matching: Beside each word, write the letter of the definition that best matches the word.

_d_	**1.** vaguely (see paragraph 1)	**a.** motions
_f_	**2.** conceal (see paragraph 1)	**b.** help one adapt
_i_	**3.** explicit (see paragraph 1)	**c.** communicating
_e_	**4.** acidly (see paragraph 2)	**d.** unclearly
_k_	**5.** innuendo (see paragraph 2)	**e.** bitterly
_m_	**6.** indicators (see paragraph 3)	**f.** hide
_b_	**7.** adaptive (see paragraph 3)	**g.** usual
_l_	**8.** indifference (see paragraph 4)	**h.** reminiscence
_o_	**9.** invariably (see paragraph 4)	**i.** open
_g_	**10.** customary (see paragraph 5)	**j.** understood
_c_	**11.** conversing (see paragraph 5)	**k.** suggestion
_a_	**12.** gestures (see paragraph 6)	**l.** unresponsiveness

_____n_____ **13.** infallible (see paragraph 7)   **m.** gauges

_____h_____ **14.** nostalgia (see paragraph 7)   **n.** perfect

_____j_____ **15.** interpreted (see paragraph 7)   **o.** always

Compare your SQ3R notes to the summary below taken from the end of the textbook chapter (p. 363).

> Summary: Nonverbal Communication of Emotion
>
> *Voice Quality:* Much of the information we convey is contained not in the words we use but in the way they are expressed.
>
> *Facial Expression:* Facial expressions are the most obvious emotional indicators. Certain inborn or universal facial expressions serve an adaptive function.
>
> *Body Language:* Body language—our posture, the way we move, our preferred personal distance from others when talking to them—also expresses emotion.
>
> *Personal Space:* Personal space—the distance people maintain between themselves and others—varies according to the emotions felt.
>
> *Explicit Acts:* Explicit acts, such as slamming a door, are another clue to someone's emotional state. People vary in their sensitivity to nonverbal cues.

Answer the following questions taken from the textbook chapter.

1. Which of the following is a nonverbal cue to emotion?

   a. swearing under your breath   **c.** body language

   b. explicit act   **d.** b and c

2. According to research, which of the following are able to identify liars at a better-than-chance level?

   a. psychiatrists   **c.** Secret Service agents

   b. government lie detector agents   **d.** all of the above

3. Crying is an example of a(n) _____ emotional cue.

   a. ambiguous (having more than one meaning)

   b. infallible (absolutely certain)

   c. cognitive (having to do with reasoning)

640L

With Help from a Friend

by Dorri Olds

Chicken Soup books contain several short stories written by different people. The stories in each book share a theme about similar life experiences. Read the story below and see if you can relate to being nervous about fitting in and being liked when you first arrived at college.

1   ***Cherish*** *your visions and your dreams, as they are the children of your soul and the blueprints of your ultimate achievements.*

Napoleon Hill

2   I remember the first day of classes at Parsons School of Design. How awkward I felt and how **self-conscious**! Were my clothes right? My hair? My talent? Was I good enough? Was I gonna cut it?

3   I walked in and **scoped** out the room while holding my breath. My vision scanned and then sharply stopped on one person. Wow. She looked cool. I plopped myself down in the empty, waiting chair next to her.

4   "Hi, I'm Dorrie." I don't remember what I thought would actually happen, but I do remember being thrilled when she smiled a big white toothy smile and said, "Hi, I'm Kathleen." That was all it took.

5   What a difference Kathleen made in my college life! She was confident where I was shaky. She was disciplined while I was wild. She was responsible: I was lazy. We signed up for all the same classes. I was so impressed with her. She worked with incredible **diligence** and with such self-assurance. I started to **emulate** her. I wanted to impress her.

6   One day the homework assignment was to create an exciting illustration based on a pair of shoes. I was bursting with ideas and ran home and pulled out my favorite pair of antique thrift show "old-lady shoes." I concentrated and worked and sweated and created a **self-perceived** masterpiece!

7   I raced down from my fifth-floor apartment, precious drawing in hand, and headed to her place. When I got there, I held up my paper with such **glowing** confidence, only to have my swelled cockiness crushed by Kathleen's reaction: "Is that the only drawing you did?"

8   "Well, yes," I responded sheepishly. "Why?"

9   "C'mon," she said. "It's still nice out. Let's go to Washington Square Park and really do some drawings." I was puzzled, but when she led, I willingly followed.

10   The whole way to the park, Kathleen animatedly talked about form, content, composition and really studying your subjects. She described the shoes in my drawing as the kind you see on the old women that sit in the park and feed pigeons. Her excitement was contagious.

11   When we got to the park, she surveyed the scene and chirped, "Over there!" She pointed to a bench that was surrounded by **discarded**, crumpled paper bags, soda cans and empty cigarette packs. An old woman sitting on the bench had fallen asleep. Kathleen handed me her drawing pad and said, "Here. Now, draw the shoes on that woman! Draw them over and over until you really know what they look like."

12   I drew and drew. I filled the sketchbook pages. They were the best I'd ever done thus far. Kathleen watched, and I felt fueled by my **captive** audience. I was showing off! It was such fun.

13   The next day was the class critique. I felt so proud hanging my drawing up on the wall for all to see. I knew I had drawn an illustration to be proud of. As the class discussion circled the room to my piece, I heard my fellow students say, "sensitive," "accurate," "beautifully stylized." I looked over at Kathleen and she gave me that wink and loving smile of hers. College was going to be a lot more fun with her around.

14   And it was. She continually inspired me, laughed with me, sketched with me and went out dancing with me. Our works of art were chosen for special exhibits, and we both made the dean's list. We wore our caps and gowns together, and a few years later, I was "best woman" at her wedding.

15   Whatever fears I had going into college about not being able to make new friends were gently washed away when I found my special, best friend.

16   After we obtained our *B.F.A.* degrees, the world opened up for both of us. Now we are both successful self-employed artists. Me, a **freelance** illustrator and graphic designer. Kathleen, a sculptor and mural painter. I work in my lovely *Chelsea cooperative* apartment that I bought five years ago. Every morning I wake up grateful for how life has turned out. I make myself a cappuccino and enjoy sipping it as I sit at my computer.

17   Oops! I gotta run. Kathleen and I are meeting for dinner. ■

Source: Canfeld, J., Hansen, M., Kirberger, K., & Clark, D. (1999).
Chicken Soup for the College Soul: Inspiring and Humorous Stories about College.
Deerfield Beach, FL: Health Communications.

B.F.A.—Bachelor of Fine Arts

Chelsea Cooperative—A luxury place to live in the Manhattan area of New York City

Vocabulary

Directions: Use your knowledge of word parts and context clues to determine the meaning of the following words from the passage. If needed, you may use a dictionary, but be sure to select the correct meaning.

Match the words to their correct meanings:

___e___	**1.** cherish (see paragraph 1)	**a.** thoroughness
___g___	**2.** self-conscious (see paragraph 2)	**b.** bright
___i___	**3.** scoped (see paragraph 3)	**c.** not needed
___a___	**4.** diligence (see paragraph 5)	**d.** self-employed
___h___	**5.** emulate (see paragraph 5)	**e.** treasure
___j___	**6.** self-perceived (see paragraph 6)	**f.** imprisoned
___b___	**7.** glowing (see paragraph 7)	**g.** awkward
___c___	**8.** discarded (see paragraph 11)	**h.** imitate
___f___	**9.** captive (see paragraph 12)	**i.** looked over
___d___	**10.** freelance (see paragraph 16)	**j.** personally believed

Main Idea

1. What does the quote from Napoleon Hill mean in paragraph 1? _____
Answers will vary.

List four reasons why the author was impressed with Kathleen in paragraph 5.

2. She was confident where I was shaky.

3. She was disciplined while I was wild.

4. She was responsible: I was lazy.

5. She worked with incredible diligence and with such self-assurance.

6. Why did Kathleen take the author to the park?

    a. to show off how well she draws

    b. to enjoy the nice day together

    (c. to help her become a better artist)

    d. to have fun away from school

List three comments that let the author know her classmates were impressed with her work (see paragraph 13).

7. Her fellow students called her art "sensitive." _____

8. "accurate" _____

9. "beautifully stylized" _____

10. What does paragraph 17 tell you about their relationship?

    (a. They stayed friends after college.)

    b. They frequently went out to dinner together.

    c. Their friendship lasted through many decades.

Critical Thinking

On a separate sheet of paper, write an essay describing an important friendship in your life. What made that friendship special?
Answers will vary.

Magazine/Periodical

READING 4

1000L

Work: When Personalities Clash

One thing we all bring to the job is the self, making conflict inevitable. Seize it as a sign to look inward.

    Have you ever had trouble getting along with someone at work? Maybe you just need to know more about how your personality types differ. Read the article below to learn more about it!

1   Wouldn't it be nice if people—other people—came with an instruction kit?

2   Don't think that hasn't been tried. A prominent organizational consultant tells this story: On a visit to a large engineering firm, he noticed that most

employees wore plastic name tags with large capitalized letters after each name: William Jackson ENFP (Extraversion, Intuition, Feeling, Perceiving) or Allison Barton INTJ (Introversion, Intuition, Thinking, Judging). Turns out the company had every employee typed according to the beloved *Myers-Briggs* personality inventory. For the sake of efficiency, workers wore their personality descriptions as lapel pins. That way no one had to waste time figuring anyone else out.

PATHETIC OR TOUCHING? ACTUALLY, HUMANLY, A BIT OF BOTH.

3   The fantasy and frustration captured in the story reflect a workplace truth. In the end—no matter how we refine policies and procedures, no matter how well we train managers or finely construct a job description—we still have to deal with other people. And, as *Sartre* noted, other people are our hell. Surely he was referring to other people's personalities.

4   Personality, that quirky grab bag of traits, tics, reactions, and beliefs that distinguish one person's projected self from another's, is the **wild card** of the workplace. Whereas most of the stressors we encounter at the office can be scheduled, delegated, avoided, or at least reimbursed, the personalities of one's coworkers remain the uncontrolled variable.

5   True, that variable largely *recedes*, swept under by the conforming tsunami of office culture, professionalism, and sheer workload. Still, our selves sneak out, and when they do they often offend someone.

6   Of course, some selves are more offensive to us than others. Predictably, at one time or another you will share a work team, a cubicle, or a reporting relationship with one of those that offends you. Then you will get to experience first-hand that most commonly reported office problem: the personality conflict.

7   Consider as but one of many such examples the traditional office bad marriage between the sweeping big-picture person and the cautious detail man. Remember, these roles occur across genders and reporting relationships. What matters most is the personality variable.

8   Let's say the emotional, *intuitive* man is the boss, because, in fact, he often is.

9   He is action-oriented, confident, and demanding. He worries about missing opportunities. This boss can't always **articulate** the basis for his decisions, which are part percentages, part gut. He doesn't bother to spell out exactly what he

---

Myers-Briggs—A personality inventory that uses four dimensions of personality [Extraversion/Introversion (E/I), Sensing/Intuition (S/N), Thinking/Feeling (T/F), and Judgment/Perception (J/P)] to create sixteen possible personality combinations such as INTJ or ENFP.

Sartre—Jean-Paul Sartre, French philosopher and novelist of the 20th century

Recedes—fades, lessens, declines

Intuitive—instinctive, perceptive, insightful

wants from his staff either, but he knows it and rewards it when he gets it. And he lets you know when he doesn't.

10   Mr. Big Picture's callous vagueness drives The Planner nuts. The latter has a more controlled, fact-driven personality, with more faith in data than in personal feelings. He worries about the costly mistake and takes a slow, thorough approach to policy change or project design.

11   Assuming that both these men are highly competent, why wouldn't they make a marvelous partnership, balancing each other's strengths and weaknesses? They do, if they like and trust each other. But personality gets in the way of such respect. Instead of admiration, their personality differences may make each man anxious about the other. And when someone makes us anxious, we figure there's something wrong with that person.

12   It's easy to imagine the many workplace scenarios that would set these men off. A deadline is being set. The big-picture guy feels it's not soon enough, whereas the planner resists, fearing a rush to judgment. Money is being allocated. The intuitive person may want to bet the bank; Mr. Cautious is only comfortable *diversifying*. A new project is assigned. The boss resents giving so much guidance; his underling is frustrated that he is being given so little.

13   In a psychologically *enlightened* person—say, the *Dalai Lama*—frustration and discomfort would prompt thoughts such as, "I wonder why you make me anxious. Maybe I could stretch a little and get comfortable with you. Maybe I need to change to make you comfortable with me."

Diversifying—spreading out the money

Enlightened—open-minded, progressive

Dalai Lama—Head of state and spiritual leader of the Tibetan people

14   I have never actually met a person who has such an emotionally enlightened reaction, but I like to imagine that she exists. For the rest of us, frustration and discomfort add up to a personal judgment: "I don't like you. Here's what's wrong with you. . ."

15   Then we quite naturally account for our anxiety by explaining—to ourselves, to our spouses, and sometimes, unfortunately, to the rest of the office—that the person who is making us anxious is either mad (crazy, troubled, manic, anal, insecure, or some other psychological *brickbat*) or bad (evil, selfish, arrogant). Once we've reliably settled on mad or bad as our dynamic explanation of a personality conflict, we tend to live there, enduring each other, sniping at each other, or undermining each other until human resources is called in to clear the air.

16   A better system would be a culture of celebration of personality differences, or at least an appreciation for them. That may have been what the name-tagged engineers were aspiring to. The problem with their simplistic system was this: You end up only looking outward, at other people's tags. The impact of personality on the workplace starts with one's own needs, *idiosyncrasies*, assumptions, and expectations. Those are much tougher to spot.

17   We are fish, and our personalities are the water in which we swim. We don't notice the water, but it just feels . . . right. So if you and I are struggling—well, it's only logical that you must be wrong.

18   Off we go, gritting our teeth in the boardroom, whispering in the hallway about each other, sitting through the conflict resolution seminar called, mysteriously, just for us. We find that other person, that aggravating, **provocative**, screwed up other, impossible to understand.

19   Can't someone give us an instruction kit? Yes. *Socrates* handed it over some time ago. It starts and ends with the hardest rule to follow, whether in the workplace or any other setting: Know thyself.

CEASE-FIRE FOR A PERSONALITY CONFLICT

20   If you are caught in an unpleasant struggle with an irritating colleague, here are some ways to extricate yourself.

Brickbat—insult

Idiosyncrasies—habits, peculiarities

Socrates—An ancient fifth century Greek philosopher who critically examined every accepted truth in order to validate popular beliefs.

- **Resist recruiting allies**. It's reassuring to find evidence that "I'm not the only one who thinks our boss is a disorganized mess." But the more you bond over the negative, the larger that negative looms in your own life.

- **Focus on strengths**. Remind yourself of the contributions your adversary does make—to the team, to the company, and especially, if you can find it, to your own work. This will take the edge off your annoyance.

- **Get out of the way.** Some personalities push buttons so personally sensitive that you are able only to cringe. If you can't diminish the intensity of your reaction, at least reduce your contact.

- **Look in the mirror**. Not everyone at your office is as affected by the other's personality as you are. If you can figure out your role in the dynamic or the source of your response, you'll learn something important about yourself. ■

Source: Sills, Judith, Ph.D. (Nov/Dec 2006). "Work: When Personalities Clash." *Psychology Today Magazine.* Retrieved from psychologytoday.com.

Vocabulary

Use context clues to find the meaning of ***wild card*** from paragraph 4.

Personality, that quirky grab bag of traits, tics, reactions, and beliefs that distinguish one person's projected self from another's, is the ***wild card*** of the workplace. Whereas most of the stressors we encounter at the office can be scheduled, delegated, avoided, or at least reimbursed, the personalities of one's coworkers remain the uncontrolled variable.

A grab bag is like a surprise or something you can't predict.	Uncontrolled Variable	Whereas most stressors can be scheduled . . .

1. Based on the clues, what is the meaning of ***wild card***? a surprise, something you can't control or predict

Use context clues to find the meaning of ***articulate*** from paragraph 9.

This boss <u>can't</u> always ***articulate*** the basis for his decisions, which are part percentages, part gut. He <u>doesn't</u> bother to spell out exactly what he wants from his staff either, <u>but</u> he knows it and rewards it when he gets it.

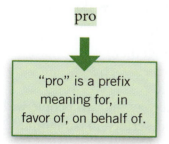

He doesn't spell it out exactly.

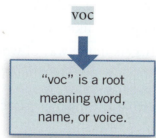

He <u>can't</u> exactly say what he wants.

<u>But</u> he <u>knows</u> what he wants even if he doesn't say it.

2. Based on the clues, what is the meaning of ***articulate***? say clearly

Use word parts to find the meaning of ***provocative*** from paragraph 18.

pro

"pro" is a prefix meaning for, in favor of, on behalf of.

voc

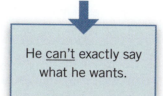

"voc" is a root meaning word, name, or voice.

tive

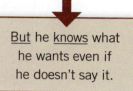

"ive" is a suffix meaning causing, making.

3. Based on the word parts, what is your best guess for the meaning of ***provocative***? something that causes speaking in favor or on behalf of something

Now use context clues to clarify the meaning of ***provocative***.

> Off we go, gritting our teeth in the boardroom, whispering in the hallway about each other, sitting through the conflict resolution seminar called, mysteriously, just for us. We find that other person, that aggravating, ***provocative***, screwed up other, impossible to understand.

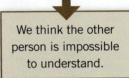

| We had to attend a conflict resolution seminar. | We think the other person is aggravating. | We think the other person is impossible to understand. |

4. Based on the word parts and context clues, what is the meaning of ***provocative***? offensive, confrontational

_____

Still not sure, look it up in a dictionary.

5. Now, using a dictionary, what is the meaning of ***provocative***?

tending or serving to provoke; inciting, stimulating, irritating, or vexing

Main Idea

6. In paragraph 11, the author discusses personality differences in the workplace. What is the author's main point?

   a. Co-workers balance each other's strengths and weaknesses.

   b. Competent people like and trust each other.

   c. Personality gets in the way of working together.

   d. When people are anxious, they find ways to cooperate.

7–12. Complete the chart below by describing the way the two people with different personalities respond to the issues described in paragraph 12.

	INTUITIVE, BIG-PICTURE BOSS	CAUTIOUS, PLANNER EMPLOYEE
A deadline is being set	feels it's not soon enough	resists, fearing a rush to judgment
Money is being allocated	may want to bet the bank	only comfortable diversifying
A new project is being assigned	resents giving so much guidance	is frustrated that he is being given so little guidance

13. What is the main idea of paragraph 15?

    a. People at work cause conflict and can be annoying.

    b. It is useful to share your frustrations with other people.

    c. We often settle on negative explanations, blaming people for conflicts.

    d. Most people that annoy us are mad or bad.

14. In paragraph 16, what does the author suggest is wrong with putting people's personalities on a name tag?

    a. The personality tags may be wrong.

    b. People tend to look only outward at the tags.

    c. People might disagree with the descriptions.

    d. They are too tough to read.

List four suggestions the author of the article suggests for how to deal with workplace personality conflicts.

15. resist recruiting allies

16. focus on strengths

17. get out of the way

18. look in the mirror

List two of your own suggestions for dealing with workplace conflict not mentioned in the article. Answers will vary.

19. _____

20. _____

Visual Images   **READING 5**

1. What is the main idea of the first picture? _____
   A couple is having a fight.

2. What details from the photo support this conclusion? Answers will vary.
   For example: The people have their backs to each other. He's holding his
   head in his hand. Her facial expression is angry.

3. What is the main idea of the second picture? A couple is spending
   time together.

4. What details from the second photo support this conclusion?
   Answers will vary. For example: They are relaxing on a couch. They both
   seem to be watching something such as a television.

5. What are the differences and similarities of these two pictures?

The first photo is of a mad couple, and in the second photo the couple is happy. The colors in the first photo are dark and they are light in the second photo. In the first one the people are turned back to back, and in the second photo they are snuggling.

Additional Recommended Reading

Albom, M. (1997). *Tuesdays with Morrie: An Old Man, A Young Man, and Life's Greatest Lesson.* New York, NY: Doubleday.

Albom, M. (2003). *Five People You Meet in Heaven.* New York, NY: Hyperion.

Berg, E. (2006). *We Are All Welcome Here.* New York, NY: Random House.

Bramson, R. (1981). *Coping With Difficult People: The Proven-Effective Battle Plan That Has Helped Millions Deal with the Troublemakers in Their Lives at Home and at Work.* New York, NY: Dell.

Carnegie, D. (1981). *How to Win Friends and Influence People.* New York, NY: Simon & Schuster.

Chapman, G. (2004). *The Five Love Languages: How to Express Heartfelt Commitment to Your Mate.* Chicago, IL: Northfield Publishing.

Chapman, G. and J. Thomas. (2006). *The Five Languages of Apology: How to Experience Healing in All Your Relationships.* Chicago, IL: Northfield Publishing.

Covey, S. (2004). *The Seven Habits of Highly Effective People.* New York, NY: Simon & Schuster.

Faber, A. and E. Mazlish. (1980). *How to Talk So Kids Will Listen & Listen So Kids Wills Talk.* New York, NY: Avon Books.

Gray, J. (2004). *Men are from Mars, Women are from Venus.* New York, NY: HarperCollins.

Hosseini, K. (2003). *The Kite Runner.* New York, NY: Riverhead Books.

Kingsolver, B. (2000). *Prodigal Summer.* New York, NY: HarperCollins.

Kluger, J., Carsen, J., Cole W., & Steptoe, S. (2006, July 10). The New Science of Siblings. *Time, 168*(2), 46–55.

Lucado, M. (2002). *A Love Worth Giving: Living in the Overflow of God's Love.* Nashville, TN: W Publishing.

Preston, R. (2007). *The Wild Trees: A Story of Passion and Daring.* New York, NY: Random House.

Tannen, D. (1990). *You Just Don't Understand: Women and Men in Conversation.* New York, NY: Ballantine Books.

Vanzant, I. (1998). *In the Meantime: Finding Yourself and the Love You Want.* New York, NY: Fireside.

Viscott, D. (1990). *How to Live with Another Person.* New York, NY: Simon & Schuster.

myreadinglab

For support in meeting this chapter's objectives, log on to www.myreadinglab.com and select Stated Main Idea.

3 Supporting Details

THEME Time Management

SPOTLIGHT ON LEARNING STYLES *W*RITE

Have you ever had a great plan for the day to get a lot of things done and then somehow lost track of the time? Before you knew it, it was time to go to class, or pick up the kids, or get to work. You had good intentions, but you ran out of time before you got everything done. One way to avoid running out of time is to write down your list of important things to do and then turn it into a schedule, hour by hour, or arranged in chunks of time. My husband, for example, often starts the day with a hot mug of coffee, a beautiful sunrise, and lots of ideas of things he wants to do. He has learned, though, that he must sit down and plan each day with a schedule, choosing what is important to accomplish throughout the day and evening. As someone who has a family, college courses, and a job, he cannot afford to lose track of time. He has learned to write out his goals in a planner: daily, weekly, and monthly. By listing his goals and frequently reviewing and revising them, he is able to achieve them with much less stress!

Now that you are in college, you have new demands on your time. Whether you are returning to school with a family of your own, managing a job and school, or living with a roommate or your parents, it is your responsibility and choice to spend time on the aspects of your life that you value the most. Setting priorities and completing tasks more efficiently will help you make the most of your time and enable you to achieve your goals.

There is a plethora (large amount) of material to read in college. One important way to make the most of your time is to learn to read more effectively and efficiently. Learning how to find the topic, the main idea, and the relevant details when you read will improve your reading effectiveness. In this chapter, you will develop your reading comprehension skills while learning more about managing your time—a very efficient plan!

In the previous chapter you learned how to identify the main idea of a paragraph. To better comprehend the text, it is also important to understand how the details in the paragraph support and develop the main idea. In this chapter you will learn to recognize and use the author's supporting details when you read. While you are improving your understanding of how the main idea relates to the supporting details within a text, you'll also be learning better ways to manage your time.

Reading the Other Sentences (What details are included in the paragraph?)

> **LO1**
> Determine what details are important for understanding the text.

When an author writes a paragraph, there is usually a point she is trying to make. As you read a paragraph, notice that there are usually several sentences related to the main idea the author is presenting. If a sentence supports the author's point, it is called a **supporting detail**.

For example, if the author's main idea involves *alternative energy sources,* sentences that offer supporting details might discuss

- biodiesel fuels
- solar energy
- wind power

Similarly, an article on *childhood obesity* might support its main idea with sentences that discuss

- junk food
- video games

How can you recognize supporting details?

- These sentences often appear near the beginning of the paragraphs that follow the main idea in a longer passage or article.
- They back up or give more information about the main idea.
- In a single paragraph, the supporting details are more detailed sentences that prove, illustrate, or explain the main idea.

EXAMPLE

Directions: For the group of statements below, write the topic in your own words on the line. Highlight or underline the main idea. Circle the letters that best represent the supporting details.

1. Topic _____

    a. Here are some simple and painless steps you can take to make sure your phones work for you rather than against you.

    b. Be discriminating in giving out your cell phone number.

   c. Monitor your phone use carefully.

   d. Break the habit of answering the phone whenever it rings.

   e. Rather than allowing the phone to interrupt your work constantly, set aside a specific time to make and return calls.

Source: St. James, Elaine. (2001). *Simplify Your Work Life: Ways to Change the Way You Work So You Have More Time to Live.* New York, NY: Hyperion, pp. 46–48.

The topic of the group of sentences is phones. All of the sentences are about using a phone. The main idea is (a) "Here are some simple and painless steps you can take to make sure your phones work for you rather than against you." The rest of the sentences are specific details that support the author's claim of providing readers with some steps to take to make sure phones work for and not against them.

PRACTICE THE NEW SKILL

Directions: For the group of statements below, write the topic in your own words on the line. Highlight or underline the main idea. Circle the answers that best represent the supporting details.

   1. Topic Handling your mail _____

   a. Deal with your mail at the same time every day.

   b. If necessary, mark off the time on your schedule in the same way you would an appointment, and let nothing interfere with that time.

   c. Avoid the temptation to flip through your mail at a time other than your regularly scheduled time.

   d. Develop the discipline to just let it sit there in your mailbox until your mail-handling time; alas, it won't go anywhere.

Source: St. James, Elaine. (2001). *Simplify Your Work Life: Ways to Change the Way You Work So You Have More Time to Live.* New York, NY: Hyperion, pp. 66–67.

   2. Topic Procrastinators _____

   a. Mr. Ferrari identifies two kinds of habitual lollygaggers.

   b. "Arousal procrastinators" believe they work best under pressure and tend to delay tasks for the thrill.

c. "Avoidant procrastinators" are self-doubters who tend to postpone tasks because they worry about performing inadequately, or because they fear their success may raise others' expectations of them.

Source: Hoover, Eric. *"Tomorrow I Love Ya!"* (December 9, 2005). *Chronicle of Higher Education,* Vol. 52, Issue 16, pp. A30–32.

3. Topic _Parkinson's Law of using time_

a. If you allocate only one hour to complete a certain task you have a much greater chance of finishing the work in that time.

b. If you set a deadline to complete a project by a certain date you will likely figure out how to do it within the time you set for that deadline.

c. Parkinson's Law says work tends to fill up (adjust to) the time available or allotted for it.

Source: Gleeson, Kerry. (2004). *The Personal Efficiency Program: How to Get Organized to Do More Work in Less Time,* 3rd ed. Hoboken, NJ: John Wiley & Sons, p. 74.

Using PIE (How do the sentences Prove, Illustrate, or Explain the author's point?)

The acronym **PIE** will help you remember what to look for in the supporting details. Ask yourself if the sentence Proves, Illustrates, or Explains (PIE), the author's main idea. Each supporting detail is like a piece of the "PIE."

LO2
Use PIE to remember the major supporting details (Prove, Illustrate, or Explain).

LO3
Use a diagram to better comprehend important ideas.

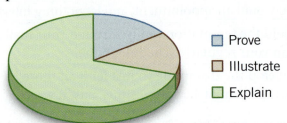

☐ Prove

☐ Illustrate

☐ Explain

You can approach the main idea/supporting details relationship from two directions: from general to specific or from specific to general. For instance, it might make more sense to identify the main idea first and then to look for the supporting details. Or it might make more sense to locate several related supporting details and then ask yourself what they are trying to prove, illustrate, or explain.

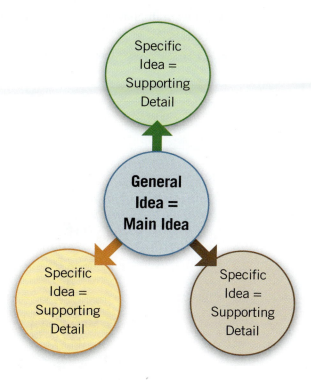

First, let's try it from general (main idea) to specific (supporting detail).

Copyright © 2012 Pearson Education, Inc.

EXAMPLE

Directions: Read the paragraph below. The main idea is underlined. Write three supporting details from the paragraph that illustrate the main idea either on the lines or on the chart below. *HINT:* What are some of the situations where the alternatives seem negative? What things are said in the "victim's mantra"?

　　<u>You can use procrastination to get even with powerful authorities who place you in situations where your alternatives all seem negative</u>. Pay the bills or go to jail, give up your vacation or lose your job. Procrastination in such situations reflects your resentment at the authority who placed you in this no-win dilemma. You feel like a victim whose life is controlled by others who make the rules. <u>And you confirm your refusal to accept the rules by speaking about the unpleasant task in the victim's mantra—"I have to."</u> "I have to pay the parking ticket. I have to have the presentation ready by

Friday but if I were in charge I wouldn't do it. If I were God there would be no parking tickets."

Source: Fiore, Neil. (1989). *Overcoming Procrastination: Practice the Now Habit and Guilt-Free Play.* New York, NY: MFJ Books, p. 16.

a. _____

b. _____

c. _____

OR complete the chart.

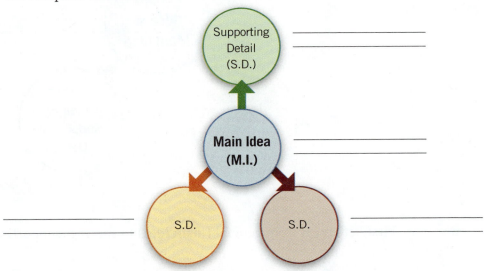

In this example, the main idea is "You can use procrastination to get even with powerful authorities who place you in situations where your alternatives all seem negative. . . . And you confirm your refusal to accept the rules by speaking about the unpleasant task in the victim's mantra—'I have to.'" *Illustrations* of situations where all seems negative are "Pay the bills or go to jail, give up your vacation or lose your job." Further *illustrations* of the victim's mantra are "I have to pay the parking ticket. I have to have the presentation ready by Friday but if I were in charge I wouldn't do it. If I were God there would be no parking tickets."

PRACTICE THE NEW SKILL

Directions: Read the paragraphs below. The main idea is underlined. Write specific supporting details from the paragraph in the spaces below or complete the charts.

1   Some e-mail applications have a built-in beeper or flashing visual signal alert function, so every time you receive a new message the computer alerts you. The alert prompts you to look at the incoming message, and because you are in the middle of something else or not prepared to spend the time to answer the message your tendency is to do it later. This is not the way to process your e-mail. <u>I suggest you turn off the alert function and instead set up times in your schedule to process your e-mail</u>. E-mail has, to some degree, become a substitute for the telephone and face-to-face meetings and needs to be acted upon promptly, although, in most environments, it should not command the same immediacy as the telephone.

Source: Gleeson, Kerry. (2004). *The Personal Efficiency Program: How to Get Organized to Do More Work in Less Time,* 3rd ed. Hoboken, NJ: John Wiley & Sons, p. 78.

HINT: What details <u>Explain</u> the main idea? Why should you turn off the alert function and set a time to answer e-mails?

S.D. — The alert prompts you to look at the incoming message immediately, but most of the time you put off reading it until later.

M.I. — *You should turn off the alert function and set a time to answer e-mails.*

S.D. — E-mail does not require the same immediacy as the telephone.

2   Neither our standard education, nor traditional time-management models, nor the plethora of organizing tools available, such as personal notebook planners, Microsoft Outlook, or Palm personal digital assistants (PDAs), has given us a viable means of meeting the new demands placed on us. If you've tried to use any of these processes or tools, you've found them unable to accommodate the speed, complexity, and changing priority factors inherent in what you are doing. The ability to be successful, relaxed, and in control during these fertile but turbulent times demands

new ways of thinking and working. <u>There is a great need for new methods, technologies, and work habits to help us get on top of our world.</u>

Source: Allen, David. (2001). *Getting Things Done: The Art of Stress-Free Productivity.* New York, NY: Penguin Group, p. 7.

HINT: What details <u>Prove</u> the main idea? Why is there a need for new methods, technologies, and work habits?

S.D.   None of the technological devices of today are able to keep up with our needs.

M.I.   *There is a need for new methods, technologies, and work habits.*

S.D.   The ability to be successful, relaxed, and in control demands new ways of thinking and working.

3   As a powerless victim you feel you can't openly rebel, because that would mean risking the probable consequences (anger and punishment), as well as losing the side benefits of the victim role (self-righteousness and martyrdom). But by procrastinating, you temporarily, secretly dethrone this authority. You can resist by dragging your feet and giving a halfhearted effort. <u>If you are in a one down position</u>—a student, a subordinate, a private in the army—<u>procrastination may be the safest way to exercise some power and control over your life</u>.

Source: Fiore, Neil. (1989). *Overcoming Procrastination: Practice the Now Habit and Guilt-Free Play.* New York, NY: MFJ Books, pp. 16–17.

HINT: How or why might procrastination be the safest way to have some power and control over your life?

As a powerless victim you feel you can't openly rebel, because that would mean risking the probable consequences (anger and punishment).

Procrastination might be the safest way to take some power and control over your life.

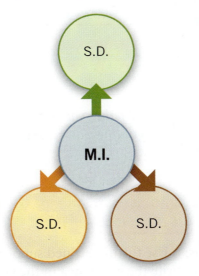

By procrastinating, you temporarily, secretly dethrone this authority. You can resist by dragging your feet and giving a halfhearted effort.

You risk losing the side benefits of the victim role (self-righteousness and martyrdom).

Now we'll try using the specific supporting details to help us find the general main idea.

Directions: Use the underlined supporting details to help identify the main idea. Write the main idea in the space below.

<u>Everyone's life is driven by something.</u> Most dictionaries define the verb *drive* as "to guide, to control, or to direct." <u>Whether you are driving</u>

<u>a car, a nail, or a golf ball, you are guiding, controlling, and directing it at</u> <u>that moment.</u> What is the driving force in your life?

Source: Warren, Rick. (2002). *A Purpose Driven Life: What On Earth Am I Here For?* Grand Rapids, MI: Zondervan, p. 27.

Main Idea: <u>The verb *drive* is defined as "to guide, to control, or to direct."</u>

S.D.   *Everyone's life is driven by something.*

M.I.   <u>The verb *drive* is defined as "to guide, to control, or to direct."</u>

S.D.   *Whether you are driving a car, a nail, or a golf ball, you are guiding, controlling, and directing it at that moment.*

PRACTICE THE NEW SKILL

Directions: Use the underlined supporting details to help identify the main idea. Write the main idea in the space below.

1   <u>Right now you may be driven by a problem, a pressure, or a deadline.</u> <u>You may be driven by a painful memory, a haunting fear, or an unconscious</u> <u>belief.</u> There are hundreds of circumstances, values, and emotions that can drive your life.

Source: Warren, Rick. (2002). *A Purpose Driven Life: What On Earth Am I Here For?* Grand Rapids, MI: Zondervan, p. 27.

Main Idea: <u>There are hundreds of circumstances, values, and emotions that can drive your life.</u>

2   <u>Respite can be a one-minute power break, a long workout, or a two-week</u> <u>vacation.</u> If you are like me and get totally absorbed, you lose track of time as you enjoy the pleasure of progress. I <u>set alarms in other rooms. Getting up</u> <u>to shut them off</u> *mobilizes* <u>me.</u> Another tactic is to drink lots of water and let <u>nature call you to move.</u> Breaks make way for new inputs to keep you going longer. Discover *tactics* that are most effective in forcing you to take a break.

Source: Szczurek, Theresa M. (2005). *Pursuit of Passionate Purpose: Successful Strategies for a Rewarding Personal and Business Life.* Hoboken, NJ: John Wiley & Son, p. 64.

Main Idea: Discover tactics that are most effective in forcing you to take a break.

3   Dr. Edward O'Keefe, author of *Self Management for College Students: The ABC Approach*, recommends that you look at the big picture of your life and figure out what's important to you. <u>He suggests writing down your</u> <u>big goals for college. Don't limit yourself to academic ones. "You should</u> <u>use college to develop the rest of yourself, in addition to your academic</u> <u>side,"</u> explains O'Keefe.

Source: O'Keefe, Edward. (Mar/Apr 2006). Time Management—Getting It Done. *Careers & Colleges*, Vol. 26, Issue 4, p. 12.

Main Idea: Look at the big picture of your life and figure out what's important to you.

REVIEW *WHAT YOU LEARNED*

1   Sometimes we get locked into things we know how to do or that our parents are doing. Doing something strange or unusual or entrepreneurial

Mobilizes—activates
Tactics—strategies

may seem more frightening. To me, everything was equally odd. I grew up on a sheep farm. No one in my family had graduated from college. I didn't know any lawyers. And so to me, buying the basketball team was no more difficult or strange than going to law school. My advice is to be fearless. I've failed at a lot of things, and it didn't kill me. Sometimes it's embarrassing, but I really got used to people saying no, and getting up, pretending it didn't happen and trying something else.

2   When you're looking at a big problem or task, break it down into small, manageable parts. Then, if one or two things don't work, it's easy to try something else. Don't let the overwhelming nature of the entire burden that you're trying to carry or the entire improvement stop you from taking the first few steps. Even if you think there's no way you're going to get to the end, it doesn't matter. You have to take the first steps.

3   I think it's important for young women to understand that there will be days when they just cannot believe how unfair the world is and they cannot believe how hard it is, and they really want to lie in bed and pull the covers over their head. That's normal. What's important is that you get up the next day—or a couple days later—and continue down the path. There are still days when I want to pull the covers over my head. But I get up anyway.

Source: Christofferson, Carla. (October 13, 2008). Women & Leadership. *Newsweek* p. 74.
[Carla Christofferson is an attorney and co-owner of the L.A. Sparks.]

Directions: Refer to the article and state the main idea and supporting details, using either the chart or the outline below.

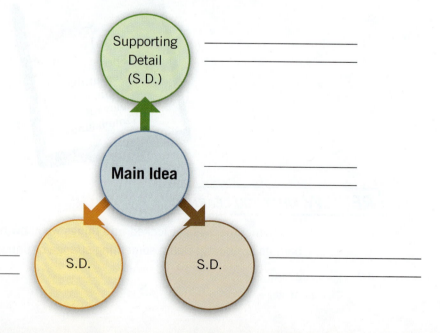

MI Even if you think there's no way you're going to get to the end, it doesn't matter. You have to take the first steps.

SD And so to me, buying the basketball team was no more difficult or strange than going to law school.

SD My advice is to be fearless. I've failed at a lot of things, and it didn't kill me. Sometimes it's embarrassing, but I really got used to people saying no, and getting up, pretending it didn't happen and trying something else.

SD I think it's important for young women to understand that there will be days when they just cannot believe how unfair the world is and they cannot believe how hard it is, and they really want to lie in bed and pull the covers over their head. That's normal. What's important is that you get up the next day—or a couple days later—and continue down the path.

REVIEW WHAT YOU LEARNED

1   Jai sent me out to buy a few groceries the other day. After I found everything on the list, I figured I'd get out of the store faster if I used the self-scan aisle. I slid my credit card into the machine, followed the directions, and scanned my groceries myself. The machine chirped, beeped and said I owed $16.55, but issued no receipt. So I swiped my credit card again and started over.

2   Soon, two receipts popped out. The machine had charged me twice.

3   At that point, I had a decision to make. I could have tracked down the manager, who would have listened to my story, filled out some form, and taken my credit card to his register to remove one of the $16.55 charges. The whole ordeal could have stretched to ten or even fifteen minutes. It would have been zero fun for me.

4   Given my short road ahead, did I want to spend those precious minutes getting that refund? I did not. Could I afford to pay the extra $16.55? I could. So I left the store, happier to have fifteen minutes than sixteen dollars.

Source: Pausch, Randy. (2008). *The last lecture.* New York, NY: Hyperion, pp. 107–108.

Directions: Refer to the passage and state the main idea, supporting details, using either the chart or the outline below.

Topic Time is precious. _____

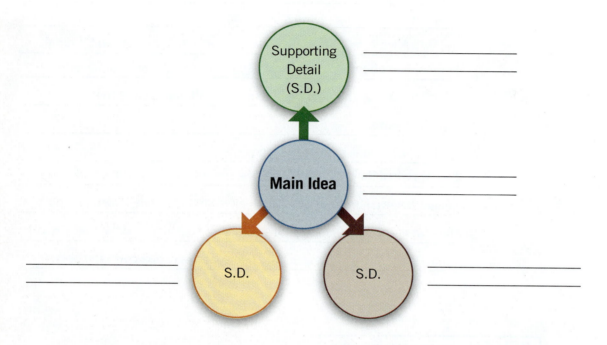

MI Given my short road ahead, did I want to spend those precious minutes getting that refund? I did not. So I left the store, happier to have fifteen minutes than sixteen dollars.

SD The store self-scan check-out did not work correctly.

SD When he tried to fix the problem, he got charged twice.

SD The writer had to make a decision to give up his money or his time.

/MASTER THE LESSON/

Supporting Details

Time Management

1   One strategy for coping with overload is time management, a series of techniques that can help people accomplish more with the amount of time they do have. Time management usually *entails* these steps:

- Employees make lists of all the tasks they need to accomplish during the day.
- The tasks are then prioritized in terms of those that are most important and must be done and those that are less important and can be put off, if need be.
- Employees estimate how long it will take to accomplish these tasks and plan their workday accordingly.

Time management is a coping strategy for individuals, but organizations can help their members learn effective time management techniques. Valerie Nossal is employed as a time management expert at MeadWestvaco Consumer and Office Products in Stamford, Connecticut, to help employees better manage their time. She suggests that employees need to be *proactive* and also set priorities and limits. Given the high volumes of work many employees are face with, they could work around the clock and not get everything done. Thus, employees need to set priorities not only in terms of what is more and less important to get done at work but also in terms of making sure they have a balance between work and the rest of their lives. Nossal advises employees to schedule time to exercise and be with their families because these are important activities that should not be neglected due to work pressures. Moreover, not paying attention to one's priorities and achieving a work-life balance may actually make employees less efficient.

2   Given the pressures to get more done in less time, some employees engage in multitasking—doing two or more things at once—such as writing a report during a meeting, answering e-mails while talking on the telephone, or opening mail while listening to a co-worker. Does multitasking

---

Entails—involves
Proactive—practical

save time? *Preliminary* research suggests that rather than saving time, multitasking might actually make people become less, rather than more, efficient, especially when they are working on complex tasks or activities. Multitasking that relies on the same parts of the brain makes a person especially *vulnerable* to efficiency losses. For example, if you are trying to compose an e-mail while carrying on a conversation with your boss over your speaker phone, both of these tasks require you to use and process language. One will likely interfere with the other, resulting in lower efficiency. However, photocopying documents while talking with a co-worker might be more feasible, though the co-worker is probably receiving a bit less of your attention than she would have received if you weren't multitasking.

Source: George, Jennifer M. and Gareth R. Jones. (2005). *Understanding and Managing Organizational Behavior,* 4th ed. Upper Saddle River, NJ: Pearson, pp. 293–294.

Define the following words, according to the textbook excerpt.

1. **Time management:** a series of techniques that can help people accomplish more with the amount of time they do have

2. **Multitasking:** doing two or more things at once

What are the three steps involved in time management?

3. Employees make lists of all the tasks they need to accomplish during the day.

4. The tasks are then prioritized in terms of those that are most important and must be done and those that are less important and can be put off, if need be.

5. Employees estimate how long it will take to accomplish these tasks and plan their workday accordingly.

When faced with a big workload, what does Valerie Nossal suggest employees do?

6. be proactive

7. set priorities and limits

_____
Preliminary—initial, pilot, beginning
Vulnerable—susceptible, open to

What two things should employees consider when they set priorities?

8. Employees need to set priorities in terms of what is more and less important to get done at work.

9. Employees need to set priorities in terms of making sure they have a balance between work and the rest of their lives.

Is multitasking a good idea, according to the author? Why or why not?

10. No. (Details of the answer will vary.) From the article: "rather than saving time, multitasking might actually make people become less, rather than more, efficient, especially when they are working on complex tasks or activities. Multitasking that relies on the same parts of the brain makes a person especially vulnerable to efficiency losses."

MASTER THE LESSON

Supporting Details

Getting rid of clutter is hard work. Keep your motivation high by reminding yourself of the advantages of a clutter-free life, including:

- **more time**—Clutter attracts clutter and takes precious time away from your workday. In fact, the average American executive wastes six weeks per year *retrieving* misplaced information due to messy desks and files, according to *The Wall Street Journal*.

- **lower stress**—Clutter and disorganization contribute to our stress levels. Remember the 80/20 rule? It applies to clutter also. We use 20 percent of our belongings 80 percent of the time. Focus on the 20, and get rid of as much of the other 80 as possible!

- **greater job security**—The "leaner and meaner" workplace is the norm rather than the exception to the rule. If you're viewed as less productive than your peers, your job security could be at stake.

- **better reputation**—When you're out of the office and your co-workers or boss can't easily find important information, you cause them to waste time. It doesn't help your professional image. Also, the first impression of a sloppy desk is hard to forget.

- **higher energy level**—You'll find yourself operating with more enthusiasm and *vigor* than before. Less physical clutter means a clearer and more refreshed mind.

- **enhanced quality of life at work**—You spend too much time at work for anything less than *optimal* conditions. Make your "home away from home"

Retrieving—recovering, salvaging

Vigor—energy, vitality

Optimal—best possible, most advantageous

a calm and comfortable *oasis*. Remember: Your desktop is a workspace, not a storage space!

Source: Simmons, Kathy. (Nov/Dec 2005). Escaping the Clutter Trap. *Office Solutions,* Vol. 22, Issue 6, pp. 14ff.

1–7. Create a graphic organizer or mind map with information from the article.

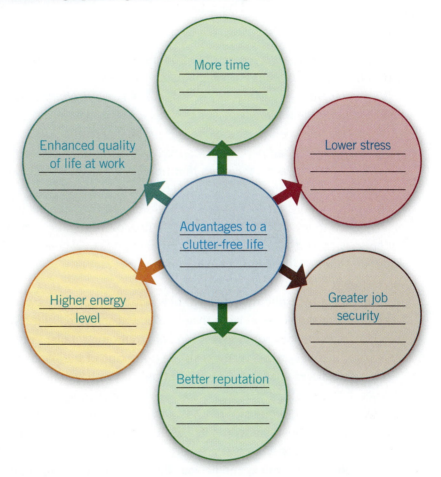

Answer the questions using the information from the article.

8. How much time does the average American executive waste trying to find lost information due to a cluttered office? 6 weeks per year

9. Why would less clutter help a person feel more energized? Less physical clutter means a clearer and more refreshed mind.

10. What is the 80/20 rule? We use 20 percent of our belongings 80 percent of the time.

Oasis—retreat, refuge, sanctuary

135

LEARNING STYLE ACTIVITIES

*L*ook, *L*isten, *W*rite, *D*o

The Last Lecture

By Randy Pausch

Randy Pausch was a professor of Computer Science, Human Computer Interaction, and Design at Carnegie Mellon University. From 1988 to 1997, he taught at the University of Virginia. An award-winning teacher and researcher, he worked with Adobe, Google, Electronic Arts (EA), and Walt Disney Imagineering, and pioneered the Alice project. At the time he wrote this book, he had pancreatic cancer. He died in July 2008.

1   All my life I've been very aware that time is finite. I admit I'm overly logical about a lot of things, but I firmly believe that one of my most appropriate fixations has been to manage time well. I've railed about time management to my students. I've given lectures on it. And because I've gotten so good at it, I really do feel I was able to pack a whole lot of life into the shortened lifespan I've been handed.

Here's what I know:

2   **Time must be explicitly managed, like money.** My students would sometimes roll their eyes at what they called "Pauschisms," but I stand by them. Urging students not to invest time on irrelevant details, I'd tell them: "It doesn't matter how well you polish the underside of the banister."

3   **You can always change your plan, but only if you have one.** I'm a big believer in to-do lists. It helps us break life into small steps. I once put "get tenure" on my to-do list. That was naïve. The most useful to-do list breaks tasks into small steps. It's like when I encourage Logan to clean his room by picking up one thing at a time.

4   **Ask yourself: Are you spending your time on the right things?** You may have causes, goals, interests. Are they even worth pursuing? I've long held on to a clipping from a newspaper in Roanoke, Virginia. It featured a photo of a pregnant woman who had lodged a protest against a local construction site. She worried that the sound of jackhammers was injuring her unborn child. But get this: In the photo, the woman is holding a cigarette. If she cared about her unborn child, the time she spent *railing* against jackhammers would have been better spent putting out that cigarette.

Railing—fighting

5   **Develop a good filing system.** When I told Jai I wanted to have a place in the house where we could file everything in alphabetical order, she said I sounded way too compulsive for her tastes. I told her "Filing in alphabetical order is better than running around and saying, 'I know it was blue and I know I was eating something when I had it.'"

6   **Rethink the telephone.** I live in a culture where I spend a lot of time on hold, listening to "Your call is very important to us." Yeah, right. That's like a guy slapping a girl in the face on a first date and saying, "I actually do love you." Yet that's how modern customer service works. And I reject that. I make sure I am never on hold with a phone against my ear. I always use a speaker phone, so my hands are free to do something else.

7   I've also collected techniques for keeping unnecessary calls shorter. If I'm sitting while on the phone, I never put my feet up. In fact, it's better to stand when you're on the phone. You're more apt to speed things along. I also like to have something in view on my desk that I want to do, so I have the urge to wrap things up with the caller.

8   Over the years, I've picked up other phone tips. Want to quickly *dispatch* telemarketers? Hang up while you're doing the talking and they're listening. They'll assume your connection went bad and they'll move on to their next call. Want to have a short phone call with someone? Call them at 11:55 a.m., right before lunch. They'll talk fast. You may think you are interesting, but you are not more interesting than lunch.

9   *Delegate.* As a professor, I learned early on that I could trust bright, nineteen-year-old students with the keys to my kingdom, and most of the time, they were responsible and impressive. It's never too early to delegate. My daughter, Chloe, is just eighteen months old, but two of my favorite photos are of her in my arms. In the first, I'm giving her a bottle. In the second, I've delegated the task to her. She looks satisfied. Me, too.

10   **Take a time out.** It's not a real vacation if you're reading email or calling in for messages. When Jai and I went on our honeymoon, we wanted to be left along. My boss, however, felt I needed to provide a way for people to contact me. So I came up with the perfect phone message:

11   "Hi, this is Randy. I waited until I was thirty-nine to get married, so my wife and I are going away for a month. I hope you don't have a problem with that, but my boss does. Apparently, I have to be reachable." I then

---

Dispatch—send off
Delegate—hand over, entrust

gave the names of Jai's parents and the city where they live. "If you call directory assistance, you can get their number. And then, if you can convince my new in-laws that your emergency *merits* interrupting their only daughter's honeymoon, they have our number."

12   We didn't get any calls.

13   Some of my time management tips are dead-on serious and some are a bit *tongue-in-cheek*. But I believe all of them are worth considering.

14   Time is all you have. And you may find one day that you have less than you think.

Source: Pausch, R. (2008). *The Last Lecture.* New York, NY: Hyperion, pp. 108–111.

Look   Create a mind map of Pausch's time management techniques. Link related ideas.

Listen   Listen to Pausch's last lecture on YouTube on the Internet. Another listening strategy is to read the time management tips out loud with someone else and then discuss the ideas.

Write   Write an outline of the time management tips in this article. Then write a summary of the main points.

Do   Discuss several practical applications to your own life that you could make with Pausch's time management tips.

Merits—deserves, warrants

Tongue-in-cheek—lighthearted, humorous, flippant, whimsical

Reading Practice

The next section of the chapter will help refine your skills in determining the supporting details while you read a variety of materials. All five of the readings address topics related to establishing your priorities and managing your time.

The first reading is from an Internet Web site, The FlyLady, which gives tips on simple, efficient ways to keep your home clean. The FlyLady combines humor and practical advice to help readers reduce clutter and chaos in their lives.

The second reading comes from the textbook, *The Community College Experience: Plus*. The excerpt is from Chapter 3, "Managing Your Time and Stress," and covers the topic of managing your priorities.

The third reading is an excerpt from contemporary literature, *Have a little faith: A true story,* by Mitch Albom, author of other best-selling books, including *Tuesdays with Morrie* and *The Five People You'll Meet in Heaven.*

The fourth reading is from an article titled "Beat the Clock" from the magazine *Career World.* Students give advice on effective ways to manage time to balance the demands of school, jobs, and other activities.

The final reading is a visual image of multitasking.

READING 1

The FlyLady

DECLUTTER 15 MINUTES A DAY—5 GREAT TOOLS THAT MAKE IT EASY!

1   Your home is filled with clutter of all shapes and sizes. This is why you are unable to keep it clean. You have too much STUFF. All we ask is that you set a timer and spend 15 minutes a day decluttering. That's it. Anyone can do anything for only 15 minutes, even if you have to break it down into 5 minute segments. These are the five tools we give you to help you **declutter** and also make it fun for you! When you get the e-mail reminders/checklists from FlyLady, try them yourself. What do you have to lose (besides clutter LOL!)?

THE 27-FLING BOOGIE

2   We do this assignment as fast as we can. Take a garbage bag and walk through your home and throw away 27 items. Do not stop until you have collected all 27 items. Then close the garbage bag and pitch it. DO NOT LOOK IN IT!!! Just do it.

3   Next, take an empty box and go through your home collecting 27 items to give away. Suze Orman taught me this in her book, *The Courage to Be Rich.* This will change the energy in your home and bring about good feelings. Every time I do this I feel better and my home is becoming decluttered in the process. As soon as you finish filling the box, take it to the car. You are less tempted to rescue the items.

4   Rule of thumb: if you have two of any item and you only need one, get rid of the least desirable.

5   I also sing a wonderful song as I am doing this fun job: "Please Release Me, Let Me Go" as sung from the stuff's point of view.

THE HOT SPOT FIRE DRILL

6   Here is a problem that we all have and continue to struggle with—Hot Spots. What is a hot spot?

7   A hot spot is an area, when left unattended will gradually take over. My favorite **analogy** is of a hot spot in a forest fire; if left alone, it will eventually get out of hand and burn up the whole forest. This is what happens in our homes. If left unattended, the hot spot will grow and take over the whole room as well as making the house look awful. When you walk into a room, this is the first thing you see.

CLUTTER ATTRACTS CLUTTER!

8   Do you have areas like this that continue to grow if left alone? Does the rest of the family see this as a place to put things when they do not want to put them where they belong? It is our job to nip this in the bud! Get rid of that pile, find the surface underneath and stop this Hot Spot from becoming a raging clutter inferno! Watch for the Hot Spot fire drill reminder—then try it—it works!

THE 5 MINUTE ROOM RESCUE

9   This is a reminder to spend just 5 minutes clearing a path in your worst room. You know this area of your home: the place you would never allow anyone to see. Just 5 minutes a day for the next 27 days and you will have a place that you can be proud to take anyone!

KELLY'S DAILY MISSIONS

10   Each day (or almost each day) Kelly will e-mail a 5-minute mission for you to do. It will be in the area of the home that we are focusing on for that week (the zone). These missions will take you to places you may have never been before! Have fun with this! We will also be posting **Kelly's missions** for the week in the Flight Plan.

WORK IN YOUR ZONES

11   Each week FlyLady will tell you what zone we are working in. After a full month, you will have worked your way around the majority of the living areas of your home. Do not worry if you have not gotten to every room in your house the first month. As one area gets cleaned, it will become easier to do and you will have more time to face those areas that don't seem to fit in any zone. See the Flight Plan for more information. Remember: FlyLady wants you to take **baby steps**. Don't worry about zones until you have conquered the basics! ∎

Source: FlyLady.net. Declutter 15 Minutes a Day—5 Tools That Make it Easy! Retrieved 4/30/11 from www.flylady.net/pages/FLYingLessons_Decluttertips.asp.

Vocabulary

1. Define **declutter.** (see paragraph 1) *Declutter* means to remove the extra things or clutter that is making your home messy. *De* is a prefix meaning "down" so *declutter* means "to put the clutter down."

2. What is an **analogy**? (see paragraph 7)

   a. contrast   **b.** comparison   **c.** cause   **d.** effect

3. What does the author mean by **Kelly's Missions**? (see paragraph 10) Every day (or almost each day) Kelly will e-mail a 5-minute mission for you to do. It will be in the area of the home that we are focusing on for that week (the zone).

4. What does the author mean by **baby steps**? (see paragraph 11) Baby steps are the basic first steps to get started.

Main Idea

5. What is the main idea from paragraph 1? These are the five tools we give you to help you declutter and also make it fun for you!

6. What is FlyLady's advice in paragraph 2? Take a garbage bag and walk through your home and throw away 27 items. Do not stop until you have collected all 27 items. Then close the garbage bag and pitch it. DO NOT LOOK IN IT!!!

7. How does her advice in paragraph 2 differ from the advice given in paragraph 3? In paragraph 3, FlyLady advises the reader to put 27 items in a box to donate or give away and then put the box in your car. In paragraph 2 the advice was to take 27 items to throw away and put them in a garbage bag.

8. What is the main idea of paragraph 8? Clutter attracts clutter so find the spots in your home where everyone puts miscellaneous stuff, clean them to the surface, and keep the spots clear so the piles don't build up again.

9. What advice does FlyLady give in paragraph 9? Spend 5 minutes a day clearing a path in your worst room and in 27 days it will be clean.

Supporting Details

10–15. Complete the chart below with the topic, central theme, and five major supporting details—the major decluttering tools.

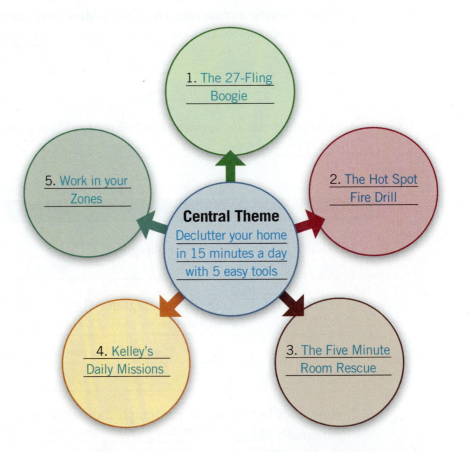

1. The 27-Fling Boogie

5. Work in your Zones

2. The Hot Spot Fire Drill

Central Theme
Declutter your home in 15 minutes a day with 5 easy tools

4. Kelley's Daily Missions

3. The Five Minute Room Rescue

Critical Thinking/Application

16–20. Discuss how you might save time incorporating this advice into your own life. Answers will vary.

READING 2

Managing Your Time and Stress

MANAGING YOUR PRIORITIES

1   Before you can begin to manage your time and *monitor* your stress levels, you have to make sure that your goals and priorities are clear. . . .[W]riting down your goals and setting your priorities, which may change frequently, are the first steps to realizing your dreams; they are also the first steps to figuring out how much time you need to spend on each goal. Before thinking about time management, take time to review what you have written down as your short-term goals and priorities.

2   If you listed your priorities right now, college would be near the top. Certainly enrolling in college and reading this book mean you are committed to furthering your education. Nevertheless, you have to figure out where the priority of going to college fits in with your other priorities. Perhaps attending classes is your only priority because you live alone and do not work; more likely, however, college competes with other priorities. If you are going to succeed in college, your education must be a top priority most of the time.

3   In addition to college, you have to consider your family as a priority. Depending on your situation, you may have family members who need you for emotional, physical, and financial support. You may even be the only one they can rely on. Because family is often a first priority for many students, it is important to manage your time with them wisely and effectively.

4   If you have not yet done so, talk to your family about the new responsibilities you have. Be honest in your descriptions of what you are doing and what you need from them. If you think time will be limited for family trips and weekend activities, let them know. If you think you will need to cut out some basic duties such as planning meals, cleaning the house, and running errands, be sure to communicate this to your family. The more they know about what to expect, the better able they will be to support your decision to enroll in college.

5   Another priority you may have is your job. Most community college students work as well as attend classes. For some, their jobs **supplement** their household income and are not necessary for survival; for many others, their jobs are more important than college because they provide the primary or sole income for the

———————————

Monitor—check, watch, examine

family. If your job is your top priority, then you should know where the other priorities must fall, and you should be prepared to make sacrifices in other areas to ensure that your job remains at the top.

6   With all the other responsibilities you have, it is easy to overlook the priority of relaxing; without it the other priorities can run you down. Don't forget that you can have fun while in college, and you certainly should participate in activities you enjoy. Without them, your college career will seem stressful and dull. Scheduling downtime to play and **rejuvenate** is an important part of effective time management. Get outside, read for pleasure, or participate in those activities you enjoy. Relaxing and having fun will recharge your body and mind to concentrate on the demands of your other priorities. ■

Source: Baldwin, Amy. (2007). *The Community College Experience: Plus.* Upper Saddle River, NJ: Pearson Prentice Hall, pp. 67–69.

Use the context clues to determine the meaning of ***supplement*** in paragraph 5.

For some, their jobs ***supplement*** their household income and are not necessary for survival; for many others, their jobs are more important than college because they provide the primary or sole income for the family.

If their jobs supplement, then they are not necessary for survival.	For <u>others</u>, their jobs are more important than college. (contrast)	For <u>others</u>, their jobs provide the primary or sole income. (contrast)

1. Based on the clues, define ***supplement***.
   a. enhance   c. add to
   b. augment   d. all of the above

Use word parts to determine the meaning of ***rejuvenate***.

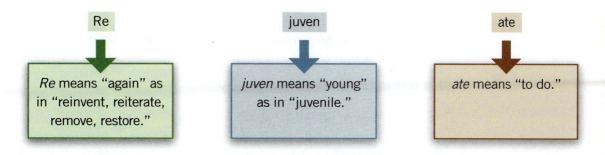

Re	juven	ate
Re means "again" as in "reinvent, reiterate, remove, restore."	*juven* means "young" as in "juvenile."	*ate* means "to do."

2. Based on the word parts, what do you think ***rejuvenate*** means?

to make young again

Now try to use the context clues to determine the meaning of **rejuvenate**:

With all the other responsibilities you have, it is easy to overlook the priority of relaxing; without it the other priorities can run you down. Don't forget that you can have fun while in college, and you certainly should participate in activities you enjoy. Without them, your college career will seem stressful and dull. Scheduling downtime to **play** and ***rejuvenate*** is an important part of effective time management. Get outside, read for pleasure, or participate in those activities you enjoy. Relaxing and having fun will recharge your body and mind to concentrate on the demands of your other priorities.

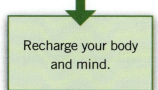

Recharge your body and mind.	Without relaxing, all the other priorities can run you down.	Play, get outside, read for pleasure, participate in activities you enjoy, relax, have fun.

3. What does the author mean by ***rejuvenate*** in paragraph 6?

    a. return   (**b.** refresh)   **c.** represent   **d.** all of the above

Main Idea

4. What is the main idea of paragraph 1?

    a. Take time to review what you have written down as your short-term goals and priorities before you think about time management.

    b. Thinking about your dreams is important for rejuvenating.

    c. Write down your goals every day.

    d. Once you know how to manage your time, then you can decide which goals you will try to achieve.

5. What is the main idea of paragraph 3?

    a. Make time to set goals with your family.

    b. Because family is often a first priority for many students, it is important to manage your time with them wisely and effectively.

    c. Spend as much time with family when you are in college.

    d. One's family is the greatest support to a college student.

6. What is the main idea of paragraph 5?

    a. For some students, their jobs supplement their household income and are not necessary for survival.

    b. Most community college students work as well as attend classes.

    c. Jobs are more important than college because they provide the primary or sole income for the family.

    d. If your job is your top priority, then you should know where the other priorities must fall, and you should be prepared to make sacrifices in other areas to ensure that your job remains at the top.

7. What is the author's main point of paragraph 6?

    a. Without fun activities, your college career will seem stressful and dull.

    b. Get outside, read for pleasure, or participate in those activities you enjoy.

    c. Studying is more important to success in college than having fun.

    d. Scheduling downtime to play and rejuvenate is an important part of effective time management.

Supporting Details

8–12. Complete the graphic organizer with the central theme of the reading above and the four major supporting details.

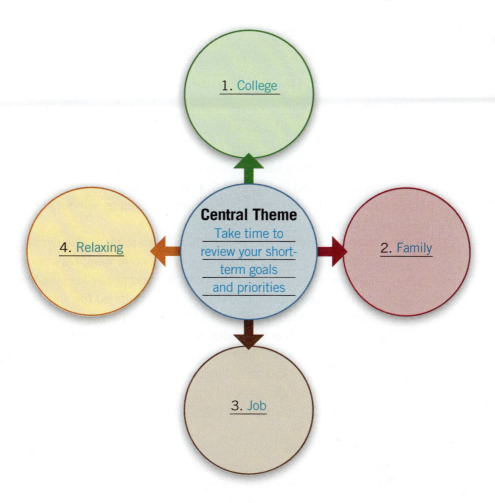

1. College

Central Theme
Take time to review your short-term goals and priorities

4. Relaxing

2. Family

3. Job

Critical Thinking/Application

13. Describe the different priorities that a student may have while balancing work, family, and college. (You may do this with a small group.)

Answers will vary.

14. Which priorities will conflict with each another?

Answers will vary.

15. What advice would you give someone having difficulty managing his or her priorities? Answers will vary.

Literature

READING 3

Have a Little Faith: A True Story

JANUARY

HEAVEN

1   January arrived and the calendar changed. It was 2008. Before the year was done, there would be a new U.S. president, an economic earthquake, a sinkhole of confidence, and tens of millions unemployed or without homes. Storm clouds were gathering.

2   Meanwhile, the *Reb* puttered from room to room in quiet *contemplation*. Having survived the Great Depression and two world wars, he was no longer thrown by headline events. He kept the outside world at bay keeping the inside world at hand. He prayed. He chatted with God. He watched the snow out the window. And he *cherished* the simple rituals of his day: the prayers, the oatmeal with cereal, the grandkids, the car trips with *Teela*, the phone calls to old congregants.

3   I was visiting again on a Sunday morning. My parents had made plans to swing by later and take me to lunch before I flew back to Detroit.

4   Two weeks earlier, on a Saturday night, the temple held a gathering in the Reb's honor, commemorating his six decades of service. It was like a coming home party.

5   "I tell you," the Reb said, shaking his head as if in disbelief, "there were people who hadn't seen one another in years. And when you saw them hugging and kissing like such long lost friends—I cried. I *cried*. To see what we have created together. It is something incredible."

6   Incredible? My old temple? That small place of Sabbath mornings and funny holidays and kids hopping out of cars and running into religious school? Incredible? The word seemed too *lofty*. But when the Reb pushed his hands together, almost prayer-like, and whispered, "Mitch, don't you see? We have made a *community*," and I considered his aging face, his slumped shoulders, the sixty years he had devoted tirelessly to teaching, listening, trying to make us better people, well, given the way the world is going, maybe "incredible" is the right description.

The Reb—the Rabbi the author was talking about. The author was asked to prepare his eulogy several years before the Reb died. This is an excerpt of one of the chapters describing their conversations.

Contemplation—thought, meditation, reflection

Cherished—appreciated

Teela—The Reb's Hindu health care friend

Lofty—snooty, proud, arrogant

7   "The way they hugged each other," he repeated, his eyes far away, "for me, that is a piece of heaven."

8   It was inevitable that the Reb and I would finally speak about the afterlife. No matter what you call it—Paradise, Moksha, Valhalla, Nirvana—the *next world* is the *underpinning* of nearly all faiths. And more and more, as his earthly time wound down, the Reb wondered what lay ahead in what he called "*Olam Habah*"—the world to come. In his voice and in his posture, I could sense he was searching for it now, the way you stretch your neck near the top of a hill to see if you can look over.

9   The Reb's cemetery plot, I learned, was closer to his birthplace in New York, where his mother and father were buried. His daughter, Rinah, was buried there too. When the time came, the three generations would be united, at least in the earth and, if his faith held true, somewhere else as well.

10   Do you think you'll see Rinah again? I asked.

11   "Yes, I do."

12   But she was just a child.

13   "Up there," he whispered, "time doesn't matter." ■

Source: Albom, Mitch. (2009). *Have a little faith: A true story.*
New York, NY: Hyperion, pp. 223–225.

Main Idea

1. Reb had a sense of building a community. He said "We [not "I"] have made a community." Reb repeated it a second time to Albom. Explain what he meant. Answers will vary.

Supporting Details

2. In paragraph 2, Reb talked about keeping the outside world at bay by keeping the inside world at hand. What specific details support this statement? He prayed. He chatted with God. He watched the snow out the window. And he cherished the simple rituals of his day: the prayers, the oatmeal with cereal, the grandkids, the car trips with Teela, the phone calls to old congregants.

Next world—heaven

Underpinning—foundation, keystone

3. In paragraph 4, Albom said the temple held an event in the Reb's honor, commemorating his six decades of service. What did he mean by saying it was like a coming home party? There were people there who hadn't seen each other in years and they were kissing and hugging like long lost friends.

4. What events made Reb believe that the building of community was "incredible"? Answers will vary.

5. Reb's daughter, Rinah, died at an early age. At the end of the reading, Albom asks Reb if he thinks he will see Rinah again. Reb indicates there is no sense of time in the afterlife. What does he mean?

Answers will vary.

Critical Thinking/Application

In paragraph 8, the author and the Reb discuss the afterlife. What does Albom mean by the phrase, "In his voice and in his posture, I could sense he was searching for it now, the way you stretch your neck near the top of a hill to see if you can look over"? Answers will vary.

Magazine/Periodical   **READING 4**

1010L   ## Beat the Clock

STUDENTS SHARE TIME-MANAGEMENT STRATEGIES THAT CAN WORK FOR YOU!

1   Ashley Rudd typically starts her day by 6 a.m. The Bedford, Mass., high school senior's classes begin at 7:21. By the time the school day ends, she has been assigned homework in most subjects. After school ends at 2:01, she rushes home, changes, and returns for tennis practice at 2:30. Practice is done at 4:30. Ashley heads home, showers, and **tackles** her homework. On days when she has tennis matches or other **obligations**, her schedule is even tighter. Somewhere in there, she needs to eat and get some sleep too.

2   Sound familiar? Wouldn't it be great if by some act of magic, you were given two or three extra hours every day?

3   Unfortunately, nobody gets more than 24 hours a day. But by following *savvy* time-management strategies, you can make the most of the hours you have.

4   Time-management skills are a plus in dealing with school, part-time jobs, and other activities. "Learning time management now will hold you in excellent *stead* as you move into even-busier adult years," says Susan Bartell, a New York psychologist who works with teens. "By learning how to use your time well, you'll develop skills necessary for later life success."

5   Even if you're **adept** at using time effectively, there is always room for improvement. Life is a balance of both busy moments and time for yourself. How can you make sure you make the most of the busy moments so you can enjoy your own time with no stress? Here are five strategies from the true-experts—busy students like you.

6   **1. Get organized.** Do you ever look at your commitments and wonder how you'll get everything done? Creating lists of important tasks and appointments can help.

7   "Make a chart or system each day in which you follow set-out times," says Andrew Meehan, 16, a student in San Juan Capistrano, Calif. "If many things are going on, this will give you an idea of what needs to be completed and how much time you have to do so."

8   Some students use technology, such as a personal digital assistant or online calendar, for organization. But even the simplest measures can work.

9   "The ability to be organized in a low-maintenance and efficient way is what counts," says Emily Doerr, 21, a student at Central Michigan University. "You can do this just as easily with a blank notebook as you can with a Palm Pilot."

10   **2. Stay on target.** Once you begin completing tasks, keep on target until you're done. It's easy to get sidetracked, but avoid putting things off.

Savvy—shrewd

Stead—advantage

11   "Procrastinating never works," Andrew says. "Your best bet is to start home-work right when you get home and complete it while the thought of schoolwork still remains in your head."

12   A great way to stay focused is to eliminate distractions. "Cutting myself off from my cell phone and Internet use has been most effective," says Kate Woodard, a senior at Lincoln Sudbury Regional High School in Massachusetts. "When I have a big paper to write, I unplug my Internet connection and leave my cell phone in another room."

13   **3. Set priorities.** Successful time management includes determining what is truly important and what can be set aside for later—or never.

14   Setting limits on yourself is key, according to Allison Blass, 20, a student at the University of Oregon who successfully juggles school, a part-time job, and volunteer work as an **advocate** for diabetes education. "It's easy to sign up for a bunch of clubs or have a ton of projects, but it might end up burning you out and making you miserable," she says. "Just focus your time on the things that are important to you."

15   Ashley Echavarria, 18, a student at Northern Arizona University, learned this lesson in high school. "I was student body president [and] editor in chief of the yearbook staff and involved in many clubs." She says, "While it all was very rewarding, it took a toll on me." She eventually learned to back off from some activities. "I learned that it was OK to say no to people," she recalls. "You should realize that this is OK and think through opportunities thoroughly when consider-ing options."

16   **4. Grab stolen moments.** In the course of a day, there are usually a few "down times." Try grabbing some of those moments and making them productive.

17   "If you're in the car for a long time or waiting in a doctor's office, take out your homework and start working," says Jenna Goeke, 13, a student at St. Frances Cabrini School in San Jose, Calif. "Or if you finish homework early, try to get ahead in other areas so you have less work the following day."

18   Kate likes to **multitask**. Sometimes she even works while eating. "I've found that breakfast is the best time to do some last-minute studying or reading," she says. "If I get to class a few minutes early, I'll try to get my homework done for the next day or at least start on it."

19   **5. Think ahead.** To avoid running out of time in completing demanding task, be sure to look ahead. Planning for the next day but not for the days or weeks ahead can be shortsighted.

20   If a major science project is due in nine weeks, develop a series of deadlines for completing portions of the work. Or if you have to read *Moby Dick* by the end of the semester, set aside 30 minutes a day and start reading now. That way, you won't find yourself staying up until 4 a.m. the night before the assignment is due.

21   "Focus on the big picture," says Echavarria. "Any task you're trying to accomplish is probably part of a bigger goal. So remember what the outcome of completing the task will be, whether it's graduating, getting your dream job, or just putting a smile on your parents' faces." ■

Source: Rowh, Mark. (Nov/Dec 2006). Beat the Clock. *Career World,* Vol. 35, Issue 3, pp. 24–25.

Vocabulary

1. Define **tackles** in paragraph 1.

   a. stomps   **c.** begins

   b. tools   **d.** implements

2. Define **obligations** in paragraph 1.

   a. responsibilities   **c.** homework

   b. chores   **d.** jobs

3. What does **adept** mean in paragraph 5?

   a. adroit   **c.** skilled

   b. proficient   **d.** all of the above

4. Define **advocate** in paragraph 14.

   a. opponent   **c.** reader

   b. activist   **d.** all of the above

5. What does the author mean by **multitask** in paragraph 18?

to work on more than one task at a time

Main Idea

6. What is the main idea of paragraph 4?

   a. Learning time management skills while you are in college will improve your chances for success later in life.

   b. Success in college depends on time management skills.

   c. Scheduling many activities improves your chances for success while in college and later in life.

   d. None of the above.

7. What is the main idea of paragraph 21?

    a. Your dreams are most important.

    b. Pay attention to the specific details and tasks in your life.

    c. Focus on the bigger picture or life goals.

    d. All of the above.

Supporting Details

8. Which paragraphs support the author's idea presented in paragraph 6?
7, 8, and 9

9. Which paragraphs give specific support for the idea in paragraph 10?
11 and 12

10. What important concept did Ashley Echavarria talk about learning in paragraph 15? She eventually learned to back off from some activities.
"I learned that it was OK to say no to people," she recalls. "You should realize that this is OK and think through opportunities thoroughly when considering options."

11. What advice from paragraph 16 is the author supporting in paragraphs 17 and 18? Grab stolen moments or "down times" in your life and make them productive.

Critical Thinking/Application

12–15. Which advice from this article do you find most helpful? Explain how you could use these suggestions in your life. Answers will vary.

Activity

Write an advice column giving time management tips to a first semester college student. First, create an outline or mind map of the main ideas and supporting details you will include. Answers will vary.

Visual Image | **READING 5**

In this picture, a woman is multitasking.

1–2. Multitasking means doing several tasks at one time. List two details in this photo showing that the woman is multitasking.

a. She is taking notes about a report or a statement.

b. She is talking on the phone, holding her credit card, and drinking coffee.

3. Discuss an occasion when you have used multitasking to save time. What things did you do at the same time? Answers will vary.

4. What were the results of your multitasking? Did you experience any problems? Answers will vary.

Additional Recommended Reading

Allen, D. (2001). *Getting Things Done: The Art of Stress-Free Productivity.* New York, NY: Penguin Group.

Cilley, M.–The Fly Lady. (2002). *Sink Reflections.* New York, NY: Bantam Books.

Covey, S. R. (1989). *The Seven Habits of Highly Effective People: Restoring the Character Ethic.* New York, NY: Simon and Schuster.

Fiore, N. (1989). *Overcoming Procrastination: Practice the Now Habit and Guilt-Free Play.* New York, NY: MFJ Books.

Gleeson, K. (2004). *The Personal Efficiency Program: How to Get Organized to Do More Work in Less Time,* 3rd ed. New York, NY: John Wiley & Sons.

Klein, S. (2006). *The Secret Pulse of Time: Making Sense of Life's Scarcest Commodity.* New York, NY: Marlowe & Company.

Pausch, R. (2008). *The Last Lecture.* New York, NY: Hyperion.

St. James, E. (2001). *Simplify Your Work Life: Ways to Change the Way You Work So You Have More Time to Live.* New York, NY: Hyperion.

Szczurek, T. M. (2005). *Pursuit of Passionate Purpose: Successful Strategies for a Rewarding Personal and Business Life.* Hoboken, NJ: John Wiley & Sons.

Warren, R. (2002). *A Purpose Driven Life: What on Earth Am I Here For?* Grand Rapids, MI: Zondervan.

myreadinglab

For support in meeting this chapter's objectives, log on to www.myreadinglab.com and select Supporting Details.

4 Implied Main Ideas

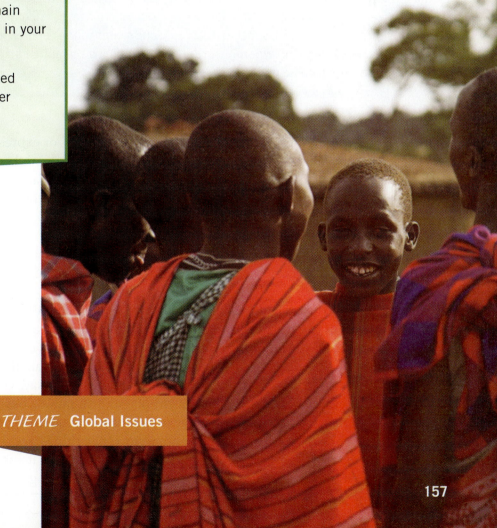

THEME Global Issues

157

SPOTLIGHT ON LEARNING STYLES

Have you ever heard a friend casually say, "I'm starving!"? This most likely meant, "I haven't eaten in a while" and "I'd like some food" or "let's get some food." What if your friend said, "This is horrible! That's all I needed!"? Something probably just happened that they found disturbing, uncomfortable, or disruptive to their day. Our perspective of what we think of as *starving* or *horrible* is probably quite different than that of someone from another culture who has actually been starving or who just dealt with a catastrophe such as an earthquake or tsunami. When I heard my friend say, "She has a major *'tude,*" I had to stop and think about it for a minute. I hadn't heard that expression before and thought about the situation she was describing before I figured out *'tude* is slang for *attitude*.

Learning by doing is about using our experiences and connecting them to what we are reading. People sometimes say they are hands-on learners. It is an important way to learn because diverse experiences may cause people to have different comprehension of the same material. Being aware of one's connections and experiences assists in determining the author's meaning.

Take a few minutes to make a list of slang words or expressions you use with your friends that someone from another culture might not understand. If you are fortunate to have a classmate who is from another culture, ask that person to share expressions they found strange or confusing when they first moved to your community.

Answers will vary.

_____

_____

When we relate to global issues, we may need to think beyond our own use of the words *starving* or *horrible* and try to imagine what others might be experiencing somewhere else in the world. This chapter addresses many global issues. You will need to pay attention to all the details and word choices to see what the author is *really* trying to say. Use your knowledge of events in the world and/or think about situations beyond what you have personally experienced to try to determine the author's implied main idea. Connecting what you are reading to other things you have read, seen, or heard will improve your comprehension of texts. It may also help to talk with others about what you are reading and learning.

Putting Implied Main Ideas in Your Own Words

(What is the unstated main idea?)

Often, an author does not directly state the main idea in a written sentence. Instead, the main idea may be implied through the details. In these cases, the author is counting on the reader to grasp his point. Why might an author want the reader to figure out his point rather than simply stating it? List some of your ideas here. Answers will vary.

> **LO1**
> Put implied main ideas of paragraphs in your own words.

_____

_____

One reason an author might imply the main idea may be so readers can draw their own conclusions. For instance, in a creative or narrative piece, the author may draw you into the story with just enough details to keep you involved. When you have to solve a mystery or figure out a situation, it makes the reading more exciting and probably makes you want to read more; this is much more interesting than having everything explained.

Another reason a writer may imply the main idea is to get you to "buy into" an idea for yourself. This is often used with persuasive writing. For example, if you decide for yourself that getting involved in a certain cause is a good idea, based on the supporting details provided, then you are more likely to act on that decision through behaviors such as writing letters to legislators or making donations to the cause. If the message is stated directly in the first sentence, however, such as "You need to donate to XXX cause, and here are three reasons why," it is more likely you will "tune out" the message and ignore the supporting reasons.

Whenever you read:

- ask yourself what message, attitude, or opinion the author is trying to share.
- notice that sometimes the main idea message is stated directly or explicitly.
- note that at other times you will need to put the main idea into your own words.
- look at the supporting details and decide for yourself what message the author is trying to get across.
- ask, "What point is the author trying to make about the topic?"

Let's review what we learned about finding the topic to help us focus on the bigger ideas.

Finding the Implied Topic

Directions: Read the terms and choose the best topic.

1. clean water, fuel, food, shelter, clothing
   Topic:

   a. things that everyone needs

   b. things that are easy to get

   c. things that everyone has

For many people around the world, the basic things one needs for survival—clean water, fuel, food, shelter, and clothing—are not easily available. Many struggle to get these necessities of life every day. Therefore, the answer is (a) things that everyone needs.

PRACTICE THE NEW SKILL

Directions: Read the terms and choose the best topic.

1. coffee farmers, cocoa producers, tea growers
   Topic:

   a. beverages

   b. products

   c. beverage producers

2. tsunami rescue, hurricane assistance, earthquake relief
   Topic:

   a. natural disasters

   b. natural disaster relief efforts

   c. global crises

3. violence against women, illiteracy, infant mortality
   Topic:

   a. critical global issues

   b. organizations to help solve global issues

   c. fundraising efforts

Finding the Implied Main Idea from a Group of Ideas

Authors may provide the reader with a list or a group of ideas or statistics. You need to ask yourself what the author is implying with this group of ideas. It may help to look at the details and ask what the individual items have in common.

EXAMPLE ──

Directions: Read the material; then select the implied main idea from the list below.

CARE has provided:

- Shelter kits contributed by Habitat for Humanity and tents
- High energy biscuits that provide enough calories per person for four days
- PUR® water purification packets
- Hygiene kits (includes toothbrushes, toothpaste, soap, detergent, shampoo, a comb, towels, safety pins, clothes line, sanitary napkins and toilet paper)
- Delivery kits for pregnant women
- Newborn kits

Source: Retrieved from the CARE Web site.

Implied Main Idea:

a. CARE provides necessary items for people facing a crisis.

b. CARE provides helpful items that some people may need.

c. CARE offers help to those who are less fortunate.

We know that the organization CARE is providing the list of items based on the introductory statement above the list. Next, look at the specific items on the list, such as shelter kits, high energy biscuits, and water purification kits. These are specific essential items people need for survival in a crisis or emergency. Therefore, the implied main idea is (a) CARE provides necessary items for people facing a crisis.

PRACTICE *THE NEW SKILL*

Directions: Read the material; then select the implied main idea from the list below.

1. Staggering Reality

- 25,000 children under age 5 die every day, mostly from preventable causes like pneumonia, infections and malnutrition.
- 4 million babies die each year in their first month of life. 2 million of those die within 24 hours of birth.
- 500,000 mothers die each year in childbirth or from pregnancy complications.

Source: Compassion, *Rock the Cradle* brochure.

Implied Main Idea:

a. Pregnancy is dangerous to women.

b. More babies die in the first 24 hours than later in life.

c. High numbers of deaths occur from pregnancy complications, childbirth, and childhood diseases.

2. Kenya by the Numbers

48 – number of years the average Kenyan is expected to live

42.6 – percentage of the population that is between zero and fourteen years old

59 – percentage of primary school entrants reaching grade five

1.2 million – number of Kenyans living with HIV/AIDS

50 – percentage of population living below the poverty line

40 – percentage of population that is unemployed

90.6 – percentage of males, age fifteen and over, who can read and write

79.7 – percentage of females, age fifteen and over, who are literate

Source: UNICEF.

Implied Main Idea:

a. HIV/AIDS is a problem in Kenya.

b. Statistics about Kenya indicate levels of poverty, education, and mortality.

c. The majority of the population of Kenya is literate.

3. **Communities in Crisis**

In Afghanistan

Education-related violence is an alarming trend in Afghanistan, with girls at particular risk of attacks and other scare tactics aimed at keeping them out of school. CARE is working with communities in the war-torn country to improve social acceptance of education and reduce the risk of attack on Afghan schools, teachers and students—especially girls.

In the Balkans

In three countries in the Balkans, CARE works with high school-age youth, especially young men, to promote attitudes and behaviors that discourage violent behavior against women and peers, and promote dignity and respect for women as equals. The young men in this project are working with local advocacy groups to design multi-media campaigns and school-based programs to advocate for women's rights and prevent violence.

In Burundi

CARE raises awareness and reduces tolerance for violence through targeted community messages via radio and interactive theater. We also train village volunteers to counsel rural women who are experiencing domestic violence, and refer them to the health clinic, if needed. In addition, CARE's village savings and loan associations help increase women's access to economic resources and provide a forum for dialogue and sensitization around issues of violence, gender and discrimination.

In Haiti

CARE is working with both men and women to prevent sexual and gender-based violence in the aftermath of Haiti's devastating earthquake, where thousands of people are cramped into makeshift camps without walls and unprotected bathing and toilet areas leave women and girls particularly vulnerable to harassment and sexual violence. We're also helping survivors of violence get the help they need to recover from the trauma.

Source: Retrieved from the CARE Web site.

Implied Main Idea:

> a. CARE works in many communities around the world, in particular, places that are currently experiencing—or have recently experienced—conflict and disaster.

b. There are many countries experiencing tragedy around the world.

c. Countries around the world that are experiencing tragedy need help.

Finding the Implied Main Idea in a Paragraph

Finding the implied main idea in a paragraph is similar to locating it in a list or group of ideas. Ask yourself what all or most of the supporting details have in common. Use the same skills to examine the supporting details for clues about the author's point as you did to find the stated main idea in a paragraph.

One word of caution, though: Don't let your own "issues" (meaning your own opinions, emotions, attitudes, etc.) get in the way of determining the *author's* point. We all have a tendency to mix our own experiences and attitudes with what we are reading. Often, the more experiences we have from life, the more difficult it is to see the author's point. That is why it is so important to recognize our prior knowledge and bias before we begin reading.

When I do the "Survey" step of SQ3R, I look over the material, and then I examine my own thoughts and attitudes as well as my prior knowledge about the topic. For instance, when I start to read something about smoking or smoking bans, I have a lot of "issues" running through my head. My father was a smoker, had emphysema and a heart attack, and died in his 70s; my brother was a smoker and had a heart attack at age 39; my mother did not smoke, but lived with second-hand smoke and had a heart attack and triple bypass surgery at 76; my brother-in-law was a smoker and died of a heart attack in his 60s; my aunt was a smoker and died of emphysema in her early 70s; and I have asthma and have trouble breathing around any kind of smoke. If I read an article about tobacco and smoking, I have to put my own issues about smoking to the side temporarily in order to "hear" or comprehend the point the author is making.

When I read research information, opinions or editorials, organizational Web sites about smoking, or legislation to ban smoking, I might not understand the author's implied main idea if I let my own issues get in the way. For instance, when I read in our local newspaper that our city council was going to vote on a proposal to ban smoking in public places, including most restaurants, I was so excited! All I could think was "It's about time! Larger cities have already done this, and even entire states. Why was our community so far behind?" I don't think I even read both sides of the argument. The article included interviews with smokers and non-smokers, restaurant and bar owners, and employees. There were many perspectives included, but my attention was only on my own desire to ban smoking. In order to determine the author's point, or implied main idea, we must carefully examine the supporting details in the reading without personal bias.

Here are some tools to help you remember all of the author's relevant information in the paragraph. One suggestion is to underline each relevant supporting detail as you read, but only if you own the book or magazine. If you are borrowing the material, such as from the library or a friend, or if you are taking a test where you are not supposed to write on it, then take notes on your own paper. Another suggestion is to write notes in the margin as you read, again, only if you own the material, otherwise, write your notes on your own paper. Make sure you include each specific detail that offers support in the paragraph. As you look over your notes and/or underlining, try to compose a sentence that addresses the meaning the author wants to convey. Do not make your sentence too general or too specific. Remember the previous examples and note how you chose the implied main ideas from the lists in the exercises. Now it is up to you to make the list of relevant supporting details.

EXAMPLE

Directions: Read the paragraph and choose the best implied main idea.

Current Situation in the Sudan

The United Nations declaration of genocide in the Darfur legally obligates the UN nation states to act to bring an end to the ethnic cleansing. Unfortunately, the international response has been sluggish. The UN's non-responsiveness is linked to a problem with funding. Meanwhile, 90 percent of African villages in Darfur have been destroyed, displacing hundreds of thousands. Refugee camps housing the displaced in neighboring counties are overcrowded, unsanitary, insufficient in their supply of food, water, and health care, and hot beds for curable disease that go untreated. Mortality is high, particularly among women and children. Aid is desperately needed to control the genocidal government of Sudan and protect the dying civilian population of Darfur.

Source: Exodus World Service Web site.

Implied Main Idea:

   a. Too many villages have been destroyed as a result of the Darfur conflict.

   b. Diseases are going untreated and people are suffering in Darfur.

   c. The United Nations is under obligation to protect the citizens of the Sudan.

   d. The UN's response to the genocide in Darfur has been grossly inadequate.

In the paragraph, there are a lot of details about the problems with the United Nations' response to the conflict in Darfur. The details of the paragraph indicate that the aid is not adequate since the people are still suffering greatly. So, while all of the statements are true, answer (d) is the best choice for the implied main idea since it covers all of the supporting details in the paragraph, and it is the point the author is trying to make.

PRACTICE THE NEW SKILL

Directions: Read each paragraph and choose the best implied main idea.

1.

   Sushila Ranamagar wasn't sure how two goats (from Heifer International) would change her life, but they did in more ways than she could have imagined. Those two goats connected Sushila with a network of women working together to improve their lives. Now Sushila is the president of a women's group in her community and, with the help of a small loan from the group, has started to diversify her farm with mushrooms and tomatoes. All of this is part of Heifer's holistic, values based approach to ending hunger and caring for the earth (by providing resources such as training, loans, and livestock to people in need).

Source: Heifer International March 2010 newsletter.
From Goats to Mushrooms to a Better Life.

Implied Main Idea:

a. Sushila Ranamagar became a farmer and leader in her community.

b. Sushila Ranamagar's life changed after receiving just two goats.

c. Heifer's gift of two goats started a chain of events that made Sushila Ranamagar's life more successful.

d. Heifer's gifts to farmers change the world.

2.

   Gertrude Osimbo and Peter Ooro had one child and longed for another. Their second baby, Caroline, died from asthma when she was 10 months old. The community thought Gertrude had done something to bring chira (a curse associated with infidelity) on her family. Peter began to threaten Gertrude with divorce. When she delivered a baby girl named Sincere, she regained respect. But just a few days before her fourth birthday, Sincere mysteriously died in her sleep. Gertrude was devastated. Child Survival Program heard her story and intervened. Medical examinations discovered that Gertrude tested HIV positive. Child Survival Program staff helped her safely deliver and taught her how to care for her child without passing along HIV. Now they have a healthy baby boy, Innocent.

   "I wish this program came earlier. I would have my two daughters here playing outside. I pray for God to give you wisdom to continue taking care of my son, Innocent."   —Gertrude Osimbo

Source: Compassion: *Rock the Cradle* brochure.

Implied Main Idea:

a. Gertrude Osimbo was devastated that she tested HIV positive.

b. The Child Survival Program helped Gertrude Osimbo learn how to take care of herself and her children.

    c. Gertrude Osimbo and Peter Ooro's children died very young.

    d. The community thought Gertrude Osimbo must have done something to bring a curse on her family.

3.

> The case for investing in girls' education is still very, very strong. We know of many women who, with education, were able to obtain jobs or start businesses and transform their lives and the lives of those around them. More broadly, it's generally accepted that one of the reasons East Asia has prospered in recent decades is that it educates females and incorporates them into the labor force, in a way that has not been true of India or Africa.
>
> *Source:* Kristof, Nicholas D. and Sheryl WuDunn (2009). *Half the Sky: Turning Oppression into Opportunity for Women Worldwide.* New York, NY: Random House, Knopf, Borzoi Books, pp. 170–171.

Implied Main Idea:

    a. East Asia is prosperous.

    b. Having educated women in the labor force is a generally accepted practice worldwide.

    c. Investing in girls' education contributes to stronger economies and societies.

    d. India and Africa do not incorporate women into the labor force like East Asia does.

Writing the Implied Main Idea in Your Own Words

Most texts we will encounter do not give us multiple choice questions. In "real life" we must determine the author's implied main idea on our own. To understand the author's point, we need to concentrate on the specific words she uses and think about the point she is trying to make with the details provided.

EXAMPLE

Directions: Read the quotation below and write what you think Mother Teresa is implying in your own words.

"If you can't feed one hundred people, then just feed one."

— Mother Teresa

Although answers will vary, one possibility is: Don't worry about how much you can do to help, just do what you can.

PRACTICE THE NEW SKILL

Directions: Read the quotations below and write in your own words what you think the writer is implying.

1.

"You must be the change you wish to see in the world." —Mahatma Gandhi

Answers will vary.

_____

2.

"Just as treasures are uncovered from the earth, so virtue appears from good deeds, and wisdom appears from a pure and peaceful mind. To walk safely through the maze of human life, one needs the light of wisdom and the guidance of virtue."   —Buddha

Answers will vary.

_____

3.

"We can never obtain peace in the outer world until we make peace with ourselves."   —Dalai Lama

Answers will vary.

_____

Putting the Implied Main Idea in Your Own Words in Paragraphs

Determining the implied main idea from each individual paragraph may be required in order to comprehend the meaning of a longer reading passage. As you read, pause after each paragraph and put the author's main point in your own words. We will work through material from the Internet Web site *Not for Sale Campaign,* a non-profit organization to fight human trafficking.

EXAMPLE

Directions: Read through the paragraph and write the implied main idea in your own words.

From *David Batstone*: how did this thing start?

I read in a local paper that one of my favorite Indian restaurants in the *Bay Area* had been trafficking women from India to wash dishes, cook meals and other tasks. The story came out when a young woman, Chianti Pratipatta died of a gas leak in an unventilated apartment owned by the proprietor of the restaurant, who forced Chianti and others into slavery under threat of reporting their illegal presence to the authorities. This was happening in my country at a restaurant I frequented. My shock turned into a consuming passion that took me around the world to learn more about how slavery flourishes in the shadows.

Source: Retrieved from Not for Sale Web site.

What is the implied main idea? _____

Batstone discovered, to his astonishment, that slavery was taking place in his favorite restaurant in California, and he then became consumed with finding out more about the hidden modern day slavery that exists around the world.

PRACTICE THE NEW SKILL

Directions: Read through each paragraph or section of the reading and write the implied main idea in your own words.

1.

In Thailand, stateless ethnic minorities and foreigners are not eligible to receive government provided health services and cannot afford even the most basic of care. These marginalized populations face a variety of other serious problems like becoming involved in the trafficking of drugs, illicit goods and people. They lack the ability to protect their young children who often die from preventable diseases and have no access to family planning methods or information regarding how to protect themselves from HIV/AIDS and STIs.

Source: Retrieved from Not for Sale Web site.

David Batstone—the founder of the *Not for Sale Campaign*
Bay Area—an area of San Francisco, California, near the Pacific Ocean

What is the implied main idea? In Thailand, stateless ethnic minorities face a variety of serious problems.

2.

Not For Sale supports a thriving artist and abolitionist named Kru Nam and her efforts to rescue hundreds of trafficked and sexually exploited children. Just recently, humanitarian aid organization, Giving Children Hope donated nearly 2 million dollars worth of medical supplies and equipment to the Not for Sale Thailand project. The success of the shipment has initiated a cooperative proposal for improving the health and quality of life of the women and children in the border area. The medicine received by Not for Sale Thailand will be stored at and administered by the government run Chiang Saen Hospital. With the donation the hospital will be able to serve not only the 110 children at Not for Sale Thailand Children's Home, but other stateless people in need of medical services free of charge. This partnership is a comprehensive progressive plan to provide health services to marginalized populations in the border area between Thailand and Burma.

Source: Retrieved from Not for Sale Web site.

What is the implied main idea? Not for Sale supports children at the Not for Sale Children's Home and provides other stateless people with medical services free of charge. This includes marginalized populations on the border area between Thailand and Burma.

3.

In the Somaliland region of Somalia, an extraordinary woman named Edna Adan Ismail runs her own obstetric hospital and trains midwives, underscoring how women's lives can be saved even in the most difficult environments. The hospital site, once used as a mass killing field during the civil war for independence (1988-1990) under Siad Barre's reign, is now a haven for bringing new life into the world.

Xavier Helgesen, co-founder of BWB, learned about this hospital in a New York Times article, and contacted the hospital after the announcement of the Better World Books Fund for Books For Africa. They teamed up and sent a container of books in the following July.

The Better World Books Fund is designed to pay for the shipping costs of containers of books, donated through Books For Africa. The fund is important, because the shipping costs for this one container alone were over $5,000.

The donated books will be used for the hospital's medical library for the Edna Adan Teaching Hospital. While the library could not currently contain a whole container of books, any extra books will be distributed to Universities in Somalia and governmental nursing facilities.

Source: Retrieved from Better World Books.

What is the implied main idea? The Edna Adan Teaching Hospital, an obstetric and training hospital in Somalia, received a large container of donated books from Better World Books Fund for Books For Africa to use in their medical library.

REVIEW *WHAT YOU LEARNED*

Directions: Read the quotations below and write what you think the writer is implying in your own words.

1.

"The Holy Prophet Mohammed came into this world and taught us: 'That man is a Muslim who never hurts anyone by word or deed, but who works for the benefit and happiness of God's creatures. Belief in God is to love one's fellow men.'"

— *Abdul Ghaffar Khan*

Abdul Gaffar Khan—Political and spiritual leader of India

Answers will vary.

2.

"The nonviolent approach does not immediately change the heart of the oppressor. It first does something to the hearts and souls of those committed to it. It gives them new self-respect; it calls up resources of strength and courage that they did not know they had. Finally it reaches the opponent and so stirs his conscience that reconciliation becomes a reality."

— *Martin Luther King, Jr.*

Answers will vary.

3.

"Islam is not the problem. Rather it is the misuse of Islam by interpreting it to fit the needs of the patriarchal order—the powers that be—and the privileges that one gender has held over the other."

— *Mahnaz Afkhami*

Answers will vary.

Directions: Use your knowledge of word parts and context clues to determine the meaning of the words.

4. patriarchal (*Hint:* think of other words that use the root patri such as *paternity, patronize, paternal,* and the root arch such as *monarch, anarchy*)

    a. ruled by women   **c.** ruled by men

    b. ruled by a dictator   **d.** ruled by the church

Martin Luther King, Jr.—Civil rights leader and peace activist in the United States
Madnaz Afkhami—Writer, scholar, and human rights activist from Iran

5. oppressor (*Hint:* think of words with the root press in them such as *pressure, depression,* and the suffix or as in *actor, supervisor*)

  a. one who lifts up and encourages others

  b. one who keeps others down by severe and unjust force

  c. one who makes peace or chooses reconciliation

  d. one who perseveres

REVIEW WHAT YOU LEARNED

A Precious Human Life

Every day, think as you wake up

Today I am fortunate

to have woken up.

I am alive,

I have a precious human life.

I am not going to waste it.

I am going to use

all my energies to develop myself,

to expand my heart out to others,

to achieve enlightenment for

the benefit of all beings.

I am going to have

kind thoughts towards others.

I am not going to get angry

or think badly about others.

I am going to benefit others

as much as I can.

His Holiness
The XIV Dalai Lama

Discuss what this saying means to you. Answers will vary.

Finding the Implied Central Idea in Longer Passages

LO2
Find the implied central idea of longer passages.

To find the implied central idea in a longer passage, use the same technique employed to locate the implied main idea for a paragraph. You still need to pay attention to the supporting details and ask yourself "What is the author *really* saying?" The difference is that the point covers several paragraphs instead of just one. After you read all of the paragraphs, look for the main message from the author. Ask yourself questions such as, "Why is the author mentioning all of these details?" "What action does she want me to take?" "What is his attitude about this topic?"

EXAMPLE

Directions: Read the passage and determine the implied central idea.

> A devastating civil war is ravaging the Sudan. Over 3.5 million Sudanese risk starvation, 2.5 million are displaced from their homes, and nearly half a million have lost their lives to violence according to statistics cited by SaveDarfur.org from the World Food Program, the United Nations, and the Coalition for International Justice. The United Nations has declared that genocide is taking place in the Sudan.
>
> Darfur residents trapped by the war at home are dependent on those few who have safely made it out of the country to speak on their behalf. Exodus World Service has a close relationship with many Sudanese refugees and they asked us for help. We are providing a platform for their voices to be heard. By reaching out to concerned citizens, Sudanese refugees hope to create a movement that encourages the United States government, the United Nations, and other peacekeeping teams to end the genocide in Darfur.
>
> *Source:* Retrieved from Exodus World Service Web site.

Implied Central Idea:

a. There is violence in Darfur.

b. Exodus World Service works on behalf of residents trapped by war and with Sudanese refugees to influence the U.S. government and the United Nations to end the genocide in Darfur.

c. Exodus World Service works with refugees around the world to assist residents trapped by war.

d. Peacekeeping efforts in foreign lands are not effective in stopping genocide.

While true, answer (a) is too general and does not indicate the author's opinion about the topic. Answer (c) is true, but it is also too general about Exodus World Service's efforts and it is not specifically about Darfur. Answer (d) is an opinion that is too broad. While the author might believe this, we don't know from the evidence or supporting details that the author takes such a strong stance about the ineffectiveness of peacekeeping efforts in *all* foreign lands. Therefore, the best choice for the implied central idea is (b). Exodus World Service works on behalf of residents trapped by war and with Sudanese refugees to influence the U.S. government and the United Nations to end the genocide in Darfur. It is specific enough to give the author's main point about the topic and it is supported by enough details from the passage.

PRACTICE THE NEW SKILL

Directions: Read the passage and determine the implied central idea.

1.

One billion women will be victims of violence in their lifetime.
Gender-based violence is one of the most pervasive and, yet, least-recognized human rights abuses in the world. As many as one in every

three women has been beaten, coerced into sex or abused in some other way—most often by someone she knows, including by her husband or another male family member.

This violence leaves survivors with long-term psychological and physical trauma; tears away at the social fabric of communities; and is used with terrifying effect in conflict settings, with women as the main target.

It doesn't have to be this way. Women and men from all walks of life are joining together to help bring an end to these pervasive, and often deadly, acts of violence.

Source: Retrieved from CARE Web site.

Implied Central Idea:

a. Men and women are joining together to bring an end to gender-based violence: one of the most pervasive yet least-recognized human rights abuses in the world.

b. Women all over the world are mistreated.

c. Violence leaves women with long-term psychological scars.

d. Men and women do not understand each other, which sometimes results in conflict and violence.

2.

Heifer International

1   Poverty is an elusive concept to pin down. Most of us have a preconceived idea of what poverty looks like. The people in these coffee-growing communities didn't fit those stereotypes—there were no

skeleton-thin children, no one was dirty or ragged, the view down into the coffee plots was breathtaking. There were even a few vehicles in some of the villages.

2   But all of these things hide the hardscrabble existence here. The vehicles are used to go to Jaltenango once a month for basic supplies, like beans and corn, not for joyriding. The children may not be thin, but they are often severely undernourished. And even though the villages are surrounded by coffee, we never had coffee in any of them. Families here do not, it seems, drink the product they grow any more than an Iowa corn farmer consumes what he grows. Coffee is the way they eke out a bare-bones survival.

3   We arrived in the community of Rio Negro. I had traveled from Heifer's headquarters in Little Rock, Ark., to what seemed like an impossibly remote village in the mountains of southern Mexico. As we talked to a family of four in Rio Negro, the husband mentioned that, before the arrival of the Heifer project, he had gone to the United States for one year to work as a roofer. When I asked him where in the U.S. he had worked, he replied, "Arkansas."

4   This was more than a chance encounter in an age of globalism; it was a realization that poverty has many faces. If a family cannot stay together because there is not enough work or money for them to survive otherwise, surely that is poverty.

Source: Retrieved from Heifer International Web site.

Implied Central Idea:

a. People in Jaltenango, Mexico, do not have adequate or reliable transportation.

b. Poverty is pervasive in Mexico.

c. Heifer works to alleviate poverty by helping families have enough income so they can stay together.

d. People who work for Heifer in Arkansas help alleviate global poverty.

3.

A Weaver's Welcome

Children from the Swat Valley (Photo: Razia Ahmed)

1   Shortly after arriving in Pakistan, one week ago, we met a weaver and his extended family, numbering 76 in all, who had been forcibly displaced from their homes in Fathepur, a small village in the Swat Valley.

2   Fighting between the Pakistani military and the Taliban had intensified. Terrified by aerial bombing and anxious to leave before a curfew would make flight impossible, the family packed all the belongings they could carry and fled on foot. It was a harrowing four day journey over snow-covered hills. Leaving their village, they faced a Taliban check point where a villager trying to leave had been assassinated that same morning. Fortunately, a Taliban guard let them pass. Walking many miles each day, with 45 children and 22 women, they supported one another as best they could. Men took turns carrying a frail grandmother on their shoulders. One woman gave birth to her baby, Hamza, on the road. When they arrived, exhausted, at a rest stop in the outskirts of Islamabad, they had no idea where to go next.

3   While there, the weaver struck up a conversation with a man whom he'd never met before. He told the man about the family's plight. Hearing that they were homeless, the man invited them to live with him and his family in a large building which he is renovating. He offered to put the reconstruction on hold so that the family could move into the upper stories of his building.

4   He and his brothers wonder what their future will be. How and when can they return to their village? And how will they start over? The crops are ruined, livestock have died, and land mines have been laid. Most of the shops and businesses have been destroyed. Many homes are demolished.

5   The relationship that began when a stranger took the risk of offering shelter to a weaver holds a lesson worth heeding.

6   The weaver and his family will never forget the extraordinary, immediate kindness extended to them when a man put his renovation project on hold so that he could help them find shelter in his building.

[Kathy Kelly co-coordinates Voices for Creative Nonviolence]

Source: Retrieved from Voices for Creative Nonviolence Web site.

Implied Central Idea:

a. True kindness and help to those less fortunate may include self-sacrifice and a change of your own personal priorities.

b. Pakistan has critical security and safety issues.

c. One weaver in Pakistan gave up personal safety and security to help struggling citizens.

REVIEW WHAT YOU LEARNED

Directions: Read the following passage and answer the questions that follow.

Lambs and Lemons Provide Education in Peru

1   Felix Ramos spent most of his 48 years in the water starved village of Sincape, located in the lower Piura River basin, in northern Peru. The tenth of twelve children, Felix was never able to finish his secondary schooling because his family couldn't afford it. With few opportunities other than farming, Felix tried to scrape out a living for his parents, wife, and seven children from the 2.5 acres of land he inherited. There simply wasn't enough income for his family to survive so Felix had to leave to seek work elsewhere in the country. "Those five years when I was working away from home in La Libertad were hard for me," says Felix, "I would abandon my wife and children for a month or a month and a half. I would come home for one or two days, leave money, and go back to work."

2   Despite the limited opportunities in Sincape, Felix just couldn't be away from his family any longer, so he used his meager saving to purchase another half acre of land and made another go at farming. He tried to grow conventional crops like corn and rice, but with the intensive use of water

and agrochemicals Felix saw that there was no way to successfully make a living this way from his 3 acres of land.

3   It was around this time that Felix became connected with Heifer Peru and their project for "Agroecological Production and Local Markets in the Lower Piura Valley." Felix was selected to receive a module of sheep as a part of the project, but for the six months before that Felix and his wife were trained in livestock care, agroecology, gender equity, and organization-building.

4   Finally, after he was well prepared, Felix's sheep arrived. "I received four ewes and one ram," says Felix, "I was so lucky that the four ewes were all pregnant and each had several lambs." Felix's flock has grown quickly since then, reaching 120 head after a few years. He has passed along five sheep to other families and sold several sheep in order to buy another 2.5 acres where he is growing sustainable crops like lemons, mangos, and tangerines.

5   He is now farming in a very different way than he did when he was growing just corn and rice. "My land was losing nutrients because of all the chemicals I was using," Felix says, "but the project's training raised my awareness as I learned about agroecology. Now I farm much differently than before."

6   But lambs and lemons aren't Felix's best crop. "My children's studies are the best crops that my family can harvest," says Felix. With Heifer's help Felix is now able to provide his children with the education he never had.

Source: Retrieved from the Heifer International Web site.

1. What is the topic? _____

funding a family's education

_____

2. Why did Felix Ramos leave his village? _____

He could not make a living for his family by farming his 2.5 acres of land

so had to seek work elsewhere.

3. How did Heifer International help Felix? _____

Felix and his wife were trained in sustainable agricultural practices and

then received sheep to produce income for their family. They then shared

their resources with their community.

4. What does Felix mean by the statement, "My children's studies are the best crops that my family can harvest"? _____

With Heifer's help he is able to provide his children with the education he never had.

5. What is the implied central idea? (What message is the writer implying?)

A man's willingness to learn and adopt a new way of agriculture provided the means for him to meet the needs of his family.

Hindustani Church Reaching Out to Rescue Prostitutes

1   PUNE, INDIA (April 15, 2010) – The Hindustani Covenant Church (HCC) invited 60 prostitutes for lunch in a yard in front of its national offices. The women arrived on rickshaws paid for by the church.

2   By paying for that transportation, the church was honoring the guests—who are considered in India's caste system to be "lowest of the low"—and in doing so declare that they are people of worth, says Ruth Hill, executive minister of the Department of Women Ministries of the Evangelical Covenant Church. "It gave them a sense of dignity."

3   The women came to the national offices to meet with Hill. All of them had received assistance from the HCC that was funded in part by Women Ministries' Break the Chains donations.

4   "The mercy and affirmation the Hindustani Covenant Church shows these women is amazing," Hill says. "They're not asking them to change first, but are reaching out to them where they are."

5   These special guests have not been able to break away from prostitution because of poverty or slave-owners forcing them to stay, but the HCC continues to minister to them in multiple ways. That kind of ministry has enabled the church to help resurrect the lives of the downtrodden and enslaved elsewhere in the country, Hill says.

6   To help the HCC expand its already extensive ministry, Hill presented the HCC with a check for $74,000 representing funds raised through the

Break the Chains initiative. She traveled to the country March 18-30 on a trip sponsored by the Indian church.

7   She was awed by the work of the HCC. "It went beyond the difference money can make. It also was a testimony to the grace that the Hindustani Covenant Church is extending. I would not have believed just how many people have had their lives radically transformed by this church."

8   During her time in India, she glimpsed a sampling of those lives as she visited eight projects and other sites.

9   One of the women she met is a former sex slave who now leads a program that teaches marketable, life-affirming skills to women who are ready to leave the sex trade.

10   In Mumbai, Hill met freed sex slaves, all of them minor girls, who are being helped through an aftercare program supported by International Justice Mission, the other partner in the first two years of the Break the Chains initiative. "The girls proudly showed us their crafts," Hill says. Items made by the girls will be sold at Triennial XIII this summer.

1. What is the implied main idea of these paragraphs? The lives of abused women are being changed in India by the faithful work of Covenant Church members both in India and in the United States.

2. Reading the first two paragraphs, what is a "rickshaw"? _____
a form of transportation

3. Why is providing transportation to the prostitutes through rickshaws important? It was honoring their guests and gave them a sense of dignity.

11   In Melghat, the church provided a micro-enterprise loan to a widow who started a small sundries store in front of her home. "The business has been so successful she is now getting a loan to expand it," Hill says.

12   "She could not have gotten a loan anyplace else," says Hill. Had she not been able to obtain the loan, the widow's plight would have been nearly hopeless.

13   "This is an example of how micro-enterprise can transform people's lives," Hill says. "You could see in her eyes the self-confidence, the hope."

4. What is the implied main idea of these paragraphs? Micro-enterprise loans provided by charitable organizations provide people who have no hope with a means to work themselves out of poverty.

5. What is a micro-enterprise? _____

Micro means "small" and enterprise is a "business," so micro-enterprise is small business.

14   In the same area, the church is providing a "Break the Chains" ministry that offers programs to improve nutrition and literacy, as well as provide loans.

15   "When HCC began there, they found 50 malnourished children ranging in age from nine months to four years," Hill says. "Parents were simply waiting for their children to die. The church said, 'this does not have to be,' and they saved the lives of all 50."

16   When Hill visited, each child wore a lanyard with their "before" photo. The nutrition program is transforming the village as people learn how to use local foods. One of the mothers is now a devoted leader in the program. The lower photo shows HCC Moderator Steven David with some of the children showing their lanyards.

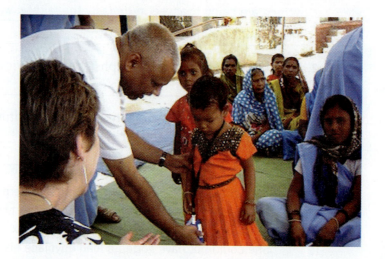

6. What does malnourished mean? _____

The word part mal means "bad," so malnourished means nourished badly or poorly.

7. What does it mean when the author says "The nutrition program is transforming the village as people learn how to use local foods"?
Answers will vary.

8. What is the implied main idea of the paragraphs above? _____
Providing nutrition and health care are also important parts of saving communities in India. The church is providing the means for communities to properly feed themselves.

17   Hill also visited a small rural village, where she met 36 adults and their children, whose families had been enslaved for generations by a moneylender. The HCC would have taken the slave owner to court, but he was connected to authorities in the justice system.

18   The Hindustani Covenant Church paid off their debt and has been working with them for 18 months, says Hill. "They are all followers of Jesus. They have been set free spiritually and physically."

19   Housing for the freed slaves still is desperately needed because they currently are living in shanties (photo on page 184), and the landowner may soon force them to leave, Hill says.

Source: Retrieved from Covenant Church Web site.

9. What is the implied main idea of the paragraphs above? Freeing slaves may involve paying old debts and relocating families.

MASTER THE LESSON

Directions: Read the article below and answer the questions that follow.

Somalia Famine

CARE scales up response, urges donors to ease restrictions on aid delivery

1   NAIROBI (July 20, 2011)—Today, famine was officially declared in two regions of southern Somalia—the first time a major famine has been announced since the famine in the Somali region of Ethiopia in 2000. This morning's declaration of famine confirms that the Horn of Africa emergency is the worst humanitarian crisis in the world now. The United Nations is warning that if the international community does not act now, famine will spread to all areas of southern Somalia within two months.

2   Across Somalia, more than 3.7 million people—more than half the entire population—are in desperate need of humanitarian assistance. In some areas in the south, nearly half the population is malnourished. These areas have the highest malnutrition rates in the world. Across the three worst-affected countries of Somalia, Ethiopia and Kenya, more than 11 million people need immediate food assistance.

3   To respond to the growing humanitarian crisis, CARE is calling for:

- International donors to commit funds to this emergency immediately to provide lifesaving aid to people affected by the famine and food crisis. The current humanitarian response is inadequate due to lack of funding and of access; just half of funds needed have been committed so far.
- All parties in south-central Somalia to grant uninhibited and unconditional access to humanitarian agencies.
- International donors to ease the current legal restrictions on the delivery of aid in Somalia on humanitarian grounds to enable more aid to reach those who need it.

4   "The declaration of famine is an urgent plea for these people. It is the most critical thing I've seen in 22 years of field experience. Every man, woman and child is suffering. The conditions of these people as they cross over the border from Somalia into the Dadaab refugee camps is down to the bone," said Barbara Jackson, CARE International's humanitarian director, who is in the Dadaab refugee camp this week. "The level of suffering they have endured is beyond our imagination, and they require immediate assistance. Everyone I met had the same message: 'Please tell the world for us, that we need help, and that we need it now. We cannot last much longer'."

5   CARE has already reached more than 1 million people across Somalia, Ethiopia and Kenya with humanitarian assistance, and we doubled our initial emergency appeal to scale up our response to provide food, water and emergency supplies to a total of 2 million people affected by the emergency in the three countries:

- In **Somalia**, CARE has assisted 164,000 people with drought relief activities and cash interventions to help families buy food, and we are scaling up our response to help as many people as possible.

- Across the border in **Kenya** at the Dadaab refugee camps, where more than 61,000 Somalis have sought safe haven in the past six months, CARE is the primary distributor of food, water and primary education for the 380,000 refugees currently living there, most of them Somalis. More than 1,500 people are arriving each day, and CARE is working with partners to scale up our response. CARE will provide food, water and emergency assistance in the newly opened Ifo II camp, which will provide safe shelter to an additional 40,000 refugees. CARE also is responding to the drought in northeastern Kenya.

- In **Ethiopia,** CARE has helped 241,587 people with food and nutrition assistance, nutrition, water and sanitation interventions such as water point rehabilitation, distribution of water treatment chemicals and hygiene promotion as well as livestock intervention comprising of slaughter destocking, animal feed and support to zonal animal health authorities.

Source: www.care.org Web site.

1. What is the implied main idea in the first paragraph?
Immediate aid is needed for famine victims in Africa.

2. According to the United Nations' definition of "famine," two deaths occur per 10,000 people per day. In these three worst affected countries of Africa, approximately how many people are dying each day?
Solution—set up the equation: $2/10,000 = x/11$ million so $x = 2,200$ people.

3–5. What does CARE propose to solve the crisis in Africa?

- International donors to commit funds to this emergency immediately to provide lifesaving aid to people affected by the famine and food crisis. The current humanitarian response is inadequate due to lack of funding and of access; just half of funds needed have been committed so far.

- All parties in south-central Somalia to grant uninhibited and unconditional access to humanitarian agencies.

- International donors to ease the current legal restrictions on the delivery of aid in Somalia on humanitarian grounds to enable more aid to reach those who need it.

6. What does the author imply by this sentence? "The level of suffering they have endured is beyond our imagination, and they require immediate assistance." Answers will vary.

_____

7–10. After reading the article, write two possible solutions that you believe will help the people in Africa, and support your ideas. Write your answers in at least four complete sentences.
Answers will vary.

_____

_____

_____

_____

LEARNING STYLE ACTIVITIES

*L*OOK, *L*ISTEN, *W*RITE, *D*O

Blood:Water Mission

NAME: Jena Lee Nardella

BORN: January 31, 1982

LIVES IN: Nashville, Tennessee

JOB: Executive Director for Blood:Water Mission

FEELS PASSIONATELY ABOUT: The discovery of unheard voices, the transformation of passionate lives, the triumph of dignity, the freedom of laughter, clean water, mountain peaks, vanilla ice cream, and basking in the wonder of God.

Jena Lee's vision is crystal-clear, even simple. Clean water.

RELEVANT (interviewer): When did you get passionate about Africa? Why?
LEE: I took a medical microbiology class (at Whitworth College, where I studied political studies) that taught me about the devastating effects of the HIV virus. It fascinated and frightened me, so I began cutting out articles in the paper that covered HIV/AIDS. I discovered the disease's ability to also attack the weakest parts of society. It didn't take long to realize that this crisis was spreading into the most vulnerable and poverty-stricken areas of the world, especially the African continent. I was frustrated that Americans were disturbingly quiet about AIDS and Africa. That's when my passion for knowing, loving, and serving Africa flourished.

R: How did you get connected with Blood:Water Mission?
L: During my senior year of college, I was hired by my school to speak at conferences on how to incorporate a fabric of social justice into a college education. I spoke at a conference in Phoenix where I met author and professor Steve Garber, who spent a lot of time asking me about the AIDS initiatives I was leading.

I didn't know this at the time, but Steve was a mentor to the members of Jars of Clay. The band had called him, asking for guidance on how they could start Blood:Water Mission. Steve connected me with the band, as they were already scheduled to play at my college that month. These passionate artists shared their vision for Blood:Water Mission, and I couldn't help but want to be a part of it. I moved to Nashville immediately following graduation, and we opened a one-room office in the basement of an old church.

R: How did Blood:Water Mission develop so rapidly as a major player in the fight against AIDS?
L: Our mission is simple: people just the same as you and me don't have access to the basic necessities for survival. People who are smart, compassionate, creative, and hard-working are struggling with AIDS and the lack of access to clean water. Women and children have to walk several miles each day to carry buckets of filthy water upon their heads. When a well is built, stomach and skin diseases disappear, those with HIV live longer, children go to school instead of carrying water, women have time to care for the orphans and the sick instead of being bound to a bucket filled with disease, and ultimately, hope is restored.

We simply took this story and shared it with as many people as we could. We explained how $1 provides a year of water for an African. The message spread faster than we could have imagined. Tens of thousands of people have responded with conviction, compassion, and enthusiasm.

R: How has Blood:Water Mission impacted Africa?
L: Blood:Water Mission has partnered with several organizations to launch more than one hundred water and sanitation projects across the African continent. Africans are the heroes in their communities because we do not go there to proclaim our importance. As a result, more than 120,000 brothers and sisters in nine different countries are organizing themselves to create water committees, to teach sanitation and hygiene practices, to build the leadership within their villages, and to celebrate the new gift of clean water. In our first year, we raised more than $1.2 million for our work in Africa.

R: What lessons have you learned from your experience?
L: Ultimately, the greatest lessons I have learned are through the transformative power of authentic love in action through relationship and human connection. I have learned that Americans are aching for purpose and connection to something deeper than themselves, and that we are all called to use our voice and talents to address social injustice, regardless of age or qualification. I have learned that God's heart breaks over the crisis in Africa, that He takes joy when people realize their responsibility to love and serve people well, and that truly He blesses our efforts.

R: What is it like to run a nonprofit at such a young age, especially one that's taking off as much as Blood:Water Mission?
L: An advisor once told me, "Jena, your greatest asset is that you don't know your own limitations." I think there's power in being young. I'm a dreamer, and I believe that change can happen if we relentlessly pursue vision with prayer, courage, and a lasting commitment. It doesn't mean that it's easy, and I have faced some dark, challenging seasons with tears and a sense of defeat, but the commitment to push through those times has made all the difference in the world.

I spend a lot of time studying leadership, nonprofit management, community development, and fund-raising strategies. I have also been blessed by leaders who are mentoring and coaching me through this process.

R: What advice would you give to someone with a similar passion?
L: Pursue that passion with everything you've got. Many people spend too much time thinking about how they may be a voice for justice and change, and they sit at home wondering when their time will come. Get up and get

involved today. Personally invest in that passion and make sure it does not become a faceless cause where you are disconnected from the people you desire to know, love, and serve.

Brenton Diaz [Interviewer]

Source: Zydek, Heather (Ed.). (2006). *The Relevant Nation: 50 Activists, Artists, and Innovators Who Are Changing Their World through Faith.* Orlando, FL: Relevant Books, pp. 54–57.

Now that you've read about how one person turned her passion into compassion, think about your passion in life. What do you care deeply about? Write it here: Answers will vary.

_____

_____

Look   Research a cause you are passionate about. Look at pictures and graphs in the materials you find for a better understanding of your issue. Then create your own visual aid representing the critical aspects of the cause and what you might do to help.

Listen   Listen to people's stories about their personal involvement in global causes. One way to hear stories is by interviewing people in your community, school, or place of worship about ways they've been involved in service to other people around the world. Another auditory method involves going to Web sites for specific global service organizations and clicking on the stories. Some are available as video. You might also find stories on YouTube or on Facebook activism links.

Write   Research a cause about which you care deeply, using the library, the Internet, and information from community organizations. Look up Web sites for organizations already fighting for causes you believe in. Consider writing to legislators, your local newspaper, or bloggers about the cause. Propose solutions to your legislators such as relevant actions or legislation to help fight the problems. Often you will find suggestions for written advocacy on organizations' Web sites.

Do   Get involved in something you care deeply about that will make a difference in the world. Recruit your friends, classmates, and family to join you. Talk to your college administrators and/or student government association about how you can help create awareness about a critical global issue on your campus.

Reading Practice

The following reading practice will help you further develop your ability to find the implied main idea and implied central idea while you are exploring various global issues.

The first reading is from the Internet. *Tragedy during trip to Uganda* is a blog posting from the *Equal Exchange* Web site. Equal Exchange is an organization involved in promoting fair trade products internationally.

The second reading is an excerpt about global poverty from the textbook, *Society: The Basics.*

The third reading is an excerpt from the book *Half the Sky: Turning Oppression into Opportunity for Women Worldwide.*

The fourth reading is an article entitled "Secondary Use," published in *The Covenant Companion* magazine.

The fifth reading includes photographs from two global Web sites, Heifer International and Samaritan's Purse.

Internet   **READING 1**

Tragedy during trip to Uganda
By Thomas Lussier, Lead Coffee Roaster

Hundreds of people hike to the site of the mudslides.

MULEMBE

1   My name is Thomas Lussier and I am the Lead Coffee Roaster at Equal Exchange. Last week Beth Ann Caspersen (Quality Control Manager) and I went to Uganda to visit the Gumutindo Co-operative. Since my years as a *barista* I have had a love for African coffees, so it was with great excitement that I prepared for this trip. Part of the trip was to include visiting a couple of primary societies and our farmer partners in the districts around Mt Elgon. When you visit producers, you expect to learn quite a bit. Perhaps it's about how difficult it is to make a living as a farmer. Perhaps you'll hear about climate change affecting weather patterns, growing seasons and rainy seasons. You might even learn about soil erosion. Working to change these things is part of the greater mission at Equal Exchange.

Some of the mudslides can be seen on the side of this mountain.

2   What you don't expect is a tragic mudslide to happen the very week you are there. You don't expect to visit the slide area that buried a health clinic and a church, several villages, men, women and children. You don't expect to attend the wake of the Chairman for the Savings and Credit Cooperative Organization (the SACCO is basically the farmers' bank). It's not unusual to witness hardship when visiting producers. During this trip, however, we witnessed utter tragedy and sadness.

3   By the end of the week, there was reason to feel encouraged. Gumutindo is very engaged with its farmers. There are agronomists and field officers in the primary societies every day. They give trainings to the farmers about a wide range of ways to farm more sustainably. The trainings focus on everything from intercropping for sustenance and added income, to organic conversion, to techniques for increased soil fertility and avoiding erosion.

Barista—person who makes coffee

People gather at the site of one of the mudslides. There are still people missing beneath them.

4   From what we are told, the trainings work. Farmers are receptive to the ideas, and increased yields and higher quality coffee leads to increased incomes, savings accounts, and increased quality of life. Also understood is how better land stewardship will increase the quality of life for future generations. These are life and death incentives. I know that sounds dramatic, but soil conservation takes time and mudslides happen in an instant. This work needs to continue and be supported wholeheartedly.

5   My thoughts continue to be with the people affected by the mudslide in the Bududa District and particularly the societies of Bumayoga, Bukalasi, Nasufwa, and Buginyanya. ◾

Source: Small Farmers Big Change Coop Web site.

Implied Main Ideas Questions

1. According to paragraph 1, what did the writer expect to see on his trip?
   He expected to see how difficult it is to make a living as a farmer, climate change affecting weather patterns, growing seasons and rainy seasons, soil erosion.

2. According to paragraph 2, what is implied concerning the writer's expectations?
   The writer did not expect to witness such incredible tragedy and have his life impacted. He only expected to learn about the country, the environment, and the economy.

3. According to the supporting details in paragraph 3, why was the writer encouraged? _____

The Gumutindo Co-operative provided much support to the farmers through specialists in agronomy. They provided training to help the farmers with sustainability and erosion and other agricultural issues affecting their income.

4. What is the implied main idea of paragraph 4? The trainings work.

_____

5. According to paragraph 4, why do the trainings work? _____

Farmers are receptive to the ideas, and increased yields and higher quality coffee leads to increased incomes, savings accounts, and increased quality of life. People see the ideas will help future generations.

Textbook

READING 2

1250L

The Extent of Poverty

Directions: Practice using SQ3R as you read this material from a textbook.

First, **Survey** the headings and subheadings, and italicized words.

Then, create **Questions** from subheadings and italicized words.

As you **Read** each section, take notes.

Then, **Recite** the answers to each of your questions in your own words.

At the end of the reading, **Review** your notes and write a summary paragraph of the central idea and major supporting details.

1   Poverty in poor countries is more widespread than it is in rich nations such as the United States. . . . In low-income countries, however, most people live no better than the poor in the United States, and many are far worse off. In the world as a whole, at any given time, 15 percent of the people—about 1 billion—suffer from chronic hunger, which leaves them less able to work and puts them at high risk of disease (Kates, 1996; United Nations Development Programme, 2001.)

2   The typical adult in a rich nation such as the United States consumes about 3,500 calories a day, an excess that contributes to obesity and related health problems. The typical adult in a low-income country not only does more physical labor but consumes just 2,000 calories a day. The result is undernourishment: too little food or not enough of the right kinds of food.

3   In the ten minutes it takes to read through this section of the chapter, about 300 people in the world who are sick and weakened from hunger will die. This amounts to about 40,000 people a day, or 15 million people each year. Clearly, easing world hunger is one of the most serious challenges facing humanity today.

POVERTY AND CHILDREN

4   Death comes early in poor societies, where families lack adequate food, safe drinking water, secure housing, and access to medical care. Organizations fighting child poverty estimate that at least 100 million city children in poor countries beg, steal, sell sex, or work for drug gangs to provide income for their families. Such a life almost always means dropping out of school and places children at high risk of disease and violence. Many girls, with little or no access to medical assistance, become pregnant, a case of children who cannot support themselves having children of their own.

5   Analysts estimate that another 100 million of the world's children leave their families altogether, sleeping and living on the streets as best they can or perhaps trying to migrate to the United States. Roughly half of all street children are found in Latin American cities such as Mexico City and Rio de Janeiro, where perhaps half of all children grow up in poverty. Many people in the United States know these cities as exotic travel destinations, but they are also home to thousands of children living in makeshift huts, under bridges, or in alleyways (Ross, 1996; United Nations Development Programme, 2000; Collymore, 2002).

POVERTY AND WOMEN

6   In rich societies, the work women do typically is undervalued, underpaid, or overlooked entirely. In poor societies, women face even greater disadvantages. For example, most of the people who work in sweatshops like the one described in the opening to this chapter are women.

7   To make matters worse, tradition keeps women out of many jobs in low-income nations; in Bangladesh, women work in garment factories because that nation's conservative Muslim religious norms bar them from most other paid work and limit their opportunities for advanced schooling (Bearak, 2001). At the same time, traditional norms give women primary responsibility for raising children and maintaining the household. The United Nations estimates that in poor countries, men own 90 percent of the land, a far greater gender disparity in wealth than is found in high-income nations. It is no surprise, then, that about 70 percent of the world's 1 billion people living near absolute poverty are women (Hymowitz, 1995).

8   Finally, the fact that women in poor countries generally do not have access to birth control raises the birth rate and keeps women at home with their children. In

addition, the world's poorest women typically give birth without help from trained health workers.

SLAVERY

9   Poor societies have many problems in addition to hunger, including illiteracy, warfare, and even slavery. The British Empire banned slavery in 1833, followed by the United States in 1865. But according to Anti-Slavery International (ASI), as many as 400 million men, women, and children (almost 7 percent of humanity) live today in conditions that amount to slavery.

10   ASI describes four types of slavery. First is *chattel slavery*, in which one person owns another. The number of chattel slaves is difficult to estimate because this practice is against the law almost everywhere. But the buying and selling of slaves still takes place in many countries in Asia, the Middle East, and especially Africa. . . .

11   A second, more common form of bondage is *child slavery,* in which desperately poor families let their children take to the streets to do what they can to survive. Perhaps 100 million children—many in poor countries of Latin America— fall into this category.

12   Third, *debt bondage* is the practice by which employers hold workers captive by paying them too little to meet their debts. In this case, workers receive a wage, but it is too small to cover the food and housing provided by the employer; for practical purposes, they are enslaved. Many sweatshop workers in low-income nations fall into this category.

13   Fourth, *servile forms of marriage* may also amount to slavery. In India, Thailand, and some African nations, families marry off women against their will. Many end up as slaves to their husband's family; some are forced into prostitution.

14   Finally, one additional form of slavery is *human trafficking*, the movement of men, women, and children from one place to another for the purpose of performing forced labor. Women or men brought to a new country on the promise of a job and then forced to become prostitutes or farm laborers, or "parents" who adopt children from another country and then force them to work in sweatshops are examples of trafficking in human beings. Such activity is big business: Next to trading in guns and drugs, trading in people brings the greatest profits to organized crime around the world (Orhand, 2002).

15   In 1948, the United Nations issued the Universal Declaration of Human Rights, which states, "No one shall be held in slavery or servitude; slavery and the slave trade shall be prohibited in all their forms." Unfortunately, nearly six decades later, this social evil persists. ■

Source: Macionis, John. (2006). *Society: The Basics,* 8th ed. Upper Saddle River, NJ: Pearson, pp. 233–236.

SQ3R notes Answers will vary.

The Extent of Poverty

Question _____

Answer _____

_____

Poverty and Children

Question _____

Answer _____

_____

Poverty and Women

Question _____

Answer _____

_____

Slavery

Question _____

Answer _____

_____

Specific Types of Slavery (*Hint:* see italicized words in the reading)

Question _____

Answer _____

_____

Question _____

Answer _____

_____

Question _____

Answer _____

_____

Question _____

Answer _____

_____

Question _____

Answer _____

_____

Literature   **READING 3**

Half the Sky: Turning Oppression into Opportunity for Women Worldwide

FROM CHAPTER 14 – *WHAT YOU CAN DO*
TERERAI TRENT

1   Tererai is a long-faced woman with high cheekbones and a medium brown complexion; she has a high forehead and tight cornrows. Like many women around the world, she doesn't know when she was born and has no documentation of her birth. She thinks it may have been 1965, but it's possible that it was a couple of years later. As a child, Tererai didn't get much formal education, partly because she was a girl and was expected to do household chores. She herded cattle and looked after her younger siblings. Her father would say: *Let's send our sons to school, because they will be the breadwinners.* "My father and every other man realized that they did not have social security and hence they invested in male children," Tererai says. Tererai's brother, Tinashe, was forced to go to school, where he was an indifferent student. Tererai pleaded to be allowed to attend, but wasn't permitted to do so. Tinashe brought his books home each afternoon, and Tererai pored over them and taught herself to read and write. Soon she was doing her brother's homework every evening.

2   The teacher grew puzzled, since Tinashe was a poor student in class but always handed in perfect homework. Finally, the teacher noticed that the handwriting was different for homework and for class assignments, and whipped Tinashe until he confessed the truth. Then the teacher went to the children's father, told him that Tererai was a prodigy, and begged for her to be allowed to attend school. After much argument, the father allowed Tererai to attend school for a couple of terms, but then he married her off about age eleven.

3   Tererai's husband barred her from attending school, resented her literacy, and beat her whenever she tried to practice by reading a scrap of old newspaper. Indeed, he beat her for plenty more as well. She hated her marriage but had no way out. "If you're a woman and you are not educated, what else?" she asks.

4   Yet when Jo Luck (president of Heifer International) came and talked to Tererai and other young women, Jo kept insisting that things did not have to be this way. She kept saying that they could achieve their goals, repeatedly using the word "achievable." The women caught the repetition and asked the interpreter to explain in detail what "achievable" meant. That gave Jo a chance to push forward. "What are your hopes?" she asked the women, through an interpreter. Tererai and the others were puzzled by the question, because they didn't really have any

hopes. Frankly, they were suspicious of this white woman who couldn't speak their language, who kept making bewildering inquiries. But Jo pushed them to think about their dreams, and reluctantly, they began to think about what they wanted. Tererai timidly voiced her hope of getting an education. Jo pounced and told her that she could do it, that she should write down her goals and methodically pursue them. At first, this didn't make any sense to Tererai, for she was a married woman in her mid-twenties.

5   There are many metaphors for the role of foreign assistance. We like to think of aid as a kind of lubricant, a few drops of oil in the crankcase of the developing world, so that gears move freely again on their own. That is what Heifer International's help amounted to in this village: Tererai started gliding along freely on her own. After Jo Luck and her entourage disappeared, Tererai began to study frantically, while raising her five children. She went away to her mother's village to escape her husband's beatings. Painstakingly, with the help of friends, she wrote down her goals on a piece of paper: "One day I will go to the United States of America," she began, for goal one. She added that she would earn a college degree, a master's degree, and a PhD—all exquisitely absurd dreams for a married cattle herder in Zimbabwe who had less than one year's formal education. But Tererai took the piece of paper and folded it inside three layers of plastic to protect it, then placed it in an old can. She buried the can under a rock where she herded cattle.

6   Then Tererai took correspondence classes and began saving money. Her self-confidence grew as she did brilliantly in her studies, and she became a community organizer for Heifer. She stunned everyone with superb schoolwork, and the Heifer aid workers encouraged her to think she would study in America. One day, in 1998, she received notice that she had been admitted to Oklahoma State University.

7   Some of the neighbors thought that a woman in her thirties should focus on educating her children, not herself. "I can't talk about my children's education when I'm not educated myself," Tererai responded. "If I educate myself, then I can educate my children." So she climbed on an airplane and flew to America.

8   At Oklahoma State, Tererai took as many credits as she possibly could and worked nights to make money. She earned her degree and then returned to her village. She dug up the tin can under the rock and took out the paper on which she had scribbled her goals. She put checkmarks beside the goals she had fulfilled, and buried the tin can again.

9   Heifer International offered Tererai a job, and she began work in Arkansas—while simultaneously earning a master's degree part-time. When she earned her MA, Tererai again returned to her village. After embracing her children and relatives, she dug up her tin can and checked off her most recently achieved goal. Now she is working on her PhD at Western Michigan University, and she has brought her five children to America. Tererai has finished her coursework and is

completing a dissertation about AIDS programs among the poor in Africa. She will become a productive economic asset for Africa, all because of a little push and helping hand from Heifer International. And when she has her doctorate, Tererai will go back to her village and, after hugging her loved ones, go out to the field and dig up her can again. ■

Source: Kristof, Nicholas D. and Sheryl WuDunn. (2009). *Half the Sky: Turning Oppression into Opportunity for Women Worldwide.* New York, NY: Random House, Knopf, Borzoi Books, pp. 240–243.

Questions

1. What is the implied main idea of paragraph 1?

   a. Tererai accepted not going to school as part of her culture.

   b. Tererai worked at learning even though she could not go to school.

   c. Tererai was angry at her brother, Tinashe, because he was allowed to go to school.

2. What is the implied main idea of paragraph 2?

   a. Tinashe was beaten because he was not smart enough for school.

   b. Tinashe tried to conceal that his sister was the smarter one.

   c. Tererai's teacher saw her talent and potential, but her father resisted and kept her oppressed.

3. What is the implied main idea of paragraph 3?

   a. A woman in Tererai's culture was not treated with respect or equality.

   b. Men control women.

   c. Tererai's husband was insecure and manipulative.

4. When was the point at which Tererai saw hope for change in her life?

   When Jo Luck (president of Heifer International) came and talked to Tererai and other young women, Jo kept insisting that things did not have to be this way. She kept saying that they could achieve their goals, repeatedly using the word "achievable." The women asked through an interpreter what "achievable" meant and Jo pushed them to think about their dreams and what they wanted. Finally, Tererai said she wanted an education.

5. Explain what the author implies by these statements:

There are many metaphors for the role of foreign assistance. We like to think of aid as a kind of lubricant, a few drops of oil in the crankcase of the developing world, so that gears move freely again on their own. That is what Heifer International's help amounted to in this village: Tererai started gliding along freely on her own.

With a little encouragement and help from Heifer International, the women could begin to see hope for themselves. This hope led to working toward their dreams and then moving along toward achieving them on their own. Like a few drops of oil, Heifer's help just got things running smoothly. Heifer was not needed to keep it going. Once their lives started moving, the women were able to keep going on their own.

Magazine/Periodical   READING 4

1210L   ### Secondary Uses

North Park Professor Nnenna Okore Makes Art With Other People's Trash

1   *Symmetry* suggests rhythm, and rhythm suggests movement in the work of Nnenna Okore. Her sculptures *unfurl,* looking deceptively simple at first glance, but upon closer inspection, they reveal the **intricate** designs and hours of painstaking handwork that formed the clay, twisted the paper, and wove the plastic grocery bags into meaningful expressions.

2   It's not often that you see the words "plastic bags" and "meaningful expressions" in the same sentence. In this case it works. Okore, a native of Nigeria, uses discarded items as raw material for her art. She loves natural materials such as clay, fiber, and wood, but she also finds inspiration in plastic grocery bags, wires, old newspapers, library discards, and phone books. It has become popular to create whimsical objects from trash. However, for Okore, it's not *kitsch*—it's consciousness. She wants to redeem the value of objects that some might see as lacking any value at all.

3   "I grew up in an environment where many of the objects most people throw away were being **revitalized** and reused because they made life easier for people who lacked material wealth, who couldn't buy brand new stuff."

Symmetry—balance, proportion
Unfurl—open out, unfold, expand, develop
Kitsch—tastelessness, outlandish behavior

4   Nnenna Okore was born in Australia and raised and educated in Nigeria, where she completed a bachelor's degree in painting at the University of Nsukka in 1999. During her years there, she met and worked with sculptor El Anatsui, who introduced her to the use of unconventional materials and encouraged her to allow her environment and her experiences to shape her work.

5   Okore came to the United States and eventually added two master's degrees in sculpture to her resume. She now serves as assistant professor and chair of the Art Department at North Park University in Chicago.

6   Her country of origin is not far from her thoughts, however. She writes on her website, www.nnennaokore.com, "Much of my inspiration stems from my childhood years at Nsukka, a small university town in southeastern Nigeria. As a child, I was fascinated by the social, natural, and man-made conditions in rural dwellings around the university campus . . . I was drawn to simple sights of barefooted children appropriating toys and hunting tools from scrap objects. Other compelling views to my sensibilities were the carefully arranged wares borne on the heads of street peddlers, and household items in the market place lined up on the termite-eaten tables."

7   Okore's pieces incorporate traditional arts and crafts techniques such as weaving, twisting, dyeing, and shaping. "I like bringing in some cultural skills or crafts into the way I make things," she says. "Working with your hands gives you a sense of power. You are in control of what you are making." Finding materials to work with is not a problem. Family, friends, colleagues, and students donate plastic bags and newspapers, and Okore admits to occasional dumpster diving when she sees useful items someone has tossed out.

8   In the West, such behavior is hardly encouraged. However, in Nigeria, as in other developing countries, secondary uses for discards are common. People save bottles to refill with other liquids, make book covers out of newspapers, and reuse paper to wrap perishables or other items for sale. Larger items, such as bicycles, are refurbished and sold. By contrast, richer nations tend toward a single use philosophy, relying on disposable food containers and household items and other cheap goods that are easily discarded.

9   "Trashed objects have within them so many levels of life that I think are not fully explored," explains Okore. "In many developing countries, [collecting discarded objects] is a source of livelihood for many people."

10   In part, her art pays homage to the resourcefulness of people whose survival depends on conserving what others would consider disposable. "People go out looking for things, picking them up, cleaning them, and selling them—making money from them," Okore says. "Others are reusing them in ways that are helpful to their households. Trash has the potential to be lifesaving."

11   Reusing materials can be lifesaving in other ways, too. Okore believes that reuse is one way artists can save the earth. "Trash becomes an avenue by which

we can become creative, especially reconstructing our environment," she says. Using materials wastefully, even thoughtlessly, sends a message. "It shows a disregard for the rest of the world when Western countries just discard stuff without thinking," Okore insists. "We use and throw away so much paper, for example, when there are people who don't even have paper to write on."

12   The mother of three children age eleven and under, she hopes to travel with them to Nigeria soon, both to see her homeland and to experience a less affluent way of life.

13   Okore's art, with its intricate patterns, flowing tapestries, and unusual elements, embodies her message of redemption and preservation. Her works have been exhibited in the United States, the United Kingdom, and Nigeria, and she has received several awards and residencies. This past December she exhibited at the Copenhagen Climate Conference and she has a work made out of old hospital linens in Swedish Covenant Hospital's art exhibit "Dreams of Healing" this month.

14   "I want to bring more value to that whole idea of reusing or redeeming things," she says. "I want to take something that would be considered valueless and create meaning from it." ∎

Source: Peters, Marianne. (April 2010). Secondary uses. *The Covenant Companion*, pp. 18–20.

Questions

1. Use context clues to determine the meaning of ***intricate*** in paragraph 1.

Her sculptures unfurl, looking deceptively simple at first glance, but upon closer inspection, they reveal the ***intricate*** designs and hours of painstaking handwork that formed the clay, twisted the paper, and wove the plastic grocery bags into meaningful expressions.

Deceptively means "misleadingly, unreliably, or not to be trusted."	Her paintings at *first* looked simple.	*But* —(indicates opposite) —when one inspects the art more closely . . .

Together, these facts reveal that ***intricate*** means the opposite of *simple* or:

a. intimidating.

b. complex.

c. deceiving.

2. Use word parts to determine the meaning of ***revitalized*** in paragraph 3.

"I grew up in an environment where many of the objects most people throw away were being ***revitalized*** and reused because they made life easier for people who lacked material wealth, who couldn't buy brand new stuff."

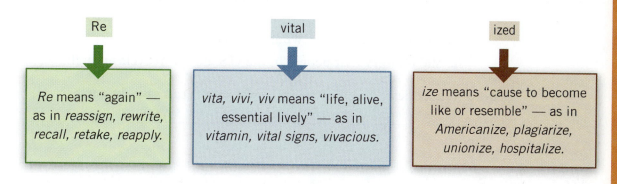

Re

Re means "again" — as in *reassign, rewrite, recall, retake, reapply.*

vital

vita, vivi, viv means "life, alive, essential lively" — as in *vitamin, vital signs, vivacious.*

ized

ize means "cause to become like or resemble" — as in *Americanize, plagiarize, unionize, hospitalize.*

Using word parts, ***revitalized*** means:

a. removed.

b. poverty.

c. renewed.

3. What is the implied main idea of paragraph 2?

a. One method of artistic expression is through using recycled materials.

b. Okore's reuse and redemption of discarded material in her art is a form of consciousness.

c. All artists should reuse materials and help save the environment.

4. True or False: Okore's art was greatly influenced by her surroundings in Nigeria.

5. True or False: Okore admired how the people in her town in Nigeria were resourceful and practical.

6. In paragraph 8, what is the implied main idea?

a. In Western countries it is common for people to discard materials when they are done using them.

b. People in developing countries try to see if there is another use for an item before discarding it.

c. In developing countries people reuse materials, but in Western countries, people have much more wasteful habits.

7. In paragraph 10, the artist Okore's implied main idea is that:

a. she respects how her culture is resourceful and does not waste resources.

b. she finds ways to use what others throw away.

c. she is angry that people in the U.S. do not recycle enough.

8–10. What does Okore believe is the way artists can save the earth?

Okore believes that reuse is one way artists can save the earth.

Visual Image   **READING 5**

Three sisters and one brother look on as a volunteer from Habitat for Humanity reads from a large book outside a house built by Habitat for Humanity in Totonicapan, Guatemala.

What does the photo imply about the children and the adult?

The children are looking at pictures in a book and seem to be interested

in the book. The adult is holding the book and appears to be reading

to the children.

What specific details in the photo support your answer?
All four children are sitting close to the woman. Three children have their
hands on the book. One child is looking away but still holding onto the pages.
The woman is wearing a name tag that says "MEL" but the children do not
have name tags, implying the woman is a guest and the children live there.

Read the caption under the photo. In what ways do the photo and
the caption support each other? The caption reads "Three sisters and a
brother look on as the Habitat for Humanity volunteer reads from a large
book outside a house built by Habitat for Humanity." The details of the
photo with the woman wearing a name tag supports that the woman is a
volunteer. The children sitting close together and listening as she reads
supports the idea that she is reading to them while their house is being
built by Habitat for Humanity.

myreadinglab

For support in meeting this chapter's objectives, log on to www.myreadinglab.com and select
Implied Main Idea.

5 Patterns of Organization

LEARNING OUTCOMES

LO1 Use the writer's plan to improve your comprehension.

LO2 Use patterns of organization in text.

LO3 Use key words to identify patterns in text.

THEME **Money Management**

SPOTLIGHT ON LEARNING STYLES 👁 Look ✏ Write

Money can be something we look at—we see it come in, we see it disappear. In our computerized society, money is something we actually see less often and experience more as numbers and values written on a statement. Much of what we earn and spend takes place electronically. We rarely see actual cash when we use debit and credit cards and have our paychecks directly deposited into our bank accounts. We may lose touch with how our money comes and goes unless we track it in a way that makes sense to us. It may seem difficult to track money if the process is new to us, but we may already have similar experiences that

we can adapt. I've noticed my teenage daughter, for instance, can figure out how to use any cell phone, Wii, or iPod device without needing directions. She automatically recognizes the patterns of organization in the information. She would not need to read an instruction manual, if one even existed, because she uses her experience to understand how the devices work. But, when it comes to investing, she does not automatically have the background in finance to create the patterns of organization needed to discern the information. She needs to develop those patterns with some perseverance and patience.

Writers Have a Plan (What are they trying to do?)

As we have already discussed in earlier chapters, most of the texts you read will have a clear purpose or main idea that the author is trying to convey. Writers generally have a plan before they

LO1
Use the writer's plan to improve your comprehension.

begin, and they develop that plan throughout their writing. Think about the writing you have done, or are now doing, in your college writing classes. You may be asked to brainstorm or free write about a topic first to generate ideas. You probably will be asked to clarify your purpose and your audience next. You also may be asked to create an outline or a mind map before you begin writing. As you can see, writing is a process that requires some planning in the early stages.

As a reader, your comprehension will greatly improve when you identify the author's plan or pattern of organization. Knowing the pattern of organization will help you look for relevant details that support the main idea and will also help you stay focused on the major points throughout your reading.

How do you know which pattern of organization is being used by an author?

- Becoming familiar with the words authors use to set apart the patterns will help.
- Good examples are words you may recognize as transition or signal words used in your writing class.
- The more you work with signal words in reading and in writing, the easier it will become to identify the pattern.
- Each pattern is used by the author to help convey a certain meaning.
- Being aware of the patterns of organization will help you understand the author's meaning.

Another important strategy is using graphic organizers, such as charts, maps, flow charts and tables, when you read. If the author puts graphic organizers in the reading, you will be able to understand her meaning more clearly if you know how to interpret them. You may also find that creating your own visual organizers as you read will help you process the information in a way that makes more sense to you.

In this chapter, we will use reading material related to money management to help you practice using the patterns of organization.

Patterns of Organization

In this chapter you will learn to recognize and use the following patterns of organization:

> **LO2**
> Use patterns of organization in text.
>
> **LO3**
> Use key words to identify patterns in text.

- paragraphs developed with time order/ sequence
- paragraphs developed with simple listing
- paragraphs developed with definition
- paragraphs developed with example

Paragraphs Developed with Time Order/Sequence

Authors may also develop paragraphs according to a pattern of time order or sequence. In this case, it is critical to pay attention to the order in which the information is presented. If it is a time order pattern, then the author wants the reader to know that each item is presented in a specific time sequence. This pattern is often used in historical or narrative genres. For instance, if someone is telling a story, the order of the facts or events is very relevant to the reader's comprehension. Similarly, when information is presented in sequential order (a sequence pattern), then imagine the text as if you were following a recipe or building something and following the directions. TRY IT!

Learning Styles TIPS

Look: Imagine you are watching a movie, or draw a picture.

Listen: Read the passage aloud, or have someone read it to you.

Write: Outline the relevant facts or events.

Do: Imagine you are in the story or events, or act it out.

Signal Words

first, second(ly), third(ly), etc.

last(ly), final(ly)

next, then, when, whenever, while, during, until, after, before, previous(ly), later, following,

---

EXAMPLE ————————————————————————————————————

Directions: Use the signal words to aid your understanding of the following paragraphs. Complete your budget in the table provided.

Start with the current month. At the top of a blank page, write down the month and year. First list, and then total, your anticipated income.

Next come your various expenses. Put your largest and most regular expenses at the top. Items such as your mortgage, car payments, and groceries come to mind. Make sure you leave space for insurance premiums, utilities, savings contributions, medical bills, credit card charges, and whatever else you spend money on each month. Now total your anticipated expenses.

Source: Strassels, Paul N. and William B. Mead. (1986). *Money Matters: The Hassle-Free, Month-by-Month Guide to Money Management.* Reading, MA: Addison-Wesley, p. 37.

MONTH _____   YEAR _____

ANTICIPATED INCOME SOURCES	INCOME AMOUNT
Job	$
TOTAL Monthly Income	$
ANTICIPATED EXPENSES	EXPENSE AMOUNT
Job	$
TOTAL Monthly Expenses	$

In this example, your budget should include the month and year at the top of the page. It should also include the title of "Anticipated Income Sources" and list the sources of your income under the title. Your table should also have the title "Anticipated Expenses" listed. Under the title should be a list with the corresponding amounts of your expenses (i.e., your mortgage or rent, car payment, and groceries, and then your "insurance premiums, utilities, savings contributions, medical bills, credit card charges, and whatever else you spend money on each month"). You should also have a total for your income and for your expenses.

PRACTICE THE NEW SKILL

Directions: Use the signal words to aid your understanding of the readings. Then, answer the questions that follow.

PRACTICE 1

1   Auto lending is a very competitive market. Banks and credit unions are eager to *underwrite* auto loans, and all the car makers have in-house consumer finance units. To keep car buyers flocking to the showrooms, those in-house financing companies frequently provide incentives such as 0% financing, or 0.9%. Don't just jump at that low rate. Remember, this is usually an either/or proposition—either you get the low rate and pay the sticker price, or we haggle on price but you pay a higher interest rate. As such, you might be better off finding outside financing and negotiating that better price.

2   <u>Before you go shopping</u>, though, the question you really must ask yourself isn't how much car you can afford but how much car loan you can afford. The answer is on your spending plan, which is in the upcoming Budgeting section.

3   You must determine how much *discretionary* income you generate each month and how much of it you're willing to *earmark* for a car. That ultimately determines how much car loan you'll be able to cover comfortably every month for the next three to four years.

4   Assume for a moment that you can afford $300.

5   <u>The next step</u> is to talk to your bank or credit union to find out what rates they're currently charging on new-car loans for thirty-six and forty-eight months. You don't want to stretch your notes out too far, particularly not out to seventy-two months. A six-year note will make you feel as if you're paying on this vehicle forever, and there's a pretty good chance you're going to want to trade your car in before the loan is paid off. That means you either have to come up with a lump sum to pay it off when you trade in your old car (cash you could otherwise use to buy your new car), or you'll have to wrap the remaining balance into your new loan, extending the debt even further. Let's assume bank rates are 4.5% for thirty-six months and 5.25% for forty-eight months, which were available in the spring of 2005.

6   <u>The next step</u> is to check the Web sites of the various car manufacturers you're interested in. They all list the various incentive programs currently in play. This is information that will make you a far *savvier* consumer when it comes time to negotiate.

Underwrite—guarantee, finance
Discretionary—optional, flexible, unrestricted
Earmark—allocate, set aside, save
Savvier—well informed and perceptive, shrewd

7   You now have all the necessary data to determine what you can afford in order to stay within your budgeted monthly note.

Source: Opdyke, Jeff D. (2006). *Complete Personal Finance Guidebook.*
New York, NY: Random House, pp. 60–61.

What are the steps to determine what you can afford?

Before you go shopping the question you really must ask yourself isn't how much car you can afford but how much car loan you can afford. You must determine how much discretionary income you generate each month and how much of it you're willing to earmark for a car.

The next step is to talk to your bank or credit union to find out what rates they're currently charging on new-car loans for thirty-six and forty-eight months.

The next step is to check the Web sites of the various car manufacturers you're interested in.

PRACTICE 2

1   Psychologically, it helps to see how much you're saving each day. It feels really good to watch your money grow, especially if you have had to give up something *tangible*, like a cup of coffee or a restaurant dinner, in order to get there.

2   Here are two suggestions that should give you some immediate *gratification* while helping you save money.

3   First, every day I want you to empty your pockets or change purse of all change, plus one of the lowest *denomination* bills you're carrying that day. The next day, when you purchase something, break the lowest-denomination paper money you've got left.

4   The day I wrote this (it happened to be a Sunday), I emptied out my change purse and scraped up the additional change from the bottom of my purse. I found fifty-nine cents. I was carrying a one-dollar bill, a five-dollar

---

Tangible—touchable, real, physical
Gratification—satisfaction, fulfillment
Denomination—quantity, value

bill, and a $100 bill (which I'd had in my wallet for about three weeks). Usually I have more change, but that's how it goes. Some days there's more, some days less. Some days your lowest bill is a dollar. Some days it'll be a five- or ten-dollar bill.

5   Following this suggestion, I'd put $1.59 into a jar. At the end of the month, I'd have $47.70. At the end of the year I'd have $572.40. Want to beef it up? Take your two smallest bills and put them in the jar. Or, every time you pay for something, break a new bill. You'll end up with a chunk of change at the end of the day.

6   As an experiment, I did this recently. At the end of the month I had more than $100 in the jar. And I never missed the cash. The next day I'd simply break a new bill and start over again.

7   <u>Here's the second suggestion:</u> At the end of the month, take whatever cash you've accumulated and put it into your account. Write yourself a check for the amount and deposit it into your money-market account or, better yet, into a mutual fund or stock brokerage account.

8   A friend told me that she deposits her "savings" into a mutual fund account that makes it difficult, if not impossible, to withdraw any funds. Another woman I interviewed told me she puts her extra cash into a bank that's a half-hour drive from her house—and she didn't ask for an ATM card for the account.

9   If you save $100 per month this way, you'll have saved another $1,200 per year, plus interest on the cash you put away. Not only will you have painlessly put away this cash, but it will start to earn interest and grow on its own. And that's how you start to build real wealth.

Source: Glink, Ilyce R. (2001). *50 Simple Things You Can Do to Improve Your Personal Finances: How to Spend Less, Save More, and Make the Most of What You Have.* New York, NY: Three Rivers Press, pp. 32–33.

What are the two suggestions the author gives for immediate gratification while saving money?

1. Every day I want you to empty your pockets or change purse of all change, plus one of the lowest denomination bills you're carrying that day. The next day, when you purchase something, break the lowest-denomination paper money you've got left.

2. At the end of the month, take whatever cash you've accumulated and put it into your account. Write yourself a check for the amount and deposit it into your money-market account or, better yet, into a mutual fund or stock brokerage account.

PRACTICE 3

Financial planning is the process of looking at your current financial condition, identifying your goals, and anticipating what you'll need to do to meet those goals. Once you've determined the assets you need to meet your goals, you'll then identify the best sources and uses of those assets for eventually reaching your goals. But remember: Because your goals and financial position will change as you enter different life stages, your plan should always make room for revision. Figure AIII.1 summarizes a step-by-step approach to personal financial planning.

Source: Ebert, Ronald J. and Ricky W. Griffin. (2007). *Business Essentials,* 6th ed. Upper Saddle River, NJ: Pearson, p. 546.

What are the five steps in developing a personal financial plan?

1. Assess your current financial condition.

2. Develop your financial goals.

3. Identify a plan of action.

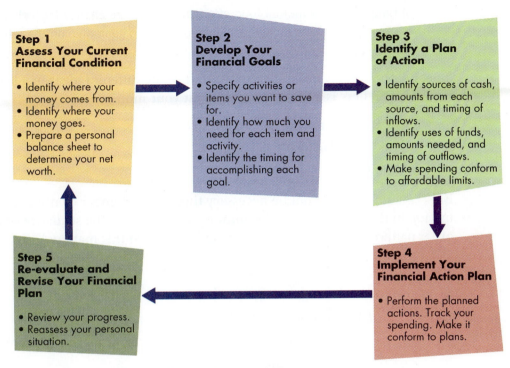

Figure AIII. 1 Developing a Personal Financial Plan

4. Implement your financial action plan.

5. Re-evaluate and revise your financial plan.

Paragraphs Developed with Simple Listing

Sometimes authors convey a simple list of ideas in no particular sequence or order. If they are simply making several points in a row, they may state *first* for the first point, *second* for the next point, and *finally* for the last point. Here is an example of how an author might share a simple list of ways to invest money.

There are several places to invest your money. First, a savings account provides the lowest risk but generally earns a lower interest rate. Second, a certificate of deposit offers the investor a fixed amount of time with a guaranteed interest rate, but the investor's funds are locked in for a period of time. Finally, a mutual fund offers investors more chance for higher returns but carries a higher risk since there is no guarantee on the return on investment.

The author also may use bullet points to indicate different ideas in a list. For example, here is a list of ways to invest your money.

- Savings Account
- Certificate of Deposit
- Mutual Fund

But remember, it may not be necessary that you remember or use the information in the same order as the author presented. (See the sequence or time order pattern of organization for examples of when this matters.)

Signal Words

one, for one thing, to begin with

first (of all), second(ly), third(ly)

further, furthermore, also, other, another, in addition, next, moreover

last(ly), (last of all), final(ly)

EXAMPLE ——————————————————————————————————————

Directions: Use the signal words to aid your understanding of the reading. Then, answer the questions that follow.

Five Things You Should Know About . . .

Credit Cards

1. **Use them carefully.** Credit cards offer great benefits, especially the ability to buy now and pay later. But you've got to keep the debt levels manageable. If you don't, the costs in terms of fees and interest, or the damage to your credit record, could be significant.

2. **Choose them carefully.** Don't choose a credit card just to get freebies (T-shirts or sports items) or because there's no annual fee. Look for a card that's best for your borrowing habits.

   Example: If you expect to carry a balance on your card from month to month, which means you'll be charged interest, it's more important to look for a card with a low interest rate or a generous "grace period" (more time before your payments are due).

3. **Pay as much as you can to avoid or minimize interest charges.** If possible, pay your bill in full each month. Remember, paying only the minimum due each month means you'll be paying a lot of interest for many years, and those costs could far exceed the amount of your original purchase.

4. **Pay on time.** You'll avoid a late fee of about $35 or more. But more importantly, continued late payments on your credit card may be reported to the major credit bureaus as a sign that you have problems handling your finances.

And if your credit rating gets downgraded, your card company could raise the interest rate on your credit card, reduce your credit limit (the maximum amount you can borrow) or even cancel your card.

Late payment on your credit card also can be a mark against you the next time you apply for an apartment or a job.

5. **Protect your credit card numbers from thieves.** Never provide your credit card numbers—both the account numbers and expiration date on the front and the security code on the back—in response to an unsolicited phone call, e-mail or other communication you didn't originate.

When using your credit card online make sure you're dealing with a legitimate Web site and that your information will be encrypted (scrambled for security purposes) during transmission.

Major credit card companies also are offering more protection by providing "zero-liability" programs that protect consumers from the unauthorized use of their card.

In general, only give your credit card or card numbers to reputable merchants or other organizations.

Source: http://www.fdic.gov/consumers/consumer/news/cnspr05/five_credit.html

Circle the five things you need to know about credit cards according to the article. Which three would you consider most important and why?

Answers will vary.

_____

_____

_____

PRACTICE THE NEW SKILL

Directions: Use the signal words to aid your understanding of the reading. Then, answer the questions that follow.

PRACTICE 1

While, unfortunately, there is no precise formula for making $1 million, there are some common themes in this book that seemed to run throughout the stories we heard.

- The millionaires we interviewed had strong encouragement from at least one family member. In the case of Chi Chi Rodriguez, it was his father who made him realize from a very young age that he would be successful. Judy Walker credits her mother and grandmother for supplying encouragement; for Del Hedgepath, it was his mother; and for Fran Kelly, it was both parents.

- Many of the millionaires we found were especially challenged in some way as a child. The experiences, instead of sending our millionaires cowering into a corner, made them stronger and helped mold their abilities to overcome adversities. David Geffen and Lisa Renshaw were bullied as children. And Dal La Magna, one of five children, learned when he was young that he'd have to get anything he wanted himself.

- Those who became millionaires set some type of goal. That goal, as we said earlier, was not always to make money. Sometimes, as in the case of Humberto Cruz, there were a series of goals. The first for him was to put food on the table and then remove a high-rate mortgage on his house. In the cases of Dennis Lardon and Scott Oki, the initial goal was as basic as finding a job—a simple goal many of us already may have had. They just happened to choose the right employers at the time.

- Many had the inner strength to make considerable sacrifices—although not always for dramatically long periods, maybe merely a year or two. For Humberto Cruz it was the two years it took to pay down his mortgage. Timothy and Karen Faber toughed it out for a year before their company started turning a profit. Lisa Renshaw lived in a parking garage for three years before her business took off.

- Many were unafraid to take risks—whether leaving money in the *volatile* stock market like Dennis Lardon and Scott Oki or starting a business in what

---

Volatile—unstable, unpredictable

might have seemed an impossible situation such as Lisa Renshaw, Jay Thiessens, or Markin Roffman. Dal La Magna's risk was *accruing* mounds of credit.

- Often, these millionaires had a unique ability to sell people on new ideas or to manage well. In some cases, such as the Jakubowskis and Humberto Cruz, management of the business involved family members. In others, a unique brand of business management fostered the growth of a company—for example, the cases of Jay Thiessens, David Geffen, Dal La Magna, Joe Dudley, and Lisa Renshaw.

- All of them read a lot or took aggressive steps to learn from others. Joe Dudley went so far as to encourage reading groups at his company. Del Hedgepath—although he never finished college—admits he read many books several times. And Jay Thiessens, even though unable to read, learned from audio or video books and seminars.

- Our millionaires followed their passions regardless of what other people said or thought. Although David Copperfield's parents would have liked him to become a doctor, he focused on becoming a magician from an early age. Maya Angelou was determined to perform and write; ultimately, all her loves and skills came together to create a unique breed of talent. Scott Oki loved computers and accounting and accepted a job with Microsoft even though the salary was not the greatest. Marvin Roffman, by firmly standing his ground over a negative analysis of Donald Trump's casino business, would up in his own successful business.

- None of these millionaires like personal debt. Even Dal La Magna, who grew up in a household where personal debt was commonplace, acknowledges debt has drawbacks. Humberto Cruz's road to wealth actually began by paying off a mortgage. Dennis Lardon, even though a multi-millionaire, reports he sticks with one charge card that he pays off monthly. And Lisa Renshaw was working to develop homes so that she could live in her own new home mortgage free. A key to Judy Walker's business success in buying homes and fixing them up: being able to offer troubled homeowners hard cash.

- All had the ability to bounce back from failures and keep going. Despite difficult times, they didn't give up.

Accruing—accumulating

We hope these profiles inspire you to learn even more from the sig-nificant people in your life and to become more financially successful at whatever it may be that you choose to do.

Source: Liberman, Gail and Alan Lavine. (2000).
Rags to Riches: Motivating Stories of How Ordinary People Achieved Extraordinary Wealth! Chicago, IL: Dearborn, pp. 209–211.

Circle the 10 things millionaires have in common. See above.

Which one of the suggestions in the reading most inspires you? Please explain. Answers will vary. _____

_____

PRACTICE 2

Paying Off Credit Card Debt

With credit cards—among the rich and the poor—at epidemic propor-tions in this country, there have been many television programs and dozens of articles about how to get out of debt. The subject is well covered in books, too; in my last book, *The 9 Steps to Financial Freedom*, I offer a step-by-step plan. In short, there is plenty of help available to show you how to get out of debt. You already know why you should do it; now I want you to take the actions that will enable you to reach that goal. Millions of people have done it, and so can you but only if you raise it to a top priority and keep your vow to become debt-free.

Having covered the topic at length elsewhere, I am not going to summarize it here, because if you have debt, you should learn everything you can about paying it off. However, here are some important points to keep in mind:

1. Face your debt by telling others about it.

2. If you are in credit card trouble, you must cut up all of your credit cards now, with the possible exception of one card for emergencies; do not carry this card in your wallet, however.

3. Call the credit card company of the one card you've kept and ask them to lower your credit limit to a level that will provide you with security in the event of an emergency.

4. You must pay more than the minimum payment every month, as much more as you possibly can. Here's an example to illustrate why: If you owe a credit card company $1000 at an 18.5 percent interest rate and you just pay the minimum of $17 every month, it will take you about 12.5 years to pay it off and cost you $1550 in interest. Pay just $10 extra a month and you will cut down the payback time to 4.6 years and pay $512 in interest. That's a savings of over $1000. Higher balances take exponentially longer to pay off; a balance of $3000 can take up to 30 years to pay off if you just pay the minimum due every month. You can calculate the amount of time it will take you to pay off your debt on the FinanCenter, Inc., Web site.

5. You must pay off the credit card with the highest interest rate first, and then the rest in descending order.

6. You must negotiate for yourself the best interest rates, even if it means switching credit cards every 6 months.

7. You must understand everything about how your credit card works—all fees, how the company charges you, all about the so-called grace period—everything.

8. You must honor all your debts equally—whether it's the money you owe Visa or the money you owe your brother.

9. After you pay off one credit card, you must apply the money you have been paying that particular company to paying off another credit card.

10. If you doubt that you can do this by yourself, you must get in touch with a wonderful nonprofit agency known as the Consumer Credit Counseling Service; they can be reached by calling (888) GO2-CCCS. They will help you organize and consolidate your debt.

11. You must never let this happen again.

12. After all your debts have been paid off, you are to apply the money you were paying all those months toward creating your future.

Source: Orman, Suze. (1999). *The Courage to Be Rich: Creating a Life of Material and Spiritual Abundance.* New York: Penguin Putnam, pp. 81–82.

Which of the 12 ideas do you find most useful? Explain.

Answers will vary.

PRACTICE 3

Creating and Sticking to a Master Plan

Okay, you've got a budget going, and you've shopped around for the best deals on your essentials and other purchases. Now you ask me the James Lipton question: "What's my motivation?"

Your goals, my friends. Your goals.

Having small goals, such as trying out that nouveau Pan-Asian joint on Saturday night with your new girlfriend or boyfriend, or larger goals, such as getting a graduate degree or vacationing in the Caribbean, can motivate you to be financially responsible and savvy in ways you've yet to dream.

Setting goals and sticking to a plan gives you a vision to keep in your head when that latte/gin-and-tonic/pair of shoes calls you to buy. It enables you to "just say no." But we all have goals, some more amorphous than others, so focus is needed. Here are some tips on solid goal making and setting your priorities:

- When it comes to finances, you've got to **concentrate**. You may not be able to have both a vacation and a new work wardrobe this year. Which do you want more? Or is there a third goal that can be eliminated so you can have goals number one and two? If you hook yourself into a smaller but well-thought-out set of goals, you have a better chance of achieving them.

- **Pop-up expenses** happen. No doubt one week you'll be asked to a baby shower (pop-up number one) and a bridal shower (pop-up number two), and you'll need new contact lenses at the same time (pop-up number three). These things *can* be manageable. Be creative and frugal where you can (with the gifts) while spending on what you really need (those contact lenses). It helps if you keep a small cushion of cash in your bank account to always cover those unexpected yet forever-popping up expenses.

- When laying out goals, make sure to look at the **time frame**. If you're thinking about saving for a down payment on a house, how much time are you giving yourself? By setting up a reasonable (and realistic) schedule to complete your financial goals, you'll be able to determine your priorities and budget for other items with longer lead times.

- **Set yourself up right.** Make sure *you* are happy and secure before you work to make anyone else happy. Include an emergency fund into your budgeting goals that can cover you for at least three months without a paycheck. And do your best to take care of debt before getting in any deeper.

- **Get started, pronto.** Now it's time to get moving on your money goals, budget, and plans. The sooner you get started, the more rewards you'll reap.

And if you're having trouble getting started, do what they tell writers to do when paralyzed by inertia: Sit in front of the computer (or piece of paper) and just start.

- **Don't beat yourself up.** Look, we all mess up once in a while. Sometimes you just have to have that freakin' latte or you'll go mad. But learn from the glitches in your plan and get back on course. Ask yourself if what you're spending is taking you closer to happiness (an A-plus on your budget!) or quickening your debt descent.

Source: Ulrich, Carmen Wong. (2006). *Gener@tion Debt: Take Control of Your Money— A How-to Guide.* New York, NY: Time Warner, pp. 33–34.

List the six suggestions the author makes:

1. Concentrate on what is most important to you.
2. Pop-up expenses happen, so anticipate them and have a cash cushion.
3. Look at the time frame for your goals.
4. Set yourself up right before you try to make anyone else happy.
5. Get started, pronto, on your money goals, budget, and plans.
6. Don't beat yourself up over indulgences and past mistakes.

Paragraphs Developed with Definition

Authors sometimes develop paragraphs by defining words or ideas in the text. This is common in both textbooks and technical articles. Often the definition follows the word in a straightforward manner. For example, according to the textbook *Principles of Accounting,* "*Interest* is the fee for using money." Sometimes the definition is in parentheses following the word or it is set apart with hyphens or dashes in the sentence. For example, the definition of *interest* might be presented a different way: "*Interest*—the fee for using money—is revenue earned by the payee for loaning the money; it is an expense incurred by the maker as the cost of borrowing money."

Signal Words

is defined as

also known as

is/are

the concept of . . .

Also watch for parentheses following a word (the definition is in parentheses) or a word followed by a dash—and then the definition.

EXAMPLE ───

Directions: Use the text to find the definition of the words.

> If you're going to finance a car, you're going to use an auto loan. They operate exactly like a home mortgage in that they're based on three variables: the principal (the size of the loan), the rate (the interest you pay annually), and the term (how many months you have to repay the principal).
>
> *Source:* Opdyke, Jeff D. (2006). *The Wall Street Journal Complete Personal Finance Guidebook.* New York: Random House, pp. 59–60.

1. Principal: _____

2. Rate: _____

3. Term: _____

In the above example, the definition of each term is in the parentheses immediately following the word: "the principal (the size of the loan), the rate (the interest you pay annually), and the term (how many months you have to repay the principal)."

/ *PRACTICE* **THE NEW SKILL** /

Directions: Read each paragraph and answer the question that follows.

PRACTICE 1

> By definition, grants are financial assistance that is not paid back. A common federal grant is the Pell Grant, which is awarded for either full-time or part-time employment. To determine your eligibility, talk with your financial aid counselor or visit any of the various websites that provide government financial aid information.
>
> *Source:* Baldwin, Amy. (2007). *The Community College Experience: Plus.* Upper Saddle River, NJ: Pearson, p. 328.

Define *grants:* financial assistance that is not paid back _____

PRACTICE 2

> Work-study is a program that allows students to earn money while they work on campus. The reason it is called "work-study" is that the jobs may allow you to study when you work. Most work-study positions,

however, are similar to office assistants and you will be busy for most of the time you work.

Source: Baldwin, Amy. (2007). *The Community College Experience: Plus.* Upper Saddle River, NJ: Pearson, p. 329.

Define *work-study*: <u>a program that allows students to earn money while they work on campus</u>

PRACTICE 3

The time value of money is perhaps the single most important concept in personal finance. The concept of *time value* recognizes the basic fact that, while it's invested, money grows by earning interest or yielding some other form of return. Whenever you make everyday purchases, you're giving up interest that you could have earned with the same money if you'd invested it instead. From a financial standpoint, "idle" or uninvested money—money that could be put to work earning more money—is a wasted resource.

Source: Ebert, Ronald J. and Ricky W. Griffin. (2007). *Business Essentials*, 6th ed. Upper Saddle River, NJ: Pearson, p. 549.

Note: In this example, the words following "is" do not define time value of money. See the next sentence for the explanation of the concept.

Define *time value of money*: <u>while it's invested, money grows by earning interest or yielding some other form of return</u>

Paragraphs Developed with Example

Authors may develop their ideas by giving examples. Sometimes it is easier to get a point across through a specific example of a situation or an experience. How do you know when an author is using an example? Authors often use the phrases *for instance, for example,* or *such as* to indicate they are providing an example or illustration. Or they may define a word first and then follow it with examples, combining both patterns of organization. For example: A *colleague* is considered your professional equal, such as a co-worker on the same level or a person in a similar job working at a different location. In the previous sentence, the word *colleague* is first defined and then an example is provided to help clarify the meaning of the word.

Signal Words

for example, one example, our first example, etc.

for instance

such as

one way to, another way, great ways to, etc.

EXAMPLE

Directions: Read the paragraphs below and answer the questions that follow. Determine the author's main idea based on the use of the relevant examples.

> Wealth is having considerably more than what you need to survive. Our first example showed us that because of debt, $50,000 was needed to survive. Without debt, only $31,700 was needed. Which means the other $18,300 that comes in creates wealth. Solid wealth. Not paper equity that is only for people with a mortgage to help them feel better about owing money. This is liquid cash. As long as you've set aside what you need for a secure future (especially if you still have a job), you can spend it, invest it, or give it away with no negative consequences.
>
> *Source:* Fuhrman, John. (2003). *The Credit Diet: How to Shed Unwanted Debt & Achieve Fiscal Fitness.* Hoboken, NJ: John Wiley & Sons, p. 41.

Define *wealth:* _____

What example does the author use to help explain *wealth*?

_____

What is the main idea? _____

_____

In the example above, the author uses the example of $50,000 versus $31,700 needed to survive to demonstrate one of the consequences of being in debt. This example supports his main idea, that without debt, less money is needed to live and the extra money that comes in then creates real wealth.

PRACTICE *THE NEW SKILL*

Directions: Read the paragraphs. Determine the author's main idea based on the use of the relevant examples.

PRACTICE 1

All these terms are important. A high credit line enables you to use your card for big charges and long vacations. A grace period of twenty or twenty-five days lets you take full advantage of your credit card. For example, you might charge a nice meal on, say, September 15, get billed for it October 10, and have until October 30 to pay—in all, six weeks of interest-free "float." Look out for banks that advertise a low interest rate but tell you only in the small print that you get no grace period at all. Always ask banks for a complete list of terms.

Source: Strassels, Paul N. and William B. Mead. (1986). *Money Matters: The Hassle-Free, Month-by-Month Guide to Money Management.* Reading, MA: Addison-Wesley, p. 194.

What example do the authors use to help the reader understand *grace periods*? You might charge a nice meal on, say, September 15, get billed for it October 10, and have until October 30 to pay—in all, six weeks of interest-free "float."

The authors discuss the terms *credit line* and *grace period*. What main idea or point are they making? A high credit line enables you to use your card for big charges and long vacations. A grace period of twenty or twenty-five days lets you take full advantage of your credit card. Look out for banks that advertise a low interest rate but tell you only in the small print that you get no grace period at all. Always ask banks for a complete list of terms.

PRACTICE 2

How long does it take to double an investment? A handy rule of thumb is called the "rule of 72." You can find the number of years needed to double your money by dividing the annual interest rate (in percent) into 72. If, for example, you reinvest annually at 8 percent, you'll double your money in about 9 years:

$$72/8 = 9 \text{ years to double the money}$$

Source: Ebert, Ronald J. and Ricky W. Griffin. (2007). *Business Essentials,* 6th ed. Upper Saddle River, NJ: Pearson, p. 549.

What is the author's main idea? You can easily calculate how long it will take to double your investment.

PRACTICE 3

Winning a scholarship is by far the most rewarding (financially and psychologically) way to pay for college because it is literally free money—you don't have to pay it back. There are thousands of scholarships out there for needy and accomplished students. All you have to do is find them. To find the ones that match your profile, get the word out that you are looking. Talking with friends, family, employers, and college officials is a great way to start the process. They may know of obscure scholarships that will fit your needs perfectly. Another way to get information is to talk to the financial aid officers and counselors at your college. They have access to and knowledge of scholarships that fit the college's student profiles (e.g., single parent and transfer scholarships). Other effective methods for finding scholarships include investigating sources at the library and searching the Internet. Searching print and web-based databases will provide you with more than enough information: your only problem will be narrowing your focus.

Source: Baldwin, Amy. (2007). *The Community College Experience: Plus.* Upper Saddle River, NJ: Pearson, p. 327.

List four ways the author suggests to find scholarships:

1. Get the word out that you are looking. Talking with friends, family, employers, and college officials is a great way to start the process.

2. Talk to the financial aid officers and counselors at your college.

3. Investigate sources at the library.

4. Search the Internet.

REVIEW WHAT YOU LEARNED

Directions: Read each passage and answer the questions that follow.

Make paying down your debt a priority, counsels Garrett. Kill the credit-card balance as quickly as possible, even if you have to give up new clothes and nights out to do it. You can even draw down your emergency savings account to pay off the credit card, as long as you keep the card balance at zero after that. Then you could use the card in an emergency until you rebuild the fund. Apply for a home-equity line of credit, so it's available for emergencies, but don't use it.

Source: Stern, Linda. (February 4, 2008). A Recession Handbook: Protect Your Pocketbook. *Newsweek,* p. 60.

The author suggests, "make paying down your debt a priority." What are three ways to do that, according to the author?

1. Give up new clothes and nights out.

2. Draw down your emergency savings account to pay off the credit card as long as you keep the card balance at zero after that.

3. Apply for a home-equity line of credit, so it's available for emergencies, but don't use it.

How much debt are you carrying right now? Does it make you nervous and uneasy? If it does but you haven't taken any action to *eradicate* it, then you haven't yet reached the "set point" of your debt. I believe that each of us has within us a point at which anxiety over our debt turns to panic, and it is at this point that we are finally moved to take action. One person's set point may be $2000; another's may be $20,000; still another's may be in the six figures. You know your set point instinctively—without a doubt you'll know it when you reach it.

Source: Orman, Suze. (1999). *The Courage to Be Rich: Creating a Life of Material and Spiritual Abundance.* New York, NY: Penguin Putnam, p. 81.

4. Define *debt set point:* a point at which anxiety over our debt turns to panic, and it is at this point that we are finally moved to take action

5. What is the author's main idea? Everyone has a "debt set point" or a point at which anxiety over our debt turns into panic and we are finally ready to take action.

Eradicate—eliminate

MASTER THE LESSON

Patterns of Organization

Directions: Read the passage and answer the questions that follow.

High-Tech Banking, 24/7

1   For young adults today, it's hard to imagine life without gadgets and high-tech helpers. We want to make sure you know about some of the attractive electronic banking services beyond ATMs.

2   **Internet banking** (online banking) enables you to transfer money between your accounts at the same bank and view account information, deposits as well as loans, at any time.

3   **Internet bill paying allows** you to pay monthly and one-time bills over the Internet. Some banks offer electronic bill payment free of charge, others charge a fee that is usually less than what you would spend on postage.

4   **Debit cards** look like credit cards but they automatically withdraw the money you want from your account. You can use a debit card to get cash from an ATM or to pay for purchases.

5   **Direct deposit** enables your paycheck and certain other payments to be transmitted automatically to your bank account. "Direct deposit is free and it's fast—there's no waiting for the check to arrive at home and no waiting in the teller lines," said Kathryn Weatherby, an Examination Specialist for the FDIC.

6   **Telephone banking** allows you to use your touch-tone phone to confirm that a check or deposit has cleared, get your latest balance, transfer money between separate accounts at the same bank, and obtain details about services.

7   **Automatic withdrawals** from your bank account can be arranged free of charge to pay recurring bills (such as phone bills or insurance premiums) or to systematically put a certain amount of money into a savings account, a U.S. Savings Bond, or an investment.

8   "Your banking can be so much more convenient and easier to monitor and control when you have access to your accounts 24 hours a day, seven days a week, from your home or practically anywhere else," added Weatherby.

9   However, she also stressed the need to take security precautions with your electronic transactions and your computer, such as those

discussed on Financial Fraud and Theft: How to Protect Yourself and Five Things You Should Know About Credit Cards. To learn more about electronic banking and consumer protections, see the Winter 2004/2005 FDIC Consumer News online at www.fdic.gov/consumers/consumer/news/cnwin0405.

Source: http://www.fdic.gov/consumers/consumer/news/cnspr05/hightech.html

1. What is Internet banking? online banking
2. What does Internet bill paying allow you to do? Pay monthly and one-time bills over the Internet.
3. What are debit cards? They are like credit cards but the amount is automatically taken out of your checking account.
4. What is direct deposit? It allows your paycheck and certain other payments to be deposited directly into your checking or savings account.
5. What is telephone banking? It allows you to use your touch-tone phone to do several banking activities without going into the bank.
6. What are automatic withdrawals? They can be automatically arranged to pay certain bills or put a certain amount of money into another account.

LEARNING STYLE ACTIVITIES

*L*ook, *L*isten, *W*rite, *D*o

FREE APPLICATION FOR FEDERAL STUDENT AID
July 1, 2011 – June 30, 2012

START HERE
GO FURTHER
FEDERAL STUDENT AID

Use this form to apply free for federal and state student grants, work-study and loans.

Or apply free online at **www.fafsa.gov**.

APPLICATION DEADLINES

Federal Deadline - June 30, 2012
State Aid Deadlines - See below.

Check with your financial aid administrator for these states and territories:

AL, AS *, AZ, CO, FM *, GA, GU *, HI *, MH *, MP *, NC, NE, NM, NV *, PR, PW *, SD *, TX, UT, VA *, VI *, VT *, WA, WI and WY *.

Pay attention to the symbols that may be listed after your state deadline.

AK   AK Education Grant - April 15, 2011 *(date received)*
     AK Performance Scholarship - June 30, 2011 *(date received)*

AR   Academic Challenge - June 1, 2011 *(date received)*
     Workforce Grant - Contact the financial aid office.
     Higher Education Opportunity Grant - June 1, 2011 *(date received)*

CA   Initial awards - March 2, 2011 + *
     Additional community college awards - September 2, 2011 *(date postmarked)* + *

CT   February 15, 2011 *(date received)* # *

DC   June 30, 2011 *(date received by state)* # *

Applying by the Deadlines

For federal aid, submit your application as early as possible, but no earlier than January 1, 2011. We must receive your application no later than June 30, 2012. Your college must have your correct, complete information by your last day of enrollment in the 2011-2012 school year.

For state or college aid, the deadline may be as early as January 2011. See the table to the right for state deadlines. You may also need to complete additional forms.

Check with your high school guidance counselor or a financial aid administrator at your college about state and college sources of student aid and deadlines.

If you are filing close to one of these deadlines, we recommend you file online at **www.fafsa.gov**. This is the fastest and easiest way to apply for aid.

The FAFSA Factor

1   Though private scholarships are often awarded solely on the basis of a student's perceived "merit," other forms of financial aid are determined by the Free Application for Federal Student Aid, better known as FAFSA.

2   Failing to submit a FAFSA each year prevents any federal and most school-offered aid (such as student loans, work-study awards, and "need-based" grants) from being given to incoming students or those already in attendance. The FAFSA form can be attained at most schools, many libraries or other public buildings, or online. Based on information supplied on the FAFSA, you will receive a Student Aid Report (SAR) that indicates the Expected Family Contribution (EFC)—how much a household is expected to pony up for the student's education bill.

3   Yet many working but cash-strapped families who submit a FAFSA are surprised to learn that they are deemed to qualify for little, if any, assistance. Among the reasons:

4   Timing. Filing a FAFSA begins on January 1 each year. The best financial awards—heavier on no-payback grants and lighter on loans—are generally given to those who file early. Some states have filing deadlines in March or April; miss that cutoff and no aid will be offered, regardless of need.

5   Income. The EFC is calculated largely by the family's income—both taxable money (wages, pensions, and capital gains) and nontaxable funds (child support, tax-exempt interest, and money contributed to IRAs and similar savings plans). In addition, nearly 6 percent of money saved in parents' bank accounts is considered in the EFC calculation, meaning that households that sock away more money (even if it is not earmarked for a college education) tend to have a higher EFC—and therefore less opportunity for student aid.

6   Students who hold part-time jobs to save for college get hurt even more. Some 35 percent of their income is expected to be applied toward college—regardless of their other expenses, such as car insurance—so paycheck-earning students often get lower aid packages than those who do not hold jobs.

7   The school's cost. Usually, more generous aid packages are offered at schools with higher tuition and living costs. As a general rule, financial need is determined by each school by subtracting the EFC from its Cost of Attendance (tuition, fees, room and board, books, and other expenses). So attending a lower-cost public university will usually yield a lower financial-aid package than if that student went to a pricier private school.

Source: Kirchheimer, Sid [AARP's "Scam Alert" Expert]. (2006). "The FAFSA Factor." *Scam-Proof Your Life: 377 Smart Ways to Protect You & Your Family From Ripoffs, Bogus Deals & Other Consumer Headaches.* New York: Sterling Publishing, p. 138.

SCAM ALERT: Don't Pay to Get Money

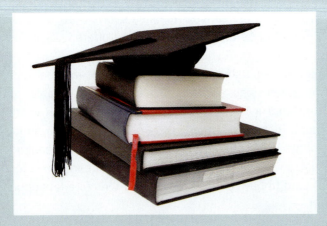

Here are some red flags that signal "Scholarship Scam Ahead!"

Up-front funds. Any request, tied to a scholarship or not, that requires you to pay an advance fee for obtaining a low-interest education loan (sometimes hawked as an "origination" or "guarantee" fee). Real student loans never require an application-processing fee.

Fees for services. Beware of any request for a payment that will allegedly grant you access to scholarship-matching lists of "secret" or "millions of dollars in unclaimed scholarships." These services usually offer the same opportunities available for free at websites—yet they charge $400 or more for the added hype. (P.S. Not one scholarship in the United States "guarantees" winners, nor is there any surplus of unclaimed scholarship money.)

Compensated "counselor." Services that promise to apply for scholarships or student loans "on your behalf," sometimes under the *guise* of financial-aid seminars, can be a front to sell overpriced loans or *glean* personal information such as bank account or Social Security numbers. *Conversely*, legitimate admissions consultants (often former university admissions officers) work one on one with students or schools to provide guidance on admissions and scholarship applications and essays; they do not get involved in loan applications.

Guise—appearance, semblance, excuse, pretext

Glean—collect, pick up, gather

Conversely—on the other hand, on the contrary

Unsolicited offers. Only after you ask about a scholarship should you receive details about it. "Any scholarship offers or applications that come to you from out of the blue are likely *bogus*," says high school counselor John Midgley, "especially when they arrive via e-mail addresses and spam them with bogus scholarship offers, most requiring up-front fees."

Any offer with one of these phrases:

- This scholarship is guaranteed or your money back . . .
- You can't get this information anywhere else . . .
- We need only your credit card or bank account number to hold this scholarship . . .
- We do all the work . . .
- You've been selected as a finalist in a scholarship, and we need only a small handling fee . . .

If you suspect that you have been the victim of a scholarship scam, report it to the Federal Trade Commission.

Source: Kirchheimer, Sid [AARP's "Scam Alert" Expert]. (2006). "Don't Pay to Get Money."
*Scam-Proof Your Life: 377 Smart Ways to Protect You & Your Family
From Ripoffs, Bogus Deals & Other Consumer Headaches.*
New York: Sterling Publishing, p. 142.

_____

Bogus—false, phony, counterfeit

👁 *L*ᴏᴏᴋ   Look around your college campus for FAFSA reminders, as well as scholarship and financial aid information. Check out posters in the Financial Aid Office and the student lounge, postings on the college Web site and/or publications created by your college. How does the information in the reading passages from *Scam-Proof Your Life* compare to your college's information?

🔊 *L*ɪꜱᴛᴇɴ   Make an appointment with a Financial Aid advisor at your college. Prepare questions to ask the advisor based on what you read in this reading passage. Record the interview with an audio recorder or take notes as you listen to the answers. Report your findings orally or in writing.

✏ *W*ʀɪᴛᴇ   Read written information available at your college about scholarships and financial aid. Prepare an outline or PowerPoint presentation of the important findings from *Scam-Proof Your Life* compared to what you learned from your college.

👆 *D*ᴏ   What specific things can you do to prevent being scammed with scholarships? Think about your own financial situation in college. How can you apply some of the suggestions from *Scam-Proof Your Life* to your own situation?

Reading Practice

The next section of the chapter will help refine your skills in determining the pattern of organization while you read a variety of materials. All of the readings address topics related to managing your money.

The first reading is from an Internet Web site, *5 Lessons the Rich Can Teach You* from *Moneycentral.*

The second reading is from an article titled *If at First You Don't Succeed: Common Mistakes Young Adults Make with Money and How to Avoid Them.*

READING 1

1220L

5 Lessons the Rich Can Teach You

They don't just have money. They spend it, borrow it and save it in ways that might benefit you, too.

1   Personally, I'm not sure how much the average person can learn from the Donald Trumps or George Soroses of the world.

2   We might envy their lifestyles or their bank accounts, but very, very few of us will ever approximate their wealth. Most of us, though, have a shot at being millionaires. In 2004, the number of households worth $1 million, not counting their primary residence, grew 21% to 7.5 million, according to Chicago-based research firm Spectrem Group.

3   Studying the habits of this relatively large and growing group of **affluent** folks can teach us a lot. These people don't just *have* money; they treat it differently than people farther down the economic ladder.

THE RICH ARE INDEED DIFFERENT

4   At least, so say various surveys of the affluent. Among the most notable differences:

5   **They give away more.** Charitable giving dropped sharply among the wealthy after the 2000–2001 bear market, according to Spectrem Group. Still, house-holds with $500,000 or more in investible assets gave away 6% of their incomes in 2004, and those with net worth of $5 million, excluding primary residences, contributed 6.1% of their incomes. That compares to an average of about 2% for all American households and 4% for households with incomes under $25,000, according to American Demographics.

6   "Our clients appreciate the success that they've had and they want to pay it forward in some way," said financial planner Ross Levin of Edina, Minnesota. "We have one client, a developer and his wife, who give away 50% of their income."

7   **They are much more likely to own businesses.** Overall, about 21% of American families own all or part of a privately held business, according to the Federal Reserve, compared to 41% of those whose net worth puts them in the top 10% of households. Business assets **comprise** 21% of the total net worth of households who have $500,000 or more in investible assets, Spectrem said.

8   Closely held and family owned businesses are a major source of wealth for many of financial planner Victoria Collins' clients, but these holdings present major challenges. It's risky having so much of one's net worth tied up in a single

investment that could be tough to sell. That's why Collins and other planners encourage their business-owning clients to **diversify** their investments.

9   "Any time you have a super-concentrated position—whether it's an individual stock or a business—you have to be concerned," said Collins, who's based in Irvine, Calif.

10   **They borrow strategically.** The wealthy are only slightly less likely to owe money than average folks, according to the Fed, but how they borrow is quite different. The richest 10% of Americans are half as likely to have credit card debts (22.4% vs. 44.4% overall), although the median balances for those who carry balances are about the same for both groups (around $2,000). The wealthier folks are also much less likely to have **installment debt**, such as auto loans (25.6%, compared to 45.2% overall).

11   What the wealthy often do have is mortgages. More than half—55.5%— have a primary mortgage, compared to 44.6% of households overall. Another 15% carry loans on other real estate, compared to 4.7% of the general population.

12   Mortgage money is pretty cheap debt at current low rates. Although many wealthier folks can do and own their homes outright, financial planners say, many prefer to put their money to work for them in investments that can earn higher returns.

13   **They don't blow a lot of money on cars.** Jay Leno, with his fleet of exotic cars, is the exception rather than the rule. The average millionaire does tend to spend more money on his wheels, but vehicles represent a much smaller proportion of his net worth.

14   The Fed survey showed the median value of all vehicles owned by the wealthi- est 10% of households was $25,400, compared to $11,800 for households overall. But vehicles represented just 2.4% of the wealthiest households' median net worth, compared with 8.8% of net worth overall.

15   "My wealthier clients are much more likely to own an American-made SUV than a Range Rover or a (Mercedes) S500," said Mark Lamkin, a financial planner in Louisville, Kentucky. "Most of them live a very **unassuming** lifestyle, but they're able to do anything they want, whenever they want."

16   **They're almost always homeowners, and many own investment property, too.** Homeownership is almost universal among those in the top 10% of net worth; 95.8%, according to the Fed, compared to 67.7% overall. About 40% of the highest-net-worth group own some kind of real estate such as rental property or a second home, compared to 11% overall.

17   But real estate isn't their major source of wealth. On average, principal residences account for 10% of the net worth of folks with more than $500,000 in investible assets, Spectrem said, while other real estate accounts for 7%.

INVESTMENTS ARE KING

18 Most of their wealth is investments:

- 46% in stocks and bonds, managed accounts, IRAs, mutual funds, deposits and alternative investments
- 10% in pensions and defined-contribution plans like 401(k)s
- 6% in insurance and annuities

There are also some indications that wealthier Americans are cutting back their exposure to real estate. The percentage of people with net worth over $1 million who own investment property shrank to 44% in 2005, down from 50% in 2004, according to TNS Financial Services, a market-research company.

19   Financial planner Deena Katz believes her clients and other wealthy folks will continue to buy second or vacation homes but may be less likely to buy rental or commercial properties.

20   "They're starting to re-evaluate their real-estate holdings," said Katz of Coral Gables, Florida. "Real estate is overpriced, and people are recognizing that."

21   The lessons here aren't revolutionary, but they're well worth learning: Don't be a **miser**, take strategic risks, live within your means, diversify. You may never make the Forbes 400 list of the wealthiest people, but you can create a richer life. ■

Source: Weston, Liz Pulliam. *5 Lessons the Rich Can Teach You.*
Retrieved from Moneycentral Web site.

Vocabulary

Directions: Circle the best definition for the word.

1. affluent (paragraph 3)

    a. foreign   **c.** transparent

    b. wealthy   **d.** educated

2. comprise (paragraph 7)

    a. give in   **c.** consist of

    b. direct   **d.** exclude

3. diversify (paragraph 8)

    a. segregate   **c.** vary

    b. integrate   **d.** keep

4. **installment debt** (paragraph 10)

  a. debt paid in increments over time

  b. debt for something installed in your home

  c. all of the above

  d. none of the above

5. **unassuming** (paragraph 15)

  a. modest

  b. arrogant

  c. unknowing

  d. unbelieving

6. **miser** (paragraph 21)

  a. generous person

  b. stingy person

  c. investor

  d. spendthrift

Main Idea

7. What is the central theme of the whole article?

  a. Anyone can become a millionaire if they use these techniques.

  b. Millionaires do things very differently than everyone else.

  c. The rich spend, borrow, and save money in ways that might benefit you.

  d. There are five ways to get rich quick.

Supporting Details

Directions: Using the details in the article, circle **True** if the statement is correct or **False** if the statement is incorrect.

8. True or False? Most wealthy people own expensive, foreign-made cars.

9. True or False? Affluent people give more of their money away to charity.

10. True or False? Rich people spend the majority of their money on real estate.

11. True or False? Wealthy people don't borrow money.

12. True or False? Affluent people don't carry much credit card debt.

Patterns of Organization

13. What is the overall pattern of organization for this article?

    a. time order   **c.** definition

    b. cause and effect   **d.** simple listing

14. Discuss what surprised you most about how the wealthy spend, borrow, and save money.

    Answers will vary.

_____

_____

15. Discuss one or more strategies you might consider incorporating into your own financial plan.

    Answers will vary.

_____

_____

Magazine/Periodical **READING 2**

If at First You Don't Succeed:

COMMON MISTAKES YOUNG ADULTS MAKE WITH MONEY AND HOW TO AVOID THEM

1   **Getting too deeply in debt.** Being able to borrow allows us to buy clothes or computers, take a vacation or purchase a home or a car. But taking on too much debt can be a problem, and each year millions of adults of all ages find themselves struggling to pay their loans, credit cards and other bills.

2   Learn to be a good money manager by following the basic strategies outlined in this special report. Also recognize the warning signs of a serious debt problem. These may include borrowing money to make payments on loans you already have, deliberately paying bills late, and putting off doctor visits or other important activities because you think you don't have enough money.

3   If you believe you're experiencing debt overload, take corrective measures. For example, try to pay off your highest interest-rate loans (usually your credit cards) as soon as possible, even if you have higher balances on other loans. For new

purchases, instead of using your credit card, try paying with cash, a check or a debit card.

4   "There are also reliable credit counselors you can turn to for help at little or no cost," added Rita Wiles Ross, an FDIC attorney. "Unfortunately, you also need to be aware that there are scams **masquerading** as 'credit repair clinics' and other companies, such as 'debt **consolidators**,' that may charge big fees for **unfulfilled** promises or services you can perform on your own."

5   For more guidance on how to get out of debt safely or find a **reputable** credit counselor, start at the Federal Trade Commission (FTC) Web site at www.ftc.gov/ bcp/conline/edcams/credit/coninfo_debt.

6   **Paying bills late or otherwise tarnishing your reputation.** Companies called credit bureaus prepare credit reports for use by lenders, employers, insurance companies, landlords and others who need to know someone's financial reliability, based largely on each person's track record paying bills and debts. Credit bureaus, lenders and other companies also produce "credit scores" that attempt to summarize and evaluate a person's credit record using a point system.

7   While one or two late payments on your loans or other regular commitments (such as rent or phone bills) over a long period may not seriously damage your credit record, making a habit of it will count against you. Over time you could be charged a higher interest rate on your credit card or a loan that you really want and need. You could be turned down for a job or an apartment. It could cost you extra when you apply for auto insurance. Your credit record will also be damaged by a bankruptcy filing or a court order to pay money as a result of a lawsuit.

8   So, pay your monthly bills on time. Also, periodically review your credit reports from the nation's three major credit bureaus—Equifax, Experian and TransUnion—to make sure their information accurately reflects the accounts you have and your payment history, especially if you intend to apply for credit for something important in the near future. For information about your rights to obtain free copies of your credit report and have errors corrected, see the FTC's fact sheet *Your Access to Free Credit Reports* online at www.ftc.gov/bcp/conline/ pubs/credit/freereports.

9   **Having too many credit cards.** Two to four cards (including any from department stores, oil companies and other retailers) is the right number for most adults. Why not more cards? The more credit cards you carry, the more inclined you may be to use them for costly impulse buying. In addition, each card you own—even the ones you don't use—represents money that you *could* borrow up to the card's spending limit. If you apply for new credit you will be seen

as someone who, in theory, could get much deeper in debt and you may only qualify for a smaller or costlier loan.

10   Also be aware that card companies **aggressively** market their products on college campuses, at concerts, ball games or other events often attended by young adults. Their offers may seem **tempting** and even harmless—perhaps a free T-shirt or Frisbee, or 10 percent off your first purchase if you just fill out an application for a new card—but you've got to consider the possible consequences we've just described. "Don't sign up for a credit card just to get a great-looking T-shirt," Kincaid added. "You may be better off buying that shirt at the store for $14.95 and saving yourself the potential costs and troubles from that extra card."

11   **Not watching your expenses.** It's very easy to overspend in some areas and take away from other **priorities,** including your long-term savings. Our suggestion is to try any system—ranging from a computer-based budget program to hand-written notes—that will help you keep track of your spending each month and **enable** you to set and stick to limits you consider appropriate. "A budget doesn't have to be complicated, **intimidating** or painful—just something that works for you in getting a handle on your spending," said Kincaid. ■

Source: http://www.fdic.gov/consumers/consumer/news/cnspr05/cvrstry.html

Vocabulary

Directions: Fill in the blank with the meaning of the word or phrase.

1. **masquerading** (paragraph 4) pretending to be
2. **consolidators** (paragraph 4) people or companies who combine things
3. **unfulfilled** (paragraph 4) not as promised
4. **reputable** (paragraph 5) trustworthy
5. **tarnishing** (paragraph 6) harming or hurting
6. **aggressively** (paragraph 10) eagerly or strongly
7. **tempting** (paragraph 10) enticing, encouraging
8. **priorities** (paragraph 11) most important things to do
9. **enable** (paragraph 11) help, make able to do
10. **intimidating** (paragraph 11) pushy, discouraging

Main Idea

11. What is the main idea of paragraph 1? Answers will vary. Possible answers may include: Taking on too much debt can cause problems.

12. What is the main idea of paragraph 6? Answers will vary. Possible answers may include: Paying your bills late may hurt your reputation.

13. Write the central theme of the article in your own words.
    Answers will vary. Possible answers may include: There are common mistakes people can make with their money and ways to avoid them.

Supporting Details

Directions: Circle **True** if the sentence is true and **False** if the statement is false.

14. **True** **False** It will not cause problems with your credit if you pay a bill late once in a while.

15. **True** **False** It is a good idea to build credit with several credit cards at the same time.

16. **True** **False** It is not a good idea to borrow money to pay debt you already have.

17. **True** **False** A budget does not have to be intimidating or painful.

Organizational Patterns

18. Which organizational pattern does the phrase *for example* signal (paragraph 3)?
    Example

19. Which organizational pattern does the phrase *three major* signal (paragraph 8)?
    Simple listing

Critical Thinking/Application

20. What did you learn from this article that you can apply to your own financial decisions?

Answers will vary.

myreadinglab

For support in meeting this chapter's objectives, log on to www.myreadinglab.com and select Patterns of Organization: Time Order, Patterns of Organization: Simple Listing, Patterns of Organization: Definition and Example.

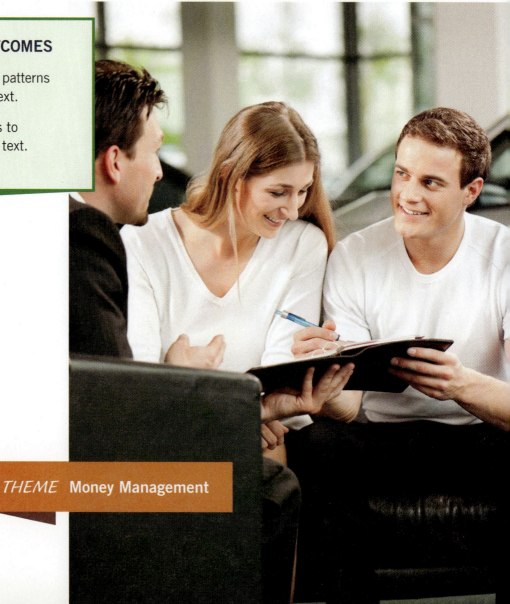

6 Advanced Patterns of Organization

THEME **Money Management**

Patterns of Organization

In this chapter you will learn to recognize and use the following patterns of organization:

- paragraphs developed with classification
- paragraphs developed with compare/contrast
- paragraphs developed with cause/effect
- paragraphs developed with a combination of patterns

Paragraphs Developed with Classification

Authors may organize paragraphs by classifying information into sorts, types, or categories. Usually there will be a sentence in the paragraph indicating that there are "several types," "three main categories," or some other classifying terms. As a reader, you should also watch for a description and perhaps examples of each classification. It may be easier to create a chart of the relevant information so you can "see" the classifications.

Signal Words

sorts

types

categories

groups

"It's not whether you get knocked down, it's whether you get up."

—*Vince Lombardi*

EXAMPLE —

Directions: Read the paragraph below. Use the signal words to locate the major categories and examples to complete the chart.

That's why everyone needs insurance—to keep life's inevitable emergencies from becoming financial disasters. If you're properly insured, you and your family can get knocked down and get back up again without having to worry about the financial consequences. When you start thinking about what type of insurance you need, remember that there are two fundamental categories of insurance coverage:

- Insurance on the things you own (such as property or liability)

- Insurance on you (such as life, health, and disability)

Source: Random House Reference. (2003). *Just Plain Smart: Personal Finance Advisor, A Lifelong Approach to Achieving Your Financial Goals.* New York, NY: Random House, p. 86.

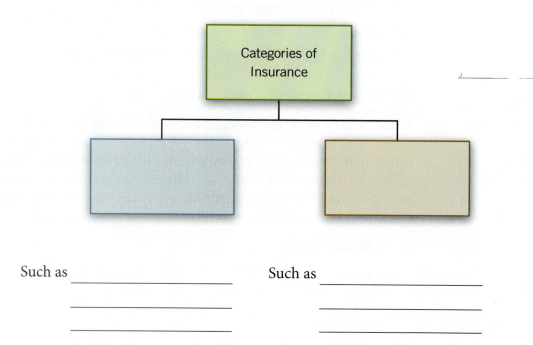

Such as _____

_____

_____

Such as _____

_____

_____

In the example above, the two categories of insurance are "Insurance on the Things You Own" and "Insurance on You." Examples of "Insurance on the Things You Own" include property or liability. Examples of "Insurance on You" include life, health, and disability.

PRACTICE THE NEW SKILL

Directions: Read the paragraph below. Use the signal words to locate the definitions, examples, or major categories needed to complete the chart.

PRACTICE 1

1   If you're time constrained or just budget phobic, here are three ways to shortcut the process:

2   **Platinum strategy—It's not your spending that matters.** If you're saving already, but want to save more, just go for it. If the higher savings level starts to strain your checkbook, you'll probably adjust your spending automatically because you'll suddenly become *cognizant* of ways to cut back on your spending, if for no other reason than to avoid bouncing checks. In other words, let nature take its course. The key here is to gradually boost the amount you save. Unless you know you can manage it, suddenly doubling or tripling the amount you save is bound to lead to disappointment.

3   **Gold strategy—If you're starting from scratch, start small.** Similar to the "platinum strategy," rather than preparing a budget, start saving a small amount, 1 percent of your salary or perhaps $2 a week. You probably won't even notice it, but if it pinches you, refer to the "silver strategy," below. Once you get used to your initial savings level, boost it a bit. Over time, you could well become a world-class saver. Idea 23, on page 76, will show you the good news (and the goodly amount of wealth) awaiting those who start saving a small amount of money and gradually increase their savings from there.

4   **Silver strategy—If you can't save at all, pay with cash.** I'll bet you dollars to doughnuts that if you have found it impossible to save, the problem involves your day-to-day spending, things like lattes, lunch at work, dry cleaning, and restaurants. If you put a lot of daily expenditures on a credit card, it simply exacerbates the problem. There's nothing like forking over cash to better understand the impact of a purchase. Get into the habit of

Cognizant—aware, mindful

paying cash for the stuff you buy and pretty soon you'll start to identify stuff you're buying that you don't really need. Avoiding them will work wonders on your checking account balance, which will in turn allow you to move up to the "gold strategy."

Source: Pond, Jonathan D. (2008). *Grow Your Money! 101 Easy Tips to Plan, Save, and Invest.*
New York, NY: Harper Collins, pp. 51–52.

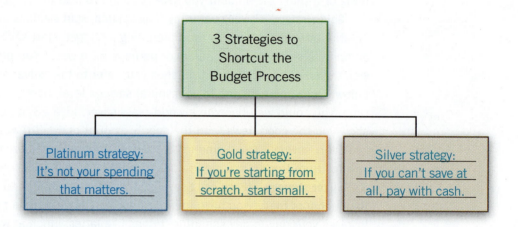

PRACTICE 2

Internet banking can mean two different things. Your regular bank or credit union may allow you access to your accounts over the Internet. You can transfer funds, pay bills, and see which checks have cleared all with a few clicks at your personal computer.

There are also banks that only do business on the Internet. They have no branches that you can walk into. The theory is that they can do business more cheaply since they do not have as much overhead as traditional banks.

Source: Kimball, Cheryl and Fay Kathryn Doria. (2002). *The Everything Get Out of Debt Book: Evaluate Your Option, Determine Your Course of Action, and Make a Fresh Start.*

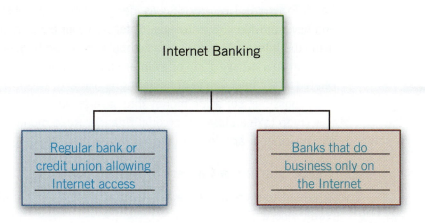

Examples of things you can do:

Access accounts

Transfer funds

Pay bills, see cleared checks

_____

Possible advantages:

Do business more cheaply

Do not have as much overhead

_____

_____

PRACTICE 3

Ages and Stages of Money Management: A To-Do List

1   **To successfully reach your financial goals, a lot depends on what you do and when. Here are just a few ideas young adults can consider at key stages of their life.**

You're in College

2   Realize that as you pay bills and debts on your own you are building a "credit record" that could be important when you apply for a loan or a job in the future. Pay your bills on time . . . and borrow only what you can repay.

3   If you decide to get your own credit card, choose carefully. Take your time, understand the risks as well as the rewards and do some comparison shopping. Don't apply for a credit card just because you received an invitation in the mail or a sales person was offering a free gift on campus.

4   Protect your Social Security number (SSN), credit card numbers and other personal information from thieves who use someone else's identity to commit

fraud. Examples: Use your SSN as identification only if absolutely necessary and never provide it to a stranger. Safeguard your personal information when using the Internet or borrowing a computer provided by your school.

5   Consider a paying job or even an unpaid internship at a workplace related to a career you're considering.

6   If possible, set aside money into savings and investments.

7   Try to take a class in personal finance. Read money-related magazine and newspaper articles.

You're Starting a Career

8   Keep your credit card and other debts manageable. Maintain a good credit record.

9   Save money for both short-term and long-term goals. Contribute as much as you can to retirement savings, which often can be used for other purposes, including a first-time home purchase. Take advantage of matching contributions that your employer will put into your retirement savings.

10   Do your best to stick to a budget and control your spending, especially if you're still paying back student loans or working at an entry-level job.

11   Although insurance sometimes seems like a waste of money, you only need one accident or catastrophe to wipe you out financially. Think about disability insurance (to replace lost income if you become seriously ill) and health insurance (to cover big medical bills). Check into low-cost or free insurance offered through your employer.

You're Starting a Family

12   Continue saving and investing money, including in retirement accounts.

13   If you don't already own your home do some research to see if this is a good option for you. A home purchase can be expensive but it also can be an excellent investment and a source of tax breaks. Check out educational resources for first-time homebuyers.

14   Make sure you are properly insured, including life, health, disability and home owner's or renter's insurance.

15   Talk with an attorney about the legal documents you should have to protect your loved ones if you become seriously ill or die. These documents typically include a will, a "durable power of attorney" (giving one or more people the authority to handle personal matters if you become mentally or physically incompetent) and a "living will" (specifying the medical care you want or don't want if you become hopelessly ill and cannot communicate your wishes).

Source: http://www.fdic.gov/consumers/consumer/news/cnspr05/ages.html

1. What are the three life stages the author discusses?

   a. You're in college

   b. You're starting a career

   c. You're starting a family

2. Discuss the stage(s) you are in and what you need to consider to reach your financial goals. Answers will vary.

_____

_____

_____

Paragraphs Developed with Compare/Contrast

When authors compare two things, they discuss the ways the items are similar. For example, an author might discuss the similarities between having a dog and a cat as a pet—you give them both food and water, you must take them to the vet for check-ups and shots, they can both be cuddly, they can make you smile with their funny behaviors, and you can love them as part of the family.

When authors contrast two things, they discuss the ways they are different. For example, an author might discuss the differences between having a dog and a cat as a pet—a dog needs to be fed once or twice a day since it might eat all the food you give it at the time, whereas a cat can be given enough food for a week and will only eat a little at a time. Another difference is that a dog can be trained more easily to understand words such as "sit" and "stay," whereas a cat more likely will ignore those commands and do what it pleases.

Watch for words that signal when the author is comparing and/or contrasting ideas. This will help you focus on the main ideas and understand the author's point.

Signal Words for Comparison

similarly, is similar to

the same as, in the same manner, in the same way

like, likewise, is alike in . . .

Signal Words for Contrast

in contrast

differently, different than

unlike

meanwhile

but, however

on the other hand

EXAMPLE ———————————————————————————————

PIN or pen? Debit-card users are caught in the cross-fire between merchants and card companies. Merchants want you to punch in a personal identification number because processing PIN-based transactions costs them less in fees. *Meanwhile*, Visa and MasterCard prefer that you sign for transactions, which are then processed through their networks.

Source: Goldwasser, Joan and Amy Esbensahde Hebert. (August 2007). *Kiplinger's Personal Finance.* Vol. 61, Iss. 8, p. 78.

Complete the chart contrasting merchants and card companies.

MERCHANTS	VISA AND MASTERCARD COMPANIES

In the first column, "Merchants," you should list that they want you to punch in your PIN number from your debit card because it costs them less in fees. In the second column, "VISA and MasterCard Companies," you should list that they prefer that you sign for your transactions, and they will process these transactions through their network. The word *meanwhile* signals a contrasting idea.

PRACTICE **THE NEW SKILL**

Directions: Complete the chart below the reading.

PRACTICE 1

1   You can view the differences between good debt and bad debt as much like the differences between good cholesterol and bad cholesterol. Doctors

tell us that we need a certain amount of good cholesterol but that too much bad cholesterol will eventually kill us.

2   We can liken bad cholesterol—LDL (low-density lipoprotein)—to bad debt, which is artery-clogging debt. Good cholesterol—HDL (high-density lipoprotein)—is akin to good debt that clears arteries and keeps you financially healthy. Part of this financial artery-clearing effect is an increase in cash (blood) flow.

3   I always thought that zero cholesterol was supposed to be my goal. Not so. Apparently if your HDL measurement is under 35, it's a health risk. Your total HDL rating should be 40 or 50 and up to 70 or 80 of HDL can actually protect you against various diseases.

4   Likewise, some people think that zero debt is best. It sounds good, doesn't it? But zero debt also means zero growth or at the most a low growth rate. Perhaps we can learn from the HDL example. If it takes some HDL to be in good physical health, let's take the mental leap that it takes some good debt to be financially healthy.

5   The definition of good debt is similar to that of good cholesterol. It keeps the arteries clear. Good debt keeps the cash flow running smoothly and the funds pumping. When you read the definitions below, notice that good debt is a debt on assets that produce a return above their cost. It is debt on assets that create cash flow in excess of the cost of the debt. It is not debt that kills. Remember this: when you use debt to pay for something it is not a payment in full, but merely a claim on your future time and earnings.

Good Debt

- Earns its keep
- Increases your net worth or cash flow
- Secures a discount that can be converted to cash or net worth
- Creates leveraged position ($300 out, $400 in monthly)
- Examples: debt for real estate at a safely leveraged level, debt for education that can be applied for a return of capital, debt for a business you are competent to operate.

Bad Debt

- Is typically for consumption
- Decreases your net worth or cash flow

- Examples: Car loans that rob your retirement fund. Continuing credit card debt, living on student loans, furniture loans, loans for rapidly depreciating items, loans for parties, weddings, or vacations.

Source: Hanson, Jon. (2005). *Good Debt, Bad Debt: Knowing the Difference Can Save Your Financial Life.* New York: Penguin Group, pp. 17–18.

What is the difference between Good Debt and Bad Debt? Complete the chart below.

GOOD DEBT	BAD DEBT
• Earns its keep	• Is typically for consumption
• Increases your net worth or cash flow	• Decreases your net worth or cash flow
• Secures a discount that can be converted to cash or net worth	• Examples: Car loans that rob your retirement fund; continuing credit card debt; living on student loans; furniture loans; loans for rapidly depreciating items; loans for parties, weddings, or vacations
• Creates leveraged position ($300 out, $400 in monthly)	
• Examples: debt for real estate at a safely leveraged level, debt for education that can be applied for a return of capital, debt for a business you are competent to operate	

PRACTICE 2

1 Why is there such a dramatic difference in what $30,000 can become in a 401(k) or IRA rather than a savings account? Let's start with the 401(k) because it give you three huge advantages over a savings account— stock market investments, enormous tax savings, and potentially thousands of dollars in free money from your employer.

2 When you have a savings account at a bank, you will never make much money. You might earn about 2 percent a year. But in 401(k) plans, people can invest in mutual funds that select stocks. I will explain these

in Chapter 7, "What's a Mutual Fund?" and you will learn how to use them easily. For now, I just want you to know that, historically, money in the stock market has grown 10.4 percent a year on average, according to Ibbotson Associates. That's not a specific guarantee for the future, but if history repeats and you are using good stock mutual funds in your 401(k), you could make 10 percent a year on average, rather than the 2 percent in your bank account. That's a tremendous difference over many years of investing.

3   That's not all. Employers often give you free money when you participate in the 401(k) plans they offer you at work. They give you what's called "a match," or "matching money." For you, it's like getting a raise every year—maybe $1,000 or more simply as a reward for participating in the company 401(k). What could be better? It's free money, and it's a reward for doing what's already good for your future.

Source: MarksJarvis, Gail. (2007). *Saving for Retirement without Living Like a Pauper or Winning the Lottery.* Upper Saddle River, NJ: FT Press, Pearson, p. 42.

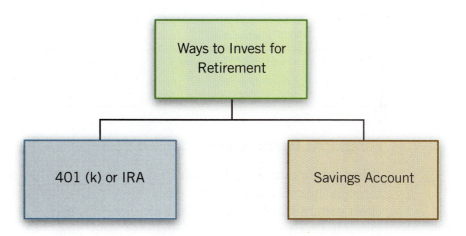

Advantages <u>Stock market investments</u>
<u>Tax savings</u>
<u>Potentially free money from employer</u>
Typical earnings: <u>10%</u>

Disadvantages <u>Make little money</u>
<u>No tax savings</u>
<u>No matching incentive from employers</u>
Typical earnings: <u>2%</u>

PRACTICE 3

Term life insurance can provide good value for your dollar. Term life insurance is relatively inexpensive (when compared with whole life insurance) and it provides an insured's survivors with a benefit upon the insured's death, but it has no value while the insured is still alive. On the other hand, while a whole life policy will cost more initially than a term policy (for the same amount of coverage), it does build up a cash balance that you can borrow against, cash in while you're alive, or have added to the death benefit.

Source: H & R Block. (2003). *Just Plain Smart Personal Finance Advisor: A Lifelong Approach to Achieving Your Financial Goals.* New York, NY: Random House, p. 95.

Complete the chart by listing the differences between term life and whole life insurance.

TERM LIFE INSURANCE	WHOLE LIFE INSURANCE
Inexpensive compared to whole life insurance	Costs more than term life initially
Provides survivors with a benefit	Builds up a cash value
Provides a good value for the dollar	You can borrow against the cash value, cash in while alive, or add to death benefit

Paragraphs Developed with Cause/Effect

When authors are trying to convey a point, they sometimes develop their ideas through the cause-and-effect pattern. How do you know when a cause-and-effect pattern is being used? If a cause pattern is being used, the author may give one or more reasons for something happening. For example, they may discuss the reasons why students have trouble paying for their college books, such as lower income from their part-time jobs or lower financial aid awards.

The author may also discuss the effects of a certain situation. For example, when the economy is doing poorly, business is down and people may get fewer hours at work. This results in lower income and less money to pay for college tuition and books.

Authors might discuss more than one cause and/or more than one effect. For example, the poor economy may cause people to get fewer hours at work and some people may even lose their jobs. This may result in more people going to community college instead of working, but it also results in more competition for the limited college financial aid. The point is that in order to make sense of what we are reading, we must be aware of how authors use the cause-and-effect pattern to demonstrate how one thing affects another.

Signal Words for Cause and Effect

because, because of

is due, due to, can be attributed to

if . . . then

leads to, has made us

since, so

accordingly, consequently

as a result, result in

therefore, thus

EXAMPLE —————————————————————————————

Getting Out of Debt: Bad-Idea Approaches

The following are options for getting out of debt that are less than optimal.

Credit Card Calculus

Strategy: To transfer debt from a high-interest rate credit card to a lower-interest rate credit card

Common Result: After making balance transfers, cardholders usually lose no time in running up their original high-interest cards again. I am amazed by the commitment of time and energy that people put into rotating their credit cards. I can only imagine the success some of the people who do this would have if they put that same creativity and effort into building their passive income. If you are smart enough to play this game, you are smart enough to invest.

Home Equity Loans

Strategy: Refinance the home to consolidate debt.

Common Result: Too many people don't control their spending, borrow more after they refinance, incur more credit card debt and refinance again. Serial refinancers use up all the equity they build and then get boxed out

of, or are charged *exorbitant* interest rates for, additional credit. In many cases, the home that was once a nest egg shuffles off to the brink of foreclosure.

Source: Langemeier, Loral. (2006). *Millionaire Maker: Act, Think, and Make Money the Way the Wealthy Do.* New York, NY: McGraw-Hill, pp. 191–192.

1. What is the result of strategy 1, to transfer the balance from a high-interest credit card to a lower-interest credit card? _____

_____

_____

2. What is the result of strategy 2, to refinance the home to consolidate debt? _____

_____

_____

  In the above example, according to the author, the common result of cardholders transferring the balance from a high-interest credit card to a lower-interest credit card is that they quickly build back up the balances on their higher-interest cards. The result of strategy 2, refinancing a home to consolidate debt, is that many consumers don't control their spending and they build their debt back up again.

Exorbitant—excessive, very high

PRACTICE THE NEW SKILL

Directions: Complete the cause-and-effect diagram below the reading.

PRACTICE 1

Credit card companies, perhaps taking their cue from drug dealers, send college students sample cards with credit lines of $500 to $2,000 to hook new users (the companies readily admit that they assume the parents will pay). The entry into massive credit card debt is easy. The cards are easy to acquire and often thought to be used for recreational spending. They come to you without prompting—in fact, often with a premium just for signing up. T-shirts and cookies are common premiums on a college campus. **Credit cards are the crack cocaine of the credit industry.** Many victims, after being strung out on credit cards, seek stronger forms of credit when their pusher threatens to cut them off. Some move from credit cards to pawning their home or other assts to feed their credit addiction. While pawning (refinancing) a home can provide temporary relief, many sneak right back to "using" again. Soon they are *plagued* by "plastic crack" again. Only now the solution of pawning the home is not available.

Source: Hanson, Jon. (2005). *Good Debt, Bad Debt: Knowing the Difference Can Save Your Financial Life.* New York, NY: Penguin Group, pp. 19–20.

Complete the cause-and-effect diagram.

Causes of Credit Card Addiction	Lead to	Effects of Credit Card Addiction
• Companies send sample cards.	⟶	• Students get "hooked."
• The cards are easy to acquire.		• Victims seek stronger forms of credit when their pusher threatens to cut them off.
• Thought of as recreational spending.		
• Come to you without prompting.		
• T-shirts and cookies are premiums.		• Pawning or refinancing provides temporary relief.
• Addicted.		• Turn to plastic crack again.

Plagued—overwhelmed, inundated, weighed down

PRACTICE 2

1   **Buying items you don't need . . . and paying extra for them in interest.** Every time you have an urge to do a little "impulse buying" and you use your credit card but you don't pay in full by the due date, you could be paying interest on that purchase for months or years to come. Spending money for something you really don't need can be a big waste of your money. But you can make the matter worse, a lot worse, by putting the purchase on a credit card and paying monthly interest charges.

2   Research major purchases and comparison shop before you buy. Ask yourself if you really need the item. Even better, wait a day or two, or just a few hours, to think things over rather than making a quick and costly decision you may come to regret.

3   There are good reasons to pay for major purchases with a credit card, such as extra protections if you have problems with the items. But if you charge a purchase with a credit card instead of paying by cash, check or debit card (which automatically deducts the money from your bank account), be smart about how you repay. For example, take advantage of offers of "zero-percent interest" on credit card purchases for a certain number of months (but understand when and how interest charges could begin).

4   And, pay the entire balance on your credit card or as much as you can to avoid or minimize interest charges, which can add up significantly.

5   "If you pay only the minimum amount due on your credit card, you may end up paying more in interest charges than what the item cost you to begin with," said Janet Kincaid, FDIC Senior Consumer Affairs Officer. Example: If you pay only the minimum payment due on a $1,000 computer, let's say it's about $20 a month, your total cost at an Annual Percentage Rate of more than 18 percent can be close to $3,000, and it will take you nearly 19 years to pay it off.

Source: http://www.fdic.gov/consumers/consumer/news/cnspr05/cvrstry.html

Complete the cause-and-effect diagram.

Causes   ⟶   **Effects**

Answers will vary.

PRACTICE 3

Let's say for example, that you have a credit card with a 25 percent interest rate and you are carrying a $10,000 balance. That means you are paying $2,500 a year in interest on that card. Over 10 years, that is a total of $25,000. Suppose, instead, you paid off that card and took the $2,500 you were paying and invested it in a decent mutual fund for just 10 years at 11 percent interest (the average annual return on the stock market for more than 80 years now). After 10 years of investing, that $2,500 a year would be worth more than $45,000. Think about that. Would you rather **have** $45,000 or **owe** $25,000? That's a $70,000 swing in your favor.

Source: Floyd, John D. (2007). *Joyfully Debt Free: How to Get Out of Debt, Stay Out, and Accumulate a Fortune!* Victoria, BC: Trafford, p. 25.

Complete the cause-and-effect diagram.

Cause(s)	Lead(s) to	Effect(s)
Paying 25 percent interest on $10,000 credit card balance	⟶	$2,500 per year interest
You pay off the credit card and invest the $2,500/yr you were paying in a mutual fund earning 11 percent interest.		After 10 years that $2,500 a year is worth $45,000.

Paragraphs Developed with a Combination of Patterns

Much of what we read uses a combination of several organizational patterns. Continue to watch for the words that signal a pattern and you'll improve your reading comprehension. The more you practice, the better you will be at recognizing patterns and knowing what to expect from the text.

EXAMPLE ——————————————————————————————

Directions: Write the organizational pattern on the blanks. Underline or highlight the signal words that indicate the pattern.

The Promise

1   How would you like to be free of overwhelming credit card debt? To have a financial cushion to fall back on? To know you have the skills to save and invest for any goal—and to guarantee your financial future?

2   I can teach you how to get there on $10 a day. If that sounds like very little, well it is.

3   <u>It's</u> a movie—without popcorn.

4   <u>It's</u> lunch at McDonald's—for two children.

5   <u>It's</u> skipping the car wash—and washing the car in your driveway instead.

Pattern: _____ (example) _____ (It's . . . It's . . . It's . . .) _____

6   It's so many of those things that you can do without. But it's also the key to your future. Let's say you're the average American. You have a decent job, but you also have $8,000 in high-rate credit card debt. You have no savings to speak of. You worry about your money on a daily basis (in fact, it keeps you up at night), and you don't believe that $10 a day can dig you out of that hole. But it can, and in less time than you may think. If you get on this plan—and stick with it:

7   In 3 years . . . you'll be credit-card-free. <u>By applying</u> that $10 a day against your $8,000 credit card debt (at an interest rate of 16 percent), <u>you'll be</u> debt-free in 33 months.

Pattern: _____ (by applying . . .) _____ (cause-effect) _____ (you'll be . . .) _____

8   In 5 years . . . you'll have a financial cushion. Once the debt is gone, you can start saving that $10 a day for your future. You'll put the money in a money-market account. It won't earn much in interest while it's sitting there, but there's no risk you'll lose it either. Five years from the time you started socking away your $10 a day, you'll have a fat emergency cushion—more than $8,000. That's your insurance against a leaky roof, a layoff or illness, or other financial mishap that comes your way.

9   In 10 years . . . you'll have a nest egg for retirement. After your emergency cushion is in place, you can start investing your $10 a day so that it can work harder and grow faster for your benefit. If you put it somewhere that it can grow tax-free—like a 401(k) account—and you earn, on that money, the 10.7 percent that the S & P 500 has returned between 1926 and today, in 10 years . . . you have $23,994; in 15 years from the day you started, you have $64,866; in 20 years, you have $134,487; in 25 years, you have $253,080; in 30 years, you have $455,091; in 35 years, you have $799,197; and in 40 years, you have $1,385,351.

Pattern: _____ (time order) _____ (in 5 years . . . , in 10 years . . . , in 15 years . . . , etc.)

Nearly $1.4 million on $10 a day. That's real money in anybody's book.

10   It sounds simple, and it is. All that's standing in your way is knowledge. You need to know how to free up that $10 a day. You need to know how to get yourself to do that every day, without fail, for the rest of your life. And you need to know how to guarantee that that money gets to where it's supposed to be so that it can work its magic for you.

Source: Chatzky, Jean. (2004). *Pay It Down!: From Debt to Wealth on $10 a Day.* New York, NY: Penguin Group, pp. ix–xi.

PRACTICE THE NEW SKILL

Directions: Answer the questions that follow the reading.

PRACTICE 1

Learning to Cook

1   One of the easiest ways to save money on food is to eat at home more and eat out less. But a lot of twenty- and thirty-something people don't know how to cook well enough to eat at home. As a result, people under age twenty-five spend 45.5 percent of their food dollars eating out, a higher percentage than any other age category, according to the National Restaurant Association. The twenty-five to thirty-four-year-olds aren't far behind, spending 43.8 percent of their food budget to dine out. The lack of expertise of Generation Xers and Generation Yers in the kitchen has prompted a new wave of books, cooking shows, and cooking classes. There are a number of celebrity chefs on TV, including Emeril Lagasse, Bobby Flay, Caprial Pence, and Sara Moulton. There's even an entire channel, the Food Channel, devoted to cooking and enjoying food.

2 GenXers are the first generation of adults since two-income families became the norm, and for many that meant breaking the traditional cycle of home-maker mom teaching her daughter how to cook. Christa DiBiase, executive producer of my radio show, says her mother, who was busy with her career, didn't teach her how to cook. But Christa's mother-in-law used to make a home-cooked dinner almost every night for her husband, Mike.

3 Some GenXers don't want to cook and eat at home. They're perfectly content eating out all the time. But others are finding they want the sense of home that a restaurant can't provide. Eating at home also allows you to control what you eat, making it easier to enjoy meals that are nutritionally better for you.

4 Christa is pregnant with her first child, and doesn't look forward to taking the baby to restaurants all the time. She says, candidly, that not knowing how to cook "makes me feel kind of inadequate." She's trying to remedy that by taking cooking classes. They're not cheap. Christa paid $60 for a single, hour-long basic cooking class. But learning how to cook just a few meals can save plenty of money over the years.

5 Of course, you don't have to learn to cook from a chef. If your local community college has a culinary department, that's a great place to look for affordable cooking classes. Some supermarkets offer instruction, to tempt you to buy the ingredients there, and you might find classes that cover certain types of cooking—low-fat or low-salt cooking—at a community center or hospital. Look for smaller classes so you can see what's happening, and if they don't automatically give out the recipes, ask for copies of them.

6 Cookbooks are an even less expensive alternative. Look in used-book stores or the library for a book that emphasizes basic cooking, find a recipe

that looks appealing, and give it a try. The worst thing that can happen in the kitchen is to cut or burn yourself. If you can avoid that, the only thing to worry about is that the food won't taste so good. If it doesn't, try it again and you'll get better at it. Cooking isn't rocket science. If you can read and follow directions, you can figure it out.

Source: Howard, Clark. (2003). *Clark's Big Book of Bargains.*
New York, NY: Hyperion, pp. 14–15.

What organizational patterns are being used in the passage above?
cause and effect; classification; comparison/contrast; example

Write the organizational patterns and signal words from the reading above.
Cause and effect: As a result, has prompted, allows you, making it, if, can

happen, you'll get, you can

Classification: age category

Contrast: But

Example: GenXers . . . Christa DiBiase . . . says her mother . . .

REVIEW **WHAT YOU LEARNED**

Directions: Read the passage and answer the questions that follow.

1   Unfortunately, I've been too close to seeing how financially devastating it can be to go without health insurance. A couple of years ago, a younger sister of mine became ill and had to have surgery. She worked full-time for a small business and didn't have health insurance yet. To make matters worse, the surgery led to a major infection and additional operations that put her in and out of the hospital for days. And not only did she have no insurance and *subsequently* got hit with an incredible bill—even after the hospital decided to charitably swallow some costs—but she was out of work for a month. My sister will probably be paying medical bills—on top of her student loans—for many, many years to come.

2   Your health is your most valuable asset. If you *forgo* insurance of any kind, let it not be health insurance. Not to get *schmaltzy*, but without

---

Subsequently—afterward

Forgo—give up, do without

Schmaltzy—mushy, sentimental

health insurance you put at risk not only your financial future, but also your family or anyone who cares for you and would have to help you in case you were unable to work or to afford a place to live on your own.

Source: Ulrich, Carmen Wong. (2006). *Gener@tion Debt: Take Control of Your Money—A How-to Guide.* New York, NY: Time Warner, pp. 162–163.

1. Why does the author discuss her sister's health problems? _____
   The author discusses her sister as an example of how not having insurance can be devastating financially.

2. What is the organizational pattern of paragraph 1? _____
   example, cause and effect

3. What is the main idea of paragraph 1? _____
   Her sister's lack of health insurance led to a serious financial problem.

4. What is the organizational pattern of paragraph 2? _____
   cause and effect

5. What is the main idea of paragraph 2? _____
   Make sure you have health insurance for the sake of your own and your family's finances.

MASTER THE LESSON

Patterns of Organization

1   Did you ever see the movie *Dave*? In it, Kevin Kline played a look-alike for the president of the United States who takes over the job while the real president has a stroke while fooling around with his secretary. (Yes, it's a comedy.) In one scene Dave is faced with shutting down a day-care center for under-privileged kids—unless he can find some wiggle room in the government's budget. So he brings his hometown CPA (Charles Grodin) to the White House and they sit around the kitchen table at midnight, chowing down and figuring out where they can make cuts. They get creative. And they succeed.

2   And that's precisely what you need to do.

3   Before we dive in, though, you need to agree that you'll be willing to make some hard choices about spending money on particular items. Let's take your cell phone as an example. If you're like many people, you've come to rely very heavily on your cell phone. You may have started using it for convenience, or only in emergencies, but over the last few years, it's become the easiest and best way to reach you. You can't imagine giving it up. Or could you? Analysts say the average cell phone bill is $54 per month. That's $648 a year. Could you give it up—or use it substantially less often—if that was what you needed to do to come up with your $10 a day? How about your high-speed Internet access? Or your second car? Or that second dinner out each week?

4   These are hard questions. And no one can answer them for you. The problem is that if you're not balancing your budget already, you may not be able to do it by getting rid of the small expenditures (like the lattes you allow yourself every so often). You may have to eliminate or trim some bigger line items.

5   I'll make you a deal: I'll go through this process in an order designed to cause you the least amount of pain, one that will ask you to give up the fewest number of things in life that you enjoy. But once you've found your $10 a day, it's up to you; you can stop, knowing that you've succeeded (and it's a success that should be celebrated!), or you can keep reading and determine if there's a way for you to more quickly build a savings cushion, or a larger nest egg. Or you can use the excess to save for other goals you might have in mind.

6   For example . . .

What could you do with an extra $50 a month?

Replace your decrepit dishwasher

Join a gym

What could you do with an extra $100 a month?

Buy season tickets to your favorite sports team's games

Take your family on a weeklong vacation

What could you do with an extra $200 a month?

Pay for your newborn child's wedding

Send your teenager to sleep-away camp for a month

What could you do with an extra $500 a month?

Put a two-year-old through college in 16 years

Put a down payment on a home in 5 years

Source: Chatzky, Jean. (2004). *Pay It Down!: From Debt to Wealth on $10 a Day.* New York, NY: Penguin Group, pp. 61–63.

1. What is the pattern of organization used in paragraph 1? <u>cause and</u>
   <u>effect</u>

2. Why does the author use the example of the cell phone? What is the author's main idea? <u>The author uses the example to show how people</u> <u>spend money on something they don't need. The main idea is that we</u> <u>should look at what we are used to spending money on and make some</u> <u>hard choices about what is really necessary.</u>

3. What is the organizational pattern for paragraph 6? <u>example</u>

4. What signal words let you know the pattern? <u>For example</u>

6–10. In the space that follows, create a graphic organizer or outline of the main idea and the supporting details of this reading passage. Answers will vary.

-In the movie, *Dave*, a look-alike U.S. president dealt with budget cuts to save a day-care center for underprivileged children.

-People must be creative with cutting their budgets.

- For example, the average cell phone bill is $648 per year.

- Giving up or using the cell phone less could free up cash.

- Giving up high-speed Internet, a second car, or a second dinner out would save cash.

- If you have already given up the small things, you may need to eliminate bigger items in your budget.

- The purpose of going through your budget is to help you find an extra $10 per day to save and it will be as painless as possible.

- The process will help you give up the fewest number of things in a life you will enjoy.

- Once you've found the $10 per day it's up to you.

- you can stop, knowing you succeeded and you should celebrate!

- you can keep reading and determine if there's more to save

- this will help build up a savings cushion or a larger nest egg

- or the excess savings can be used for other goals

- There are several examples of things you could do with extra money.

- an extra $50 per month

- an extra $100 per month

- an extra $200 per month

- an extra $500 per month

Reading Practice

The next section of the chapter will help refine your skills in determining the pattern of organization while you read a variety of materials. All three of the readings address topics related to managing your money.

The first reading comes from the textbook, *Business Essentials,* in the section titled *Conserving Money by Controlling It.*

The second reading is from literature and is *The Story About Investment* from *The Message.*

The final reading is a visual image, *Compounding Money over Time.*

READING 1

1250L   ## Conserving Money by Controlling It

Use **SQ3R** to read this textbook excerpt.

Survey	Skim over the material. Read the title, subtitle, subheadings, first and last paragraphs, pictures, charts, and graphics. Note italics and bold print.
Question	Ask yourself questions before you read. What do you want to know? Turn headings and subheadings into questions and/or read questions if provided.
Read	Read the material in manageable chunks. This may be one or two paragraphs at a time or the material under one subheading.
Recite	Recite the answer to each question in your own words. This is a good time to write notes as you read each section. Repeat the question-read-recite cycle.
Review	Look over your notes at the end of the chapter, article, or material. Review what you learned and write a summary in your own words.

1   Several steps in the financial-planning process call for conserving money by paying attention to where it goes—by keeping spending within affordable limits and understanding what you're spending your money on. As too many people have found out the hard way, a major pitfall in any financial plan is the temptation to spend too much, especially when credit is so easy to get. Consumers often lose track of how much they spend, and, to make matters worse, some don't consider the costly finance charges associated with easy credit. Because many credit-card issuers target college students and recent graduates with tempting offers appealing to the desire for financial independence, we'll use the following section to explain the financial costs entailed by credit cards. Keep in mind, however, that the same lessons apply equally to other loans—home mortgages, cars, and student financial aid.

CREDIT CARDS: KEYS TO SATISFACTION OR FINANCIAL HANDCUFFS?

2   Although some credit cards don't charge annual fees, all of them charge interest on unpaid (outstanding) balances. Because credit-card debt is one of the most expensive sources of funds, you need to understand the costs before you start charging instead of being surprised when you open your bill. For one thing, many card users don't realize how much interest they're paying or how long it will take them to pay off their bills.

3   Some states post Web sites to help consumers understand credit-card costs. Figure AIII.8 reprints part of a page from California's "Minimum Payment Credit Card Calculation." Using the table as a guide, let's consider the following situation. Suppose you owe $5,000 for credit-card purchases, and your card company requires a minimum monthly payment (minimum payment due—or MPD) of 5 percent of the unpaid balance. The interest rate is 18 percent APR (annual percentage rate) on the outstanding balance. (By the way, this rate isn't unusually high: Some rates are well above 20%.)

Figure AIII.8 Paying Off Credit-Card Debt

BALANCE = $5,000	MPD 3%		MPD 5%		MPD 10%	
APR	MONTHS	COSTS	MONTHS	COSTS	MONTHS	COSTS
6%	144	$5,965.56	92	$5,544.58	50	$5,260.74
9%	158	$6,607.24	96	$5,864.56	51	$5,401.63
12%	175	$7,407.50	102	$6,224.26	53	$5,550.32
18%	226	$9,798.89	115	$7,096.70	55	$5,873.86
21%	266	$11,704.63	123	$7,632.92	57	$6,050.28
Note: MPD = Minimum Payment Due and APR = Annual Percentage Rate						

4   Figure AIII.8 reflects an account with $5,000 outstanding balance at the end of last month. *This is the amount on which your interest of 18 percent APR is charged.* Remember, too, that your card company requires a *minimum monthly payment due (MPD) of 5 percent* of the current balance. Let's assume that you pay only the monthly minimum and ask ourselves two questions:

1. How many months will it take to pay off the $5,000?

2. How much interest will you have paid when you do pay it off?

5   To answer these questions, let's look at Figure AIII.8. Remember that your card has an MPD of 5 percent, so we start by finding the MPD 5 percent column. Next, we remember that the APR is 18 percent, so we find the row on the left that corresponds to an 18 percent APR. Where this row intersects with the MPD 5 percent column is the number of months it will take you to pay off $5,000: 115 months. That's approximately 9½ years! And remember: This number assumes that your balance gradually diminishes to zero because you add *no other purchases to the card.* Your total payment of $7,096.70 covers your $5,000 debt plus $2,096.70 in interest charges. An immediate cash payoff, (therefore) would save you $2,096.70 in interest payments.

6   (Why) does repayment take so long? In Figure AIII.9, we run through some sample calculations for the first two months in your 115-month repayment process.

Your minimum monthly payment decreases because your ending balance gets smaller with each monthly payment. Your $250 payment in February includes $75 in interest owed on the $5,000 balance in the previous month. At 18 percent APR, interest on $5,000 would be $900 for a year (0.18 X $5,000), but for one month (January), it's only 1/12 of that amount—$75. You're paying the rest of your February installment of $175 ($250 - $75) on the principal amount, thereby reducing the month-end balance to $4,825. If we carry out these calculations over 115 months, we find that, when your account is paid in full, you've made "payments on principal" or $5,000 and interest payments of $2,096.70.

Figure AIII.9 Calculating Minimum Monthly Payments

	MINIMUM MONTHLY PAYMENT (5% OF PREVIOUS ENDING BALANCE) =	INTEREST OWED ON PREVIOUS BALANCE* (1/12 × .18 × PREVIOUS BALANCE) +	PAYMENT ON PRINCIPAL	ENDING BALANCE OWED ON PRINCIPAL
January –	–	–	–	$5,000
February	$250.[0.05 × $5,000] =	$75.[1/12 × 0.18 × $5,000] +	$175	$4,825[5,000 – 175]
March	$241.25[0.05 × 4,825] =	$72.38[1/12 × 0.18 × 4,825]	+ $168.87	$4,656.13[4,825 – 168.87]

*Monthly interest is calculated using 1/12 of annual interest rate.

Source: Ebert, Ronald J., and Ricky W. Griffin. (2007). *Business Essentials*, 6th ed. Upper Saddle River, NJ: Pearson Prentice Hall, pp. 553–554.

Practice Paying Off Your Debt
(questions from the textbook chapter)

Using the method illustrated in Figure AIII.9, you should be able to answer the following questions about credit-card repayment:

1. According to the data in Figure AIII.9, your minimum monthly payment for April would be which of the following?

   a. $232.81 = (.05 × $4656.13)   c. $230.56

   b. $253.47   d. $226.18

2. According to the data in Figure AIII.9, for April, the interest owed on your previous balance would be which of the following?

   a. $70.43   c. $69.84 = (1/12 × .18 × $4656.13)

   b. $71.94   d. $68.32

3. According to the data in Figure AIII.9, for April, your ending balance owed on principal would be which of the following?

 a. $4,182.16 c. $4,517.22

 b. $4,493.16 = $4656.13 − ($232.81 − $69.84) d. $4,334,97

Main Idea

4. What is the main idea of paragraph 1 in your own words? There are financial costs associated with all types of loans, and consumers need to be careful.

5. What is the main idea of paragraphs 2–6 in your own words?
There are many costs that add up quickly when you don't pay off your credit card each month. Repayment of a credit card can be much more expensive than you realize.

Supporting Details

6. How many months will it take to pay off a $5,000 credit card balance if you pay the minimum 5% of the balance each month and the interest rate is 18%?
115 months

7. What is the ending balance owed on principal in March (in Figure AIII.9)?
$4,656.13

Patterns of Organization

8. What is the primary pattern of organization for this reading? cause and effect

9. Circle or list the signal words that indicate the pattern. See items circled in the article.

Critical Thinking

10. How does this new information impact your life? Discuss a way you can apply what you learned. Answers will vary.

Literature   **READING 2**

The Story About Investment

1   "It's also like a man going off on an extended trip. He called his servants together and **delegated** responsibilities. To one he gave five thousand dollars, to another two thousand, to a third one thousand, depending on their abilities. Then he left. Right off, the first servant went to work and doubled the master's invest- ment. The second did the same. But the man with the single thousand dug a hole and carefully buried his master's money.

2   "After a long absence, the master of those three servants came back and settled up with them. The one given the five thousand dollars showed him how he had doubled the investment. His master **commended** him: 'Good work! You did your job well. From now on be my partner.'

3   "The servant with the two thousand showed how he also doubled his master's investment. His master commended him: 'Good work! You did your job well. From now on be my partner.'

4   "The servant given the one thousand said, 'Master, I know you have high standards and hate careless ways, that you demand the best and make no **allowances** for error. I was afraid I might disappoint you, so I found a good hiding place and secured your money. Here it is, safe and sound down to the last cent.'

5   "The master was furious. 'That's a terrible way to live! It's criminal to live cautiously like that! If you knew I was after the best, why did you do less than the least? The least you could have done would have been to invest the sum with the bankers, where at least I would have gotten a little interest.

6   "'Take the thousand and give it the one who risked the most. And get rid of this "play-it-safe" who won't go out on a limb. Throw him out into utter darkness.'" ■

Source: Peterson, Eugene. (2002). *The Story About Investment. The Message: The Bible in Contemporary Language.* Colorado Springs, CO: Navpress, p. 1796.

Vocabulary

Use context clues to find the meaning of *delegated* from paragraph 1.

It's also like a man going off on an extended trip. He called his servants together and *delegated* responsibilities. To one he gave five thousand dollars, to another two thousand, to a third one thousand, depending on their abilities. Then he left. Right off, the first servant went to work and doubled the master's investment.

The man was going on a trip and did something with responsibilities.	The servant went right to work.	He gave money to his servants depending on their abilities.

1. Based on the clues, what is the meaning of *delegated*? to give responsibility to someone

Use context clues to find the meaning of *commended* from paragraph 2.

His master *commended* him: 'Good work! You did your job well. From now on be my partner.'

His master said 'Good work!'	His master said he did his job well.	His master was so impressed he wanted the man to be his partner.

2. Based on the clues, what is the meaning of *commended*? praised or told one they did well

Use word parts to find the meaning of ***allowances*** from paragraph 4.

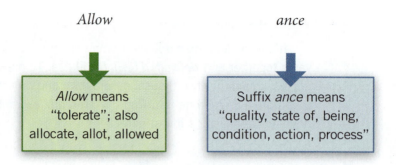

Allow   *ance*

Allow means
"tolerate"; also
allocate, allot, allowed

Suffix *ance* means
"quality, state of, being,
condition, action, process"

What is the meaning of ***allowances***? <u>action of tolerating or allowing</u>

Use context clues to find the meaning of ***allowances*** from paragraph 4.

"The servant given the one thousand said, 'Master, I know you have high standards and hate careless ways, that you demand the best and make no ***allowances*** for error. I was afraid I might disappoint you, so I found a good hiding place and secured your money. Here it is, safe and sound down to the last cent.'

The master has high
standards and
demands the best.

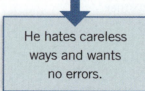

He hates careless
ways and wants
no errors.

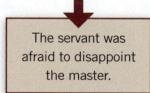

The servant was
afraid to disappoint
the master.

3. Based on the clues, what is the meaning of ***allowances***? <u>toleration of</u>
<u>one's errors</u>

4. Look in the dictionary for the meaning of ***allowances*** as used in the
reading. <u>sanctions, tolerances</u>

Main Idea

5. What is the central theme of this reading passage in your own words?

Answers will vary.

Supporting Details

Directions: If the statement is correct, circle **True.** If the statement is incorrect, circle **False.**

6. True or False: Each of the servants was given the same amount of money to invest.

7. True or False: The master was impressed with each servant's investment strategy.

8. True or False: The master was pleased with the servant who took the greatest risk.

Pattern of Organization

9–10. What are the organizational patterns being used in this passage? List the patterns and the signal words that indicate the patterns.

Organizational Pattern	Signal Words
Time order	then, right off, after, from now on (2X)
Compare and contrast	to one, to another, to a third, the first servant, the second did the same, but, the one, the servant with the two, the servant given the one thousand

Visual Image

READING 3

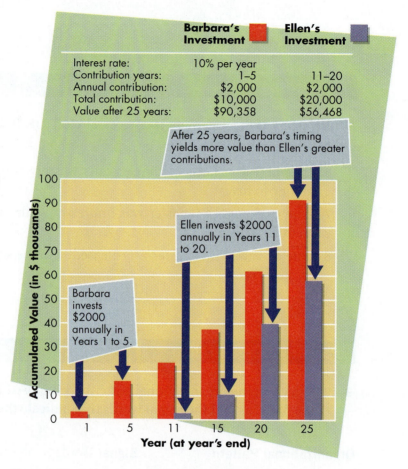

Figure AIII.5 Compounding Money over Time

Source: Ebert, Ronald J. and Ricky W. Griffin. (2007). *Business Essentials,* 6th ed.
Upper Saddle River, NJ: Pearson, pp. 550–551.

Read the visual image above and answer these questions:

1. Which person will have more value in her contributions after 25 years? Barbara _____

_____

2. What is the approximate value of Barbara's contributions at 25 years?
$90,000 _____

3. What is the approximate value of Ellen's contributions at 25 years?
$58,000

4. How much did Barbara invest? _____
$10,000

5. How much did Ellen invest? _____
$20,000

Now read the text which accompanies the chart.

Making Better Use of Your Time Value

1 Most people want to save for the future, either for things they need—down payments on a house, college tuition, and so on—or the nonessentials (luxury items and recreation). The sooner you get started, the greater your financial power will be: You will have taken advantage of the time value of money for a longer period of time.

2 Consider the following example. Coworkers Ellen and Barbara are both planning to retire in 25 years. Over that period, each can expect a 10-percent annual return on investment (the U.S. stock market has averaged more than 10 percent for the past 75 years). Their savings strategies, however, are different: Whereas Barbara begins saving immediately, Ellen plans to start later but invest larger sums. Barbara will invest $2,000 annually for each of the next five years (years 1 through 5), for a total investment of $10,000. She'll let interest accumulate through year 25. Ellen, meanwhile, wants to live a little larger by spending rather than saving for the next 10 years. Then, for years 11 through 20, she'll start saving $2,000 annually, for a total investment of $20,000. She, too, will allow annual returns to accumulate until year 25, when both she and Barbara retire. Will Ellen have a larger retirement fund in year 25 because she's ultimately contributing twice as much as Barbara?

3 Not by a long shot: Barbara's retirement wealth will be much larger—$90,364 versus Ellen's $56,468—even though she invested only half as much ($10,000 versus $20,000). We explain the disparity by crunching all the numbers in Figure AIII.5. Barbara's advantage lies in timing—namely, the length of her savings program. Her money is invested longer—over a period of 21 to 25 years—with interest compounding over that range of time. Ellen's earnings are compounded over a shorter period—6 to 15 years. Granted, Ellen may have had more fun in years 1 to 5, but Barbara's retirement prospects look brighter. ■

Did your answers become more clear after reading the text or was the chart easy to understand and interpret? Answers will vary.

_____

Discuss any additional information you obtained from reading the text that helped you comprehend the material in the chart.
Answers will vary.

_____

_____

Additional Recommended Readings

Chatzky, J. (2004). *Pay It Down!: From Debt to Wealth on $10 a Day.* New York, NY: Penguin Group.

Dominguez, J. and V. Robin. (1999). *Your Money or Your Life: Transforming Your Relationship with Money and Achieving Financial Independence.* New York, NY: Penguin Books.

Floyd, J. D. (2007). *Joyfully Debt Free: How to Get Out of Debt, Stay Out, and Accumulate a Fortune!* Victoria, BC: Trafford.

Fuhrman, J. (2003). *The Credit Diet: How to Shed Unwanted Debt & Achieve Fiscal Fitness.* Hoboken, NJ: John Wiley & Sons.

Glink, I. R. (2001). *50 Simple Things You Can Do to Improve Your Personal Finances: How to Spend Less, Save More, and Make the Most of What You Have.* New York, NY: Three Rivers Press.

H & R Block. (2003). *Just Plain Smart Personal Finance Advisor: A Lifelong Approach to Achieving Your Financial Goals.* New York, NY: Random House.

Hanson, J. (2005). *Good Debt, Bad Debt: Knowing the Difference Can Save Your Financial Life.* New York, NY: Penguin Group.

Howard, C. (2003). *Clark's Big Book of Bargains.* New York, NY: Hyperion.

Kimball, C. and F. K. Doria. (2002). *The Everything Get Out of Debt Book: Evaluate Your Option,* *Determine Your Course of Action, and Make a Fresh Start.*

Kirchheimer, Sid. [AARP's "Scam Alert" Expert]. (2006). *Scam-Proof Your Life: 377 Smart Ways to Protect You & Your Family from Ripoffs, Bogus Deals & Other Consumer Headaches.* New York, NY: Sterling Publishing.

Langemeier, L. (2006). *Millionaire Maker: Act, Think, and Make Money the Way the Wealthy Do.* New York, NY: McGraw-Hill.

Liberman, G. and A. Lavine. (2000). *Rags to Riches: Motivating Stories of How Ordinary People Achieved Extraordinary Wealth!* Chicago, IL: Dearborn.

MarksJarvis, G. (2007). *Saving for Retirement Without Living Like a Pauper or Winning the Lottery.* Upper Saddle River, NJ: FT Press, Pearson.

Opdyke, J. D. (2006). *The Wall Street Journal Complete Personal Finance Guidebook.* New York, NY: Random House.

Orman, S. (1999). *The Courage to Be Rich: Creating a Life of Material and Spiritual Abundance.* New York, NY: Penguin Putnam.

Pond, J. D. (2008). *Grow Your Money! 101 Easy Tips to Plan, Save, and Invest.* New York, NY: HarperCollins.

Random House Reference. (2003). *Just Plain Smart: Personal Finance Advisor, A Lifelong*

Approach to Achieving Your Financial Goals. New York, NY: Random House.

Strassels, P. N. and W. B. Mead. (1986). *Money Matters: The Hassle-Free, Month-by-Month Guide to Money Management.* Reading, MA: Addison-Wesley.

Ulrich, C. W. (2006). *Gener@tion Debt: Take Control of Your Money—A How-to Guide.* New York, NY: Time Warner.

myreadinglab

For support in meeting this chapter's objectives, log on to www.myreadinglab.com and select Patterns of Organization: Classification, Patterns of Organization: Comparison, Patterns of Organization: Contrast, Patterns of Organization: Cause and Effect.

7

Facts and Opinions

THEME Current Social Issues: Politics, Populations, and Poverty

SPOTLIGHT ON LEARNING STYLES  Do (EXPERIENCE)

Have you ever had trouble deciding if what you were hearing or reading was the truth or just someone's opinion? In our society, it is pretty common for these things to get confused. Sometimes individuals have an agenda, and they only share the facts that support their cause. People also use phrases such as *as a matter of fact* or *the truth of the matter is* before they state their own opinions. It is often difficult to distinguish the facts from the opinions. One good way that has helped me make this distinction is by using my own experience and common sense. I may sometimes encounter new information for which I have no background knowledge, but there always seems to be something that nudges me to ask, "Does this make sense?" When my daughter encounters different beliefs, I ask her to compare the ideas she hears with what she knows to be true. Then I suggest she compare new thoughts and ideas to what she's read, researched, and experienced for herself. While she knows that her own experiences may be limited to the places she's lived, the values she's been taught, the people she's encountered, and the things she's read, she still can trust her intuition and faith. When I hear the term *critical thinking*, I think of having an open mind for learning and enhancing that learning with discernment. Having an open mind is important, but be careful that your mind is not so open that it falls out!

Facts and opinions are both used to support an author's point or main idea. The use of facts versus opinions will depend on the author's purpose for writing.

In this chapter you will learn to:

- distinguish the difference between a fact and an opinion
- detect opinions in persuasive text

There are many strong opinions as well as facts regarding politics, populations, and poverty. This chapter will give you the opportunity to read several perspectives and data sources related to current social issues. As you read the material in this chapter, it will be up to you to decide if you are going to form an opinion or change your position on specific issues that are critical in our world.

Some of the topics included in this chapter are:

- homelessness
- the working poor
- welfare

- protecting our planet's natural resources
- immigration
- peace and justice

Note: This is a college level textbook, and the topics deal with serious issues. The material may not be comfortable or easy to read. Remember, the objective of this chapter is to help you learn to distinguish facts from opinions in written text.

Separating Facts and Opinions
(How do I tell when the information is real?)

How do I know if what I read is a **fact**? A *fact* is information that can be proven or verified through evidence.

> **LO1**
> Determine how to identify facts and opinions.

Here are some examples of facts:

- From 2002 to 2003, the number of people living in poverty in the United States increased by 1.3 million to 35.6 million.

- In 2003, the number of people living in food-insecure households rose for the third year in a row to 36.3 million Americans, including more than 13 million children.

Source: Dziedzic, Nancy. (2007). *World Poverty.* Detroit, MI: Thomson Gale, pp. 22–23.

The preceding facts can be checked for accuracy. *Note:* Authors generally cite the source of the facts presented so that readers can verify the information with the original source, which improves credibility.

How do I know if what I am reading is an **opinion**? An opinion cannot be proven and is someone's belief or perspective. Opinions may use judgmental words such as *easy, difficult, cheap, expensive, beautiful, ugly, adequate, inadequate,* etc. Opinions may suggest one solution to a complex issue or present the issue from one side or perspective. *Note:* This does not mean the opinion is necessarily bad or good, but that it is a personal view rather than a fact.

Here are some examples of opinions:

- Elected officials would do well to take a cue from history.

  Federal funding for social programs, already inadequate, has been on the chopping block recently.

Source: Dziedzic, Nancy. (2007). *World Poverty.* Detroit, MI: Thomson Gale, pp. 22–23.

Note in the preceding examples, in the first statement, the phrase *would do well to* cannot be verified for accuracy. In the second example, the phrase *already inadequate* is an opinion because people may disagree on how much funding is enough or *adequate*.

Essays often use a mixture of facts and opinions. The writer chooses which facts to present to support her opinion. You might form or alter your own opinion based on which facts you read. As a reader, you will learn to decide for yourself what you believe as you become more adept at separating the facts from the opinions.

EXAMPLE

Directions: Read the statements and write **F** for a fact and **O** for an opinion. If the statement contains both a fact and an opinion, write **F/O** and identify each one.

_____ **1.** Food costs too much these days.

_____ **2.** The average American consumer's food bill has increased 10% over the past two years.

_____ **3.** It is difficult to find affordable housing when the average rent price has increased more than the average wage in our area.

Question 1 is **O** or opinion because *too much* is a judgment. Depending on their perspectives, one person may believe the cost of food is reasonable, while another may think it is too expensive. Question 2 is **F** or a fact. There are governmental reports to verify the change in food prices and consumer spending over time. Question 3 is **F/O** because the sentence contains both a fact and an opinion. The words *difficult* and *affordable* are judgments; therefore, this part of the sentence is opinion. The increase in the average rent price and wage in an area can be verified, making the second part of the sentence a fact.

PRACTICE THE NEW SKILL

Directions: Read the statements and write **F** for a fact and **O** for an opinion. If the statement contains both a fact and an opinion, write **F/O** and identify each one.

1. _____ F/O _____ While ascending the ranks of the U.S. Civil Service, from aquatic biologist to information specialist to chief editor of Fish and Wildlife Service publications, Carson quietly and methodically began to plan another book—not what she called just "another 'introduction to oceanography,'" but a definitive work on the sea.

_____F/O_____ It was already within her, this masterpiece, as Michelangelo would say of his sculptures; all she needed to do was chip away the surrounding stone.

_____O_____ Routine for a genius, and more, for although Carson was modest in her manner, she possessed strong confidence and a rare ability to synthesize an archipelago of scattered research—theses, dissertations, professional papers, raw statistics—into a single island of vivid prose that everyone could enjoy.

_____F_____ The result was *The Sea Around Us*, her second book, published in July 1951.

Source: Heacox, Kim. (1996). *Visions of a Wild America: Pioneers of Preservation.* Washington, DC: National Geographic Society, p. 120.

2. _____F_____ Dams on rivers are built for irrigation, to generate electricity, and to supply water to cities and industry.

_____F/O_____ Engineers like to say that dams built to generate electricity do not take water from the river, only its energy, but this is not entirely true since reservoirs increase evaporation.

_____F/O_____ The annual loss of water in arid or semiarid regions, where evaporation rates are high, is typically equal to 10 percent of the reservoir's storage capacity.

Source: Brown, Lester R. (2003). *Plan B: Rescuing a Planet under Stress and a Civilization in Trouble.* New York, NY: W. W. Norton & Company, p. 33.

3. _____O_____ The U.S. public is evenly divided over whether government or people themselves should take responsibility for reducing poverty (NORC, 2003).

_____F_____ Government statistics show that 39 percent of the heads of poor families did not work at all during 2003, and an additional 31 percent worked only part time (U.S. Census Bureau, 2004).

_____0_____ Such facts seem to support the "blame the poor" position because a major cause of poverty is *not holding a job.*

Source: Macionis, John J. (2006). *Society: The Basics,* 8th ed. Upper Saddle River, NJ: Pearson, pp. 218–219.

Your Facts and Opinions

One way to see the difference between facts and opinions is to write your own. Think about the topic of pollution. Consider things you've read, watched, heard, or experienced.

PRACTICE

Write three facts about pollution. *(Hint: The facts do not have to come from a government report, but you must be able to verify what you call a fact.)*

Answers will vary.

_____

_____

_____

Write three opinions about pollution. *(Hint: Words like* should *or* shouldn't, difficult, easy, expensive, horrible, *etc. may be used for opinions.)*

Answers will vary.

_____

_____

_____

In this exercise, which was easier to write? Why?

_____

_____

Detecting Opinions in Persuasive Text

When an author is trying to persuade the reader to take some action or adopt a certain perspective on an issue, there are various techniques that might be used. One technique is to select only facts that support your point of view and ignore the opposing facts. You may

LO2
Separate facts from opinions in persuasive text.

notice that you are only getting "one side of the story." I once asked my class to read a popular news magazine article about gun control. We noticed the "news report" only included the problems involved with losing freedom and rights. Several students were hunters, and they initially saw no problem with the article. But, after closer examination, we detected a one-sided perspective, with only a pro-freedom argument from the National Rifle Association. The other side of the issue was not presented in the "news" article.

When an author uses words that indicate judgment or value, an opinion is generally being offered. It is important to notice these words because your interpretation may vary from what the author or speaker intended.

For example, just after I graduated from college and moved to Indianapolis, my husband's new coworker recommended that we try a "great seafood restaurant." When asked if it was expensive, the coworker said, "No, it's pretty cheap." We took his recommendation and went to the seafood buffet that Friday night. When we received our bill, the price for two people (with water to drink) was more than the cash we had between us (and we didn't have credit cards); it was much more than what we considered "cheap." We had to go out to the car to look for change on the floor and between the seats! We found enough to pay the bill that night, but then had to eat a package of bologna and loaf of bread the rest of the week until we received our first paychecks! I learned that my perspective of *expensive* and *cheap* was very different from that of this aerospace engineer. I also learned to be careful when people use judgment or value words rather than specific facts.

Some value or judgment "*Words to Watch*" indicating opinions include:

large	a little	long	light
small	a lot	short	heavy
expensive	weak	beautiful	easy
cheap	strong	ugly	difficult

What other value or judgment words can you add to this list? Answers will vary.

_____   _____   _____   _____

_____   _____   _____   _____

_____   _____   _____   _____

Also beware of authors who use terms such as *all, most,* or *none.* Carefully assess whether *all* people or *most* scientists agree. Sometimes authors use these types of terms to exaggerate the severity of an issue in order to persuade the reader.

Consider the author's use of facts and opinions, and do not be afraid to question the information. A good reader will be aware if the author is supporting his claim with reasonable and credible information. A good reader will also consider changing his or her position on an important issue only after the facts and opinions are clear and reliable.

EXAMPLE

Directions: Read the following paragraph. Use two different color highlighters—one for opinions and one for facts.

> Although food stamps provide help for many people, actual benefits now average about a dollar per meal per person. In addition, 35 percent of those eligible are not enrolled in the program. Barriers to enrollment include an application process that can be dauntingly cumbersome, especially for those of limited education. For non-English speakers, too, language can present another barrier, made all the more formidable because of a prevailing anti-immigration sentiment. The National Council of LaRaza has reported that Latinos, like African-Americans, suffer "alarmingly high rates of food insecurity."

Source: Anderson, George M. (February 4, 2008).
America. *New York.* Vol. 198, Iss. 3, pp. 5+.

This example includes a combination of opinions and facts. The opinions that you highlighted should include "Barriers to enrollment include an application process that can be dauntingly cumbersome, especially for those of limited education" and "For non-English speakers, too, language can present another barrier, made all the more formidable because of a prevailing anti-immigration sentiment." The phrase "dauntingly cumbersome" is the author's belief and cannot be proven. Also, the phrase "made all the more formidable" is a matter of perspective. The other sentences are facts because they can be proven. The facts include the first two sentences, "Although food stamps provide help for many people, actual benefits now average about a dollar per meal per person. In addition, 35 percent of those eligible are not enrolled in the program." The last sentence includes a fact and an opinion. "The National Council of LaRaza has reported that Latinos, like African-Americans, suffer 'alarmingly high rates of food insecurity.'" The quote within the sentence is an opinion since it uses the subjective phrase "alarmingly high." The source of the quote, though, can be verified as a fact through reading the report of the National Council of LaRaza.

PRACTICE THE NEW SKILL

Directions: Read the following paragraphs. Use two different color highlighters—one for opinions and one for facts. Then, complete the chart below.

PRACTICE 1

FDA Approves Cloned Meat; Grocers Balk

1. The News

Just over a decade after scientists cloned the first animal, the last major barrier to selling meat and milk from clones has fallen: The U.S. government declared this food safe Tuesday. After considering the matter for nearly seven years, the Food and Drug Administration released a report saying that meat and milk from cloned cattle, pigs, and goats is safe to eat, being indistinguishable from that of naturally bred animals.

2. Clone-Burgers Coming Soon?

Don't look for much food from the offspring of cloned animals at your neighborhood supermarket or restaurant any time soon. Despite the ruling that meat and milk are safe for human consumption, it is going to take years to get them into the nation's food chain. And many of America's biggest grocers are already dead-set against it. "Our intention is not to accept cloned products from our suppliers," says Meghan Glynn, spokeswoman for Kroger, Co., the Cincinnati-based owner of Ralphs, Foods4Less and several other chains. Consumer anxiety about cloning is serious enough that several major food companies, including the big dairy producer Dean Foods Co. and Smithfield Foods Inc. say they are not planning to sell products from cloned animals.

3. The Cloning Advantage

Cloning is simply another technology producers can add to their already high-tech breeding programs, which include in vitro fertilization. It offers breeders greater access to the genetics of exceptionally fine specimens, said Stephen Sundlof, director of the FDA's Center of Food Safety and Applied Nutrition. "It is helpful in creating genetic twins of the very best animal who can transmit the very best traits to their offspring," he says. Because cloning is expensive, upward of $50,000 for each live birth, it is rare, said Greg Jaffe with the Washington D.C.-based Center for Science in the Public Interest. "Most consumers will never eat a cloned animal.

Those animals, which are very expensive to produce, primarily will be used as breeding stock and will end up as a miniscule portion of our food supply only at the end of their useful lives," he says.

Source: FDA Approves Cloned Meat; Grocers Balk. (January 16, 2008). *Journal & Courier,* Lafayette, Indiana, p. A3.

FACTS	OPINION
Answers will vary.	

PRACTICE 2

Chemistry in the Environment

Water Pollution

1   Water quality is critical to human health. Many human diseases—especially in developing nations—are caused by poor water quality. Several kinds of pollutants, including biological contaminants and chemical contaminants, can get into water supplies. Biological contaminants are microorganisms that cause diseases such as hepatitis, cholera, dysentery, and typhoid. Drinking water in developed nations is usually treated to kill microorganisms. Most biological contaminants can be eliminated from untreated water by boiling. Water containing biological contaminants poses an immediate danger to human health and should not be consumed.

2   Chemical contaminants get into drinking water from sources such as industrial dumping, pesticide and fertilizer use, and household dumping. These contaminants include organic compounds, such as carbon tetrachloride and dioxin, and inorganic elements and compounds such as mercury, lead, and nitrates. Since many chemical contaminants are neither volatile nor alive like biological contaminants, they are *not* eliminated through boiling.

3   The Environmental Protection Agency (EPA), under the Safe Drinking Water Act of 1974 and its amendments, sets standards that specify the maximum contamination level (MCL) for nearly one hundred biological and chemical contaminants in water. Water providers that serve more than twenty-five people must periodically test the water they deliver to their

consumers for these contaminants. If levels exceed the standards set by the EPA, the water provider must notify the consumer and take appropriate measures to remove the contaminant from the water. According to the EPA, if water comes from a provider that serves more than twenty-five people, it should be safe to consume over a lifetime. If it is not safe to drink for a short period of time, you will be notified.

Safe drinking water has a major effect on public health and the spread of disease. In many parts of the world, the water supply is unsafe to drink. In the United States the Environmental Protection Agency (EPA) is charged with maintaining water safety.

Source: Tro, Nivaldo J. (2006). *Introductory Chemistry Essentials,* 2nd ed. Upper Saddle River, NJ: Pearson, p. 418.

FACTS	OPINIONS
Answers will vary.	

PRACTICE 3

The U.S. Department of Justice reports:

- 797,500 children (younger than 18) were reported missing in a one-year period of time studied resulting in an average of 2,185 children being reported missing each day.

- 203,900 children were the victims of family abductions.
- 58,200 children were the victims of non-family abductions.
- 115 children were the victims of "stereotypical" kidnapping. These crimes involve someone the child does not know or someone of slight acquaintance, who holds the child overnight, transports the child 50 miles or more, kills the child, demands ransom, or intends to keep the child permanently. (pp. 7-8)

Commentary on Child Trafficking

During the years I've spent helping young girls escape from this form of slavery, I have seen and heard of the worst examples of inhumanity. But that personal burden is far outweighed by the immeasurable sense of joy and accomplishment that I experience when I see this cycle broken—when girls have their freedom restored and emerge from the dark depths of the trafficking world with a new found sense of who they are. To help people regain their sense of humanity is worth more than I can measure.

FACTS	OPINIONS
Answers will vary.	

REVIEW *WHAT YOU LEARNED*

Directions: Read the following paragraphs. Use two different color highlighters—one for opinions and one for facts. Then, complete the chart below.

1   Call it the Joneses syndrome. We see what people a notch or two more affluent than ourselves have, and we begin to want it too. Like forbidden fruit, it looks too good to resist. So we find ourselves on a treadmill, keeping up with the Joneses only to find that the Joneses (who are keeping up with other Joneses) are constantly upping the ante so that we never quite reach the point of satisfaction. In reality, of course, we seldom fasten on one particular family, but on our broader social surroundings.

2   The psychology behind the Joneses syndrome is as simple as family life. A child does not expect an ice cream bar for lunch. But if a sibling gets one, then having an ice cream bar suddenly seems not just desirable

but a *dire* necessity. A child does not instinctively long for a particular brand or style of sneakers. But if "everyone" in his class starts wearing them and commenting on those who don't, lack of those sneakers makes him feel deprived and inferior. Kids want what other kids have. In this respect, they are strikingly like adults. Psychologist David G. Myers writes that this is a big part of the reason most people in the industrialized world, living with comforts unknown to wealthy families in earlier generations, do not consider themselves wealthy.

Source: Simon, Arthur. (2006). *How Much is Enough?: Hunger for God in an Affluent Culture.* Grand Rapids, MI: Baker Books, p. 114.

FACTS	OPINIONS
Answers will vary.	

REVIEW *WHAT YOU LEARNED*

Directions: Read the following paragraphs. Use two different color highlighters—one for opinions and one for facts. Then, complete the chart below.

1   Slowing down the rate at which a nation consumes road fuel is neither easy nor quick, and it's especially difficult if it's going to be accomplished in a manner that's lifestyle neutral. By lifestyle neutral, I mean carrying out a social change without altering the way people buy or drive vehicles. In North America, the issue of an individual's right to buy the car or truck of his choice is about as *contentious* as gun control. And a lot more people own vehicles than guns.

2   The difficulty of this challenge is highlighted when you consider that since the Model T was introduced in 1908, there have been a handful of years where road fuel consumption has stayed level or gone down in the United States. Not surprisingly, those years were mainly during the 1970s oil price shocks.

Dire—urgent, serious, critical
Contentious—controversial, debatable

3   Without forcing people to buy more efficient cars, there are two ways of curbing road fuel consumption: getting people to drive less, or getting them to use less fuel while driving. It sounds simple enough, but remember the political challenge is to do it in a lifestyle neutral way. So getting people to drive less than the average 12,000 miles per year is pretty tough now that a substantial portion of the population commutes by car—usually alone—to and from sprawling suburbs. After all, it's not realistic to think that masses of people are going to move closer to their jobs just to save a few bucks a week on gasoline. Building more mass transit would help, but it would be *prohibitively* expensive, take a long time, and violate our principal assumption that the solution cannot alter peoples' lifestyle. Carpooling is not in the solution set either, because it violates the same basic assumption. *Ditto*, raising fuel taxes to curb demand.

4   So, in the absence of legislated change, Americans are confined to the other solution: trying to use less road fuel for the same distance traveled. There are four options that serve to improve the fuel economy of vehicles on the road:

1. Reduce the average weight of the vehicle;

2. Switch to a fuel type that gets better fuel economy or displaces the crude oil supply chain altogether;

3. Reduce the average highway driving speed; or

4. Improve engine and drive train technologies.

> *Source:* Tertzakian, Peter. (2006). *A Thousand Barrels a Second: The Coming Oil Break Point and the Challenges Facing an Energy Dependent World.* New York, NY: McGraw-Hill, p. 189.

FACTS	OPINIONS
Answers will vary.	

Prohibitively—excessively, unreasonably

Ditto—slang meaning the same thing

MASTER THE LESSON

Fact vs. Opinion

Directions: Read the statements and write **F** for a fact and **O** for an opinion. If the statement contains both a fact and an opinion, write **F/O** and identify each one.

Reduce Average Driving Speed

1. _____F_____ In 1974, during the energy crisis, the U.S. Congress cut the highway speed limit to 55 miles per hour, down from 75 miles per hour in most states.

2. _____F_____ It depends on the vehicle, but an average car traveling at 55 miles per hour consumes 17 percent less fuel than one traveling 20 miles per hour faster.

3. _____F_____ In 1987 the limit went back up to 65 miles per hour.

4. _____F_____ In 1995, the federal government *relinquished* its *jurisdiction* over speed limit controls altogether, leaving the decision up to the states once again.

5. _____F/O_____ Today, highway and freeway speed limits vary from 55 to 75 miles per hour, but it's a challenge to find anyone that drives less than 70 today.

6. _____O_____ There is no doubt that reducing speed reduces fuel consumption; however, it's far from a lifestyle neutral solution.

7. _____O_____ The last thing suburban drivers want is to increase their now lengthier commuting time by slowing down their driving speed.

Source: Tertzakian, Peter. (2006). *A Thousand Barrels a Second: The Coming Oil Break Point and the Challenges Facing an Energy Dependent World.* New York, NY: McGraw-Hill, p. 192.

8–10.

Directions: Read the following paragraph. Use two different color highlighters—one for opinions and one for facts.

_____
Relinquished—gave up, abandoned
Jurisdiction—authority, control

Messing with Mother Nature

Animal rights groups argue that cloning is cruel because it only works in a small percentage of attempts and is very stressful for the animals involved. The groups opposed ranged from Farm Sanctuary—whose spokeswoman Natalie Bowman called the FDA decision *"appallingly* irresponsible"—and the American Anti-Vivisection Society to Consumer Union and the Consumer Federation of America. "In the face of ever-increasing food safety concerns, it is troubling to see the FDA approval of products from cloned animals to be sold to the public, when questions surrounding the health risks, legal implications and ethical concerns remain unanswered," said Tim Buis, president of the National Farmers Union. "If you have moral objections to a particular food, or ethical objections to them, FDA's saying, 'Tough, you've got to eat,'" said Carol Tucker-Foreman of the Consumer Federation of America. "The FDA did not give adequate consideration to the welfare of these animals or their *surrogate* mothers," said Wayne Pacelle of the Humane Society of the United States.

Source: FDA Approves Cloned Meat; Grocers Balk. (January 16, 2008).
Journal & Courier, Lafayette, Indiana, p. A3.

Appallingly—awfully, inexcusably

Surrogate—substitute, replacement

MASTER THE LESSON

Fact vs. Opinion

Directions: Read the statements and write **F** for a fact and **O** for an opinion. If the statement contains both a fact and an opinion, write **F/O** and identify each one.

Hunger and Malnutrition

1. _____O_____ Hunger's relation to poverty is reciprocal: poverty causes hunger, but hunger causes people to remain in poverty.

2. _____F/O_____ As with every other aspect of global poverty, hunger is an immensely complicated problem, involving not just the lack of food but also the larger functions of macro- and microeconomics, national and international aid, weather and environmental changes, the availability of such social services as education and health care, use of *arable* land and equitable land distribution, and the healthy development of the agricultural sector.

3. _____F_____ Figure 2.1 shows regional progress on the United Nations Millennium Development Goal of eliminating world hunger.

Figure 2.1

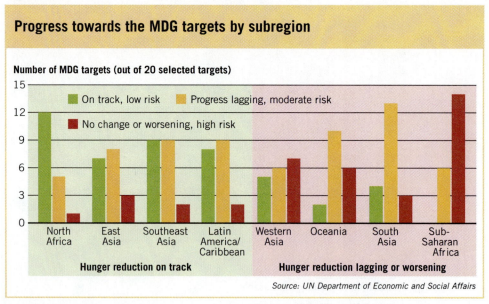

Progress towards the MDG targets by subregion

Number of MDG targets (out of 20 selected targets)

Legend:
- On track, low risk
- Progress lagging, moderate risk
- No change or worsening, high risk

Subregions: North Africa, East Asia, Southeast Asia, Latin America/Caribbean, Western Asia, Oceania, South Asia, Sub-Saharan Africa

Hunger reduction on track | **Hunger reduction lagging or worsening**

Source: UN Department of Economic and Social Affairs

_____
Arable—fit for cultivation

4. _____F_____ According to the report *The State of Food Insecurity in the World 2005* (Food and Agriculture Department of the United Nations, 2005), at least 842 million people (other sources cite 852 million) suffer from chronic hunger.

5. _____F/O_____ The UN Food and Agriculture Organization (FAO) estimates that as many as two billion people suffer from periodic hunger and food insecurity (the condition of not knowing whether one will have enough food at any given time); 75% of the world's hungry people live in rural areas with few economic prospects.

6. _____O_____ The FAO contends that hunger is a cause of poverty rather than a consequence.

7. _____F_____ As Figure 2.2 shows, hunger causes disease, unemployment, high rates of child mortality, lack of education,

Figure 2.2

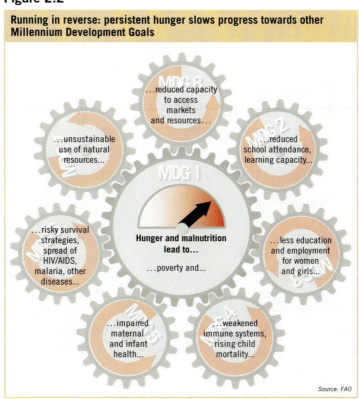

Running in reverse: persistent hunger slows progress towards other Millennium Development Goals

MDG 8 ...reduced capacity to access markets and resources...

...unsustainable use of natural resources...

MDG 2 ...reduced school attendance, learning capacity...

MDG 1

Hunger and malnutrition lead to...

...poverty and...

...risky survival strategies, spread of HIV/AIDS, malaria, other diseases...

...less education and employment for women and girls...

...impaired maternal and infant health...

...weakened immune systems, rising child mortality...

Source: FAO

unsustainable use of natural resources, risky personal
choices, and a lack of economic opportunities.

Source: Dziedzic, Nancy. (2007). *World Poverty*. Detroit, MI: Thomson Gale, pp. 9–10.

8-10. Discuss whether this paragraph is mostly facts, opinions, or both.

> By global or historical standards, much of what Americans consider
> poverty is luxury. A rural Russian is not considered poor if he cannot
> afford a car and his home has no central heating; a rural American is. A
> Vietnamese farmer is not seen as poor because he plows with water buf-
> falo, irrigates by hand, and lives in a thatched house; a North Carolina
> farm worker is, because he picks cucumbers by hand, gets paid a dollar a
> box, and lives in a run-down trailer. Most impoverished people in the world
> would be dazzled by the apartments, telephones, television sets, running
> water, clothing, and other amenities that surround the poor in America. But
> that does not mean that the poor are not poor, or that those on the edge of
> poverty are not truly on the edge of a cliff.

Source: Shipler, David K. (2004). *The Working Poor: Invisible in America.*
New York, NY: Alfred A. Knopf, p. 8.

_____

Amenities—services

LEARNING STYLE ACTIVITIES

Look, Listen, Write, Do

Ethanol Isn't Worth Costly Cornflakes and Tortillas

1   It was supposed to be the fuel that could wean, at least partially,
America and other petroleum importing countries from their dependence
on foreign oil. Anointed by the U.S. government and in receipt of political
support from both sides of the political spectrum, corn-based ethanol has
emerged as the biofuel of choice.

2   Ethanol, added to motor fuel, is a great oxygenate and can stretch
gasoline supplies blended from 10 to 85 percent by volume. This ability of
ethanol to stretch gasoline stocks was supposed to provide some measure
of energy independence. It is renewable and it evokes credits in net carbon
dioxide emissions, as well.

3   In theory these are all positive things. In reality, however, the situation is borderline catastrophic.

4   First, the net energy ratio of corn-based ethanol (i.e., useful energy divided by the energy required to produce a unit of ethanol) is at best 1.25. Some have even calculated a ratio less than one, meaning it takes more energy to produce ethanol from corn than the energy content of the fuel.

5   Due to large government subsidies, the growth of corn-based ethanol has been nothing short of meteoric. From 2000 to 2010, U.S. corn-based ethanol production increased from 1.6 to 13.2 billion gallons per year. In 2011, this total is expected to grow to almost 14 billion gallons. Congressional mandates, moreover, have decreed that by 2022, biofuels blended into the U.S. gasoline stock will increase to 35 billion gallons per year.

6   Thanks to considerable improvements in crop productivity, U.S. planted land has decreased roughly 39 million acres since 1980 (an 11 percent decrease). Corn's share of this total, though, increased from 23.6 percent to 27.8 percent, displacing 13.4 million acres of other crops. Also, the improvement in corn productivity led to per acre production of 91 bushels in 1980 to climb to almost 165 bushels per acre in 2009.

7   So which crops are being displaced by corn? Food crops, animal feed crops, and cotton all have experienced declines. In fact, since 2003, barley acreage has decreased 46.3 percent, oats 31.7 percent and cotton 18.6 percent. Hence farmers are just responding to the economics of corn. High gasoline prices drive ethanol prices up, and high ethanol prices drive corn prices up.

8   If cattle feed lots, poultry producers and hog farmers have to pay $5.40 per bushel for corn (the average price in 2010), is it surprising that food prices are increasing? And with cotton acreage decreasing by 18.6 percent, is it surprising that cotton prices went up 86 percent over the last 12 months?

9   The bottom line is the food versus fuel issue is very real and it will only get worse. To meet the 2022 mandate of 35 billion gallons of biofuels using corn-based ethanol, crop land dedicated to corn will have to increase from 88 million acres to 233 million acres. That would increase the total crop land in the U.S. to 461 million acres, which is highly unrealistic. The most U.S. crop land ever planted was 375 million acres, back in 1932.

10   Clearly corn-based ethanol is not a sustainable solution for the U.S. energy needs.

11   The rest of the story is even more unsavory. U.S. taxpayers are subsidizing corn-based ethanol, and as a direct consequence, food and clothing prices are going up. As Robert Bryce wrote last month in *Energy Tribune*:

12   "Last year, the Congressional Budget Office reported that the cost to taxpayers of using corn ethanol to reduce gasoline consumption by one gallon is $1.78. This year, the corn ethanol sector will produce about 13.8 billion gallons of ethanol, the energy equivalent of about 9.1 billion gallons of gasoline. Using the CBO's numbers, the total cost to taxpayers this year for the ethanol boondoggle will be about $16.2 billion."

13   Additionally, in 2000, fuel ethanol used 5.9 percent of the U.S. corn crop, and corn was priced at $1.85 per bushel. But last year, fuel ethanol used 38.4 percent of the U.S. corn crop, and corn was $5.40 per bushel.

14   Finally, on an equivalent energy basis, the cost of corn feedstock for corn-based ethanol is $3.80 per gallon of gasoline. This doesn't include the cost of production of the ethanol, the cost of transportation or any other costs besides the corn price, clearly making corn-based ethanol a money-losing proposition.

15   The use of corn-based ethanol costs the country perhaps an incremental amount of nearly $4 per gallon, doubling the cost per gallon in the portion that is ethanol compared to petroleum in motor fuel. It is thus evident that corn-based ethanol has evolved into the least attractive of all energy ideas of today.

Source: Economides, Michael. (May 17, 2011). Ethanol Isn't Worth Costly Cornflakes and Tortillas. *Forbes.*

Form a small group with your classmates and complete one of the learning style activities below. Remember, you may choose to use your preferred learning style

or you may work outside of your "comfort zone" to help you develop one of the other styles. As you work with your group, think about how you will present the results to the class.

👁 *L*ᴏᴏᴋ   Create a mind-map of the important information in the article. OR Create a collage of ads and promotional material about the advantages of using ethanol.

🔊 *L*ɪꜱᴛᴇɴ   Create a speech with the important information in the article. OR Prepare a debate for the pros and cons of using ethanol.

✏️ *W*ʀɪᴛᴇ   Create an outline of the important information in the article and write a summary. OR Write a letter to the editor of *Forbes* or your local newspaper about using ethanol.

👆 *D*ᴏ   Consider the important ideas in the article and find real-life examples to create a presentation of choices which use ethanol versus not using ethanol. OR Create a skit such as a talk-show or game-show demonstrating the concepts presented in the article.

Reading Practice

The following readings are related to the themes of politics, populations, and poverty and come from a variety of sources: the Internet, textbooks, literature, magazines, and visual images. They were chosen not only to help you improve your ability to distinguish facts from opinions but also to build your other reading skills of learning vocabulary, locating main ideas and supporting details, and understanding organizational patterns. The diverse readings were also selected to give you the opportunity to learn about issues and think about ideas that are relevant in our society today.

The first reading is from the Internet Web site, Planet Green, titled *Reduce Your Carbon Footprint by Half in Three Steps: Lose Ten Tons of Carbon Emissions in a Year.*

The second reading is from a textbook titled *Society: The Basics*. It is from Chapter 8: Social Stratification, and the topic is Controversy & Debate, The Welfare Dilemma.

The third reading is from literature from Henry David Thoreau's works *Walden* and *Civil Disobedience*.

The fourth reading is from *U.S. News and World Report* magazine, titled, "10 Ways to Go Green and Save Cash—No Excuses."

The fifth reading is a visual of an article titled "Be the Change You Want to See in the World."

Internet

READING 1

Reduce Your Carbon Footprint by Half in Three Steps: Lose 10 Tons of Carbon Emissions in a Year

Directions: Read the following paragraphs. Use two different color highlighters—one for opinions and one for facts. Then, complete the chart below.

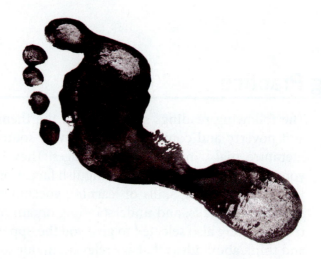

1   Your carbon footprint can be sort of a difficult thing to visualize—you can't really see your carbon emissions trailing up into the atmosphere as you go about your life. You surely know that burning fossil fuels releases greenhouse gas emissions, and that it's not just your car that contributes to your carbon footprint—the electricity you use in your home, your airplane travel, even the food you eat has

a significant impact on the number that goes with your particular footprint. And, while every person's footprint is a bit different, one thing is true for everyone: You can reduce your carbon footprint by half (or more!) with these three tips.

2   First, though, we should establish a few baselines. The average American's yearly carbon footprint is just about 20 tons, according to the United Nations; the global average is just a shade under 4 tons each year. This is not something we can be proud of for being first—America is way, way out in front here, and that's a huge problem. If we're going to make any progress in the fight against the climate crisis, that means it's time for big action, so let's get to it. Here's how to lose 10 tons in a year.

BECOME A *WEEKDAY VEGETARIAN*: LOSE .7 TONS

3   Your diet has a huge impact on the climate. A vegetarian diet is often cited as a greener way to eat (and it is, in a lot of ways) but it's a very polarizing topic for lots of people, and it's no good to stand around shouting at folks who just won't give up meat. Happily, we've found a happy medium: Be a weekday vegetarian. It's simple, easy to remember, much cheaper than buying all meat, all the time, and still has a significant impact. According to a study from the University of Chicago, an all-vegetarian (lacto-ovo—dairy and eggs allowed) diet will reduce your carbon footprint by about a ton; cut that back to five out of seven days—about 70 percent—and you've got 1400 pounds, or 0.7 tons.

4   You can still eat a little meat—please, choose a climate-friendly version when you do—when the weekends roll around; during the week, it's easy to find tons of

vegetarian recipes you can feast on, knowing you're on your way to losing 10 tons of carbon.

BUY GREEN POWER: LOSE 4 TONS

5   Eating green is just a small slice of the pie, so to speak. The average American household is responsible for nearly 9 tons of carbon emissions per year, according to the Department of Energy. Most of that comes from our most prominent source of electricity in this country: Coal, which we use for about 48 percent of our electricity nationally. Since there are a little more than two people per household, on average, according to the U.S. Census Bureau, we can cut the 9 ton average about in half, down to 4 tons per person per year.

6   So, switching from the "dirty power" that your utility provides (it really depends on location and individual utility for this one—Maryland's average emissions are a bit higher, actually, since they use more coal, for example) to renewables can save you a bundle of carbon. Each utility does it differently, so you'll have to contact whichever company or organization makes sure there's light when you flip on the switch, but more and more are offering programs that allow you to help them invest in renewable energy, and cut way back on your carbon footprint in the process. One caveat: You will pay a bit of a premium for green power; in most cases it's about one cent per kilowatt-hour, maybe $180 or $200 per year, but you can easily save that by buying less meat as part of your weekday vegetarian diet, and you can save even more cash with the last of the three tips.

CUT THREE FLIGHTS PER YEAR: LOSE 5 TONS

7   Okay, so we're halfway home, and to a huge source for our individual and collective carbon footprints: Airplane travel. It's sort of the elephant in the room when it comes to talking about this stuff, since modern airplane travel can be marvelously convenient—it's the only way to get from one end of the country to the other, say, in less than a day. Until a proper high-speed rail infrastructure connects the corners of our country, airplane travel will just be a reality for some of us, some of the time.

8   That's okay; we're just saying you could do less of it. While that sounds restrictive and maybe even a little backwards, it's not as hard as you might think. Frequent business travelers: How many silly trips do you make each year that you don't have to? I'll bet at least one. How often do you zoom away and return home within three or four days? Seems kinda quick, no? By using tools like teleconferencing, and combining business with a little pleasure, you'll be surprised at how easy it is to not fly so much.

9   Here's the crux of this one: Flying generates humongous carbon emissions. One flight from New York to Los Angeles (y'know, five hours or so, a movie, maybe catching up on your reading) averages nearly two tons, all by itself. Exact numbers are tricky to pin down—it really depends on what sort of plane you're flying, exactly how full it is, a little thing called radiative forcing—but it's a safe bet to say that cutting out three round-trips will save you 5 tons (and probably a little more). Check out Mike's great three-part series on greener flying over on TreeHugger for a very thorough treatment of the subject, including some killer alternatives for winged travel.

10   So there you have it: Three steps, 10 tons of carbon emissions saved. It's not quite as easy as installing a programmable thermostat, or another easy lifestyle change you can make in a day, but it has a heck of a lot more impact. If you're

serious about helping curb runaway climate change, these tips are the place to start. Seriously. ■

Source: Dunn, Collin. *Reduce Your Carbon Footprint by Half in Three Steps.* Retrieved from the Planet Green Web site: http://planetgreen.discovery.com/home-garden/reduce-carbon-footprint-threesteps.html

FACTS	OPINIONS
Answers will vary.	

CRITICAL THINKING/APPLICATION

Based on what you read and analyzed above, what changes will you consider making in your daily life? Explain.

Answers will vary.

_____

_____

Textbook

READING 2

1290L

Chapter 8 Social Stratification: Controversy & Debate: The Welfare Dilemma

Use SQ3R to read this textbook excerpt.

Survey	Skim over the material. Read the title, subtitle, subheadings, first and last paragraphs, pictures, charts, and graphics. Note italics and bold print.
Question	Ask yourself questions before you read. What do you want to know? Turn headings and subheadings into questions and/or read questions if provided.
Read	Read the material in manageable chunks. This may be one or two paragraphs at a time or the material under one subheading.
Recite	Recite the answer to each question in your own words. This is a good time to write notes as you read each section. Repeat the question-read-recite cycle.
Review	Look over your notes at the end of the chapter, article, or material. Review what you learned and write a summary in your own words.

1   In 1996, Congress ended federal public assistance, which guaranteed some income to all poor people. The new state-run programs require people who receive aid to get training or find work—or have the benefits cut off.

2   Almost no one likes welfare. Liberals criticize welfare for doing too little to help the poor, conservatives charge that it hurts the people it is supposed to help, and the poor themselves find welfare a complex and often *degrading* program.

3   So what, exactly, is welfare? The term "welfare" refers to an assortment of policies and programs designed to improve the well-being of some of the U.S. population. Until the welfare reform of 1996, most people used the term to refer to one part of the overall system: Aid to Families with Dependent Children (AFDC), a program of monthly financial support to parents (mostly single women) to care for themselves and their children. In 1996, some 5 million households received AFDC for some part of the year.

4   Did AFDC help or hurt the poor? Conservative critics charge that rather than reducing child poverty, AFDC actually made the problem worse, in two ways. First, they claim that this form of welfare weakened families, because for years after the program began, public assistance regulations provided benefits to poor mothers only if no husband lived in the home. As conservatives see it, AFDC operated as an economic incentive to women to have children outside of marriage, and they blame it for the rapid rise in out-of-wedlock births among poor people. To conservatives, the connection between being poor and not being married is clear: Fewer than one in ten married-couple families were poor, and more than nine out of ten AFDC families were headed by an unmarried woman.

5   Second, conservatives believe that welfare encouraged poor people to become dependent on government handouts, the main reason that eight out of ten poor heads of households did not have full-time jobs. Furthermore, more than half of nonpoor single mothers worked full time, compared with only 5 percent of single mothers receiving AFDC. Conservatives thus claim that welfare strayed far from its original purpose of short-term help to nonworking women with children (typically, after the death or divorce of a husband) and became a way of life. Once trapped in dependency, poor women are likely to raise children who will themselves be poor as adults.

6   Liberals charge that their opponents use a double standard in evaluating government programs. Why, they ask, do so many object to the government giving money to poor mothers and their children when most "welfare" actually goes to richer people? The AFDC budget amounted to around $25 billion annually—no

Degrading—humiliating, demeaning

small sum, to be sure, but just half of the $50 billion in home mortgage deductions that homeowners pocket each year. And it pales in comparison to the $300 billion in annual Social Security benefits Uncle Sam provides to senior citizens, most of whom are not poor. And what about "corporate welfare" to big companies? Their tax write-offs and other benefits run into hundreds of billions of dollars per year. As liberals see it, "wealthfare" is far more expensive than welfare.

7   Liberals also claim that conservatives have a distorted picture of public assistance. The popular images of do-nothing "welfare queens" mask the fact that most poor families who turn to public assistance are truly needy. Moreover, the typical household receiving AFDC received barely $400 per month, hardly enough to attract people to a life of welfare dependency. In constant dollars, in fact, AFDC payments actually declined over the years. Liberals therefore fault public assistance as a "Band-Aid approach" to the serious social problems of too few jobs and too much income inequality in the United States.

8   As for the charge that public assistance undermines families, liberals admit that the proportion of single-parent families has risen, but they dispute that AFDC was to blame. Rather, they see single parenting as a broad cultural trend found at all class levels in many countries.

9   Thus, liberals conclude, programs such as AFDC were attacked not because they benefited a part of the population many consider undeserving. Our cultural tradition of equating wealth with virtue and poverty with vice allows rich people to display privilege as a badge of ability, whereas poverty is a sign of personal failure. According to Richard Sennett and Jonathan Cobb (1973), the negative stigma of poverty is the "hidden injury of class."

10   [Statistics have shown] that people in the United States, more than people in other industrial nations, tend to see poverty as a mark of laziness and personal failure. It should not be surprising, then, that Congress replaced the federal AFDC program with state-run programs called Temporary Assistance for Needy Families (TANF). States set their own qualification requirements and benefits, but they must limit benefits to two consecutive years, with a lifetime of five years.

11   By 2002, TANF had moved about half of single parents on welfare into jobs or job training. President Bush and other supporters of welfare reform declared the reforms successful. However, opponents point out that many of the "success stories"—that is, people who are now working—earn so little pay that they are hardly better off than before (and half of these jobs provide no health insurance). In other words, welfare reform has slashed the number of people receiving welfare, but it has done far less to reduce poverty. In addition, say the critics, many

of these working women now spend less time with their children. In sum, the welfare debate goes on. ■

Source: Macionis, John, J. (2006). *Society: The Basics.* 8th ed. Upper Saddle River, NJ: Pearson, pp. 218–219.

Continue the Debate … (questions from the text)

1. How does our cultural emphasis on self-reliance help explain the controversy surrounding public assistance? Why do people not criticize benefits (such as home mortgage deductions) for more well-to-do people?

   Answers will vary.

   _____

   _____

   _____

   _____

   _____

2. Do you approve of the benefit time limits built into the TANF program? Why or why not?

   Answers will vary.

   _____

   _____

   _____

   _____

   _____

3. Why do you think the welfare reforms have done little to reduce poverty?

   Answers will vary.

   _____

   _____

   _____

   _____

Literature

READING 3

Henry David Thoreau is a famous American writer from the 1800s. His book *Walden* is a true story based on his leaving the life he knew in the city and moving to a small cabin on Walden Pond with only the possessions he could carry on his back. He also wrote an essay called *Civil Disobedience*, which is often published together with *Walden*. Both works may stimulate your thoughts and even change your life!

Directions: For each of the quotes from Henry David Thoreau, reflect on what the quote means to you. Include an actual example from your life as well as your opinion about what you think Thoreau means.

Answers will vary.

1. Be true to your work, your word, and your friend.

   _____

   _____

2. Go confidently in the direction of your dreams. Live the life you have imagined.

   _____

   _____

3. In the long run, men hit only what they aim at. Therefore, they had better aim at something high.

   _____

   _____

4. It is never too late to give up our prejudices.

   _____

   _____

5. Never look back unless you are planning to go that way.

   _____

   _____

6. This world is but a canvas to our imagination.

   _____

   _____

10 Ways to Go Green and Save Cash—No Excuses

Everyone is feeling the squeeze right now, with our investments being decimated and our 401(k)'s withering away. Consumers across the country are looking for ways to cut back. Luckily, some of the best ways to save money are also simple steps toward living a little greener. And, as we recently learned, simple steps can have a big impact. So, try these green tips to save some needed cash—no excuses.

- **Bike to work.** Or bike to public transit.

  Excuses: "But bikes are expensive! And I have to look nice for work."

  Why Your Excuses Are Lame: Often, you can buy a bike for the price of a tank of gas on Craigslist. It won't be titanium frame, but it will get you around. It's easy to bring a change of clothes and change at work, especially if your office has a locker room. If not, you can bike to public transit if it's available in your area, and walk the remainder. Another way you'll save money: By walking and biking more, you can cancel your gym membership.

- **If you have to drive, drive more efficiently.**

  Excuses: "Hypermiling sounds scary. And I don't want to add anything on to my car."

  Why Your Excuses Are Lame: Hypermiling—the strange driving practices that save gas, like driving on the lines in the rain or going into neutral on ramps—can be really unsafe. You don't have to try them to save gas, though; instead, take simple precautions like making sure your tires are blown up, taking off your roof rack to cut down on drag, and boosting your mileage by getting regular tune-ups.

- **Cook at home.** Buy nutritious ingredients to save money. Eating in will also discourage packaging and food waste.

  Excuses: "I don't know how to cook, I don't have the time, and ingredients are as expensive as eating out."

  Why Your Excuses Are Lame: Try pricing out the ingredients for a home-cooked meal—you'll find them to be significantly less expensive than takeout or a meal. As for not knowing how to cook—well, you don't have to be Emeril or Bobby Flay to make a decent meal for your family. Try cookbooks for beginners, not only because they're less intimidating but also because the recipes in them don't require fancy, expensive ingredients.

- **Put your home on an energy diet.** Monitor your thermostat, secure proper insulation, and eliminate all sources of vampire power—the electricity wasted by devices that are always plugged in.

  Excuses: "But how will I know what's using up the most power? It's too complicated."

  Why Your Excuses Are Lame: For big savings, you can buy devices to time and monitor your thermostat. You can also buy cords that prevent vampire power from being wasted. If you don't want to spend money, just monitor your own use—the oldest advice in the book. Put on a sweater instead of turning on the heat for the first few chilly days. Turn off the lights whenever you leave a room. Unplug appliances when they're not in use. And shut down your computer each night—computers are one of the biggest energy hogs.

- **Work from home.** Telecommuting saves you money in gas and food and can make your day less stressful.

  Excuses: "They need me in the office. How will I stay connected?"

  Why Your Excuses Are Lame: There are so many ways to stay connected from home—ask your office about wiring your home for video conferencing. You don't have to work from home every day to see significant savings; even one or two days a week will save you hundreds of dollars over the year in gas and lunches.

- **Don't shop—freecycle.** Use the net to find free furniture and goods, and swap the stuff you no longer need.

  Excuses: "Why would I want someone else's old junk? I don't like hand-me-downs."

  Why Your Excuses Are Lame: Just because items are used, it doesn't mean they're junk. Many of the site's offerings are only gently used, and if you end up with an item you don't like, so what? It's free, so just put it back on the site, and keep looking for something else.

- **Eat less meat.** Even if you only buy a little less each week, you'll save money and make an environmental impact.

  Excuses: "But I love burgers."

  Why Your Excuses Are Lame: Burgers are great, and if you want them, eat them. But in exchange, try a meatless meal every day, or week, or whatever you can handle. According to the U.N., even slight cutbacks in meat eating have an impact on climate change. So, if you like meat, try a turkey burger, because poultry has less of a carbon footprint than beef. Eat salads or pasta for lunch, and meat for dinner. You'll see the difference reflected in your grocery bill, and also your health.

- **Reuse what you can.** Get reusable water bottles instead of buying bottled water. If you pack your or your kid's lunch, buy a lunch bag and use Tupperware instead of buying Ziploc and brown paper bags.

Excuses: "But it's convenient."

Why Your Excuses Are Lame: Why spend money continually on stuff you'll just throw away? Cut out plastic utensils, disposable water bottles, paper napkins, and brown bags. They may be just little expenses, but they're still wasteful ones when you can reuse so easily and cheaply.

- **If you need to buy new gadgets, trade in your old ones for cash.**

Excuses: "But my phone/iPod/computer is really old."

Why Your Excuses Are Lame: Tech trade-in sites that give you cash for gadgets will often take any of them. You might not get as much as if you were trading in a new iPhone, but you can put the cash towards the price of your new tech toys. The sites, such as Gazelle, Cell for Cash, and even Office Depot also keep toxic technology out of landfills, and recycle the parts safely.

- **Do it yourself.** This applies to anything around the home. Grow your own vegetables. Make your own cleaning solution out of baking soda. Hang your clothes out to dry.

Excuses: "What is this, the olden days? Also, I have no idea how to do that."

Why Your Excuses Are Lame: Old housekeeping customs can be big green money savers. Your dryer, for example, is one of the home's biggest energy hogs, so putting clothes on a backyard line every once in a while would be reflected in your bill, and would give your clothes a fresh-air smell. Harsh chemicals comprise many of our household cleaners, and if you think organic cleaners are expensive, make your own here. You can also use things in your fridge for cleaning—vodka removes mildew, lemons freshen a garbage disposal, and onions clean the top of a grill. As for vegetable gardening, if you have the space and a little time, you might find that your produce is cheap and even more delicious than vegetables that have traveled halfway across the country.

Article note: Maura Judkis is a producer at *U.S. News*. She writes about the green movement and looks for ways to be an eco-friendly consumer without breaking the bank. ◼

Source: Judkis, Maura. (October 9, 2008). *10 Ways to Go Green and Save the Planet—No Excuses. U.S. News & World Report.*

Questions

1–9. Complete the concept map. Include the topic and central idea, and the major supporting details.

Vocabulary

Use word parts to find the meaning of **hypermiling**.

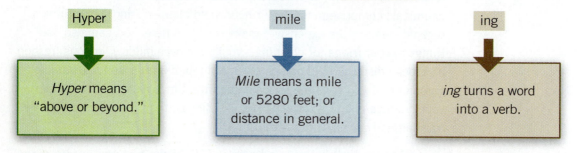

10. Based on the word parts, what is the meaning of **hypermiling**?

    a. Getting better miles per gallon through using excessive means

    b. Getting higher miles per gallon than average cars

c. Getting more distance on a trip by being hyper

d. All of the above

Now use context clues to find the meaning of ***hypermiling***.

"***Hypermiling*** sounds scary. And I don't want to add anything on to my car."

Why Your Excuses Are Lame: ***Hypermiling***—the strange driving practices that save gas, like driving on the lines in the rain or going into neutral on ramps—can be really unsafe. You don't have to try them to save gas, though; instead, take simple precautions like making sure your tires are blown up, taking off your roof rack to cut down on drag, and boosting your mileage by getting regular tune-ups.

Strange driving practices

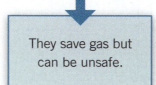

They save gas but can be unsafe.

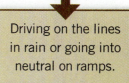

Driving on the lines in rain or going into neutral on ramps.

11. Based on the clues, what is the meaning of ***hypermiling***? getting super high mileage on your car

Use word parts to find the meaning of ***telecommuting***.

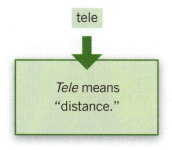

tele

Tele means "distance."

commute

Commute contains *com*, or "to be with other people."

ing

ing turns a word into a verb.

12. Based on the word parts, what is the meaning of ***telecommuting***? working from home

Now use context clues to find the meaning of ***telecommuting***.

Work from home. *Telecommuting* saves you money in gas and food and can make your day less stressful.

Excuses: "They need me in the office. How will I stay connected?"

Why Your Excuses Are Lame: There are so many ways to stay connected from home—ask your office about wiring your home for video conferencing. You don't have to work from home every day to see significant savings; even one or two days a week will save you hundreds of dollars over the year in gas and lunches.

13. Based on the clues, what is the meaning of *telecommuting*?
    working from home

Use word parts to find the meaning of *reusable*.

14. Based on the word parts, what is the meaning of *reusable*?
    able to use again

Use context clues to find the meaning of *reusable*.

Reuse what you can. Get *reusable* water bottles instead of buying bottled water. If you pack your or your kid's lunch, buy a lunch bag and use Tupperware instead of buying Ziploc and brown paper bags.

Excuses: "But it's convenient."

Why Your Excuses Are Lame: Why spend money continually on stuff you'll just throw away? Cut out plastic utensils, disposable water bottles, paper napkins, and brown bags. They may be just little expenses, but they're still wasteful ones when you can reuse so easily and cheaply.

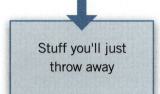

Get reusable water bottles instead of buying bottled water.

Stuff you'll just throw away

still wasteful ones when you can reuse so easily and cheaply

15. Based on the clues, what is the meaning of ***reusable***?

able to use again

Main Idea

16. What is the central thesis of the article? Answers will vary. Possible answer: Try these green tips to save some needed cash—no excuses.

Critical Thinking/Application

17. What can you do to go green and save cash?

Answers will vary.

Facts and Opinions

Complete the chart using the information from the article.

FACTS	OPINIONS
Answers will vary.	

Visual Image READING 5

In order to find facts in a picture, look at the details that you can prove.

When deciding the subjects' opinions, look at the emotions portrayed in the photograph.

Questions

1–6. State the FACTS and your OPINIONS about the photograph.

FACTS	OPINIONS
Answers will vary.	

7–8. Based on the information you determined above, what do you think is happening in the context of the photo?
Answers will vary.

Read a shortened version of an article related to the photograph:

"Be the Change You Want to See in the World"

Blake Mycoskie, founder and Chief Shoe Giver of TOMS Shoes, says that this Mahatma Ghandi quote is his favorite—and he even sells shoes that display those words.

Fascinating business: For every pair of shoes TOMS sells, it gives a pair to a needy child.

Mycoskie, 32, launched TOMS in May 2006 after visiting Argentina and seeing kids without shoes—and wanting to do something to help them. In just two and a half years, TOMS has given away more than 70,000 shoes in Argentina, South Africa and Ethiopia. ■

Source: Sellers, Patricia. (October 17, 2008). Be the Change You Want to See in the World. *The Huffington Post.*

9–10. Using the photograph **and** the text, describe the situation in the photograph.

Answers will vary.

_____

_____

Additional Recommended Reading

Breton, M. J. (1998). *Women Pioneers for the Environment.* Boston, MA: Northeastern University Press.

Easwaran, E.(1997). *Ghandi the Man: The Story of His Transformation.* Berkeley, CA: Nilgiri Press.

Ehrenreich, B. (2001). *Nickled and Dimed: On (not) Getting by in America.* New York, NY: Holt.

Heacox, K. (1996). *Visions of a Wild America: Pioneers of Preservation.* Washington, DC: National Geographic Society.

Kramer, M. (2006). *Dispossessed: Life in Our World's Urban Slums.* Maryknoll, NY: Orbis Books.

Mandela, N. (2006). *Nelson Mandela in His Own Words.* K. Asmal, D. Chidester, & W. James (Eds.). New York, NY: Little, Brown and Company.

Payne, R. K. (2005). *Understanding Poverty.* Highlands, TX: Aha! Process, Inc.

myreadinglab

For support in meeting this chapter's objectives, log on to www.myreadinglab.com and select Critical Thinking.

8 Inferences

THEME **Goal Setting and Achievement**

SPOTLIGHT ON LEARNING STYLES Do

Setting goals can be overwhelming if you've never done it. If you've lived day to day, week to week, and/or paycheck to paycheck, maybe you've never seriously thought about setting a longer term goal or planning for your future. So how do you realistically turn a dream into something that you might actually achieve? Do you ask yourself if it's really possible to turn that dream into a reality in *your* life? When I met my husband, he had a lot of passions, interests, and dreams. He was 39 years old, worked as a scientist in a genetics lab, and lived in an apartment. He told me he'd love to travel to a beach or to the mountains someday. He told me he dreamed of having a vineyard, an orchard, a big garden, and a house in the country. He also told me he loved to experience art, gourmet meals, a variety of live music, botanical gardens, and nature. Wow! What fun this would be! So, we set out on an adventure to make his dreams come true! Together we looked at each "dream" and turned them into achievable "goals." We turned our neighborhood corner backyard into a vegetable, flower, and wildlife garden/habitat and now we can/freeze/dry and donate produce beyond our dreams. We found low-priced online vacation specials and traveled to the Smoky Mountains, Rocky Mountains, Appalachian Mountains, Canadian Rockies, and the hills of Sedona and Phoenix, Arizona, and Austin, Texas. We snorkeled on the beaches in Cozumel and Florida and enjoyed the shores of Lake Michigan, and the coasts of California and Washington. Turning your dreams and passions into goals is a matter of setting up achievable steps to reach those goals. It may mean giving up the trips to the vending machine or the fast food restaurant for a year and saving the $3 per day or $20 per week for something bigger. Breaking a bigger goal into smaller achievable steps will work!

How to Find Inferences (What can you see between the lines?)

LO1
Find inferences.

Making an inference or drawing a conclusion is a skill you have been using all of your life, but you may not have known that was the name of what you were doing. How do you know when you are making an inference? Every day you encounter situations where you do not have all of the information or facts, but you must make decisions or choose what actions you will take based on what you do know. In these instances you may rely on your own judgment or experiences to fill in the missing information.

Imagine this scenario: You come home from school and see a clock flashing 12:00 (and it is not 12:00). What would you guess happened? Check the answer that most likely explains the situation.

_____ **1.** The cat unplugged the radio.

_____ **2.** The electricity turned off temporarily while you were gone.

_____ **3.** Someone came into your house and reset the clock.

My guess would be answer 2: the electricity turned off temporarily while you were gone. Answers 1 and 3 would not be inferences because they are not likely causes, and there is no evidence to suggest it. Answer 1 is only likely if you have an extraordinary cat that pulls electrical cords out and puts them back into sockets. Answer 3 is also unlikely since resetting a clock would then display a specific time rather than a flashing 12:00. So, even though you do not know for sure that the electricity turned off, you can draw that conclusion using your experiences and knowledge of digital clocks, and you can safely eliminate the other two choices. This is *making an inference* based on the information given.

Making an inference when you read is also called *reading between the lines*. When you think about the situation presented, every detail may not be explained. It is up to you, the reader or listener, to figure out the missing information. Think of making inferences as if you are working as a detective or investigator. The best inferences will be based on some reasons, hints, or clues. Inferences are not random guesses, but rather judgment calls made from the existing evidence.

As you read and work through the material in Chapter 8 you will develop your ability to find inferences in written text. The theme of Chapter 8 is Goal Setting and Achievement. As you work on your goal of becoming a more proficient reader, you will read about people who have set and achieved their goals. You will also read material containing ideas you may consider implementing to help you achieve your goals in school and in life.

EXAMPLE

Directions: Read the passage below and write the author's inference in your own words.

"Habit, if not resisted, soon becomes necessity."—St. Augustine (A.D. 354–430)

St. Augustine is implying that one must not allow oneself to give in to a habit or else that behavior will soon seem necessary to one's life. You may infer a good habit or a bad habit, but the words "if not resisted" imply that the habit is something that wouldn't be good, perhaps like an addiction.

PRACTICE THE NEW SKILL

Directions: Read the passages below and write the inference for each in your own words.

1. "There is an eagle in me that wants to soar, and there is a hippopotamus in me that wants to wallow in the mud."—Carl Sandburg (1878–1967)

   Answers will vary.

2. "The further the soul advances, the greater are the *adversaries* against which it must contend."—Evagrius of Pontus (d. 399)

   Answers will vary.

3. "Oh, I can't drink these days. I'm allergic to alcohol and narcotics. If I use them, I break out in handcuffs."—Robert Downey, Jr.

   Answers will vary.

How to Separate Valid from Invalid Inferences
(Can the inference be supported?)

A valid inference is one that is supported by information in the passage. An invalid inference has no support in the passage. Think of it this way: If you were a detective, you would need some reason to follow your hunch—it would need to be based on something. So as you read a passage, look to the clues in the text to draw your conclusions. Remember, to be valid, an inference must be supported by something. If you are in doubt, try to underline the support for your inferences.

LO2
Separate valid from invalid inferences.

Adversaries—opponents, enemies, rivals

EXAMPLE

Directions: Read the passage below and write **V** for valid inferences and **I** for invalid inferences.

> Hoping to clear his (Obama's) own racial confusion, he would forgo doing homework and bury himself in the works of *prodigious* black authors who sought to explain or amplify the feelings of powerlessness and anger *embedded* in the hearts of black men: Langston Hughes, Ralph Ellison, James Baldwin, Richard Wright, W.E.B. Du Bois.
>
> *Source:* Mendell, David. (2007). *Obama: From Promise to Power.* New York, NY: Harper Collins, p. 44.

a. _____ As a teenager, Obama needed answers about the feelings of black men.

b. _____ Obama read many books as a teenager.

c. _____ All teens struggle with identity issues.

d. _____ Black teenagers would rather read books than do homework.

e. _____ Teens prefer to read books about people of their same race.

Statements (a) and (b) should be marked with a **V** since they are valid inferences. The passage states that Obama did not do his homework, but instead read books by black authors because he was confused about race. Statement (c) is not addressed in the passage since it does not discuss all teens; thus it is an invalid inference and should be marked with an **I**. Statement (d) is an invalid inference since the passage says nothing about all black teenagers, only Obama. Statement (e) is also invalid because it is a general statement that is not supported by the passage.

PRACTICE THE NEW SKILL

Directions: Read the following paragraphs and write **V** for valid inferences and **I** for invalid inferences.

Prodigious—exceptional, remarkable, extraordinary

Embedded—entrenched, implanted, set in

1. If I were to try to read, much less answer, all the attacks made on me, this shop might as well be closed for any other business. I do the very best I know how—the very best I can; and I mean to keep doing so until the end. If the end brings me out all right, what is said against me won't amount to anything. If the end brings me out wrong, ten angels swearing I was right would make no difference.

   Source: Wheeler, Joe. (2008). *Abraham Lincoln: A Man of Faith and Courage.* New York, NY: Howard Books, p. 21.

   a. _____I_____ Abraham Lincoln ran a shop.

   b. _____V_____ Lincoln believes he simply needs to always do the best he can.

   c. _____V_____ What people say against you won't matter if you come out right.

   d. _____V_____ If people say you were right, what they said won't matter if you were really wrong.

   e. _____V_____ It's not what people say, but what you do that matters.

2. In our struggle, if we are to bring about the kind of changes that will cause the world to stand up and take notice, we must be committed. There is so much work that needs to be done. Every home and neighborhood in this country needs to be a safe, warm, and healthy place—a place fit for human beings as citizens of the United States. It is a big job, but there is no one better to do it than those who live here. Goodness and change are possible in each and every American citizen. We could show the world how it should be done and how to do it with dignity.

   Source: Parks, Rosa, with Gregory J. Reed. (1994). *Quiet Strength: The Faith, the Hope, and the Heart of a Woman Who Changed a Nation.* Grand Rapids, MI: Zondervan Publishing House, p. 44.

   a. _____V_____ Parks believes every American citizen has the potential to be good.

   b. _____I_____ Parks believes that only some Americans can change.

   c. _____I_____ Parks believes the world should show Americans how to change.

It is commendable if a person bears up under the pain of unjust suffering because he or she is conscious of God.—1 Peter 2:19 NIV *(Rosa Parks, p. 35)*

d. ____I____ Parks believes every American has the right to own their own home.

e. ____V____ Parks believes that through suffering and struggle, we must work to bring about needed change.

3. It is difficult to imagine the impact of such *gargantuan* tragedy on any individual. But for an artistic giant such as O'Keeffe it must have been comparable to a sentence of death. For a lifetime, she had depended on those penetrating blue eyes. It was through them that she saw a world usually considered *mundane* as a wondrous, spectacular place of fun and fulfillment. O'Keeffe's world was a garden of brilliant colors and mysterious shadows and images previously unseen. It was through those razor-sharp eyes that she found beauty and order in subjects others were blind to.

Source: Looney, Ralph. (1995). *O'Keeffe and Me: A Treasured Friendship.*
Niwot, CO: University Press of Colorado, p. 49.

Gargantuan—huge, gigantic, enormous
Mundane—ordinary, dull, boring

a. ___I___ O'Keeffe was a gardener.

b. ___V___ O'Keeffe was an artist.

c. ___I___ When O'Keeffe started to lose her sight, it was mundane.

d. ___V___ O'Keeffe saw the world in a unique way.

e. ___V___ Losing her sight must have been a huge misfortune for O'Keeffe.

REVIEW WHAT YOU LEARNED

Directions: Read the following paragraphs and write **V** for valid inferences and **I** for invalid inferences.

From the mother of champion cyclist Lance Armstrong, this is an extraordinary story of the resilience of the human spirit and the remarkable effect of great parenting.

1   Lance Armstrong has dazzled the world with his six straight Tour de France championships, his winning personality, and his poignant victory over life-threatening cancer. Yet the adage that "behind every strong man there is a strong woman" has never been more true than in Lance's case. His mother, Linda Armstrong Kelly, is a force of nature whose determination, optimism, and sheer *joie de vivre* not only nurtured one of our era's greatest athletes but fueled her own transformation from a poverty-stricken teen in the Dallas projects to a powerful role model for mothers everywhere. This *luminous* memoir, written with humor and compassion, tells Linda's story of survival.

a. ___V___ Linda Armstrong was very supportive of her son Lance.

b. ___I___ Linda Armstrong was always strong and successful.

2   Pregnant at age seventeen, kicked out of her home, and mired in an abusive relationship, Linda was a perfect candidate for disaster. But armed with a fierce belief in herself as a work in progress, and *buoyed* by a tidal wave of love for her little boy, Linda *flouted* statistics and became

----

Joie de vivre—French term meaning joy of life

Luminous—brilliant

Buoyed—sustained, kept up

Flouted—defied, ignored

both a corner-office executive and a no-nonsense, empowering mom whose desire to excel was contagious. Her resolve to find "the diamond in the dumpster, the blessing in every bummer" set an extraordinary example for Lance—and will inspire everyday moms to dream big and make a difference.

a. _____V_____ Linda Armstrong's belief in herself as a work in progress helped her overcome her difficult circumstances.

b. _____V_____ Lance Armstrong learned to overcome adversity from his mother.

3   Funny, *resonant*, down-to-earth, and utterly unforgettable, *No Mountain High Enough* is exhilarating proof that sheer willpower can—and occasionally does—triumph over adversity.

a. _____I_____ Linda Armstrong's book is based on scientific research.

b. _____I_____ Lance Armstrong's mother was also a bicyclist.

> *Source:* Kelly, Linda Armstrong. (2005). *No Mountain High Enough: Raising Lance, Raising Me.* New York, NY: Broadway Books, book jacket.

4   "Eddie Haskell had a million chances," I said, and this might be the first time I heard a truly hard edge on my voice. "All he had to do was love us, and he blew it. He's not getting another chance to hurt us ever again. I don't want your son in our life anymore, Miss Mamie. And I'm sorry, but that means we can't be in yours either. I think it's best for everybody if we all just do our own thing and get on with it."

a. _____I_____ Eddie Haskell was loving toward Linda and the baby.

b. _____V_____ Linda thought it was best to get away from the abuser.

5   After a long time, she hugged her arms across the front of her and nodded tightly.

6   "Maybe," she whispered. "Maybe it is for the best."

7   "It is. It's for the best," I repeated as firmly as I could, when what I really wanted to do was throw my arms around her and beg her not to go.

8   "I know," she said, brushing the back of her hand across her cheek. "I do know that. But . . . it's just that . . ."

Resonant—meaningful, important, significant

9   She couldn't say any more, and she didn't have to. I didn't doubt how much she loved her grandbaby. It was hard for her to let go of him, and it was hard for me to let go of her. It was breaking both our hearts. But we each had to do what we thought was best for our own boy.

a. ___V___ It was difficult for Linda Armstrong to do what was best for herself and her baby.

b. ___I___ Miss Mamie did not love her grandchild.

Source: Kelly, Linda Armstrong. (2005). *No Mountain High Enough: Raising Lance, Raising Me.* New York, NY: Broadway Books, pp. 84–85.

REVIEW *WHAT YOU LEARNED*

Directions: Read the following paragraphs and write **V** for valid inferences and **I** for invalid inferences.

1. Amelia's (Earhart) next *foray* was so unusual, in the 1920s for an educated young woman, as to be almost strange. She began driving a sand and gravel truck. Noting that a building boom was turning outlying airfields into housing subdivisions, she decided money could be made hauling paving and building materials for the *burgeoning* market. Lloyd Royer, a young Midwesterner, a top-notch mechanic looking to get into his own business, was her partner in the enterprise. They bought a truck and proceeded to drum up business. The truck, a Moreland, was, since Amelia always bought the latest thing, state of the art. The Moreland Company, located in Burbank, was famous for producing the first trucks that ran on low-grade fuel and used more than a three-speed transmission; it gave a one-year guarantee. Amelia's friends were less than impressed. Several, in fact, dropped her. Whether or not she was "*ostracized* by the more *right-thinking* girls," as she claimed years later, there is no doubt that she was made to feel distinctly uncomfortable.

Source: Butler, Susan. (1997). *East to the Dawn: The Life of Amelia Earhart.* Reading, MA: Addison-Wesley Longman, p. 111.

Foray—venture
Burgeoning—growing, rapidly increasing
Ostracized—disliked, not accepted, detested, out of favor
Right-thinking—conservative

a. ___V___ Amelia Earhart did not impress her friends with her new business.

b. ___I___ A growth in housing subdivisions meant sand and gravel trucks would not be needed.

c. ___V___ Amelia Earhart bought the latest technology.

d. ___I___ Amelia Earhart was concerned by her friends' reactions to her business.

e. ___I___ Earhart started a truck driving business on her own.

2. When Margaret Spellings was searching for wisdom to share with newly *minted* college graduates, she didn't turn to classic works of philosophy or modern self-help books. She found advice on her morning cup of coffee. "In thinking on what advice to offer as you embrace this next stage in your lives," the secretary of education told the graduating class of Golden Gate University in San Francisco on May 6, "I looked for inspiration from something every single one of us has needed or will need at some point to get through life . . . Starbucks."

a. ___I___ Spellings found inspiration for her speech at the library.

b. ___V___ Spellings thinks everyone needs or will need coffee to get through life.

3–5. What can you infer from the coffee cup advice? Write your own interpretation of each quote.

> Holding up a cup from the *ubiquitous* beverage shop, Ms. Spellings proceeded to elaborate on the common-sense tips that appear on the chain's recognizable white cardboard cup.
>
> No. 204 says: "Remember your dreams and fight for them. There is just one thing that makes your dream become impossible: the fear of failure." Answers will vary. _____

_____

_____

> Ms. Spellings pointed to the story of Oprah Winfrey, who considered her years-ago transfer from a TV anchor desk to a talk show a demotion.

Minted—made

Ubiquitous—ever-present, everywhere, omnipresent

Ms. Winfrey has turned her syndicated show into an unrivaled success and is now worth $1.5 billion, according to *Forbes* magazine.

"If you can remain open to what life throws your way, roll with the punches, and stay focused and sure of who you are, then success can be found in the most unlikely places," the secretary told the graduating class at Golden Gate, which was composed of working adults. It was her only scheduled commencement address this year. Answers will vary.

_____

_____

In her conclusion, Ms. Spellings pointed to Starbucks' tip No. 209: ". . .The only things we do in this world that count are those things that make the world a better place for those who come behind us."
Answers will vary.

_____

_____

"Education is a great place to serve," said Ms. Spellings. "Everyone can be engaged in its improvement, as a parent, as a volunteer, as an employer. And I hope it's an area where you'll invest your time and talents."

Source: Hoff, D. (2007, May 16). *Federal File. Education Week, 26*(37). Retrieved from Academic Search Premier database.

/ **MASTER** *THE LESSON* /

Inference

Directions: Read the following paragraphs and write **V** for valid inferences and **I** for invalid inferences.

Managing Ethically
There's No Such Thing as a Free Burger

1.   Coca-Cola Co. made the news after auditors discovered some irregular actions two managers took in pursuit of their goals. Evidently the managers very much wanted a test market of a promotion to deliver positive results.

   <u> V </u> Auditors for Burger King discovered something newsworthy.

2.   Coca-Cola wanted Burger King to do a national promotion with Frozen Coke, a slushy-type drink Coca-Cola hoped would yield millions in additional revenues. Before doing a national promotion, however, Burger King wanted to test market the promotion in Richmond, Virginia. The deal was this: When customers purchased a Value Meal during a certain two-week period, they were given a coupon for a free Frozen Coke. Whether or not Burger King would go ahead with the national promotion hinged on how many Value Meals were sold and how many Frozen Coke coupons were redeemed.

   <u> I </u> The results of the test market did not matter to Coca-Cola.

3.   After the first week, things did not look good for Frozen Coke. Despite all of Coca-Cola's effort to push the promotion, the numbers were bad, and Burger King managers were disappointed. In an effort to save the promotion, two midlevel managers at Coke then crossed the line into ethically questionable territory. Evidently, they paid a consultant $9,000 to distribute cash to Boys and Girls Clubs and other not-for-profit organizations in Richmond to be used to purchase Value Meals at Richmond Burger Kings. The administrators of the organizations were not aware of the motivation underlying the "free" Value Meals, and it is not clear that the consultant knew all that was going on either. However, what is clear is that any efforts to attain goals must be, first and foremost, defensible on ethical grounds.

   <u> V </u> Two managers for Coca-Cola Co. threw the results of the test market.

Source: George, Jennifer M. and Gareth R. Jones. (2005). *Understanding and Managing Organizational Behavior*, 4th ed. Upper Saddle River, NJ: Pearson, p. 225.

Aboard the SS Manhattan: July 1936

4.   The night before *embarking* for Berlin, Jesse Owens found himself seated next to George Herman Ruth at a banquet honoring the American Olympic team.

___V___ Owens and Ruth were seated together at a banquet.

5.   "You gonna win at the Olympics, Jesse?" Ruth asked, slicing through his sirloin.

___I___ Ruth was going to compete in the Olympics.

6.   "Gonna try," Owens replied. He was nervous on two counts. Naturally, he was awed by the Babe, but additionally, watching the *gargantuan* Ruth eat, he was praying that nothing would be spilled on his rented tuxedo. It was obvious that coaching first base for the Dodgers was not a position that required physical fitness or table manners.

___V___ Babe Ruth did not have good table manners.

7.   "Trying doesn't mean s—t," Ruth said with a grin. "Everybody tries. I succeed. Wanna know why?"

___I___ Babe Ruth was humble.

8.   Owens could only *muster* a nod.

___V___ Owens wasn't sure how to respond to Ruth's remarks.

9.   "I hit sixty home runs a few years back because I *know* I'm going to hit a home run just about every time I swing that frigging bat," Ruth said. In his first season of retirement, he could not quite bring himself to speak of his playing career in the past tense. Swallowing and continuing, he said, "I'm surprised when I *don't*! And that isn't all there is to it. Because I know it, the pitchers, *they* know it too. They're pretty sure I'm going to hit a homer every time."

___V___ Ruth was confident in his baseball talent.

10.   Owens was duly impressed. Ruth was right. Confidence matters and when he boarded the SS Manhattan the following day, bound for Germany, he had never felt quite so confident.

___I___ Owens wasn't sure of his own ability as an athlete.

Source: Schaap, Jeremy. (2007). *Triumph: The Untold Story of Jesse Owens and Hitler's Olympics.* Boston, MA: Houghton Mifflin, pp. 142–143.

Embarking—going on board (as on a cruise ship)
Gargantuan—huge
Muster—gather

MASTER THE LESSON

Inference

Directions: Read the following paragraphs and write **V** for valid inferences and **I** for invalid inferences.

Longitude

1.   Anyone alive in the eighteenth century would have known that "the longitude problem" was the thorniest scientific dilemma of the day—and had been for centuries. Lacking the ability to measure their longitude, sailors throughout the great ages of exploration had been literally lost at sea as soon as they lost sight of land. Thousands of lives, and the increasing fortunes of nations, hung on a *resolution*.

   ___V___ Measuring longitude was a critical problem in the 18th century.

2.   The quest for a solution had occupied scientists and their patrons for the better part of two centuries when, in 1714, England's Parliament *upped the ante* by offering a king's ransom (20,000 pounds, or approximately $12 million in today's currency) to anyone whose method or device proved successful. Countless *quacks* weighed in with *preposterous* suggestions. The scientific establishment throughout Europe—from Galileo to Sir Isaac Newton—had mapped the heavens in both hemispheres in its certain pursuit of a *celestial* answer. In stark contrast, one man, John Harrison, dared to imagine a mechanical solution—a clock that would keep precise time at sea, something no clock had ever been able to do on land.

   ___I___ The longitude problem was not as important to England's king as it was to sailors.

3.   *Longitude* is a dramatic human story of an epic scientific quest, and of Harrison's forty-year obsession with building his perfect timekeeper, known today as the chronometer. Full of heroism and *chicanery*, brilliance and the

---

Resolution—solution, answer, outcome
Upped the ante—increased the gamble or stake
Quacks—imposters, fakes, con artists, pretenders
Preposterous—ridiculous, outrageous, unbelievable
Celestial—space or outer space
Chicanery—deception by trickery

absurd, it is also a fascinating brief history of astronomy, navigation, and clockmaking. Through Dava Sobel's *consummate* skill, *Longitude* will open a new window on our world for all who read it.

_____V_____ Harrison spent many decades improving his invention, which ultimately changed navigation and timekeeping in the world.

Source: Sobel, Dava. (1995). *Longitude: The True Story of a Lone Genius Who Solved the Greatest Scientific Problem of His Time.* New York, NY: Walker and Company, book jacket.

4.   "Alfred Nobel, the inventor of dynamite, who died yesterday, devised a way for more people to be killed in a war than ever before. He died a very rich man." (Alfred Nobel read his own obituary in the local newspaper, at the end of the 19th century)

a. ____I____ Nobel read his obituary from the grave.

b. ____V____ There was an error in the newspaper.

c. ____I____ Nobel had a desire to help people kill one another efficiently.

d. ____V____ Nobel made much money from selling dynamite.

e. ____V____ Effective tools for war are big business.

Consummate—expert, supreme

5.   "Every man ought to have the chance to correct his epitaph in mid-stream and write a new one." (Nobel reacted to the obituary and created the Nobel Prize.)

a. ___V___ Nobel wanted to be known for something other than inventing a way for people to kill each other.

b. ___I___ People should be able to correct the inscription on their tombstones.

c. ___V___ People should be given the opportunity to change how they will be remembered.

d. ___V___ Awarding prizes to scientists and writers who help foster peace is how Nobel is now remembered.

e. ___I___ All inventors are eligible for the Nobel Prize.

Directions: Read the quotations below and write your own inferences.

6.   "Life is like riding a bicycle. To keep your balance you must keep moving."—Albert Einstein, in a letter to his son Eduard, February 5, 1930.
Answers will vary.

_____

_____

7.   "To advance confidently in the direction of one's dreams and to endeavor to live the life one imagines . . . is to meet with success."—Henry David Thoreau, *On Walden Pond*. Answers will vary.

_____

_____

8–10.   Find a quotation you especially like that will keep you motivated to achieve your goals. It may be something you have memorized or have read somewhere. Write it below and discuss the inferences. Answers will vary.

_____

_____

LEARNING STYLE ACTIVITIES

Look, Listen, Write, Do

As you read the poem below, think about the choices and life goals of the boys. What inferences can you make?

We Real Cool

The Pool Players
Seven At The Golden Shovel

We real cool. We
Left school. We

Lurk late. We
Strike straight. We

Sing sin. We
Thin gin. We

Jazz June. We
Die soon.

Gwendolyn Brooks (b. 1917)

Biography: Gwendolyn Brooks was a highly regarded, much-honored poet, with the distinction of being the first black author to win the Pulitzer Prize. She also was poetry consultant to the Library of Congress—the first black woman to hold that position—and poet laureate of the State of Illinois. Many of Brooks' works display a political consciousness, especially those from the 1960's and later, with several of her poems reflecting the civil rights activism of that period.

Source: Retrieved from Poetry Foundation Web site.

Commentary on "We Real Cool"

What is it that Brooks is trying to tell us about the seven pool players in the poem "We Real Cool"? It's clear that they are a group of young men who have dropped out of school, who spend their time in a pool hall until late at night. There is a vague sense of menace implied by her use of the word "lurk," and by the way they brag about how they "strike straight." But the structure that Brooks has chosen for the poem seems to imply that a palpable uncertainty underlies their cocky demeanor. If the reader pauses after each line-ending "We," a sense of their insecurity becomes apparent:

> We real cool. We
> Left school. We
>
> Lurk late. We
> Strike straight. We

Sing sin. We
Thin gin. We

Jazz June. We
Die soon.

Each use of "We" becomes a hesitation—a moment of uncertainty followed up by the boasting declaration on the following line. Brooks doesn't necessarily want us to think that the pool players are questioning their own validity. She doesn't seem to feel that these young men possess the degree of self-awareness necessary to question their own bravado. Instead, she leaves it to the reader to feel the uncertainty behind each of the short lines of the poem. The rhythm and pace of the poem itself is what ultimately leads the reader to sense the pool players' self-doubt. Though they may not question the choices they have made, Brooks seems to say we can feel pity for them because of the unspoken circumstances that have led them to make those tragic choices.

*L*OOK   Picture what the author saw as she looked in a poolroom. Draw the seven boys doing what the poet describes. Use some of her lines such as "real cool," "left school," "lurk late," "strike straight," "sing sin," "thin gin," "Jazz June," "die soon."

*L*ISTEN   Find a Web site on which the poet reads the poem. Also read the poem out loud, pausing after each "We" as the poet suggests. Read the poem musically and imitate the sound and rhythm the boys would have in their neighborhood. Put special emphasis not only on the "we" at the end of each line, but also on the words "real cool," "left school," "lurk late," "strike straight," "sing sin," "thin gin," "Jazz June," "die soon."

*W*RITE   Write what the author means by her words such as "real cool," "left school," "lurk late," "strike straight," "sing sin," "thin gin," "Jazz June," "die soon." Discuss why she only used two words to create an image in each line.

*D*o   Imagine being in the poolroom or actually go visit one. Compare your experience with the author's as she describes the boys. What do you imagine she meant when the boys said "We". . . "real cool," "left school," "lurk late," "strike straight," "sing sin," "thin gin," "Jazz June," "die soon."

Reading Practice

The following readings are related to the theme of Goal Setting and Achievement. The questions that follow each reading will help you improve your reading skills of learning vocabulary, locating main ideas and supporting details, recognizing the organizational patterns, separating facts from opinions, and finding inferences.

The first reading is *I Learned to Love Myself* from an Internet source, www.heifer.org, the Web site for a global humanitarian/agricultural service organization, Heifer International.

The second reading is from a textbook titled *The Community College Experience: Plus.* The subheading is titled *Being Realistic About Goals.*

The third reading is from a piece of literature titled *Of Beetles & Angels: A Boy's Remarkable Journey from a Refugee Camp to Harvard* by Mawi Asgedom.

The fourth reading is from *Contracting Business* magazine, titled, "Goal Setting Essential for Success."

The fifth reading is a visual image of *Determination.*

Internet

READING 1

I Learned to Love Myself . . .

1   Being a woman and an independent mother means having a life with many responsibilities and few opportunities, especially in the Andes. Farming and raising livestock, often without technical know-how, do not provide families with an adequate standard of living, especially families headed by single women.

2   Nevertheless, some opportunities can turn men's and women's lives around. That happened to Victoria Medrano Campos, a 48-year-old farm woman who was born and raised in the community of San Pedro de Pillao in the Pasco Region in central Peru. Her words and deeds show that she is a wise, responsible woman who is appreciated by the other members of her community because of the good example she sets.

3   "Farming is hard work and there is little profit, but thanks be to God, Heifer came with a plan that changed my life," Victoria says enthusiastically.

4   Victoria, who has three daughters, saw the project, "Capacity Building and Food Sovereignty in Farming Communities in Pasco" implemented by Heifer Peru and Separ, as a valuable opportunity to learn more about caring for her animals and making better use of her land. She and other members of her community began participating in the project in April 2008.

5   "Since I decided to participate in this project, I have taken it very seriously and I haven't missed a single workshop. Because of the great effort I made, they sent me to Cusco to share my knowledge with people from different parts of southern Peru. We all shared our experiences."

6   The personal development workshops helped Victoria recognize and value her skills and talents. She also learned to love her neighbors and to treat her animals differently.

7   "I am very grateful, and I wish Heifer and Separ would never leave. As a single mother, I thought I had little chance of getting ahead, but they made me understand that wasn't true."

8   Before participating in the project, she did not care for her animals appropriately and did not take the greatest advantage of her land or the natural fertilizer her animals provided. With training, she and other community members learned to keep their animals clean and healthy, give them medication and feed them with good fodder. This was taught in introductory workshops before the farmers became participants and received sheep.

9 "Now I talk to my animals. I ask them if they're hungry. My sheep love me, and as soon as they hear me come home, they start crying so I'll go see them."

10 Victoria is a courageous woman who has shown she is able to support her family. Because of her knowledge, and with the support of other farmers in her community, she was chosen to be trained as a local outreach worker. She has finished the training and has begun to share what she has learned. She says she wants to share her knowledge with as many people as possible, so they can also practice the techniques that helped her change her life.

11 She is very proud, because her family is among those who have the first lambs. Five have been born and are ready to be shared with other farmers in her community.

12 "I am sure I will do much better as the years go by. I am happy to have shown that I can accomplish the things I set out to do." Victoria's experience gives us strength and courage. ■

Source: Heifer International Web site: Our Work, Success Stories,
North and South America, *I learned to love myself.*

Main Idea

1. What is the central thesis of the article?
   Answers will vary. One possible answer is: One woman's life changed
   when she learned better farming techniques.

2. What is the main idea of paragraph 1?
   It is difficult to support your family as an independent mother with
   limited technical skills, especially in the Andes.

Supporting Details

3. What opportunities turned one person's life around in the Andes?
   Answers will vary. One possible answer may include—Heifer International
   offered classes in agriculture to teach better sustainable farming techniques.

4. How did Victoria's experiences enable her to give back to her community?

According to paragraph 10 she was chosen by her community

to be an outreach worker.

Patterns of Organization

5. Overall, what organizational pattern is used within the article?

Time order

6. What signal words indicate the overall organizational pattern?

Since, Before, Now, As soon as, Finished, Begun, First, As the years

go by, etc.

Facts and Opinions

List 3 facts and 3 opinions from the article.

Facts: Answers will vary.

7. _____

8. _____

9. _____

Opinions: Answers will vary.

10. _____

11. _____

12. _____

Inferences

13. Write **V** for a valid inference or **I** for an invalid inference.

    ___I___ Victoria is a single parent because her husband died.

14. Write **V** for a valid inference or **I** for an invalid inference.

    ___V___ Victoria is hopeful now that the future will continue to get better.

15. Explain the steps Victoria took from struggling as a single parent to being an active community leader. Answers will vary. _____

    _____

    _____

    _____

    _____

    _____

    _____

    _____

    _____

Textbook **READING 2**

Being Realistic About Goals

1   Some of us set goals that sound great on paper, goals we sincerely want to achieve, but we don't always consider the whole picture. We get excited about the end result, but we don't consider the challenges we will have to overcome to reach a goal. A world-class athlete who dreams of a gold medal around his neck also

envisions the countless practices, the changes in his lifestyle, which may restrict his other interests and time spent hanging out with friends and family. He may also have to travel extensively, which will leave him little time at home. He may have to sacrifice an enormous amount of time, effort, and other personal interests to reach his goal of athletic glory without changing his priorities, without monitoring his goals closely, and without pushing himself to his limit, both physically and mentally. Eating chocolate bars on the couch every day does not contribute to an athlete's goals.

2   Although you won't be asked to put your body through the paces a world class athlete does to train for an event, you will have to be realistic about your expectations as you work toward a certificate or degree. The following is an extreme example of a student with a realistic goal but unrealistic expectations.

- *Student A's goal:* I want to get a degree in psychology and become a high-school counselor.

- *Student A's expectations:* I don't like to read anything that doesn't interest me, so I skip any chapters in my textbooks that are boring. I don't like to write and I am not familiar with the library, so I will avoid any professor who assigns a research paper. I don't have a lot of time to devote to studying, so I am going to take classes that are easy and require very little outside work.

> **Question 1: Do you think Student A will successfully reach her goal if she maintains these expectations?** Answers will vary.
> _____

3   Although Student A demonstrates excessively unrealistic expectations, it is worth noting that we all have moments when we do not consider all the hard work required and possible challenges when faced with a large goal. Sometimes we get so excited about the end result we forget to think about what it takes to get there.

> **Question 2: What can Student A do to change her expectations and reach her goal?** Answers will vary.
> _____
> _____

> **Question 3: What can you do if you feel you have unrealistic expectations?** Answers will vary.
> _____
> _____

4   The following is a checklist to keep your expectations realistic and keep you on track.

- Visualize, write down, or talk through the possible steps to achieving your goal, including those that may be unpleasant (e.g., staying up late to finish a paper, saying "no" to social activities because you need to study).

- Acknowledge that there may be **unforeseen** obstacles that will stand between you and your goal.

- Determine a plan of action if you encounter an obstacle to your goal.

- Enlist the help of friends and family as backup support as you work toward your goal.

- Talk to an advisor or professor if you feel your expectations are not realistic or if you have any difficulty reaching your educational goals.

As these steps suggest, a little planning and a review of your expectations will help you set realistic goals you can **attain**. ◼

Source: Baldwin, Amy. (2007). *The Community College Experience: Plus.*
Upper Saddle River, NY: Pearson, pp. 43–44.

Vocabulary

4. Define **envisions** (paragraph 1).

   a. wants   **c. predicts**

   b. despises   **d.** all of the above

5. Define **unforeseen** (paragraph 4).

   a. unexpected   **c.** predictable

   b. horrible   **d.** hoped for

6. Define **attain** (paragraph 4).

   a. avoid   **c.** predict

   b. buy   **d. achieve**

Main Idea

7. What is the main idea of paragraph 1? People need to consider what it will take to achieve the goals they set for themselves.

8. What is the main idea of paragraph 3? We all have moments when we get excited about our goals but forget the hard work it will take to achieve them.

Patterns of Organization

9. What is the primary pattern of organization used in paragraph 1? What were your clues? Example. The clues were the details about the world-class athlete who envisions winning a gold medal. The paragraph contains several examples of things he considers and does to reach his goals.

10. What is the primary pattern of organization used in paragraph 3? What were your clues? Comparison and contrast. The phrases: *although Student A . . . we all have moments when we don't consider . . .*

Literature

READING 3

930L

Of Beetles & Angels: A Boy's Remarkable Journey from a Refugee Camp to Harvard

EPILOGUE: OF SNAKES, BUTTERFLIES, AND SMALL ACTS OF KINDNESS

I delivered the commencement address at my graduation from Harvard in 1999. This is the text of my speech.

1   When I was a child, my mother told me that I should always sleep with the covers over my head. At the time, my family was living in a Sudanese refugee camp, in Africa, and we owned nothing that we did not carry with us. On many a night, we slept out in the open, and my mother warned that if we let the covers down, snakes could slip in and slither into our mouths. We had no trouble following her advice.

2   Years later, in the comfort of the United States, my mother gave me another piece of advice, this one less obvious. "Always remember where you came from," she told me just before I left for Harvard. I was puzzled. The first piece of advice had been easy. Who wants a mouth full of snake! But why was it important to remember where I came from?

3   When I moved on to Harvard and saw new worlds open before me, I quickly forgot about trying to understand my mother. Before I knew it, I was signed up for the Tae Kwon Do Club, the Harvard African Students' Association, A Phillips Brooks House Program, the Freshman Crew Team (where I totaled a $15,000 boat against a dock), and a Freshman Bible Study (I figured I needed all the prayer that I could get). And, of course, I was taking four classes and trying to meet as many of my 1,600 classmates as wanted to meet me. As I focused my energies on myself and my immediate surroundings, remembering where I had come from seemed far less important than knowing where I was supposed to be every half hour.

4   During my sophomore year, however, something happened to remind me of my mother's advice. I was working as a delivery man for the Harvard Student Agency. One day as I was waiting for my packages in the office, an elderly black woman **tottered** in and wearily leaned on her cane. She hoped to find someone who would type a short letter for her. Such a simple, easy thing to do. But HSA has no typing service, and the receptionist had to tell her that she had come to the wrong place. As the old woman turned to leave, frustrated and confused, one of my coworkers called her over, gently sat her down, and typed the letter. It was such a simple act. Yet never has a Harvard student seemed so great to me as in that moment of reaching out.

5   I began to reflect on what my mother might have meant. In the Sudan, we had carried with us all that we owned, but that included our devotion to one another. In that sense we carried a home, a community, a sense of mutual responsibility wherever we went. On that day in the Harvard Student Agency, my coworker carried a community with her as well: the simple community of human connection and duty.

6   So what have I learned from my four years at Harvard? Many facts and formulas, many new ways of thinking, a fresh understanding of the world. But what's most important to me is that after four years at Harvard I'm finally beginning to understand my mother's advice.

7   Remembering where you come from means holding on to the vision that you are a part of a human community that you can carry with you every day. That community has given us much. Are we not obligated to give it something back?

8   My mother's advice in childhood was to pull the covers over my head—that had been the easy part. But her later advice meant, I now realize, that I should know when to pull the covers down and stick my neck out. That's the hard part. Too many of us go through life with covers over our heads. We want to reach out, but we fear to make ourselves vulnerable. And we are also busy. We have appointments to keep; we have things to do. We race through a world of demands. And then we ask ourselves almost helplessly, "What can we do as individuals?"

9   Some people say that a butterfly flapping its wings in Japan can cause a hurricane in Louisiana. Any one of us, however small and helpless we may feel, can spark unimagined changes. Today's small act of kindness can become tomorrow's whirlwind of human progress.

10   But as you all know, progress is not easy, and it will not come **unsolicited.** I hope that many of us will inspire positive change. There is still so much to be done both in distant lands such as the Sudan, and closer to home in our own communities. The big, sweeping, revolutionary actions are always most noticeable. But quite often, it will be the small things that all of us can do that will have the most impact. Yes, we will be busy in our lives. But we can all take a little time to do a little deed of kindness. We can help write a letter; we can inscribe a little goodness on the hard surface of this world.

11   In a few minutes we shall be welcomed to the ranks of educated men and women. As we start the journey to wherever our dreams may lead, we must remember where we have come from. We must recall our membership in the human community that has nourished us; we must accept the responsibility to keep that community alive. Improving the quality of life for the entire human community is the single greatest task that faces our generation and generations to come. Of course, no worthy **endeavor** is without risks and pitfalls—without snakes, if you will—but I know that you, my classmates, are ready to peek out, to see beyond yourselves, and cast off the covers. You are ready to face the snakes and drive them away. You are ready to change the world. Thank you! Good luck! And congratulations! ■

Source: Asgedom, Mawi. (2002). *Of Beetles & Angels: A Boy's Remarkable Journey from a Refugee Camp to Harvard.* Boston, MA: Little, Brown and Company, pp. 135–138.

Vocabulary

Directions: Choose the best definition for each word as used in the reading.

1. tottered (paragraph 4)

  a. ran

  c. wobbled

  b. skipped

  d. fell

2. unsolicited (paragraph 10)

  a. unwelcome

  c. sold

  b. welcome

  d. unsold

3. endeavor (paragraph 11)

    a. adventure   c. consequence

    (b. attempt)   d. experiment

Main Idea

4. What is the main point or thesis of the passage?

It is important to remember where you came from and to use your

experiences to better the world.

Supporting Details

5. The author was giving a commencement speech for which college?

    a. Sudan University   c. Japan Institute

    (b. Harvard University)   d. University of Louisiana

6. What "little deed of kindness" does the author suggest we can do in our busy day?

    a. smile at a stranger   c. write a letter

    b. open the door for someone   (d. all of the above)

Patterns of Organization

7. What is the organizational pattern in paragraph 9?

    a. example   (c. cause and effect)

    b. simple listing   d. compare and contrast

8. In paragraph 8, the author is comparing what two pieces of advice?

His mother's advice: (1) pull the covers over your head and (2) know when

to pull the covers down and stick your neck out (take a risk, make yourself

vulnerable to reach out and help someone).

Facts and Opinions

9. Complete the chart using some of the facts and opinions from the reading.

FACTS	OPINIONS
Answers will vary.	

Inferences

10. Would you infer from the reading that the author has led a successful life? Why or why not? Answers will vary. Students may say yes because he has moved from owning nothing and living in a refugee camp to graduating from Harvard, a prestigious university, and at the top of his class.

Magazine/Periodical
READING 4

1050L   ## Goal Setting Essential for Success

ABSTRACT (SUMMARY)

1   There's a story about a World War II German U-boat that contacted headquarters to inform them that they were lost. When asked by headquarters as to where they wanted to go, the U-boat responded, "We don't know." Headquarters replied, "Then you're not lost!"

2   If you're not getting anywhere in life, maybe it's because you've got nowhere to go!

3   Before you can get what you want out of life and your career, you have to decide what it is that you actually want.

4   I'm not crazy about the term "goal setting," because it's a motivational speaker's term, which can translate to artificially and **superficially** psyching people

up, but not really providing any practical, substantial advice they can use to improve their life.

HOW TO SET GOALS

5   Lao-tzu said, "A journey of a thousand miles begins with a single step."

6   I'll take the 2,112,000 steps further and say that a journey of a thousand miles requires that you concentrate on making each and every step the right one to take you to where you want to be.

7   Unless you're really into taking the "scenic route to success," the most efficient way to get where you want to go is to plan it out.

8   While it's necessary to step back and take a look at the big picture, you're not going to achieve your goals until you devise a believable and workable plan.

9   The way to get anything done is to decide on the ultimate achievement, then break it down into smaller increments, like this:

- Lifetime or ultimate goal
- Five-year goal
- One-year goal
- 12 monthly goals
- Four weekly goals
- Daily goals
- Hourly goals

Some hourly goals can and should be broken down into smaller, 15 minute tasks.

10   At this point, you see that we can substitute the word "goal" with "plan"; so, "goal setting" is not really a "motivational speaker" term—it's nothing more than planning . . . and planning is huge!

11   Notice also that, when you plan it all out, some very **vague** sounding goal, such as, "I want to be able to retire comfortably at the age of 65," transforms into a plan consisting of a series of small, doable steps, such as saving an average of $6 per hour, per 40-hour work week, and scheduling a weekly deposit of $240 into a savings account. Do that, stay out of debt, pay off your house, and you'll have a very comfortable retirement.

SCHEDULING YOUR SUCCESS

12   Until a goal is scheduled, it's just some vague notion of something you would "like to see happen."

13   Once you've broken your larger goals into smaller, 15 to 60 minute tasks, schedule them in your daily planner.

14   I call this step "scheduling your success." You don't hope that someday you'll become successful, you schedule it in.

15   Your goals don't always have to be financial. People say they want to spend more time with their children, their hobbies, or their religion. Have they scheduled it in?

16   Start using a daily planner and scheduling your activities, and you'll find out how many hours there are in a day, and just what you can and cannot do. You start prioritizing things differently.

17   If you really want to hold your own feet to the fire and make yourself miserable, start scheduling in advance—in writing—your television-watching schedule.

18   If you want to cut down on your alcohol consumption, schedule in what you're going to drink and when, days and weeks in advance. You'll find deliberately scheduling your alcoholism to be a sobering experience.

19   In order for goals to work, they must be time-specific.

20   When I entered sales back in 1972, I had what I thought was a bona-fide goal to pay cash for a brand new Cadillac. By mid-1998, I realized that the problem with my "goal" was that it had no schedule. A goal is not a real goal until it's planned out and scheduled. I wrote out a plan, and by the end of 1999, I had the money for the Cadillac.

21   For the record, I never bought the car. That's one reason why I say you'll spend your money more wisely if you make it a personal policy to stay out of debt and only pay cash for everything but your house. There was no way I was going to blow more than 27 years worth of savings on a car! I took the money and put a down payment on my current home.

THE KEY IS COMMITMENT

22   Another point about goal setting is your attitude toward your goals. Are your goals something you would like to happen? Are your goals a guideline? Or, are they mandatory?

23   In order for goals to work, they must be mandatory.

24   In 1987, I decided I wanted to make one sale per day, six days per week. In order to force myself to succeed, I also decided that I would not eat on any given day until I made a sale. Here's where it gets complicated. I was given a total of 157 leads that year. I closed 143 of them.

25   Now the question is, did I go hungry most of the time? The answer is no!

26   That was the year I started driving through working-class neighborhoods. I was looking for homes that had two things: an air conditioner in the window and a late-model car in the driveway. The window air conditioner told me they needed central air. The newer car told me they had a credit rating.

27   Why, in this day and age, would anyone not have central air conditioning? Is it because they don't know they can get it with no down payment and very

affordable monthly payments? Is it possible they still think that central air conditioning is a "rich man's game"?

28   The only way to find out was to knock on the door and ask.

29   How many doors do you think I had to knock on to make a sale? Let me put it this way, I was usually eating breakfast by 10 a.m. and never went hungry.

30   The point of the story is that a serious, inner commitment is required to hit your goals.

ACHIEVING SUCCESS

31   Success does not happen by accident. Success happens on purpose. Success is not a matter of luck or good timing. Success is a result of planning, followed by deliberate right action.

32   Set career, financial, and personal goals.

33   Plan your work, then work your plan.

34   Everyone knows you should set goals. However, it's like exercise. Everyone knows you should, but only 8% of the population do it.

35   People who set **mandatory**, time-specific goals, and schedule them into a daily planner, tend to hit them much sooner than they'd planned.

STAYING MOTIVATED

36   Goal setting is the answer to the age old question of, "How do you stay motivated?"

37   When you've got long-range goals, you're no longer working, per se. Every day, you're consciously and intentionally taking one step closer to achieving your ultimate career goal, which is a very nice feeling.

38   Do you know why they pave the roads? It's so you can't see the rut you're driving yourself into.

39   Set some goals and make certain you take one step towards achieving them every day, and you'll start having a good reason to get up and go to work in the morning, because you'll be making progress. You'll drive yourself right out of that rut and actually get somewhere every day.

40   You might think you're working for someone else, but you're not. One way or another, you're working for yourself.

41   You're not in a dead-end, low paying job. You've got a good job, and it can be better. It starts with planning the steps to your own success, scheduling them, then taking them. ■

Source: Greer, Charlie. (2007, October). *Goal Setting Essential for Success. Contracting Business, 64*(10), pp. 105–107. Retrieved from Career and Technical Education database.

Vocabulary

Directions: Use your knowledge of word parts and context clues to choose the correct meaning of the word.

1. superficially (paragraph 4)

   a. in depth   **c.** greatly

   (**b.** on the surface)   **d.** efficiently

2. vague (paragraph 11)

   a. clear   **c.** difficult

   (**b.** imprecise)   **d.** easy

3. mandatory (paragraph 35)

   a. optional   **c.** discretionary

   b. fixed   (**d.** required)

Main Ideas

4. What is the main idea of paragraph 20?

To reach a goal you must figure out the steps to achieve it.

5. What is the overall main idea or central theme of the article?

The only way to reach your goals and be successful is to know the steps and outline the plans to reach your goals.

Supporting Details

6. True or false?

_____F_____ The author suggests that hoping you'll be successful is the most important step.

Patterns of Organization

7–10. Create a mind-map or graphic organizer with the information in the article. *(Hint: use the subheadings as categories.)*

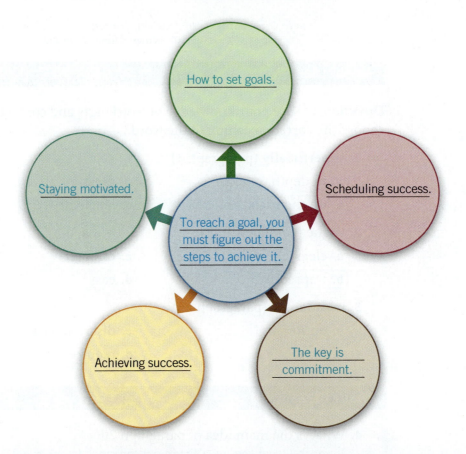

How to set goals.

Staying motivated.

To reach a goal, you must figure out the steps to achieve it.

Scheduling success.

Achieving success.

The key is commitment.

Facts and Opinions

11. Fact or opinion? (paragraph 34)

_____O_____ Everyone knows you should set goals.

Inferences

12. Explain this quote from paragraph 5: "A journey of a thousand miles begins with a single step."

Answers will vary. Even the biggest goals start with taking the first step and

doing just one thing.

13. What does the author mean by "scenic route to success," in paragraph 7?

Answers will vary. The scenic route refers to taking your time and not being

concerned about how long it takes to reach your goal.

14. Is the following a valid (**V**) or an invalid (**I**) inference? (paragraphs 17 and 18)

_____I_____ Scheduling your television watching time or your alcohol consumption won't have much effect on changing your habits.

15. In paragraph 26, why did the author drive through working class neighborhoods looking for homes with a late-model car in the driveway and window air conditioner?

"The window air conditioner told me they needed central air. The newer car

told me they had a credit rating." The author knew he could potentially get

business from these families.

Visual Image   **READING 5**

Directions: Use the picture to answer the questions.

1. What do the umbrella and backpack tell you about the person in the picture? You can infer from the backpack that the person is a student, perhaps walking to school or home from school. Carrying the umbrella shows the person is prepared for the heavy snow.

2. What can you infer about the weather conditions? The trees have several inches of snow, which indicates there is a great deal of snow on the ground. It also looks like it is currently snowing based on the white flakes in the photo against the person's jeans and jacket.

3. What can you infer the person in the picture is trying to do? Based on the person's backpack and small size, it looks like this is a school-age child walking to school or home from school during a snowstorm. Also, it looks like the person is walking on a path so it is probably a common walk to or from school.

4. How is the person in the picture demonstrating determination?

This individual is demonstrating determination to walk to or from school despite the weather conditions.

5. Discuss a time in your life where you exhibited determination.

Answers will vary.

Additional Recommended Readings

Allen, J. (2008). *As a Man Thinketh: From Poverty to Power.* New York, NY: Penguin Group.

Drachman, V. G. (2002). *Enterprising Women: 250 Years of American Business.* Chapel Hill, NC: University of North Carolina Press.

Dungy, T. (2007). *Quiet Strength.* New York, NY: Tyndale House.

Goodall, J. with P. Berman. (1999). *Reason for Hope: A Spiritual Journey.* New York, NY: Warner Books.

Herrmann, D. (1998). *Helen Keller: A Life.* New York, NY: Alfred A. Knopf.

Isaacson, W. (2007). *Einstein: His Life and His Universe.* New York, NY: Simon & Schuster.

Mandela, N. (2003). *In His Own Words.* Boston, MA: Little, Brown and Company.

Perry, J. (1999). *Unshakable Faith: Booker T. Washington & George Washington Carver.* Sisters, OR: Multnomah Publishers.

Stross, R. (2007). *The Wizard of Menlo Park: How Thomas Alva Edison Invented the Modern World.* New York, NY: Crown Publishers.

Tolle, E. (2005). *A New Earth: Awakening to Your Life's Purpose.* New York, NY: Plume Penguin Group.

Young, J. S. and W. L. Simon. (2005). *iCon Steve Jobs: The Greatest Second Act in the History of Business.* Hoboken, NJ: Wiley.

myreadinglab

For support in meeting this chapter's objectives, log on to www.myreadinglab.com and select Inference.

9 Purpose and Tone

THEME Entertainment: Movies, Music, Food, Sports, and Hobbies

SPOTLIGHT ON LEARNING STYLES 🔊 LISTEN 👁 LOOK

Have you ever listened to someone and realized that they didn't mean what they said? Maybe they were being sarcastic or trying to be funny. How could you tell what they really meant to say? Suppose you go out to the parking lot and there is a ticket on your friend's windshield. Your friend remarks, "That's great. That's all I needed." Does your friend really think that getting a ticket is great? Did she need a ticket? Usually when we hear the inflection in someone's voice, we have a better idea what he or she means. We use our listening learning style to help determine the tone. How do you let your friends know your tone when you send a text message, instant message, or e-mail? Years ago my sister-in-law kept writing "lol" at the end of her e-mail sentences. For months I kept wondering what she meant. Then another friend wrote this symbol :) at the end of some of his sentences. I finally asked my students what the letters and symbols meant. They told me "lol" meant

"laugh out loud" and :) was a smiley face. Since we were communicating different tones by writing, without the clues of changing voices or facial expressions, another method was needed. Think about all the different ways you communicate tone when you text or send an instant message. When my daughter, husband, and I added a text package to our cell phones, I had to learn a new language really fast. My daughter had lots of symbols to mean things I did not know, so I asked her to write a code page for me :). Authors do the same things with words. Getting to know which words create specific feelings may help you avoid confusion about tone when you read. It may also help to read material out loud or have someone else read to you. "Hearing" the author's tone can be aided by getting to know the intended emotions behind specific word choices. Like texting, this new way of looking at and listening to text will make reading more real.

To fully comprehend the material you read, it is crucial that you pay attention to the author's purpose and tone. If, for instance, you read material thinking it is serious and factual, but its real intention is to make fun of something, you will misinterpret the meaning.

Think about sending a text message or an e-mail, or using Myspace or Facebook. How do you let someone know your emotions, if you are angry or are trying to be funny? Jot down some ideas below. (*Hint:* lol, emoticons)

_____

_____

In this chapter, you will learn to determine the author's purpose and tone by paying attention to the specific word choices used in the text. The theme

"Entertainment" includes reading passages related to movies, music, food, sports, and hobbies. So have some fun while you work through this chapter.

Connotative and Denotative Words (Are emotions evoked?)

Since we cannot see facial expressions or other non-verbal cues when we read, we must rely on the author's word choices to understand if emotions are being expressed. The specific words used also enable us to detect if the emotions are positive or negative.

> **LO1**
> Identify connotative and denotative words.

A **denotation** is the straightforward definition of a word. It does not indicate a positive or negative emotion, so it would be considered neutral. Some examples of words with straightforward meanings (denotations) are:

House

Car

Restaurant

Collector

A **connotation** is a meaning that evokes an emotion. It is used in place of the neutral denotation when the author wants the reader to feel a certain positive or negative emotion.

- For example, if your friend says she is "happy," it evokes a basic emotion of joy.
- But if your friend says she is "all right," you might think she is not as happy as she could be.
- On the other hand, if she says she is "stoked," you know she is really, really happy!

Read the example below and try to determine the positive and negative connotations.

EXAMPLE

Directions: Read the words below. Circle the + if the word sounds positive, and circle the − if the word sounds negative.

Denotation	Connotation	Connotation
House	shack + −	mansion + −

In the example above, a *house* is a neutral word. The reader may imagine many different images when she reads the word *house,* but it basically refers to a place where one dwells or resides. When the word *shack* is used, it represents a very small, possibly run-down dwelling, so it has a negative connotation and the – should be circled. Conversely, the word *mansion* refers to a very large dwelling, possibly owned by someone rich and famous; it has a positive connotation and the + should be circled.

PRACTICE THE NEW SKILL

Directions: Read the words below. Circle the + if the word sounds positive and circle the – if the word sounds negative.

1. car ride ⊕ – beater + ⊝

2. restaurant dive + ⊝ café ⊕ –

3. collector hoarder + ⊝ saver ⊕ –

Write your own denotations with corresponding connotations (mark + or – beside each).

1. _____ _____ _____

2. _____ _____ _____

3. _____ _____ _____

Another way to practice finding positive and negative connotations is to look at some good and bad reviews.

EXAMPLE

Directions: As you read the paragraph below, list the positive and negative connotations.

At the time Georgia O'Keeffe was trying to become a professional artist, both painting and photography were male-dominated fields. By incorporating the element of photography into her paintings, though, O'Keeffe broke new ground as a woman artist. Photography, as well, helped her connect to Alfred Stieglitz. O'Keeffe had a major influence on this photographer, becoming both his business partner and lover. At first their relationship was completely professional, as he was married. But after a while, Stieglitz became infatuated with the striking young painter. Discontented with his marriage of twenty-five years, Stieglitz viewed O'Keeffe as an easily influenced young woman who *needed* him. After only a few weeks in New York, she soon became his love interest. While she thrived under his care and attention, O'Keeffe also impacted Stieglitz. She made him feel youthful and filled with bliss, something that he hadn't felt in a long time.

List the Positive Connotations   **List the Negative Connotations**

_____   _____

_____   _____

_____   _____

In the example above, the positive connotations are words such as *broke new ground, major influence, striking young painter,* and *thrived.* The negative connotations are words such as *infatuated, discontented,* and *easily influenced.*

PRACTICE THE NEW SKILL

Directions: As you read reviews below, list the positive and negative connotations.

1. Fearful wizards refer to their nemesis, the wicked Voldemort, as You-Know-Who. But for literate kids and plenty of adults, the book world's You-Know-Who for the past few years has been Harry Potter, unassuming boy hero of J.K. Rowling's fantasy series. Now that the first book—Harry Potter and the Sorcerer's Stone (Philosopher's Stone in the original British version)—is a movie, true Hogwartsians will return to the source and compare written and visual texts with the care of a New Critical scholar. They will find that the book was better—richer in mood, in thrilling melodrama, in joy—than director Chris Columbus' meticulous, stolid film.

Source: Corliss, Richard. (2001). *Wizardry without Magic.*
Retrieved from *Time Online.*

About the movie . . .

List the Positive Connotations   **List the Negative Connotations**

unassuming boy hero and   for literate kids and plenty of adults. . . .

compare written and visual   true Hogwartsians will return to the source

texts with the care of a   They will find the book was better—richer

New Critical scholar   in mood, in thrilling melodrama, in joy

2. If you've read the novel—and if you haven't, why not?—impeccable casting means you'll feel like you've met all of these characters already. The three young leads—Radcliffe, Grint, and especially Watson—deliver likable, natural performances, while the film's biggest joy is watching the spot-on performances of their peers: Maggie Smith plays Professor McGonagall like Miss Jean Brodie with a pointy hat, while Robbie Coltrane steals the show as loose-lipped Hagrid. Alan Rickman, meanwhile, sneers for England as Professor Snape.

Source: Hennigan, Adrian. (2001). *Harry Potter and the Philosopher's Stone.* Retrieved from www.bbc.co.uk.films.

About the movie . . .

List the Positive Connotations	List the Negative Connotations
impeccable casting; you'll feel like you've met all of these characters already. The three young leads deliver likable, natural performances; the film's biggest joy is watching the spot-on performances of their peers	sneers for England as Professor Snape

3. Guitar Hero may be simple in design, but between its terrific sense of atmosphere, the amazing song selection, fantastic cover versions, and absolutely wicked gameplay, it's one of the most complete packages that the genre has ever seen. It's fun to play alone, but even better in groups. If you've ever been interested in the rhythm genre, this is the game to buy.

Source: Gamespot.com.

List the Positive Connotations	List the Negative Connotations
terrific sense of atmosphere; amazing song selection; fantastic cover versions; absolutely wicked gameplay; it's one of the most complete packages that the genre has ever seen; It's fun to play alone, but even better in groups; If you've ever been interested in the rhythm genre, this is the game to buy	

Author's Purpose (Why is the author writing?)

Authors have many reasons for writing, and this affects their style.

> **LO2**
> Determine the author's purpose.

EXAMPLE

Directions: Brainstorm some types of written text you may read or encounter in your daily life.   Answers will vary.

(example) *sports page* _____   *bumper stickers* _____

_____   _____

_____   _____

Compare your list with those of your classmates. Is it clear that there are many different types of writing? One way to organize the different types of text is by determining the author's purpose: *to persuade, to inform,* and *to entertain.*

> *Persuade:* The author is trying to convince the reader to take some action. It may be to change an opinion, agree with his ideas, or engage in a prescribed behavior such as vote for a specific candidate or buy a particular product.
>
> *Inform:* The author is trying to convey information to the reader. It may be facts and figures, data, or statistics. It could also be a set of directions or a description or narration of an event.
>
> *Entertain:* The author is trying to make the reader feel something. It may be an emotion such as laughing, crying, relaxing, or escaping. Or the author is providing a puzzle or mystery to solve.

EXAMPLE

Directions: Circle the author's purpose for the type of text: **P** for persuade, **I** for inform, and/or **E** for entertain.

Letters to the Editor: P   I   E

Letters to the editor generally try to persuade the reader to agree with the writer's perspective; therefore, **P** is the correct answer.

PRACTICE THE NEW SKILL

Directions: Circle the type of text: **P** for persuade, **I** for inform, and/or **E** for entertain.

1. advertisements: (P)   (I)   (E)
2. cookbooks: P   (I)   (E)
3. mysteries: P   I   (E)

Many types of writing have more than one purpose. For instance, an advertisement has all three purposes: to persuade you to purchase the product, to inform you of the benefits of owning the product, and maybe to entertain you so the ad will be memorable (as in the Super Bowl ads). A cookbook might simply inform the reader of ingredients and instructions to prepare a recipe, but it may also entertain the reader with stories, pictures, and/or quotations.

As a reader, it is important to think about the nature of the material as well as the word choices as you determine the author's purpose. Consider the words the author uses in the text to help you determine her purpose. Pay attention to the use of denotative words, which may be neutral, and connotative words, which may indicate strong positive or negative emotions.

Directions: Read the passage below and circle the purpose(s): **P, I,** or **E.** As you read, highlight words that evoke emotion.

Through four innings, Robinson electrified the crowd, and Branca, the starting pitcher, held the Yankees without a hit. His fastball was humming. His curveball was sweeping in big, fat arcs. He seemed entirely untouchable until the fifth inning, when DiMaggio hit a ground ball deep in the hole between short and third. Reese made a nice play but threw too late to get the out. Suddenly, Branca's perfect game was gone, and so was his confidence. From the Yankee dugout, coach Charlie Dressen, formerly of the Dodgers, seized the opportunity and began *heckling* the pitcher. "You'll go wild!" he shouted. "You'll go wild!" Branca did. He walked the next batter on four pitches and hit the batter after him, loading the bases. Then, facing Johnny Lindell, he threw a sloppy curve that drifted too far over the plate. Lindell bashed it for a two-run double. Rizzuto came up next and drew a walk on five pitches, loading the bases yet again. Now Bobby Brown came on to pinch hit for Shea. When Branca threw two pitches out of the strike zone, Shotton had seen enough. Branca was finished. In came Hank Behrman. As Branca walked off the field and Behrman walked on, Robinson stood with hands on hips and lips pursed, his face a picture of sheer disgust.

Source: Eig, Jonathan. (2007). *Opening Day: The Story of Jackie Robinson's First Season.* New York, NY: Simon & Schuster, p. 243.

P   I   E

In the example above, the author's purpose is to inform the reader of the events and to entertain the reader with the exciting details. Therefore, the correct answer is **I** and **E.** Some of the words that evoke emotion, and thus indicate an entertaining purpose are *electrified, humming, entirely untouchable, sloppy curve, bashed it, had seen enough, sheer disgust.*

PRACTICE **THE NEW SKILL**

Directions: Read the following paragraphs and circle the author's purpose(s): **P, I,** or **E.** As you read, highlight words that evoke emotion.

Heckling—mocking, taunting

1. Pollock preferred sculpting to painting or drawing. He and his friends sometimes visited a quarry near the Los Angeles River, where they purchased blocks of limestone and sandstone for carving. Pollock, who stored his materials in Tolegian's backyard, soon accumulated a huge pile of stones, much to the *dismay* of Tolegian's mother. . . . With a chisel and a hammer Pollock chipped away at one block after another, and on weekend afternoons the backyard studio would *reverberate* with the sounds of his labors—the chime of the hammer as it struck the chisel, the plink-plink-plink of the chips as they splintered from the stone. His friends felt sorry for him, thinking he was no better at sculpture than at drawing. Nonetheless they recognized the pleasure he took in carving. Tolegian described Pollock as "more at ease with a rock than a human being."

Source: Solomon, Deborah. (1987). *Jackson Pollock: A Biography.* New York, NY: Simon & Schuster, pp. 40–41.

P ⬛(I) E

2. Camping is not just another form of outdoor recreation. It is a way of living. Alone, it *nurtures* a sense of *autonomy* and self-reliance, as one must learn to make a home out of a scrap of canvas and deal with broken lantern globes, biting insects, and the *vagaries* of weather. Traveling with family, camping *engenders* a spirit both of cooperation and dependence on each other.

Source: McCafferty, Kevin. (1999). *L. L. Bean Family Camping Handbook.* New York, NY: The Lyons Press, p. 4.

⬛(P) I E

3. You should get to know this "Modern Family"

"Modern Family" (8 p.m. Central Wednesday, ABC; four stars) has the finest cast of any new fall show and, thank goodness, this excellent comedy gives these talented performers the kind of sharp material they deserve.

In mockumentary style, the series follows three families who share various bonds. Julie Bowen is pitch-perfect as Claire, a mother of three, and

---

Dismay—disappointment, shock

Reverberate—echo, resound

Nurtures—cultivates, develops

Autonomy—independence, self-sufficiency

Vagaries—whims

Engenders—causes, produces, creates

Ty Burrell is terrific as her husband, who attempts, to his kids' horror, to take the "cool dad" approach (not realizing that belting out songs from "High School Musical" is the most humiliating thing anyone's dad could possibly do).

Jesse Tyler Ferguson and Eric Stonestreet are a gay couple who adopted a child, and Sofia Vergara and Ed O'Neill are a newly married couple whose temperaments and ages are far apart.

The themes about family life and its stresses are nothing new, but you couldn't ask for better execution. Creators Steve Levitan and Christopher Lloyd are comedy veterans ("Frasier" and "Back to You" are among their many credits), and "Modern Family" manages to have a light touch while still packing in lots of jokes and some deft physical bits. There's one gag with a BB gun that has made me laugh all four times I've seen it.

With all that going for it, it almost feels like overkill to hear that actors such as Shelley Long, Edward Norton and Elizabeth Banks will be stopping by to guest star on the show. But if "Modern Family" keeps up the quality of the writing, what the heck—the more the merrier.

Source: Retrieved from *Chicago Tribune* Web site.

Author's Tone (What are the author's emotions?)

LO3
Detect the author's tone.

Another important skill for a good reader is to determine the author's tone in a passage. Tone is like the mood of the text. It is the way the author expresses his attitude. Think back to our example of writing a text message, e-mail, or Myspace or Facebook message. To be sure your friends don't misunderstand your message, it is important that you express your tone through your choice of words. You might be able to add an emoticon such as a smiling ☺ or frowning face ☹, or add an instant message code for laughter like lol or :) or :D, but your words still matter to ensure that you clearly get your complete message across. How do you know which tone the author is using when he doesn't use emoticons or text/IM codes? You learn which words—especially the connotations—express different emotions, feelings, and tones.

Here is a list of some words that express tone. Read through the list and put a check mark next to all that you know. Then look up the others to make sure you understand them. As you become more familiar with words that express tone, your thinking will change to become more discerning of what you read.

affectionate	delightful	incredulous	remorseful
ambivalent	depressed	indignant	respectful
amused	dignified	insulting	revengeful
angry	disbelieving	intense	romantic
apologetic	distressed	irreverent	sarcastic
arrogant	doubtful	ironic	scheming
ashamed	earnest	joking	scornful
astonished	encouraging	joyful	sentimental
authoritative	enthusiastic	lighthearted	serious
bewildered	evasive	loving	solemn
bitter	excited	mocking	sorrowful
calming	fearful	morbid	sympathetic
caring	fervent	nostalgic	threatening
caustic	forgiving	optimistic	tolerant
cheerful	frightened	outraged	uncertain
comical	funny	outspoken	uneasy
compassionate	gentle	passionate	unhappy
conceited	grateful	pathetic	unrealistic
concerned	grim	pessimistic	warm
condescending	honest	playful	wishful
critical	hopeful	pleading	woeful
cruel	hostile	positive	worrisome
curious	humorous	praising	yearning
defensive	impassioned	proud	

Tone may best be understood if you create a mind map so you can see all of the eight types of tone in one place.

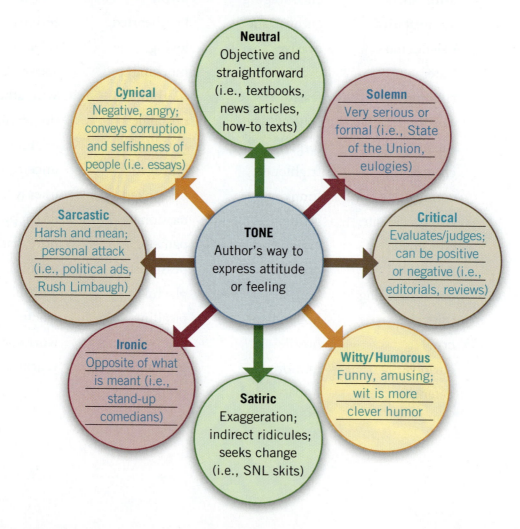

Neutral or serious tone is used when the author is writing about important topics in a straightforward manner. Usually the author will be objective about an issue and discuss both sides without hidden meanings. A neutral tone is usually found in textbooks and news reporting.

Example:

"The preparation of cocoa and hot chocolate is designed to minimize the tendency to sedimentation."—*Food Fundamentals*, 8th ed.

Solemn tone is much more sober than the neutral or serious tone. It is used with somber or critical issues. The president or governor may use a solemn tone with a public address. It may also be used at a graduation speech or for the *eulogy* at a funeral.

Example:

"Ask not what your country can do for you. Ask what you can do for your country."—John F. Kennedy

Critical tone is not necessarily negative. It is used when the author needs to evaluate or judge an issue. It may be used in reviews of movies, books, restaurants, or CDs; letters to the editor; or essays.

Example:

"If you've read the novel—and if you haven't, why not?—impeccable casting means you'll feel like you've met all of these characters already."
—Adrian Hennigan, *Harry Potter and the Philosopher's Stone*

Witty or humorous tone is used when the author intends to be funny or amusing. When the humor is more sophisticated or clever, it is called *wit*. If the reader does not realize when a witty or humorous tone is being used, much misunderstanding may result.

Example: Here are some funny warning labels

- Do not use as ear plugs (on a package of Silly Putty)
- Not dishwasher safe (on a remote control for a TV)
- Warning: May contain nuts (on a package of peanuts)
- Do not use while sleeping (on a hair dryer)
- Do not eat toner (on a toner cartridge for a laser printer)

Eulogy—tribute

- Caution: Shoots rubber bands (on a product called "Rubber Band Shooter")
- Beware! To touch these wires is instant death. Anyone found doing so will be prosecuted. (on a sign at a railroad station)

Satiric tone is used when the author is making fun of someone or something. It is usually an exaggeration of an issue, and the message is indirect. When the author uses a satiric tone, the goal is to encourage change.

Example:

The skits on the comedy show, *Saturday Night Live* and *The Daily Show* on Comedy Central are satirical because they make fun of current events or certain people in order to change their audience's thinking.

Ironic tone is used to suggest the opposite of what is expected in a word or a situation. Ironic tones are used in combination with satire and humor. An example of an ironic situation is someone hurting himself during a good luck ceremony.

Example:

Someone breaking into the police station.

Sarcastic tone is used when the author wants to put down or humiliate someone, but in a humorous way. The tone may appear harsh and bitter. While at first it may seem like humor, when you read sarcasm, you notice that the meanness in the language intends to disgrace or demean.

Example:

"Oh, a sarcasm detector. That's a *really* useful invention!"—Comic Book Guy, *The Simpsons*

Cynical tone is even harsher than sarcasm. Rather than demean a person, a cynical tone is used when the author intends to express the corruption or selfishness in people or humankind. It is more general and is used against a group of people or an organization.

Example:

"Power corrupts; absolute power corrupts absolutely."—John Emerich Edward Dalberg Acton (Lord Acton)

EXAMPLE

Directions: Read the passage below and identify the tone being used.

> We live in a world of celebrity worship, filled with "soft news" and gossip about the personal lives of stars in film, music, television, sports and business. It's little wonder then that our love of celebrity, and the entertainment media's fixation with *superficiality* over substance, has spread to the world of books. In a choice between spending hours reading an author's actual work or focusing on the gossip of their personal lives, the public—and the media—seem to prefer the gossip.

Source: Leddy, C. (2008, July). *Celebrity Culture Influences the Publishing Arena, Too. Writer, 121*(7), pp. 8–9. Retrieved from Academic Search Premier database.

Tone: <u>critical</u>

Notice the phrases, *It's little wonder then;* and *media's fixation with superficiality over substance;* and *the public—and the media—seem to prefer the gossip.* This author is critical of people and the media for choosing gossip over substance.

/ *PRACTICE* THE NEW SKILL /

Directions: Read the following paragraphs and identify the tones being used.

1. His dad, Dale Earnhardt Sr., had a well-deserved reputation at the racetrack for never hesitating to trade paint—that is, deliver a high-speed bump—to anyone who got in his way. But as Dale Jr., the most popular driver on the NASCAR circuit, announced on May 10 that he was leaving the racing team founded by his late father who was killed in 2001—and is now run by his stepmother Teresa Earnhardt—he tried to take the high road. "She's a smart businesswoman and always tried to be fair," Junior told PEOPLE. Somehow, though, he couldn't entirely *muffle* the *bluntness* that was his

---

Superficiality—showiness

Muffle—quiet, silence

Bluntness—candor, honesty

dad's trademark. "[Our relationship] has never been that great," he says of Teresa. "We just made do."

Source: Hewitt, B., and M. Ballard. (2007, May 28). *The Earnhardt Family Smash-Up. People,* 67(21), pp. 119–120. Retrieved from Academic Search Premier database.

Tone: Answers will vary. Earnhardt's first comment is insincere.
         His second comment was honest. The author's tone is skeptical.

2. For centuries, tea (usually green tea) has been a popular beverage in Japan. When it is consumed simply as a beverage at meals there, tea is brewed efficiently by simply putting tea leaves in a pot, pouring boiling water over them, and steeping until served. An elaborate, beautiful tradition, the ceremonial preparation of tea is a *cherished* part of Japanese life even in today's *hectic* scene.

Source: McWilliams, Margaret. (2006). *Food Fundamentals,* 8th ed. Upper Saddle River, NJ: Pearson, p. 412.

Tone: Answers will vary. The author's tone is one of admiration.

3. Got an iPod? Your choice is iTunes ... or iTunes. With 100 million iPods, Nanos and Shuffles sold, Apple commands more than 70% of the personal-music market. An iPod will play music you transfer to your computer from CDs and other files. But if you want to buy music online, the only place to go is Apple's iTunes store. That's because Apple has refused to share its technology with other player manufacturers, which use technology from Microsoft.

Source: Solheim, M., and A. Smith. (2007, August). What You Need to Know about BUYING MUSIC ONLINE. *Kiplinger's Personal Finance,* 61(8), p. 22. Retrieved from Academic Search Premier database.

Tone: Answers will vary. The author's first comment ("iTunes or iTunes") is
mocking. The author's next couple sentences are straightforward. The last
sentence is critical.

Cherished—appreciated, respected, treasured
Hectic—chaotic, frantic

REVIEW *WHAT YOU LEARNED*

Directions: As you read the passage below, pay attention to the authors' choice of words to help you determine their purpose and tone.

Tourists Also Change

1   Have you traveled to another country or spent time in a culture different from your own? Do you feel that it affected you? It is fairly obvious that visitors of foreign cultures are affected differently by what they experience. The visitor seeking relaxation or pleasure is only minimally interested in the history and culture of the hosts. Bars and swimming pools are pretty much the same all over the world, and the tourist is therefore not in close contact with the "real" culture of the place. Other visitors actively search for and examine the host culture, compare it with their own, and perhaps experience change in their attitudes about the host people and themselves.

2   A study assessing tourist attitude changes toward a host people was conducted among British tourists to Greece and others visiting Morocco. The visitors were there for recreation and pleasure, yet their attitude toward the host people changed as a result of the two- to three-week tours of those countries. The tourists to Greece found the Greeks less suave, more religious, and less affluent than they originally believed. Attitudes towards Moroccans also changed. Moroccans came to be seen as poorer, more conservative, more talkative, more musical, tenser, and more mercenary than before the trip. Fellow countrymen were seen, post trip, as more affluent and less tense.

3   But how do we know that the tourists surveyed understood the real culture of their hosts, and vice versa? Generalizations about attitudinal and other changes brought on by travel, of course, should be made very carefully. People with strong prejudices about ethnic groups may only strengthen their prejudices as a result of travel because the selectively see what they feel is important. The basically generous and open person sees the good, whereas the person who needs to protect a certain view perceives what is necessary to maintain that self-image. But how can the negative influences be reduced and the positive be encouraged?

Source: Walker, John R. and Josielyn T. Walker. (2011).
Tourism: Concepts and Practices.
Upper Saddle River, NJ: Pearson, p. 341.

1. What is the topic of the reading? _____ *Tourists change* _____

2. What is the central theme of the reading?_____ *Tourists may change* _____
   as a result of traveling to a culture different from their own.

3. What is the author's purpose?   Persuade   (Inform)   Entertain

4. What is the tone of the passage? _____ *Straightforward, informational* _____

5. Have you ever traveled or spent time with a culture different from your own? Do you know someone who has? Discuss how your experiences compare to those in the text. Write your thoughts in a paragraph form. *Answers will vary.*

_____

REVIEW WHAT YOU LEARNED

Directions: As you read the passage below, pay attention to the author's choice of words, especially positive and negative connotations, to help you determine his purpose and tone.

Ansel Adams

1   When I was twelve, I contracted measles and was put to bed for two weeks with the shades drawn to protect my eyes. My father read to me when he came home from the office. My mother and Aunt Mary fluttered around, *commiserating* and annoying, though with the best of intentions.

2   The spaces between the shade and the top of the windows in my bedroom served as crude pinholes, and vague images of the outer world were projected on the ceiling. When anyone moved outside to the east, the highly *diffuse* image would move along to the west above me. It took me quite a time to understand the phenomenon; it was my first inquiry into the complex structure of image formation. My father explained it and I then grasped the theory of the camera lens and why the picture was upside-down on the film. He opened his Kodak Bullseye camera, placed a piece of semitransparent paper where the film usually resides, set the shutter on open, pressed the button, and viola—a camera obscura! This effect had been observed for thousands of years, yet it was not until 1826 that photography began with an image that was actually preserved by the Frenchman Niecephore Niepce.

Source: Adams, Ansel. (1985). *Ansel Adams: An Autobiography.*
Boston, MA: Little Brown and Company, p. 49.

1. What is the topic of the reading? _____
Ansel Adams' childhood photography memory

2. List the positive connotations. _____
Answers will vary.

3. List the negative connotations. _____
Answers will vary.

4. What is the author's purpose? _____
                        P   Ⓘ   Ⓔ

5. What is the tone of the passage? _____
reminiscent

Commiserating—sympathizing

Diffuse—dispersed, scattered, thin

MASTER THE LESSON

Purpose and Tone

Directions: Read the paragraphs below and list the tone used in each one.

1. Before the *advent* of food courts in shopping malls, a food experience at the mall might include the lunch counter at Walgreens drugstore, an ice cream shop or a local cafeteria (such as S&S Cafeteria, in the South). Food courts quickly replaced those other eating options and became popular with shoppers—but that was 30 years ago.

   Tone: _Informative_

2. Times change. Today, unfortunately, food courts are one of the things that are wrong with many suburban shopping malls. They are often unattractive, noisy and crowded—usually filled with unruly groups of teens and moms with toddlers in tow and aisle-obstructing baby strollers. They serve an array of inexpensive, fast and passably good—but never memorable—food. Finding a more pleasant dining option or a table service restaurant at some malls is not easy.

   Tone: _Critical—negative_

3. The trouble with food courts is that they are still operating on several assumptions from the distant past: 1) the belief that people are not selective about the quality of what they eat as long as it is quick and inexpensive, and 2) the belief that people want to eat in a hurry, and that they don't want to relax and enjoy their food.

   Tone: _Critical—negative_

4. Of course, the operational efficiencies of having food service grouped in one location is a significant, cost-saving advantage for the mall operator. And food courts are an effective way to feed a lot of people in a short time. Sometimes, a sandwich on the run does fill the bill.

   Tone: _Critical—positive_

5. But consumers have changed a great deal in the intervening years. Today, consumers are as picky about where they eat and what they

---

Advent—arrival

eat as they are about the stores in which they shop and what they buy. Diners who regularly frequent P.F. Chang's, Cheesecake Factory and California Pizza Kitchen are no longer happy with the food court's usual line-up of burger chains, Wonder Wok and Steak on a Stick (not that there is anything wrong with such establishments; they do have their place). But in a society where knowledgeable consumers can routinely debate the attributes of balsamic vinegars and handmade mozzarellas, the mall food court leaves a lot to be desired.

Tone: Critical—mostly negative _____

6. When malls do offer better choices, these often are *relegated* to out-parcels that require shoppers to get in their cars and leave the mall in order to eat—unmindful of how difficult it then becomes to get them to return and resume shopping. Once most shoppers have left the mall—they are gone for good.

Tone: Critical—negative _____

7. One of the reasons that lifestyle or village centers are gaining popularity is that they offer more and better dining options, and the dining venues are integrated into the overall shopping space and experience. This results in an outing that is more convenient and appealing, and that *resonates* with the customer's lifestyle. Village centers devote an average of about 18 percent of their space to eateries, a higher percent than most malls. Outdoor cafés and coffee shops also are popular attractions at village shopping centers, offering places where people can rest and catch their breath, boosting their energy for all that shopping.

Tone: Positive _____

8. Food has moved front and center in the American lifestyle. Restaurants of all types are rapidly expanding their domains, growing at a rate of 17.6 percent a year (the fastest growing sector of retail, after discount stores). Americans are in love with their food—and their waistlines show it. Obesity is rapidly becoming a major health problem, and overeating is at least partially to blame. It is rare today for a

---

Relegated—demoted, downgraded, transferred

Resonates—resounds

family or social group event or activity not to include a focus on food. And the popular trend of "grazing" has encouraged a nonstop process of eating, from dawn to bedtime. Packaged snacks—food in small bites, designed for immediate consumption—are the fastest-growing merchandise category at grocery stores. We are *barraged* with TV advertisements for foods and snacks, 24 hours a day, and Americans respond enthusiastically.

Tone: Sarcastic

9. Chocolate boutiques, tea salons and gourmet food shops add upscale options to shopping centers and are often more appealing than many mass-market apparel chains and shoe stores. When it comes to the customer's attention, time and money, *Prada* blouses are competing with *pesto* chicken paninis.

Tone: Sarcastic

10. Successful shopping centers find a way to weave food opportunities into the shopping experience, making it easy for the customer to have the best of both worlds—and to avoid the dreaded food court.

Tone: Sarcastic

Source: Sway, R. (2007, April). *Mania at the Mall. Display & Design Ideas*, p. 1. Retrieved from MasterFILE Premier database.

_____

Barraged—bombarded, flooded

Prada—upscale clothing designer

Pesto— food paste made of basil leaves, garlic, pine nuts and olive oil

Purpose and Tone

5 WAYS TO FIND CHEAP, LOCAL FUN

There is no shortage of things to do in a buzzing metropolitan area, and with the Internet at your fingertips (and in your phone), you can find popular after-work and weekend events and activities in a matter of seconds. But if you're looking to avoid long drives, large crowds, and possible admittance or parking fees, you may want to look for less publicized events at the community level.

Check your city's newsletter or website. Besides local reports and announcements, your city's news publications will likely also feature a section for upcoming events. For example, right on my city's homepage is a banner advertising the annual 5K run, a post announcing the kickoff of free outdoor concerts, and a link to the summer recreation guide. These events probably won't attract out-of-towners, but they are excellent opportunities for residents to have fun with other members of the community.

Stay updated with event calendars. Libraries, museums, community centers, and other family-oriented venues tend to be really good about keeping the public posted on events hosted at their facilities, by way of a calendar of events on their website or bulletin board. (For example, in September, hundreds of museums offer free admission to celebrate National Museum Day.) You can also create your own calendar events to keep track of the local happenings you and your family are interested in.

Read flyers. They're everywhere—stapled on telephone poles, taped to bus stops, tacked on bulletin boards by the layer. Strangers hand them to you on busy intersections. Sure, it's easy to pass them by (or chuck them in the next recycling container) without a glance, but you may be missing out on something interesting: free drinks at a new restaurant's grand opening, a carnival hosted by a local church, weekly concerts in the basement of a music store—the possibilities are endless. And all it takes is a few seconds of reading.

Ask around. Virtually every person you interact with can be a resource. A neighbor may be part of a baseball league. A co-worker's sister may be the drummer in a new rock band. You can easily pick up on fun things to do just by asking for more information (date, time and location) in your day-to-day conversations. Don't forget to ask your kids (or your friends' kids) about school events. Attending plays, concerts, sports games, and charity dinners put on by students is a great way to support the youth in your community.

Crash a party. It may be rude to show up uninvited at a private party, but when you pass by a large group of people (or cars) gathered at, say, a park or a school, it doesn't hurt to investigate. If you have a minute to spare, stop and ask someone who seems to be in the know, "What's going on?" You may discover you're just in time for an outdoor concert or a high school football game. The great thing about local events is that you can go home, pack your family in the car or prepare for a walk, call friends who might want to join you, and still make it back in time to have some fun.

NOTE: Amy Lu writes at Wise Bread, a blog dedicated to helping readers live large on a small budget. Wise Bread's book, 10,001 Ways to Live Large on a Small Budget, debuted as the #1 Money Management book on Amazon.com.

Source: USNews.com.money Web site.

1. What are the positive connotations of this article?
Answers will vary. Examples include excellent opportunities, family-oriented venues, celebrate, possibilities are endless, great way, etc.

2. What is the purpose of this article?

(Persuade)   (Inform)   Entertain

3. What tones are used in this article?
Persuasive, informative, positive

4. Describe what steps you could take in your community to find inexpensive things to do. Write your answer in at least two complete sentences.
Answers will vary.

LEARNING STYLE ACTIVITIES

Look, Listen, Write, Do

Music is an integral part of our culture. It has been ingrained in the human spirit for centuries. People of all continents, backgrounds, and ages relate to music on some level. Some people say music speaks to their souls. Others say they don't know what to say, but the music tells it all. My daughter moved in response to music when just an infant and my mother responded to the sound of my father's singing when she was in extreme sedation after a triple bypass heart surgery. My sisters and I sang to my father and mother to soothe them as they moved on from this life on earth. Music cheers us, inspires and encourages us, and brings back memories of times past.

For this activity, choose one song that represents *you*. When choosing your song, make sure it matches your values, attitudes, and beliefs. Print the lyrics and hand them to your instructor. Also make the song available to your instructor to play for the class (through a CD, YouTube link, etc.). As you choose your song, think about your life purpose and the tones the song conveys both to you and about you, as well as to the listener.

Look   Draw or find a picture of what the song means to you. Explain why the visual images match the messages about you that you want to convey. Visual images may include your own artwork, album cover designs, videos, etc.

Listen   Listen to your song. Play it for your classmates. Listen to other people's songs and try to determine which song represents the person in your class. What musical tones are conveyed in the instruments and voices that represent you?

Write   Write about what the song means to you. Explain why the lyrics represent you and your values, attitudes, and beliefs. Explain how the lyrics match your life purpose. Also discuss how the tone in the lyrics conveys what you stand for.

Do   Discuss why your song matches the experiences you have had or hope to have. Explain your beliefs, values, and attitudes and how the words in the song represent you.

Reading Practice

The following readings are related to the theme Entertainment—Movies, Music, Food, Sports, and Hobbies. While you read material from various sources, you will continue to build your reading skills including learning vocabulary, locating main ideas and supporting details, understanding the differences between facts and opinions, and discerning inferences, organizational patterns, and purpose and tone.

The first set of readings, from Internet sources, are different reviews of the movie, *Lord of the Rings*.

The second reading is "The Value of Play" from a textbook titled *Early Childhood Education Today*.

The third reading is a piece of literature called *The Story of an Hour* by Kate Chopin.

The fourth reading is a review of the movie *Inception* from the *NY Daily News*.

The fifth reading shows an image of motocross.

Internet

READING 1

Movie Reviews: *The Lord of the Rings: The Fellowship of the Ring*

REVIEWER 1

1   You think *Harry Potter* had expectations? It's a **beloved** book, sure, but it was published in 1997. In 10 years it will be as forgotten as *The Bridges of Madison County*. But J.R.R. Tolkien's *The Lord of the Rings* series dates all the way back to 1937 (when *The Hobbit* was published), and it's taken all these decades for someone to even attempt a live-action recreation of the **trilogy** of books. And not without reason.

2   How do you satisfy a **legion** of fans, some of whom have been waiting almost 65 years to see their absolute favorite work of literature put to film? More often than not, *you don't*, and though Peter Jackson's production of *The Lord of the Rings* is painstakingly faithful and earnest, it is almost a foregone conclusion that the movie will never *quite* be good enough for the obsessed fans (see also the

1978 animated), just as it will be far too obtuse for those who haven't read the books.

3   For the uninitiated, *The Lord of the Rings* is a trilogy of books that occur 60 years after the events of *The Hobbit*. A hobbit (read: little person with hairy feet) named Frodo Baggins (Elijah Wood), nephew of the famed Bilbo Baggins (Ian Holm), is **entrusted** with a mysterious ring when Bilbo **opts** to take a permanent holiday, fading away from society after 111 years of life. How'd he get so old? That ring isn't just a band of gold. It's a magic ring forged of unspeakable evil— evil that has finally awakened after centuries of dormancy . . . *and now it wants its ring back.*

Source: Review by Christopher Null (December 17, 2001). *The Lord of the Rings: The Fellowship of the Ring.* Retrieved from Film Critic.com Reviews.

REVIEWER 2

4   Directed by Peter Jackson, *The Lord of the Rings: The Fellowship of the Ring* is a masterfully made movie. The message is inspiring, and the **cinematography** is absolutely breathtaking. The filming for the movie took place in the beautiful countryside of New Zealand, which provided a setting that has the appearance of a fantasy world. The scenery itself has become so well-loved by fans of the movie that there is even a tour to show vacationers all the places where filming took place. The film's gorgeous scenery is impressively matched by the **dedication** of the actors. Viggo Mortensen, who portrayed the character "Aragorn," wore his costume wherever he went, and tried to act as his character would in his daily situations.

5   While acting and scenery surely contributed to the success of the film, a well-written plot is the defining **attribute** for any blockbuster. While Peter Jackson did direct *The Fellowship of the Ring*, the story is taken from a novel of the same title, written by J.R.R. Tolkien. Tolkien's book is a classic piece of literature, telling an epic tale of an unlikely hero fighting to defeat a great evil. The **protagonist** is Frodo Baggins, a young hobbit (similar to a dwarf) who is given a magic ring that contains the spirit of the sinister Sauron. The ring tempts whoever bears it, which is a great conflict Frodo must endure as he goes on a quest to destroy the ring. He is accompanied by his friend, Samwise Gamgee, and a band of warriors who unite under the cause of ending the horrible evil that is caused by the ring. They call themselves "The Fellowship of the Ring", and together they must **traverse** their world, from tall, snowy moun- tain peaks to deep, dark mines. The story is the epitome of the classic battle between good and evil, but it still manages to create very original characters, situations, and settings. ■

Vocabulary

Directions: For each word below choose the best meaning as it is used in the movie reviews above. Use context clues, word parts, and if needed, a dictionary.

1. **beloved** (paragraph 1)
   - a. well-loved
   - b. lovers
   - c. loved before
   - d. friendly

2. **trilogy** (paragraph 1)
   - a. two-part series
   - b. three-part series
   - c. series of books
   - d. series of movies

3. **legion** (paragraph 2)
   - a. parade
   - b. legal group
   - c. large group
   - d. flags

4. **entrusted** (paragraph 3)
   - a. itemized
   - b. questioned
   - c. locked
   - d. trusted

5. **opts** (paragraph 3)
   - a. props
   - b. chooses
   - c. declines
   - d. forgets

6. **cinematography** (paragraph 4)
   - a. the making of a movie
   - b. the paying for a movie
   - c. the managing a cinema
   - d. taking pictures

7. **dedication** (paragraph 4)
   - a. organization
   - b. commitment
   - c. cheerfulness
   - d. procrastination

8. **attribute** (paragraph 5)
   - a. attractiveness
   - b. weakness
   - c. money-maker
   - d. characteristic

9. **protagonist** (paragraph 5)

    a. enemy   c. hobbit

    b. hero   d. horse

10. **traverse** (paragraph 5)

    a. make a map of   **c. go across**

    b. meet new people   d. battle

Main Idea

11. What is the main idea in paragraph 1? _____

    There is a reason no one has attempted to make a movie of the

    action-packed classic book *Lord of the Rings* until now.

12. What is the main idea in paragraph 2? The *Lord of the Rings* movie will
never be quite good enough for true fans of the books.

13. What is the main idea in paragraph 4? _____

    Lord of the Rings is a great movie!

Supporting Details

14. List some of the specific things Reviewer 1 likes about the movie.

    Answers will vary, but may include: painstakingly faithful and earnest

15. List some of the things Reviewer 2 likes about the movie.

    Answers will vary but may include: Reviewer 2 likes the plot/storyline.

    It is masterfully made; the message is inspiring, and the cinematography

    is absolutely breathtaking; the film's gorgeous scenery is impressively

    matched by the dedication of the actors.

Facts and Opinions

16. Discuss and explain which of the two reviewers uses the most facts to
support their opinions? Give specific examples. Answers will vary.

Inferences

Overall, what can you infer about each reviewer's attitude about the movie?

17. Reviewer 1 _Answers will vary, but may include—unimpressed, doubts it will satisfy fans of the books_

18. Reviewer 2 _Answers will vary, but may include—loved it_

Purpose and Tone

19. What is the purpose(s) of the movie reviews?

(Prove)   (Illustrate)   (Explain)

20. List words or phrases that indicate one example where a reviewer is critical.
Answers will vary.

21. List words or phrases that indicate one example where a reviewer is skeptical.
Answers will vary.

22. List words or phrases that indicate one example where a reviewer is witty.
Answers will vary.

Textbook

READING 2

Use SQ3R as you read this textbook excerpt.

Survey	Skim over the material. Read the title, subtitle, subheadings, first and last paragraphs, pictures, charts, and graphics. Note italics and bold print.
Question	Ask yourself questions before you read. What do you want to know? Turn headings and subheadings into questions and/or read questions if provided.
Read	Read the material in manageable chunks. This may be one or two paragraphs at a time or the material under one subheading.
Recite	Recite the answer to each question in your own words. This is a good time to write notes as you read each section. Repeat the question-read-recite cycle.
Review	Look over your notes at the end of the chapter, article, or material. Review what you learned and write a summary in your own words.

1310L

"The Value of Play" from Chapter 10—The Preschool Years: Getting Ready for School and Life

"Education is for improving the lives of others and for leaving your community and world better than you found it."

—**Marian Edelman**

VOICE FROM THE FIELD

1   Early childhood educators have long recognized the value of play for social, emotional, and physical development. Recently, however, play has achieved greater importance as a *medium* for literacy development. It is now recognized that literacy develops in meaningful, **functional**, social settings rather than as a set of abstract skills taught in formal pencil-and-paper settings.

Enhancing Literacy

2   Literacy development involves a child's active **engagement** in cooperation and **collaboration** with peers; it builds on what the child already knows. Play provides this setting. During observation of children at play, especially in free-choice, cooperative play periods, one can note the **functional** uses of literacy that children incorporate into their play themes. When the environment is appropriately prepared with literacy materials in play areas, children have been observed to **engage** in attempted and conceptual reading and writing in **collaboration** with other youngsters. In similar settings lacking literacy materials, the same literacy activities did not occur.

3   To demonstrate how play in an appropriate setting can nurture literacy development, consider the following classroom setting in which the teacher has designed a veterinarian's office to go along with a class study on animals, focusing in particular on pets.

4   The dramatic play area is designed with a waiting room, including chairs; a table filled with magazines, books, and pamphlets about pet care; posters about pets; office hour notices; a No Smoking sign; and a sign advising visitors to check in with the nurse when arriving. On a nurse's desk are patient forms on clipboards, a telephone, an address and telephone book, appointment cards, and a calendar. The office contains patient folders, prescription pads, white coats, masks, gloves, a toy doctor's kit, and stuffed animals for patients.

Medium—method, way

Scaffolding Literacy Activities

5   Ms. Meyers, the teacher, guides students in using the various materials in the veterinarian's office during free-play time. For example, she reminds the children to read important information they find in the waiting area, to fill out forms about their pets' needs, to ask the nurse for appointment times, or to have the doctor write out appropriate treatments or prescriptions. In addition to giving directions, Ms. Meyers also models behaviors by participating in the play center with the children when first introducing materials.

6   This play setting provides a literacy-rich environment with books and writing materials; allows the teacher to model reading and writing that the children can observe and *emulate*; provides the opportunity to practice literacy in a real-life situation that has meaning and **function**; and encourages the children to interact socially by **collaborating** and performing meaningful reading and writing activities with peers. The following anecdotes relate the type of behavior Ms. Meyers observed in the play area.

- Jessica was waiting to see the doctor. She told her stuffed animal dog, Sam, not to worry, that the doctor would not hurt him. She asked Jenny, who was waiting with her stuffed animal cat, Muffin, what the kitten's problem was. The girls agonized over the ailments of their pets. After a while they stopped talking, and Jessica picked up the book *Are You My Mother?* and pretended to read to her dog. Jessica showed Sam the pictures as she read.

- Preston examined Christopher's teddy bear and wrote a report in the patient's folder. He read his scribble writing out loud and said, "This teddy bear's blood pressure is twenty-nine points. He should take sixty-two pills an hour until he is better and keep warm and go to bed." At the same time he read, he showed Christopher what he had written so he could understand what to do.

Additional Ideas for Literacy Play

7   When selecting settings to promote literacy in play, choose those that are familiar to children and relate them to themes currently being studied. Suggestions for literacy materials and settings to add to the dramatic play areas include the following:

- A fast-food restaurant, ice cream store, or bakery suggests menus, order pads, a cash register, specials for the day, recipes, and lists of flavors or products.

- A supermarket or local grocery store can include labeled shelves and sections, food containers, pricing labels, cash registers, telephones, shopping receipts, checkbooks, coupons, and promotional flyers.

Emulate—imitate, copy, follow

- A post office to mail children's letters needs paper, envelopes, address books, pens, pencils, stamps, cash registers, and labeled mailboxes. A mail carrier hat and bag are important for children who deliver the mail and need to identify and read names and addresses.

- A gas station and car repair shop, designed in the block area, might have toy cars and trucks, receipts for sales, road maps for help with directions to different destinations, automotive tools and auto repair manuals for fixing cars and trucks, posters that advertise automobile equipment, and empty cans of different products typically found in service stations. ■

(Contributed by Lesley Mandel Morrow, professor and coordinator of early childhood programs, Rutgers University)

Source: Morrison, George S. (2007). *Early Childhood Education Today,* 10th ed. Upper Saddle River, NJ: Pearson, pp. 286–287.

Vocabulary

Each field or career has words that occur frequently in work conversations. For instance, in the field of literacy and early childhood education, the words *functional, engagement,* and *collaboration* are often used to discuss learning. Becoming familiar with the common words of your career will make reading texts in your field easier.

Use context clues to find the meaning of ***functional/function*** from paragraphs 1, 2, and 6.

> It is now recognized that literacy develops in meaningful, functional, social settings rather than as a set of abstract skills taught in formal pencil-and-paper settings. (paragraph 1)

During observation of children at play, especially in free-choice, cooperative play periods, one can note the **functional** uses of literacy that children incorporate into their play themes. (paragraph 2)

This play setting provides a literacy-rich environment with books and writing materials; allows the teacher to model reading and writing that the children can observe and emulate; provides the opportunity to practice literacy in a real-life situation that has meaning and **function;** and encourages the children to interact socially by *collaborating* and performing meaningful reading and writing activities with peers. (paragraph 6)

Meaningful uses of literacy	Not a set of abstract skills taught in paper-and-pencil settings	Practice literacy in real-life situations; incorporated into play themes

1. Based on the clues, what is the meaning of **functional**?

real-life, useful

Use context clues to find the meaning of **engage/engagement** from paragraph 2.

Literacy development involves a child's active **engagement** in cooperation and collaboration with peers; it builds on what the child already knows.

When the environment is appropriately prepared with literacy materials in play areas, children have been observed to **engage** in attempted and conceptual reading and writing in collaboration with other youngsters. In similar settings lacking literacy materials, the same literacy activities did not occur.

It is active and can include working with peers	Environment prepared with literacy materials in play areas	The same activities did not occur without literacy material

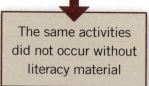

2. Based on the clues, what is the meaning of ***engage/engagement***?
focus and interested

Use context clues to find the meaning of ***collaboration/collaborating*** from paragraphs 2 and 6.

Literacy development involves a child's active engagement in cooperation and ***collaboration*** with peers; it builds on what the child already knows. Play provides this setting. During observation of children at play, especially in free-choice, cooperative play periods, one can note the functional uses of literacy that children incorporate into their play themes. When the environment is appropriately prepared with literacy materials in play areas, children have been observed to engage in attempted and conceptual reading and writing in ***collaboration*** with other youngsters. (paragraph 2)

This play setting provides a literacy-rich environment with books and writing materials; allows the teacher to model reading and writing that the children can observe and emulate; provides the opportunity to practice literacy in a real-life situation that has meaning and function; and encourages the children to interact socially by ***collaborating*** and performing meaningful reading and writing activities with peers. (paragraph 6)

They interact socially	They cooperate with other children	It is with other youngsters and peers

3. Based on the clues, what is the meaning of ***collaboration***?
working together

SQ3R Answers will vary.

Survey—What is the topic of the selection?

Question/Read/Recite (Hint: Turn subheadings into questions.)

Question _____

_____

Answer _____

_____

Question _____

_____

Answer _____

_____

Question _____

_____

Answer _____

_____

Review (Write a summary of the material in your own words.)

_____

_____

Main Idea, Supporting Details, and Patterns of Organization

Create a concept map with the topic, the central theme of the reading, the major supporting details, and the minor supporting details. *Hint:* Use your SQ3R notes to help determine how the ideas are related. Remember, examples often provide minor details to support a major detail. Answers will vary.

Fact and Opinion

Are the author's points developed primarily through facts or opinions?

Do you believe the author is an expert or has an informed opinion? List evidence in the reading that supports your answer. Answers will vary.

Inference

What conclusions can you draw from the reading about the author's attitude regarding early literacy development? Answers will vary.

Purpose and Tone

What is the purpose of this textbook reading?   P   ⓘ   E

What tone does the author use?

Witty   Uncertain   Indignant   ⟨Serious⟩

Critical Thinking/Application

Based on ideas from the reading, in what ways could a parent or caregiver improve the literacy development of a child? Give specific examples of ways to set up the child's home environment/play area.

Literature

READING 3

The Story of an Hour

Kate Chopin (1894)

1   Knowing that Mrs. Mallard was **afflicted** with a heart trouble, great care was taken to break to her as gently as possible the news of her husband's death.

2   It was her sister Josephine who told her, in broken sentences; **veiled** hints that revealed in half concealing. Her husband's friend Richards was there, too, near her. It was he who had been in the newspaper office when intelligence of the railroad disaster was received, with Brently Mallard's name leading the list of "killed." He had only taken the time to assure himself of its truth by a second telegram, and had **hastened** to **forestall** any less careful, less tender friend in bearing the sad message.

3   She did not hear the story as many women have heard the same, with a paralyzed inability to accept its significance. She wept at once, with sudden, wild abandonment, in her sister's arms. When the storm of grief had spent itself she went away to her room alone. She would have no one follow her.

4   There stood, facing the open window, a comfortable, roomy armchair. Into this she sank, pressed down by a physical exhaustion that haunted her body and seemed to reach into her soul.

5   She could see in the open square before her house the tops of trees that were all **aquiver** with the new spring life. The delicious breath of rain was in the air. In the street below a peddler was crying his wares. The notes of a distant song which someone was singing reached her faintly, and countless sparrows were twittering in the eaves.

6   There were patches of blue sky showing here and there through the clouds that had met and piled one above the other in the west facing her window.

7   She sat with her head thrown back upon the cushion of the chair, quite motionless, except when a sob came up into her throat and shook her, as a child who has cried itself to sleep continues to sob in its dreams.

8   She was young, with a fair, calm face, whose lines **bespoke repression** and even a certain strength. But now there was a dull stare in her eyes, whose gaze was fixed away off yonder on one of those patches of blue sky. It was not a glance of reflection, but rather indicated a suspension of intelligent thought.

9   There was something coming to her and she was waiting for it, fearfully. What was it? She did not know; it was too subtle and elusive to name. But she felt it, creeping out of the sky, reaching toward her through the sounds, the scents, the color that filled the air.

10   Now her bosom rose and fell tumultuously. She was beginning to recognize this thing that was approaching to possess her, and she was striving to beat it back with her will—as powerless as her two white slender hands would have been. When she abandoned herself a little whispered word escaped her slightly parted lips. She said it over and over under her breath: "free, free, free!" The vacant stare and the look of terror that had followed it went from her eyes. They stayed keen and bright. Her pulses beat fast, and the coursing blood warmed and relaxed every inch of her body.

11   She did not stop to ask if it were or were not a monstrous joy that held her. A clear and exalted perception enabled her to dismiss the suggestion as trivial. She knew that she would weep again when she saw the kind, tender hands folded in death; the face that had never looked save with love upon her, fixed and gray and dead. But she saw beyond that bitter moment a long procession of years to come that would belong to her absolutely. And she opened and spread her arms out to them in welcome.

12   There would be no one to live for during those coming years; she would live for herself. There would be no powerful will bending hers in that blind persistence with which men and women believe they have a right to impose a private will upon a fellow-creature. A kind intention or a cruel intention made the act seem no less a crime as she looked upon it in that brief moment of illumination.

13   And yet she had loved him—sometimes. Often she had not. What did it matter! What could love, the unsolved mystery, count for in the face of this possession of self-assertion which she suddenly recognized as the strongest impulse of her being!

14   "Free! Body and soul free!" she kept whispering.

15   Josephine was kneeling before the closed door with her lips to the keyhole, imploring for admission. "Louise, open the door! I beg; open the door—you will make yourself ill. What are you doing, Louise? For heaven's sake open the door."

16   "Go away. I am not making myself ill." No; she was drinking in a very elixir of life through that open window.

17   Her fancy was running riot along those days ahead of her. Spring days, and summer days, and all sorts of days that would be her own. She breathed a quick

prayer that life might be long. It was only yesterday she had thought with a shudder that life might be long.

18   She arose at length and opened the door to her sister's importunities. There was a feverish triumph in her eyes, and she carried herself unwittingly like a goddess of Victory. She clasped her sister's waist, and together they descended the stairs. Richards stood waiting for them at the bottom.

19   Some one was opening the front door with a latchkey. It was Brently Mallard who entered, a little travel-stained, composedly carrying his grip-sack and umbrella. He had been far from the scene of the accident, and did not even know there had been one. He stood amazed at Josephine's piercing cry; at Richards' quick motion to screen him from the view of his wife.

20   When the doctors came they said she had died of heart disease—of the joy that kills. ■

Vocabulary

Directions: Choose the meaning that best matches the word as it is used in the reading selection above.

1. **afflicted** (paragraph 1) diagnosed, affected

2. **veiled** (paragraph 2) hidden

3. **hastened** (paragraph 2) rushed, hurried

4. **forestall** (paragraph 2) prevent, hinder, anticipate, jump in before

5. **aquiver** (paragraph 5) agitated, excited, trembling, nervous

6. **bespoke** (paragraph 8) modified, tailored, adapted, custom-made, personalized

7. **repression** (paragraph 8) oppression, tyranny, cruelty

Main Idea

8. What is the central theme of this passage? Answers will vary. Possible answer may be: When Mrs. Mallard's husband died, she discovered much about herself and her life, but then she died with an awareness of a full life of freedom.

9. What is the main idea of paragraph 12? Answers will vary.
Possible answer may include—she will live for herself rather than for
someone else.

10. What is the main idea of paragraph 10? Answers will vary.
Possible answer may be: Mrs.Mallard realized she was free at last.

Supporting Details

11. Answers will vary.

12. _____

13. _____

14. _____

Patterns of Organization

15. What is the primary pattern of organization Bradbury uses in this
passage? Time order

16. List the signal words which helped you determine the pattern.
There were, but now, she was, there was, now, she was, there would be,
she would, was, it was only yesterday

Facts and Opinions

17. List the facts in paragraph 9. Answers will vary.

_____

_____

18. List the opinions in paragraph 9. Answers will vary.

_____

_____

Inferences

Directions: List five inferences that can be made from the reading above.

19. Answers will vary. _____

20. _____

21. _____

22. _____

23. _____

Purpose and Tone

24. What is the overall tone of the passage? Answers will vary.

_____

_____

_____

25. What is the author's primary purpose in this passage? Entertain

_____

_____

_____

Magazine/Periodical   **READING 4**

1210L

"Inception" Review: Leonardo DiCaprio and Christopher Nolan Blow Our Minds

Elizabeth Weitzman

1   When was the last time you had your mind blown by a movie? Because when "Inception" ends and the lights come up, you'll be sitting in your seat, staring at the screen, wondering what the hell just happened.

"Inception" star Leonardo DiCaprio is about to blow your mind—not with the gun—in one of the best mind benders ever made.

2   Of course, it won't be the first time director Christopher Nolan has shaken us out of the apathy that modern moviegoing induces. "Inception" blends the blockbuster enormity of his "Dark Knight" with the indie insights of "Memento" to create an all-encompassing experience that makes most other summer films seem mediocre.

3   Like "Memento," this is one you'll need to see several times, backwards and forwards, to fully grasp. And since part of the fun is Nolan's insistence on keeping us unmoored, you won't find any spoilers here.

4   But the basics are these: Leonardo DiCaprio is Dom Cobb, a futuristic thief who specializes in rifling through people's brains while they dream. Though this is not a job without risks, his new assignment is about to raise the stakes.

5   When a mysterious businessman (Ken Watanabe) asks Dom to change—rather than simply steal—the thoughts of a competitor (Cillian Murphy), Dom's colleagues (including Joseph Gordon-Levitt and Ellen Page) balk. They'd have to travel deeper into the recesses of their target's subconscious, which poses extreme danger for everyone involved. But Dom has been a haunted man since his wife (Marion Cotillard) died, and this mission may be his best chance to find some peace.

6   No synopsis could possibly do justice to the complex universe Nolan fashions as we go deeper into each visually ornate, emotionally intricate dreamscape.

Granted, not every element works perfectly; Cotillard's storyline feels underdeveloped, and the action could have been tightened up. But the ambition on display is so huge, and the filmmaking so intelligent, you'll emerge feeling as if you've just watched an entire season of the greatest sci-fi series never made.

7   With "Inception," Nolan acknowledges that no one could create a movie as exciting, as unexpected, as startling as the dreams we invent for ourselves. But it's evident by now that he's never going to give up trying. ■

Source: Weitzman, Elizabeth. (2010, July 16). "Inception" Review: Leonardo DiCaprio and Christopher Nolan Blow Our Minds. *NY Daily News.*

Vocabulary

Choose five words or phrases from the reading that are unfamiliar to you. Use the dictionary or other sources to determine their meanings. Answers will vary.

1. _____

2. _____

3. _____

4. _____

5. _____

Main Idea

6. What is the central theme of this article? _____

Answers will vary. Possible answer may be *Inception* is one of the best

mind bender movies ever made.

Supporting Details

7. What are the similarities between *Inception* and *Memento*, according to the writer? _____

Both have indie insights. Both are movies you'll need to see several times,

backwards and forwards, to fully grasp.

Patterns of Organization

8. What is the primary pattern of organization used when the writer gives the synopsis of the movie? _____
   time order

Facts and Opinions

List three facts and three opinions from the movie review.

Facts: Answers will vary.

9. _____
10. _____
11. _____

Opinions: Answers will vary.

12. _____
13. _____
14. _____

Inferences

15. Would you infer the writer would recommend the movie? Why or why not?
    Answers will vary. Possible answers are: Yes, because he thinks the movie
    is great. He infers it is better than any other summer movie. He also says
    watching *Inception* is like watching a whole season of the greatest
    sci-fi series never made.

Purpose and Tone

List three positive connotations the author uses to describe *Inception*.
Answers will vary. Possible answers may include:

16. "blockbuster enormity"
17. "all-encompassing experience"
18. "emotionally intricate"

List a tone used in the article. Give an example.

Tone	Example
Answers will vary.	

19. admiring

20. But the ambition on display is so huge, and the filmmaking so intelligent, you'll emerge feeling as if you've just watched an entire season of the greatest sci-fi series never made

Visual Image **READING 5**

1. Write a caption for this photo using the purpose: *inform*.

   Answers will vary. For example: Motocross is a sport that is becoming increasingly popular.

2. Write a caption using the purpose: *persuade*.

   Answers will vary. For example: By doing motocross, you will be cool and adventurous like you've always wanted!

3. Write a caption using the purpose: *entertain*.

   Answers will vary. For example: The man raced across the finish line and

   won the competition in the nick of time . . .

4. What is the perceived tone of this image?

   Answers will vary. For example: excited, fervent, passionate, intense

Additional Recommended Readings

Adams, A. (1985). *Ansel Adams: An autobiography.* Boston, MA: Little Brown and Company.

Bradbury, R. (1975). *Dandelion Wine.* New York, NY: Bantam Books.

Buskin, R. (2002). *Sheryl Crow: No Fool to This Game.* New York, NY: Billboard Books.

Eig, J. (2007). *Opening Day: The Story of Jackie Robinson's First Season.* New York, NY: Simon & Schuster.

McCafferty, K. (1999). *L. L. Bean Family Camping Handbook.* New York, NY: The Lyons Press.

McWilliams, M. (2006). *Food Fundamentals,* 8th ed. Upper Saddle River, NJ: Pearson.

Solomon, D. (1987). *Jackson Pollock: A Biography.* New York, NY: Simon & Schuster.

myreadinglab

For support in meeting this chapter's objectives, log on to www.myreadinglab.com and select Purpose and Tone.

10 Critical Thinking

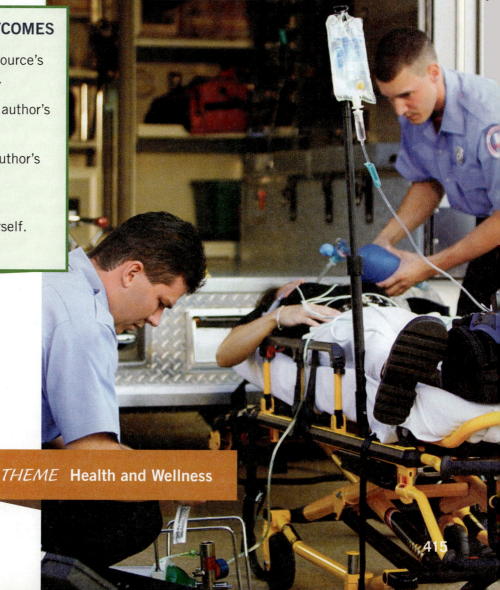

LEARNING OUTCOMES

LO1 Determine a source's bias and credibility.

LO2 Determine an author's argument.

LO3 Validate the author's support.

LO4 Evaluate the information for yourself.

THEME **Health and Wellness**

SPOTLIGHT ON LEARNING STYLES ✍ WRITE 👆 Do

When it comes to critical thinking, a lot depends on what we've read and what we've experienced for ourselves. Our lives are filled with information from so many sources, and it may be very difficult at times to decide what and whom to believe. When I encounter new information, especially related to health and wellness, I like to compare it to other things I've read. Between the Internet, brochures in doctors' offices, news clips, magazines, and research, it seems like I get a lot of conflicting information when it comes to what to eat, how much to exercise and sleep, and how much sun exposure is safe. Do I believe the doctor or nurse practitioner's recommendation when I experience strange side effects from a new medication? Do I believe the advertisements from the drug companies that assure me the medicine is "safe when taken as directed"? Do I drink 10 cups of green tea, 2 cups of coffee, and/or 8 glasses of water each day? Do I avoid eggs, or should I eat more eggs every day? Is eating dark chocolate really good for me? Whom do I believe? Using my writing learning style, I can research the latest advice on real health topics that matter to my family and me, I can check out the sources of this information to determine if they are trustworthy, and I can write a chart to compare the information obtained and evaluate my sources. Some of my questions include:

- Are patients receiving fair and consistent health coverage?

- Are consumers getting accurate information so they can make informed decisions about product safety and effectiveness?

- Are government officials making decisions based on what's moral, ethical, or economically beneficial?

- Can you trust someone else who has gone through the same health crises you, a friend, or a family member are facing?

- Who decides what is right and wrong, acceptable or unacceptable regarding your health?

In this final chapter, you have the opportunity to use all of your reading skills in combination to think critically about health and wellness issues. Reading selections in this chapter come from many different sources and contain multiple perspectives and biases. You will refine your critical thinking skills as you consider different points of view in readings from the health and wellness field. The goal is that as you become a more critical reader and thinker, you will know when you need to gather more information, question a source, or incorporate the perspective into your own.

In the first step of SQ3R, we survey the reading. This includes looking at the title or heading. It is also the first step in detecting bias.

Detecting Bias

According to the thesaurus, *bias* is "prejudice, partiality, unfairness, preconceived notion, foregone conclusion, favoritism, predisposition, or

> **LO1**
> Determine a source's bias and credibility.

preconception." A writer may be for or against an issue, topic, or organization. A reader can tell a lot about the writer's attitude or bias just by looking at a title. Let's look at some titles of articles and blogs about health care. Examine the word choices and tone to determine the bias or attitude of each writer.

EXAMPLE

Directions: Read the headline and identify the writer's bias (note the word choices and tone).

1. How American Health Care Killed My Father

Bias: _____

2. The Health Insurance Trap

Bias: _____

For headline 1, the writer is angry at the American health care system and blaming it for his father's death. His tone is critical. For headline 2, there is a negative connotation evidenced by the word *trap* to describe health insurance. The writer is critical in a negative manner.

PRACTICE *THE NEW SKILL*

Directions: Read the headline and identify the writer's bias (note the word choices and tone).

1. Uninsured and Sick Student Begged for His Life

Bias: The writer is compassionate and sympathetic toward the student based on the words *begged for his life*. The author is critical of the health care system.

2. Health Insurance Companies Want Severe Penalties for People Who Do Not Buy Coverage

Bias: The writer sees the health care insurance companies as greedy. The use of the words *want severe penalties* shows the writer is critical of their behavior.

3. The Fatal Flaw of Obamacare

Bias: *Flaw* gives a negative connotation as the writer thinks there is an error in President Obama's health care bill; *fatal* means the writer thinks the bill will not get passed through Congress. The use of the word *fatal* has a strong negative connotation and the word *Obamacare* may indicate the writer has a cynical tone.

4. "Don't Get Sick": The Truth about GOP Health Plans?

Bias: By saying "Don't get sick," the writer is saying that the health plan won't be sufficient if someone actually does get sick. The writer is sarcastic.

5. Experts: Even with Reform, Health Care Insurers Will Likely Discriminate

Bias: The writer is straightforward about letting the reader know what the experts said.

6. Millions Agree with Prognosis Offered by Country Doctors

Bias: Country doctors have good ideas about health care. Maybe the writer is exaggerating with the word *millions* and is positive about country doctors' view of health care. The writer is critical in a positive manner.

Determining Credibility

If you see a Web page outlining a special nutritional plan to lower cholesterol written by Dr. Sharon Snyders, would you accept the information? Why or why not? You might want to question the purpose of the Web site or text and ask, for instance, if the creator of the site is trying to sell a nutritional supplement or a self-help book. Also find out if the information is coming from an organization with a mission or agenda, and if so, what is it?

LO2
Determine an author's argument.

The answer to whether you would accept the information would depend on her credentials. I would ask, "What is the focus of Dr. Snyders's expertise?" Just because she is a "doctor" does not necessarily mean she is experienced or educated in nutrition and lowering cholesterol. A "Dr." before her name may indicate a doctor of philosophy in education, literacy, history, psychology, mathematics, business, or engineering—and not in medicine.

What would you need to ask before you accepted the information? Using the example above, important questions to ask would be: "What is her doctorate degree in? What makes her an expert on lowering cholesterol?" Remember that having a title next to one's name does not ensure a person's expertise in everything. If the author were a Registered Dietician, or you learned she had a Ph.D. in Nutrition, she would more likely be a credible source for information about lowering cholesterol. On the other hand, do not dismiss a person's first-hand account or experience. If a person is giving an opinion or sharing feelings, and he or she has been through an illness, that may be more valuable to you for inspiration and encouragement than a long research study.

Note: If you search the Internet, you may find information from Web sites ending in .com, .edu, and .org. Commercial site addresses (URLs) end in .com. It is not safe, however, to assume that non-commercial sites (.org and .edu) are unbiased or credible. Organizations create Web sites that promote their points of view. Educational institutions are made up of individuals who also may create Web sites with biases or partiality toward a particular perspective. So, although the information may be created by an educational institution and it is less likely to be biased, you still need to use caution and check the credibility and reliability of the source.

Following are some statements taken from different sources on the Internet related to the search words "cell phones and cancer."

EXAMPLE ————————————————————————————————————

Directions: Read the brief statement and source and evaluate it for credibility.

Studies have not shown any consistent link between cellular telephone use and cancer, but scientists feel that additional research is needed before firm conclusions can be drawn.

(National Cancer Institute Fact Sheet. U.S. National Institutes of Health.)

The National Cancer Institute is a credible source because it is a research-based government organization. Based on studies that have been conducted thus far, the Institute objectively states that more research needs to be done.

PRACTICE THE NEW SKILL

Directions: Read the brief statement and source and evaluate it for credibility.

1. Heavy users of wireless mobile phones face increased risks of developing severe brain tumors, according to the most comprehensive study ever conducted on the possible link between cancer and the long-term use of cellular phone. Researchers at the Swedish National Institute for Working Life and the University of Oerebro compared the mobile phone use of 4,400 people—half of them cancer patients, and the other half healthy people who made up the control group—and made some disturbing discoveries.

    Credibility: Is the source credible? Why or why not? Answers will vary. The source may be credible since it is associated with the University of Oerebro in Sweden.

2. A group called the International EMF Collaborative issued a report the other day warning that cell phones might be more dangerous than users have been led to believe by health authorities.

    The report, titled "Cellphones and Brain Tumors: 15 Reasons for Concern," says the latest research indicates that regular use of cell phones can result in a "significant" risk of brain tumors. It also says children are at greater risk than adults because their still-developing brain cells are more vulnerable to electromagnetic radiation.

    "Cell phones are causing brain tumors," the lead author of the report, Lloyd Morgan, told me. "Industry-backed studies try to hide that fact. But if you read them carefully, you can see there are risks." *(The Morning Call)*

    Credibility: Is the source credible? Why or why not? Answers will vary. This source may be less credible. The EMF Collaborative is not mentioned as being associated with a university or government organization. The research is not clearly supported.

3. Lawmakers say they will seek more federally funded research into the possible connection between cell phone use and cancer. The announcement comes several days after a review released by the

Environmental Working Group found potential safety hazards connected to cell phone use. *(WebMD)*

Credibility: Is the source credible? Why or why not? <u>Answers will vary.</u>
<u>The source may not be credible. The Environmental Working Group is not</u>
<u>identified with experienced researchers.</u>

After surveying the title and a few key statements in the article to determine potential bias and credibility and then deciding if it is worth reading, what else should we do? Here is a 4-step process to help you evaluate readings more thoroughly. It incorporates the other steps of SQ3R as we ask questions and look for answers in the material as we read.

SAVE: 4-Step System to Evaluate Readings

SAVE is an effective and easy-to-remember system for critically evaluating non-fiction material. Once you have applied the SAVE test, you will be able to decide if the source is something you should save or toss.

> **LO3**
> Validate the author's support.
> **LO4**
> Evaluate the information for yourself.

S—Source: Who is the owner of the publication or Web site and/or author of the article? Do you detect any bias in the presentation of the material? Is the author qualified or credible as an expert in his specific field? What is the owner/author's background? Who might be paying them to write the article? Is there an agenda to promote?

A—Argument: Identify the author's argument or point. What does the author state as his or her opinion or attitude? Does the stated argument answer your question or fulfill your purpose for reading?

V—Validate: What evidence is presented by the author as proof that his viewpoint is correct? Is the evidence used in the proper context? Is the support logical? Is it truthful?

E—Evaluate: Overall, using all of the information you found above, how useful is this information for you? Do you believe what you read? Will you change your lifestyle or behavior based on the text you read? Will you SAVE the article or toss it?

Example of One Student Using SAVE

Here is an example of what one student, Rachelle, did when she wanted to learn more about the medical uses of marijuana. First she did an Internet search on the topic "marijuana medical uses," and then she analyzed two different sources.

SOURCE 1: NORML WEB SITE

Review of Human Studies on Medical Use of Marijuana

by Dale H. Gieringer, Ph.D.
August 1996
California NORML (The National Organization for the Reform
of Marijuana Laws)
2215-R Market St. #278
San Francisco CA 94114
(415) 563-5858 / canorml@igc.apc.org

Summary: Human Studies on Medical Uses of Marijuana

There have been hundreds of studies on the medical uses of cannabis since its introduction to western medicine in the early nineteenth century. A review of the literature reveals over 65 human studies, most of them in the 1970s and early '80s.

- The best established medical use of smoked marijuana is as an anti-nauseant for cancer chemotherapy. Marijuana's efficacy was demonstrated in studies by half a dozen states, involving hundreds of subjects. Most research has found smoked marijuana superior to oral THC (Marinol). Many oncologists are currently recommending marijuana to their patients.

- Marijuana is widely used to treat nausea and appetite loss associated with AIDS, but the government has blocked research in this area. Studies have shown that marijuana helps improve appetite, and Marinol has been FDA approved for treatment of AIDS wasting syndrome. Nearly 10,000 PWAs were reported to be using marijuana through the San Francisco Cannabis Buyers' Club. However, the government has blocked efforts by Dr. Donald Abrams of the University of California at San Francisco to proceed with an FDA-approved study of marijuana and AIDS wasting syndrome, by refusing to grant him access to research marijuana. Research is badly needed on the relative merits of smoked and oral marijuana versus Marinol.

- There is much evidence, largely anecdotal, that marijuana is useful as an anti-convulsant for spinal injuries, multiple sclerosis, epilepsy, and other diseases. Similar evidence suggests marijuana may be useful as an analgesic for chronic pain from cancer and migraine as well as for rheumatism and a variety of auto-immune diseases. There is a conspicuous lack of controlled studies in this area; further research is needed.

- Cannabidiol, a constituent of natural marijuana not found in Marinol, appears to have distinctive therapeutic value as an anti-convulsant and hypnotic, and to counteract acute anxiety reactions caused by THC.

- It has been established that marijuana reduces intra-ocular pressure, the primary object of glaucoma therapy. Due to its psychoactivity, however, marijuana has not gained widespread acceptance in this application.

- Many patients report using marijuana as a substitute for more addictive and harmful psychoactive drugs, including prescription painkillers, opiates, and alcohol. Marijuana and Marinol have also been found useful as a treatment for depression and mood disorders in Alzheimer's and other patients. More research is needed.

SOURCE 2: HARVARD WEB SITE

Health Concerns: What Are the Medical Dangers of Marijuana Use? (Condensed Article)

Source: cyber.law.harvard.edu/evidence99/marijuana/Health_1.html

I must preface these statements with the remark that there is still a great deal of research to be done concerning the effects of marijuana on the health of humans due to the fact that widespread marijuana use has only become prevalent in this country within the last three decades, so the effects of long-term use are just beginning to become apparent. I should also add that in making these observations, I have concentrated on the risks of smoking natural marijuana, since it is the most effective method of ingesting its active cannabinoids. It would be fallacious to conclude that because the chemicals in marijuana have been found to present fewer dangers than some very harmful substances, the medical or recreational use of marijuana is perfectly safe. In a recreational context, marijuana has been shown to affect health, brain function, and memory. And in a medical context, marijuana is like any other powerful prescription drug: it has potentially dangerous side effects, and the decision to use it to treat patients must involve the same balancing test as the one required for chemotherapy or AZT: do the therapeutic effects of the drug outweigh its harmful effects? Though there are many more studies to be done on this issue, current data shows that the answer to this question may not always be "yes."

Effects of Habitual Marijuana Use on the Immune System

The most potent argument against the use of marijuana to treat medical disorders is that marijuana may cause the acceleration or aggravation of the very disorders it is being used to treat. Smoking marijuana regularly (a joint a day) can damage the cells in the bronchial passages which protect the body against inhaled microorganisms and decrease the ability of the immune cells in the lungs to fight off fungi, bacteria, and tumor cells. For patients with already weakened immune systems, this means an increase in the possibility of dangerous pulmonary infections, including pneumonia, which often proves fatal in AIDS patients.

Respiratory Illnesses

The main respiratory consequences of smoking marijuana regularly (one joint a day) are pulmonary infections and respiratory cancer, whose connection to marijuana use has been strongly suggested but not conclusively proven. The effects also include chronic bronchitis, impairment in the function of the smaller air passages, inflammation of the lung, the development of potentially pre-cancerous abnormalities in the bronchial lining and lungs, and, as discussed, a reduction in the capabilities of many defensive mechanisms within the lungs.

Mental Health, Brain Function, and Memory

It has been suggested that marijuana is at the root of many mental disorders, including acute toxic psychosis, panic attacks (one of the very conditions it is being used experimentally to treat), flashbacks, delusions, depersonalization, hallucinations, paranoia, depression, and uncontrollable aggressiveness. Marijuana has long been known to trigger attacks of mental illness, such as bipolar (manic-depressive) psychosis and schizophrenia. This connection with mental illness should make health care providers for terminally ill patients and the patients themselves, who may already be suffering from some form of clinical depression, weigh very carefully the pros and cons of adopting a therapeutic course of marijuana.

S—Source

For the **NORML** Web site, Rachelle noticed that the owner of the Web site is NORML—the National Organization of the Reform of Marijuana Laws. Right away, Rachelle knew that this information most likely would be biased toward legalizing marijuana use. Since the agenda of the organization is to legalize marijuana, Rachelle realized that she probably would not get all of the facts supporting both sides of the issue. She also noticed that the author is a Ph.D., but she did not see on the site any information about the author's background such as what field the Ph.D. was in.

For the **Harvard** Web site, Rachelle noticed that the owner/author is Harvard University. Rachelle expected that a well-respected university would be less biased and more likely to give facts related to both sides of the topic of the medical uses of marijuana. Rachelle also thought that since the site owner is a university, the authors of the information would be more careful that the facts they used to support their point were accurate. In addition, since the university site is addressing law, Rachelle also thought that the site would be less likely to have a one-sided agenda and more likely to report factual information.

A—Argument

Rachelle then looked for each Web site's main argument.

NORML Web Site Argument: This is stated at the beginning of the article.

There have been hundreds of studies on the medical uses of cannabis since its introduction to western medicine in the early nineteenth century.

Harvard Web Site Argument: The following statement is in the third paragraph, after some introductory information that sets the context for the writer's argument.

In a recreational context, marijuana has been shown to affect health, brain function, and memory. And in a medical context, marijuana is like any other powerful prescription drug: it has potentially dangerous side effects, and the decision to use it to treat patients must involve the same balancing test as the one required for chemotherapy or AZT: do the therapeutic effects of the drug outweigh its harmful effects? Though there are many more studies to be done on this issue, current data shows that the answer to this question may not always be "yes."

V—Validate

NORML Web Site Argument: Rachelle paraphrased the argument to make it clear and concise: *Many studies show the effective medical uses of cannabis.*

Next Rachelle analyzed each supporting detail and tried to validate the information.

1. The best established medical use of smoked marijuana is as an anti-nauseant for cancer chemotherapy. Marijuana's efficacy was demonstrated in studies by half a dozen states, involving hundreds of subjects. Most research has found smoked marijuana superior to oral THC (Marinol). Many oncologists are currently recommending marijuana to their patients.

After reading this first supporting reason, Rachelle asked: "What studies?" and "Which states?" She also asked for more specific information about the research the writer claimed has found marijuana superior to Marinol. The phrase "many oncologists are recommending" also indicates that many are not.

2. Marijuana is widely used to treat nausea and appetite loss associated with AIDS, but the government has blocked research in this area. Studies have shown that marijuana helps improve appetite, and Marinol has been FDA approved for treatment of AIDS wasting syndrome. Nearly 10,000 PWAs were reported to be using marijuana through the San Francisco Cannabis Buyers' Club. However, the government has blocked efforts by Dr. Donald Abrams of the University of California at San Francisco to proceed with an FDA-approved study of marijuana and AIDS wasting syndrome, by refusing to grant him access to research marijuana. Research is badly needed on the relative merits of smoked and oral marijuana versus Marinol.

Rachelle wanted to know more about how the government had "blocked research." She suspected the tone of the writer was critical because of the use of the word *blocked*. Rachelle questioned the context and relatedness of the information coming from the San Francisco Cannabis Buyers' Club. She wanted to know what PWAs were, and why it was important that nearly 10,000 were buying marijuana. There was little information given about Dr. Donald Abrams and no reason given for why his research grant was rejected by the FDA. There might have been unrelated reasons for not funding his grant. Finally, she felt the phrase "research is badly needed" was an opinion and not a reason for research.

3. There is much evidence, largely anecdotal, that marijuana is useful as an anti-convulsant for spinal injuries, multiple sclerosis, epilepsy, and other diseases. Similar evidence suggests marijuana may be useful as an analgesic for chronic pain from cancer and migraine as well as for rheumatism and a variety of auto-immune diseases. There is a conspicuous lack of controlled studies in this area; further research is needed.

Also the term *conspicuous lack* showed the writer was using more negative connotations.

4. Cannabidiol, a constituent of natural marijuana not found in Marinol, appears to have distinctive therapeutic value as an anti-convulsant and hypnotic, and to counteract acute anxiety reactions caused by THC.

Rachelle did not see the writer's use of the qualifying term *appears to have* as a strong support.

5. It has been established that marijuana reduces intra-ocular pressure, the primary object of glaucoma therapy. Due to its psychoactivity, however, marijuana has not gained widespread acceptance in this application.

It has been established did not tell Rachelle by whom. She wondered which qualified researchers found this to be true.

6. Many patients report using marijuana as a substitute for more addictive and harmful psychoactive drugs, including prescription painkillers, opiates, and alcohol. Marijuana and Marinol have also been found useful as a treatment for depression and mood disorders in Alzheimer's and other patients. More research is needed.

Rachelle questioned the term *many patients* and thought it was vague. She knew that just because *many patients* or many people did something, that did not mean the action was a good idea or a safe medical practice. Also, when the writer stated, "Marijuana and Marinol have also been found useful as a treatment for ..." Rachelle asked again, "who found it useful?" and "where was the study written?"

Harvard Web Site Argument: Rachelle paraphrased the argument to make it clear and concise.

Paraphrased point: *The therapeutic effects of marijuana do not outweigh the harmful effects.*

Next Rachelle analyzed each supporting detail and tried to validate the information.

• Smoking marijuana regularly (a joint a day) can damage the cells in the bronchial passages which protect the body against inhaled microorganisms and decrease the ability of the immune cells in the lungs to fight off fungi, bacteria, and tumor cells.

In this first supporting reason, the author discussed the specific effects of smoking marijuana on the cells in the body and specifically on the immune cells in the lungs. No emotional or connotative language was used to describe the effects. Several specific Web sites and studies were cited at the end of the section.

• The main respiratory consequences of smoking marijuana regularly (one joint a day) are pulmonary infections and respiratory cancer, whose connection to marijuana use has been strongly suggested but not conclusively proven.

The language used in this section was denotative and objective. The author did not use alarmist or emotional language. Saying, "whose connection to marijuana use has been strongly suggested but not conclusively proven" shows that the author was not trying to convince the reader of something that has not been proven. Citations of articles and Web sites were offered to the reader for further research and verification.

• It has been suggested that marijuana is at the root of many mental disorders, including acute toxic psychosis, panic attacks (one of the very conditions it is being used experimentally to treat), flashbacks, delusions, depersonalization, hallucinations, paranoia, depression, and uncontrollable aggressiveness. Marijuana has long been known to trigger attacks of mental illness, such as bipolar (manic-depressive) psychosis and schizophrenia.

The first question for a critical reader would be "*Where* has it been suggested?" that "marijuana is at the root of many mental disorders"? The author of this article stated the sources of the information and offered additional sources to the reader.

E—Evaluate

NORML Web Site Argument: Overall: Rachelle found the source biased in favor of legalizing medical marijuana. The credibility of the author was questionable since there was no information about his background. Rachelle also found the writer's support weak. None of the "research" or "studies" were specifically identified. The writer also used negative connotations showing a critical and biased tone in the support. Qualifying terms such as *many, some,* and *appears to* were used throughout the support, which indicates the writer's information was vague and not supported with solid and relevant data. After running the SAVE test, she decided not to save this article. It was not useful for a college level research paper.

Harvard Web Site Argument: Overall: Rachelle found the source balanced with facts and objective research regarding the medical use of marijuana. The authors cited several sources for the studies and information used to support their points. The author is the Harvard Law Review so the article most likely looked at the issue from a legal and objective perspective. Even though the author used qualifying terms such as *mostly* or *inconclusive,* the information was based on cited research, so the conclusions appear to be credible most of the time. The author also used denotative and non-emotional words, indicating use of a non-biased argument. After running the SAVE test, Rachelle saved the article to use in her college research paper.

PRACTICE THE NEW SKILL

Directions: Read the passages below and use SAVE to help you decide if the article is something you would SAVE or discard.

1. There's a new perk for coffee drinkers. Brewed coffee contains significant amounts of dietary fiber—more, in fact, than what is found in common beverages such as wine and orange juice, according to researchers in Spain. Their study found the amount of soluble fiber in coffee can range from 0.47 to 0.75 grams per 100 ml, depending on the manner of brewing: espresso, filtered, or freeze-dried instant. For those drinking three cups a day, coffee could contribute up to 10 percent of their average daily soluble fiber intake as well as appreciable amounts of health-protective antioxidants.

Source: Food in the News. (2007, May). *Saturday Evening Post*, Retrieved from Academic Search Premier database.

S—Source: (Who is the owner/author? Are they qualified/biased?)

"Researchers in Spain" is not a credible source. Who are the researchers?

A—Argument: (What is the author's argument/point/opinion/attitude?)

There is a new perk for coffee drinkers—brewed coffees have more fiber than other foods and beverages.

V—Validate: (What is the evidence? Is it in context/logical/truthful?)

The article states "soluble fiber in coffee can range from 0.47 to 0.75 grams per 100 ml, depending on the manner of brewing: espresso, filtered, or freeze-dried instant. For those drinking three cups a day, coffee could contribute up to 10 percent of their average daily soluble fiber intake as well as appreciable amounts of health-protective antioxidants."

E—Evaluate: (How useful is this text to you? Will you SAVE it or toss it?)

It is not clear if the researchers conducted a credible study. I would toss the study.

2. Facebook profiles reveal more about your friends than they realize. In addition to telling you a person's favorite band and romantic status, online profiles can also reveal whether he or she is a narcissist. Narcissism is a personality disorder characterized by intense self-absorption. Narcissists don't really value other people, seeing them purely as a tool to serve their own needs. Researchers at the University of Georgia who studied Facebook profiles found telltale signs of narcissism in a small but significant portion of them. Instead of a snapshot, narcissists often feature a glamour shot or a professional photo. They tend to have large numbers of online friends and plenty of back-and-forth wall posts, but few truly intimate friends. In this way, a narcissist's Facebook presence mirrors his real social life, says study author W. Keith Campbell. It "turns out that narcissists are using Facebook the same way they use their other relationships—for self-promotion, with an emphasis on quantity over quality." Beware of such "friends," Campbell tells *LiveScience.com*, because it's ultimately unrewarding to be involved with people who love themselves too much. "Narcissists might initially be seen as charming, but they end up using people for their own advantage. They hurt the people around them and they hurt themselves in the long run."

Source: The Facebook Narcissist Test. (October 17, 2008). *The Week.* Vol. 8, Issue 383, p. 24.

> **S—Source:** **(Who is the owner/author? Are they qualified/biased?)**
> *The Week* is a weekly periodical.

A—Argument: (What is the author's argument/point/opinion/attitude?)

Facebook profiles reveal more about your friends than they realize. In addition to telling you a person's favorite band and romantic status, online profiles can also reveal whether he or she is a narcissist.

V—Validate: (What is the evidence? Is it in context/logical/truthful?)

Researchers at the University of Georgia . . . says study author W. Keith Campbell . . . Campbell tells LiveScience.com

There is no real evidence of Campbell's opinion.

E—Evaluate: (How useful is this text to you? Will you SAVE it or toss it?)

It is not useful. It is mostly opinion and I would toss it.

3. "You're never fully dressed without a smile," sang Little Orphan Annie in the Broadway musical. It turns out Annie may have been giving some shrewd advice—studies have repeatedly shown that people remember smiling faces better than neutral ones. Now researchers at Duke University have found a physical explanation for the phenomenon. Roberto Cabeza and his colleagues "introduced" volunteers to a number of people by showing them a picture and telling them a name. Using MRI, the investigators found that both learning and recalling the names associated with smiling faces preferentially activated the orbitofrontal cortex, an area of the brain involved in reward processing. Cabeza says that although the studies are preliminary, it makes evolutionary sense that a smile would be rewarding to the onlooker. "We are sensitive to positive social signals," Cabeza explains. "We want to remember people who were kind to us, in case we interact with them in the future."

Source: Leitzell, Katherine. (April/May 2008). Just a Smile.
Scientific American Mind. Vol. 19, No. 2, p. 8.

S—Source: (Who is the owner/author? Are they qualified/biased?)

Researchers at Duke University . . .
Duke University is a well-known university.

A—Argument: (What is the author's argument/point/opinion/attitude?)

—studies have repeatedly shown that people remember smiling faces better than neutral ones.

V—Validate: (What is the evidence? Is it in context/logical/truthful?)

Duke University researchers have found a physical explanation for the phenomenon. Roberto Cabeza and his colleagues "introduced" volunteers to a number of people by showing them a picture and telling them a name. Using MRI, the investigators found that both learning and recalling the names associated with smiling faces preferentially activated the orbitofrontal cortex, an area of the brain involved in reward processing. Cabeza says that although the studies are preliminary, it makes evolutionary sense that a smile would be rewarding to the onlooker. "We are sensitive to positive social signals," Cabeza explains. "We want to remember people who were kind to us, in case we interact with them in the future."

E—Evaluate: (How useful is this text to you? Will you SAVE it or toss it?)

I would SAVE the article and use it in my research.

REVIEW *WHAT YOU LEARNED*

Directions: Apply the SAVE technique to decide if you will SAVE or discard the documentary. Answers will vary.

Food, Inc.—A Robert Kenner Film

Synopsis

In ***Food, Inc.***, filmmaker Robert Kenner lifts the veil on our nation's food industry, exposing the highly mechanized underbelly that's been hidden from the American consumer with the consent of our government's regulatory agencies, USDA and FDA. Our nation's food supply is now controlled by a handful of corporations that often put profit ahead of consumer health, the livelihood of the American farmer, the safety of workers and our own environment. We have bigger-breasted chickens, the perfect pork chop, insecticide-resistant soybean seeds, even tomatoes that won't go bad, but we also have new strains of E. coli—the harmful bacteria that causes illness for an estimated 73,000 Americans annually. We are riddled with widespread obesity, particularly among children, and an epidemic level of diabetes among adults.

Featuring interviews with such experts as Eric Schlosser ("Fast Food Nation"), Michael Pollan ("The Omnivore's Dilemma") along with forward thinking social entrepreneurs like Stonyfield Farms' Gary Hirschberg and Polyface Farms' Joel Salatin, ***Food, Inc.*** reveals surprising—and often shocking truths—about what we eat, how it's produced, who we have become as a nation and where we are going from here.

Directions: Choose 5 of the reviews below. Apply the SAVE technique to evaluate whether you would use the review in your own decision to watch the film, *Food, Inc.* and perhaps explore the issues of food consumption. Answers will vary.

Note: The following reviews are posted exactly as they appear on the blog, including spelling and grammar errors.

Reviews

1

Sad ... Scary, but we the "wallets" can make the difference.

Great documentary. I grew up in a farming community and bought into the lies being sold to the consumers today. I've also been the "low-income" individual that couldn't afford to eat "right." The cold reality is that the consumer can only make a difference by buying responsibly and/or boycotting products that are unsafe or unethical. The FDA/USDA will not protect you, nor will the industry rush to ensure your safety. The case of rBGH is a proven point. An educated public chose not buy products that contained rBGH, and the industry had to respond by eliminating it from the farms. Money will always force the hand of politics and big industry, ethics/morality will never/seldom win. Take care of you and your family by becoming educated, and then demanding full product disclosure. Use your wallet and your brain. Pass the info along and vote appropriately.

by Rob from Snohomish, WA
November 8, 2009, 6:55 AM

2

Food, Inc
★★★★☆

Thank you so much for making a video that is telling the truth about the deceit that is going on all around us with the food industry. My family eats organic. We are so thankful that we can support a good cause for our farmers who raise food God's way!

by Sharon Isaac from Corpus Christi, TX
December 7, 2009, 12:16 PM

3

Lemmings or Educated Humans?
★★★★☆

If you are more interested in Tiger Woods latest utterance or who crashed last nights white house party than what poison your children are eating then this is a wake up call. The 3 books you need to study to stop being an ignorant victim are:

Omnivores Dillema

In Defense of Food

The China Study

Our conversations should be more about prevention and responsible eating than what is being spewed out of Washington DC re: healthcare reform.

by john
December 13, 2009, 11:38 AM

4

If you Eat you need to See!

★★★★☆

As an Executive Chef working for the world's largest food service provider, I can not stress the importance of this film. What disturbs me most is not how our foods are treated, but how we consumers are treated by simply being kept in the dark. Farmers being purposely pushed in to bankruptcy, government allowance of monopolies and the very people in charge of our food regulations were once the dealers of such filth. The good news is we can make a difference, but before we do, we need to educate ourselves by learning what we are allowing people to put in our bodies. This is not a cheap film that was made by PETA or other one-sided groups to gross you out into being a vegan; this is a film that exposes the truth in the food industry and its regulators. This is a must see for the entire family and anyone in the culinary world.

by Richard from Minneapolis, Minnesota
December 31, 2009, 8:55 AM

5

Kansas Farm Wife

★★★★☆

I actually used to think a lot more of PBS. In past they have seemed to have done a better job understanding the difference between fact and one persons version of fact.

I just hope PBS will do its homework and provide equal time to those who feel Food Inc. is more fiction than fact.

As a proud Kansas Farm Wife who is PROUD to say we feed 144 people plus you, I can say Food Inc. is not who we are. We feed America, but we eat here too!!!!!!

The responsibility of feeding so many people is huge, trying to do that while being considerate of how tight household incomes are today makes it more difficult. The United States is the envy of the entire world for quality, efficiency and safety. If we do not follow the regulations in place we will be out of business and out of a way of life we love.

At the end of the day my family eats what we raise. Am I really going to knowingly put my family at risk? NO!!!!!!

by Twilya L'Ecuyer from Morrowville, Kansas
March 9, 2010, 12:33 PM

6

I would advise people to check the facts. Consumers have been misinformed. This movie is very far from the truth. The men and women of Americas farming community take pride in providing the people of the world a safe, wholesome and nutritious food supply.

PBS, I am really disappointed in your choice to promote this movie. We operate a family farm that has been in the family nearly 100 years. I grew up watching many educational shows on PBS. We have been long time supporters of PBS. We really wish you would have taken the time to check the facts and not follow the opinions of one person. That being said, we will no longer donate to your cause.

by Brandon from Falun, Kansas
March 9, 2010, 1:06 PM

7

After having read the comments, a quote comes to mind. "It's impossible to make a man believe something if his livelihood depends on him not believing it."

The farmers who have posted negative comments and pledge to stop supporting PBS because of this movie have missed the point. The movie does not condemn farmers. In fact, it actually portrays farmers as victims or unknowing accomplices to the agenda of big business.

During the follow-up conversation that was aired in NE, one of the panelists said that the movie was "a good depiction from 20,000 feet." That's exactly what it's meant to be. It's not meant to be a depiction of the daily life of a farmer. It's meant to help us all see the bigger picture and connect the dots. While an individual farmer may, in fact, be operating an ethical and well-intentioned farm, what happens once they sell their cattle to the stock yard? What are the true health, environmental and economic impacts of producing GMO foods? Does the individual family farm really have autonomy when only 4 companies control 90%+ of the US's agricultural production and distribution? Have you, as a farmer, ever thought about these questions? And if not, why not?

I urge the farmers to look beyond their own acres and see, truly see, the impact they personally have on the well-being of America. There's a bigger, more noble goal than simply making money.

by Allison Nebraska
April 22, 2010, 2:20 PM

8

I was raised on a family farm. My father was a beef farmer. His cattle grazed on grass in the spring, summer, and fall; and on hay in the winter. Every year, each of his adult children would buy a half of beef that was processed by the local butcher. We knew exactly what we were getting, and the beef cattle did not have to be fattened up on a corn diet in a feed lot to be excellent tasting. Corn fed beef flavor is something that is acquired. My Dad is gone now, and my brother farms the land. He buys young cattle in the spring and sells them off to feed lots in the fall. I live in a small town with two supermarkets. Neither of them carry organic beef—or chicken or pork. I can, however, buy organic vegetables and fruits. E coli is a much bigger risk than anyone knows. My own brother-in-law got sick along with a dozen or more others eating hamburger from a local fast food. I am going to explore the options mentioned in above posts to see where I can buy meat that has been raised organically and not been put through a chlorine bath before packaged (ugh). Food, Inc. is an excellent documentary that everyone should watch. The idea that you can no longer buy seed corn or clean and reuse your own seed corn as my Dad did—which hasn't been genetically modified so that it can be sprayed with weed killer makes me sick. I am going to be extra diligent when I not only shop for food but also for plants and seeds for my garden. If we who can afford to pay a little more do so, then the price will come down for everyone.

by Nancy Wilson from Mason, Mi
April 22, 2010, 2:43 PM

9

Kudos, Allison

I just finished reading the farmer reactions, particularly those in Kansas. Allison, you hit the nail on the head. If you hadn't written what you did, I would have.

And for those of you Kansas farmers who feel picked on and have completely missed the point: my husband and his family, for at least 3 generations back are or have been Kansas farmers—crops, chickens, and cattle. They fed their families from what they produced—and it killed them all, with the exception of my husband, by the age of 60. All the men and most of the women died of cancer. My husband, who had major health issues already at the age of only 38, switched to organics and organic farming. He educated himself on real health and clean nutritious food and cured himself of all his ailments and conditions, including cancer, high blood pressure, high cholesterol, enlarged prostate, and more. At 51, he moved to Oregon to be in an environment more conducive and supportive of organic sustainable farming.

Just so you know—not all Kansas farmers are short-sighted.

by Jodee from Dallas, Or
April 22, 2010, 2:50 PM

10

single mom
★★★★☆

Look I wanna to thank everyone that helped with this movie. I kinda knew there was greed and corruption. But galee this movie really shows the deciet that's out there. I just wanna say I don't think this movie was trying to convince me of anything if so I would've turned the channel. I saw nothing but fact being delivered. I am so thankful for that. I am filled with so many emotions right now its sad. I know one thing I will be doing a over haul on my farms food intake asap. Again thank you coming from a single mother of 5 that now has her eyes open to it. I will never be the same . . .

by crystal from boston, ma
April 22, 2010, 7:36 PM

11

Illuminating!!
★★★★☆

As a physician, I have always stressed the importance of a healthy diet to my patients. Now I know that I did not go far enough. I wish I could play this film in my waiting room over and over again. Not only will this film change how I shop and how I feed my family but also how I counsel my patients. We need more eye-openers like this. If we are as persistent as some of the food companies have been, we will effect a change and be healthier for it.

by Roxane from bryn mawr, PA
April 22, 2010, 11:31 PM

REVIEW WHAT YOU LEARNED

Directions: Apply the SAVE technique to decide if you will SAVE or discard this text.

1   While I was training to become a family doctor, I learned the conventional wisdom about nicotine addiction. Physicians have long believed that people smoke primarily for pleasure and become psychologically dependent on that pleasure. Tolerance to the effects of nicotine prompts more frequent smoking; when the habit reaches a critical frequency—about five cigarettes per day—and nicotine is constantly present in the blood, physical dependence may begin, usually after thousands of cigarettes and years of smoking. Within hours of the last cigarette, the addicted smoker experiences the symptoms of nicotine withdrawal: restlessness, irritability, inability to concentrate, and so on. According to this understanding, those who smoke fewer than five cigarettes per day are not addicted.

2   I was armed with this knowledge when I encountered the proverbial patient who had not read the textbook. During a routine physical, an adolescent girl told me she was unable to quit smoking despite having started only two months before. I thought this patient must be an outlier, a rare exception to the rule that addiction takes years to develop. But my curiosity was piqued, so I went to the local high school to interview students about their smoking. There a 14-year-old girl told me that she had made two serious attempts to quit, failing both times. This was eye-opening because she had smoked only a few cigarettes a week for two months. When she described her withdrawal symptoms, her story sounded like the lament of one of my two-pack-a-day patients. The rapid inset of these symptoms in the absence of daily smoking contradicted most of what I thought I knew about nicotine addiction. And when I tracked that received wisdom back to its source, I found that everything I had learned was just a poor educated guess.

3   With funding from the National Cancer Institute on Drug Abuse (NIDA), I have spent the past decade exploring how nicotine addiction develops in novice smokers. I now know that the model of addiction described in the opening paragraph is fiction. My research supports a new hypothesis asserting that limited exposure to nicotine—as little as one cigarette—can change the brain, modifying its neurons in a way that stimulates the craving to smoke. This understanding, if proved correct,

may someday provide researchers with promising avenues for developing new drugs and other therapies that could help people kick the habit.

Source: DiFranza, Joseph R. (May 2008). Hooked from the first cigarette. *Scientific American*, p. 82.

About the author: Joseph R. DiFranza is a family physician practicing out of the University of Massachusetts Medical School in Worcester. A perennial thorn in the side of the tobacco industry for 25 years, DiFranza has been an advocate for efforts to prevent the tobacco industry from selling its products to children, and it was his research and complaint to the Federal Trade Commission that resulted in the demise of the notorious Joe Camel advertisements for Camel cigarettes. DiFranza has received a grant from Pfizer to determine whether his theory of cigarette addiction explains the effectiveness of smoking-cessation medications.

S—Source: (Who is the owner/author? Are they qualified/biased?)

Joseph R. DiFranza, a family physician at the University of Massachusetts Medical School and he is qualified because of his expertise.

A—Argument: (What is the author's argument/point/opinion/attitude?)

He believes that cigarettes cause a nicotine addiction at much lower amounts than reported in textbooks.

V—Validate: (What is the evidence? Is it in context/logical/truthful?)

The evidence is his discovery that high school students who smoke 2–3 times per week have the same addiction level as his 2-pack-per-day patients.

E—Evaluate: (How useful is this text to you? Will you SAVE it or toss it?)

I will SAVE this article since the author is credible and his methods of gathering information are objective and unbiased.

/ **MASTER** THE LESSON /

Critical Thinking

Directions: Apply the SAVE technique to decide if you will SAVE or discard this text.

When We Lose Our Heads

1   Although a lack of time is not synonymous with stress, the way people deal with time and the stress they experience are interrelated. But the connection is more complex and intriguing than Friedman and Rosenman imagined.

2   Why do we always seem to lock ourselves out of our apartments when we are already under pressure, and make the situation go from bad to worse? A downward spiral starts to seem inevitable. People under stress often appear to be at loose ends, so much so that even experts confuse their actions with the symptoms of a full-fledged attention deficit. The inability to concentrate was the first major time waster we examined; stress is the second. Stress makes it increasingly difficult to organize time sensibly.

3   The cerebral cortex is the most susceptible region in the head. It is the first to get thrown off kilter when copious amounts of adrenaline and noradrenaline flow during a stress reaction. In an extreme case, entire regions in the prefrontal cortex are simply shut off. The executive function, which is the manager in our heads, suffers in the process. This mechanism reveals a very sensible *austerity* measure of nature: we need to act quickly if we are threatened, not take a long time to choose and plan. At the same time, arousal increases under stress. The same hormone noradrenaline, which scales down the executive function, heightens our receptivity to new stimuli. . . . it becomes even harder to keep our priorities straight. When we are under stress, we are no longer able to filter out unimportant matters; we become scatterbrained, flighty, and reckless.

4   At first, we are not even aware that we are experiencing a stress reaction; we just get the feeling that we are running out of time. The devilish thing about a perceived time bind is how quickly this feeling becomes self-fulfilling. No sooner does a small thing go wrong than we are overwhelmed by what we assume to be time pressure, although there is little objective basis for that assumption. All of a sudden we find that everything is taking longer to get done. We get bogged down and make errors that take even

_____
Austerity—severity, strictness, sternness

more time to straighten out. Now we have a legitimate cause for concern, and our sense of helplessness raises the level of stress even further.

5   There is a simple way to combat this stress reaction: get moving. Robert Sapolsky, a professor of neurology at Stanford University, made the cases for a connection between movement and diminished stress in his book *Why Zebras Don't Get Ulcers*. A game of squash, a run around the track, or a bit of yoga can bring the level of stress hormones back down to a level at which concentrated work becomes possible. Exercise actually frees up far more time than it expends.

6   But we persist in the mistaken belief that this effective remedy is the very thing we don't have a single free minute for. We tell ourselves that the stress comes from a lack of time, even though it is really just the other way around: We are not stressed because we have no time; rather, we have no time *because* we are stressed.

Source: Klein, Stefan. (2006). *The Secret Pulse of Time: Making Sense of Life's Scarcest Commodity.* New York, NY: Marlowe & Company, pp. 199–201.

S—Source: (Who is the owner/author? Are they qualified/biased?)

The author is Stefan Klein and his qualifications are unknown based on the information above.

A—Argument: (What is the author's argument/point/opinion/attitude?)

His opinion is that stress causes a spiraling cycle of thoughtless mistakes, wasting time, and therefore more stress. This cycle is linked to hormonal control and could be reduced by an exercise routine that would reduce the hormone levels.

V—Validate: (What is the evidence? Is it in context/logical/truthful?)

Klein cites evidence by two experts in the field, Friedman and Rosenman, as researchers who had noticed the connection between wasting time and stress. He also cites Robert Sapolsky, a professor of neurology at Stanford University, as an expert who has proposed a cure to stop this cycle. The evidence is in context and seems logical.

E—Evaluate: (How useful is this text to you? Will you SAVE it or toss it?)

This text is useful, but some of the evidence presented here needs to be confirmed by other authors, especially the facts concerning the effects of the hormones on the brain during stress.

> Women complain about premenstrual syndrome, but I think of it as the only time of the month that I can be myself.
>
> **Roseanne Barr**

What does the comedian, Roseanne Barr, mean by her quote?

She is trying to present premenstrual syndrome, which is usually a very serious topic in most situations, from a different view that will make us laugh about it.

Describe her perspective or bias.

Her perspective is as a woman who gets premenstrual syndrome. Her bias is that you can find something funny in whatever happens to you.

/ **MASTER** THE LESSON /

Critical Thinking

Directions: Apply the SAVE technique to decide if you will SAVE or discard this text.

Find a Community

When a family member showed signs of depression, Allyson Tolbert wanted to help—but she didn't know how. On the Web, she found a group that helped her make a life-saving difference.

1   Some people search the Internet for fun and games. Some seek news and information. Others share life with loved ones. And people in trouble can use the Internet to get in-the-trenches advice from strangers who are experiencing the same problems.

2   Allyson Tolbert, 24, a singer-dancer-actress from St. Petersburg, Fla. used the Web to find an online medical community to help her and a family member cope with depression.

3   "I was about 13 when my mother first noticed signs of depression in me," Tolbert says. The previously outgoing teen withdrew and avoided things she used to enjoy. Even though Tolbert says the two are "incredibly close," her mother knew that Tolbert needed to talk to someone else, so she took her to a counselor.

Her Experience Helped Another Relative Years Later

4   Tolbert was diagnosed with major depression. Regular sessions with her counselor helped her deal with feelings that were triggered by her father, who left when she was young and later didn't want any contact with her.

5   "It took many years to realize it wasn't my fault," she says. But her treatment, which eventually included medication, did help. Tolbert earned a degree in music theater from the University of Florida and was crowned Florida's Miss Largo this year.

6   Recently, Tolbert noticed signs of depression in a close family member. She knew what to look for, but others in the family didn't know much about the disease or how they could help. Depression "is a touchy subject, especially in minority communities," Tolbert says.

Seeking Support and Resources on the Internet

7   Needing guidance, Tolbert Googled the phrase "how to help someone who is depressed or suicidal." And she found exactly what she needed on

the site of Families for Depression Awareness (familyaware.org) There she discovered a wealth of resources, including stories of others with depression that show "you are not alone." That might sound trivial, Tolbert says, but "it really does make a difference." She ordered the group's free literature and shared it with her family.

8   Now she gives back to that group by speaking about depression, spreading the word about the site and distributing Families for Depression Awareness brochures wherever she goes, including while she was on the road as a cast member with the national tour of the Broadway show *The Producers.* In July, six months after that show ended, she moved to New York City.

What Her Future Holds

9   "This has been the test of my depression [management]," she says, "because this is a hard city, and it is a hard business." She loves her new life, but she admits that making the transition has "taken everything I learned in counseling."

10   WebMD says "Have a specific question for others like you who have 'been there' and 'done that'? Need to get help from or give help to those who can empathize and sympathize? Then become familiar with terms like community, blogs, message boards and groups. We call it 'health networking,' and it can be a lifesaver."

Source: A special guide with WebMD, Michael W. Smith, M.D., chief medical editor at WebMD.com (October 20–23, 2008). *USA Weekend. Health Smart,* p. 6.

S—Source: (Who is the owner/author? Are they qualified/biased?)

The owner of the article is *USA Weekend*. The author is Dr. Michael W. Smith, WebMD chief medical editor. Dr. Smith interviewed a woman whose personal experiences showed how this "health networking" helped her and her family. The author was biased for health networks on the Internet.

A—Argument: (What is the author's argument/point/opinion/attitude?)

The author's opinion is that "health networking" on the Internet can help connect people with health concerns to others who have experienced the same problems and will share possible solutions.

V—Validate: (What is the evidence? Is it in context/logical/truthful?)

Allyson Tolbert was able to get help for herself and her family by searching on the Internet and finding an organization called Families for Depression Awareness. The organization sent her literature that she shared with her family. The information is in context and is logical for the author's argument.

> **E—Evaluate: (How useful is this text to you? Will you SAVE it or toss it?)**
>
> Personal experiences of people using "health networking" are useful, but only one example is not enough to conclude that "health networking" will work for everyone. The article also made a big claim that health networking can save lives, but did not present a specific case to illustrate the point.

"The doctor said he needed more activity, so I hide his TV remote three times a week."

CartoonStock.com

What does the cartoon creator infer with the caption and the picture?

The husband doesn't get much exercise, so the wife found a creative way to get her husband some activity by hiding the one thing in the house he cares about, the TV remote.

LEARNING STYLE ACTIVITIES

*L*ook, *L*isten, *W*rite, *D*o

Research Project

Choose a health and wellness topic you want to learn more about. Write a question you want answered.

      For example—

      Topic—tanning beds

      Question—Are tanning beds safer than the sun for avoiding skin cancer?

Research your topic using the Internet, a virtual or online library, or sources at your library.

List the sources you evaluated.

Apply the SAVE technique you learned in this chapter to the sources you are considering using for your research. Choose at least three different sources in the final project.

Create a way to present your research findings using one or more of your preferred learning styles. You may work in groups and combine your research on similar topics.

Some ideas for each learning style include:

👁 *L*ooĸ   Create a visual project using a PowerPoint slide show, photos, posters, etc. showing your research findings. Use graphic organizers such as concept maps in your presentation. You may also consider creating a Web page, collage, or video.

🔊 *L*ɪsᴛᴇɴ   Create an oral presentation such as a speech, and discuss your research findings. You may also interview and record people discussing your re-search topic, either by audio or video recordings.

✏ *W*ʀɪᴛᴇ   Write a paper discussing your research findings. You may include a formal or informal outline with your information. You may also consider writing a poem, short story, or other format to share your research findings.

👆 *D*ᴏ   Demonstrate your research findings by building a model, acting out a skit, or pretending you are on a talk show or game show.

Reading Practice

The following readings are related to the theme of Health and Wellness. In this final set of readings, use all of your reading skills to understand the nuances and perspectives presented in the material. As you read, consider your own opinions and attitudes about the topics before you read, and then see if your own perspectives change as you read.

The first reading is "The Dangerous Art of the Tattoo" from an Internet version of *U.S. News & World Report*. Several reader responses are also given to the controversial story.

The second reading is from a textbook titled *Psychology: An Introduction*. The excerpt is from the section *Staying Healthy: How Does a Healthy Lifestyle Help Us Control Stress?*

The third reading is from a piece of literature titled *Brain Surgeon: A Doctor's Inspiring Encounters with Mortality and Miracles*. In this excerpt, Dr. Black discusses a hip hop singer's brain tumor and the possible connection to her cell phone use.

The fourth reading is "Smoker's Corpse, Diseased Lungs Appear on Cigarette Warning Labels" from *Journal & Courier* magazine.

The fifth reading is a visual image of a woman eating a dark chocolate bar. An article, "Dark Chocolate Is Healthy Chocolate," accompanies the picture which discusses the health benefits of eating dark chocolate.

Internet

READING 1

1260L

The Dangerous Art of the Tattoo

Section: HEALTH, MONEY & EDUCATION

On Health

Laser removal, which demolishes tattoo pigment, may sound easy. But it opens up a toxic chemical dump

1   Tattoos are fast becoming a mark of the 21st century, with one quarter or more of those under the age of 30 adorning their skin with at least one. Whether driven by the urge for personal expression or just plain youthful impulsiveness, most people get tattooed without a clue about the health implications of this invasive skin-puncturing procedure. I'd suggest that all tattooing require a signed consent form outlining risks—the most obvious one being a major case of remorse.

2   Upwards of 50 percent of those who get tattoos later wish they hadn't. Their regrets become medical when they visit a dermatologist to have the tattoos removed, which is both painful and expensive. In the July issue of the *Archives of Dermatology*, researchers at Texas Tech University Health Sciences Center report on what's behind the change of heart: moving on from the past, problems wearing clothes, embarrassment, and concerns that tattoos could adversely affect job or career.

3   But tattooing is designed to last forever, delivering permanent ink deep under the epidermis. The skin reacts by protectively encapsulating the alien clumps of pigment in dense fibrous tissue while a few nearby lymph nodes collect what migrates out. For a long time, removal meant surgical excision or deep abrasion of the skin, invariably causing scarring and sometimes the need for skin grafting. In the preferred approach now, the tattoo gradually fades away under many months of laser treatments tailored to the wavelength of the pigments. Sounds easy. But with disruption, the fading tattoo becomes more like a toxic chemical dump.

4   Chemists from several laboratories, including the government's National Center for Toxicological Research, have identified low levels of carcinogens in tattoo ink. But the laser removal process, which demolishes the pigment by scorching it with heat, triggers chemical reactions that generate carcinogenic and mutation-inducing breakdown products, which are then absorbed by the body. Recently, German scientists reported that concentrations of toxic molecules from red and yellow pigments increased up to 70-fold after laser irradiation. And the bigger the tattoo, the greater the toxic release. This can only make one wonder whether it's better to let the sleeping paint lie, walled off by the body's own protective devices. Only time and a lot more study will tell.

5   We know so woefully little about tattoos. The Food and Drug Administration, which goes after cosmetics with a vengeance, does not regulate the tattoo industry. In fact, no one really knows exactly what's in the numerous commercial and homemade inks. But they do contain solvents and metals like lead and mercury and a range of impurities acceptable for computer printers or car paint—but not for human injection.

6   Allergic reactions and skin infections can occur after tattooing. And though they may be coincidental, skin cancers, including melanomas, have been reported within tattoo sites, bearing very close watching. The FDA warns about the risk of tattoo parlors transmitting viruses like HIV and the cancer-causing hepatitis C. Because of this, blood banks typically ban donations from people who have been tattooed in the previous 12 months. The FDA also warns patients that if they have an MRI scan, their tattoos can swell or burn, presumably related to the metal in some inks.

7   Stigma. Once mainly a guy thing, tattoos now decorate men and women equally, and increasingly they are a women's health issue. It should be obvious that getting or removing tattoos during pregnancy is not a good idea. And some anesthesiologists have expressed concerns about performing epidurals, used during labor, through those symmetrically designed female lower-back tattoos because of the slim possibility that the needle might carry pigment into the spinal canal. Perhaps not surprisingly, most patients seeking removal are women, prompted by a disproportionate level of psychological distress and even tattoo

stigma. Witness the tasteless moniker used to describe those lower-back tattoos: "tramp stamp."

8   I asked a few of my *U.S. News* colleagues about their take on women and tattoos. One said there was something trendy if not sexy about them—but maybe not for his fiancée. Another said he'd date a girl with one if it were not too obvious. A third saw only harmless self-expression. I'm with one young reporter who visited a tattoo parlor for a piece she was writing. She's down on tattoos because of the murky risks—and the idea of looking at the deeds of her youth for 80 years. ∎

Source: Healy, Bernadine, M.D. (August 4, 2008). The Dangerous Art of the Tattoo. *U.S. News & World Report,* vol. 145, Issue 3. Retrieved from Master File, Premier Database

---

S—Source: (Who is the owner/author? Are they qualified/biased?)

Bernadine Healy, M.D., is a writer for *U.S. News & World Report.* Being a medical doctor, she is qualified to talk about the effects of tattoos on the human body. She expertly explains the information from the medical journals and medical agencies cited in the article. She is biased against tattoos.

A—Argument: (What is the author's argument/point/opinion/attitude?)

Tattoos are a danger to the people who get them. They can cause both physical and psychological problems for the person with the tattoo. Tattoos also can cause social and career problems that were unforeseen earlier. Tattoos are still accepted by some members of society though, but not in all circumstances.

V—Validate: (What is the evidence? Is it in context/logical/truthful?)

The author uses sources for her facts such as the researchers at Texas Tech University Health Sciences in the *Archives of Dermatology*, chemists from several laboratories, including the government's National Center for Toxicological Research, and the Food and Drug Administration. She discusses that tattoos are permanent and hard to remove, which may cause psychological problems for the person who wants to get rid of one later. Tattoo dyes become toxic or cause cancer if removed by laser treatments. People can also get allergic reactions from the tattoo inks. The stigma associated with tattoos may also cause social and career problems unforeseen by the person before deciding to get the tattoo. All of these factors give the author the conclusion that tattoos are not a good choice.

> **E—Evaluate: (How useful is this text to you? Will you SAVE it or toss it?)**
>
> The text was very useful in discussing both the physical and non-physical factors that people who get tattoos face. The text also cited excellent sources of information that can be investigated for further explanation. I would SAVE this article.

Has your opinion about tattoos changed as a result of reading this article? Explain.

Answers will vary.

_____

_____

Reader Comments (from the Web site as they appear with spelling, grammar, etc.)

for the "artist" among us. . . .

Phyllis Ferry of PA Jul 27, 2008 13:46:00 PM

Tatoos

I see a lot of talk about tatoos, but I never see any articles on tatoos that have aged. Your skin is a dynamic organ that constantly changes. Over time, so does your tatoo. If your kids want a tatoo, take them to a retirement village or Veterans Home to pick out their Tatoo. When they see how it will look after a few years, they will not look so appealing.

of WA Jul 28, 2008 13:46:20 PM

Art & The Human Body

Artists and creativity are now so stifled by corporations and standards that they must resort to alternate means of expression. I have 6, they are tasteful, meaningful, and hidden. I am an executive and I feel they are personal, and therefor not exposed in the workplace. It does impact peoples opinions and unfortunately opinions carry weight. I think the secret is to be happy with yourself and your image, what ever it may be. And of course to ink responsibly in clean areas. Everyday we get in a car or on a train or walk somewhere we risk getting in an accident, tripping and falling and smashing our faces. Really, isn't everything a risk. Weigh it, if it makes sense for you and you are rational and sober when you make it, then you shouldn't regret it. The key is meaning and self worth. You are what you eat, and you are to others how they perceive you.

Melissa of MI Jul 28, 2008 14:18:19 PM

Doctor Healy is Completely Correct

I'm a guy and do have my children's tattooed on my arm although I wouldn't do it again, but at least it isn't a snake or an ex-girlfriend and it is worse for women than men. There are a lot of women today that won't be happy with their tattoos when they're grandmothers. Closing, I'll also add my wife had a fatal heart attack while still in her 40s and now that I'm dating again I'm glad I don't have her name written on my body.

JW of TX Jul 28, 2008 17:33:51 PM

More Anti-tattoo Scare Tactics

Too often, anti-tattoo articles appear in print which are typically written by someone without a tattoo. Documented tattooing has existed in nearly every culture for 5000 years. So, why, in this new millennium, is tattooing viewed so adversely? A fine artist friend of mine once thought that people react negatively because of the "keeping up with the Jones' factor." In other words, if more and more people get tattooed I will HAVE to get one too.

Choosing to be tattooed is not a frivolous decision. A PROFESSIONAL tattooist will not tattoo everyone who walks through the door. Most often, tattooists work by appointment to ensure the client is not acting hastily. He/she will also have a consent form that explains the process is permanent, can react, will change with time, etc. So, to those planning to get a tattoo, gather information first and make an educated decision to do so.

Speaking of information, much of what we find in regard to tattooing on the internet and in print elsewhere, is usually incorrect, opinionated and mythic. Just as in this article. "Ink deep under the epidermis," is very misleading to the lay person. The epidermis in its thickest areas (palms and soles) is about 1.5mm thick. Palms and soles, by the way, do not readily accept being tattooed. The ink is implanted in the epidermis. Any deeper, the tattoo will take on a blurry edge. The top layer of skin is dead skin and is shed every two weeks. Don't be frightened or misled by medical jargon.

As a tattoo artist with 32 years experience, I have never seen a tattoo develop skin cancer. In fact, I have detected cancerous growths while tattooing and have helped several clients identify them as such. They were able to get treatment before the growths became problematic. They may not have every discovered them if I wasn't tattooing their skin. I can also tell you of a client who developed skin cancer on his legs, but the areas with tattoos were not affected.

Tattooing as a women's health issue, according to this article, refers only to pregnancy neatly covered under the subtitle of Stigma. This seems rather incongruent. The term "tramp stamp" is derogatory. Personally, I refer to them as sacrum tattoos which is descriptive of the placement. Women birthing naturally with no fear of pain (possibly because they're tattooed) usually don't receive dangerous epidurals which can often leave you paralyzed.

The real dangers of tattoos come from greedy suppliers selling kits to the untrained.

If you don't want a tattoo, don't get one. If you don't like the way they look, avert your gaze. If you want a tattoo, do your homework and choose a professional, respectable tattoo artist with several years experience and knowledge. Choose your designs and placement wisely. If you dislike your tattoo you can opt for cover-up, rework or removal. Removal is costlier and can leave scars that are more unattractive than the tattoo. If you regret your decisions in life, own up to them.

Pat Sinatra of NY Jul 28, 2008 17:58:15 PM

You Tattoo Me

I am 54 and received my first Tattoo 30 years ago. It was a small dragon on my right shoulder. You could only see it if I was shirtless or sleeveless. Because of the new standard in factory inks which had just come out people often assume it is a new Tattoo. I give it no special care except to stay out of the sun which I must do because I burn in 15 minutes. I liked my Dragon so much and being a devote of Oriental and Buddhist Culture I sought someone to do a Full Sleeve (whole arm) of a Dragon. This was six years after my first Tattoo. I studied the magazines looking for a qualified artist. I found Shotsie an International Award Winning Artist who had the Board of Health inspect his shop every year. It wasn't the law, it was how he ran his shop. Over the next year going once or twice a month we became friends. I explained to Shotsie what I wanted and he freehanded my interpretation. After the first week we never talked about the Dragon again. He would just show me what he just spent three hours working on before he bandaged it up and it was always better than I had pictured it. Maybe this color or that. In the end it cost about $5,000.00. Now over 24 years later people think I've had it done within the last year. Plus my little Dragon is incorporated into the Sleeve. I have had Shotsie do a few more on my other arm to balance things out. I am happy with my Tattoo's and don't regret ever having them done. They are part of me as I am part of them. *

Jeff Smith of NJ Jul 29, 2008 11:29:55 AM

Late-in-Life Tattoos

There's a solution to the tattoo dilemma—don't decide until you're at least 50 years old. Then you'll be sure of what you REALLY want. I celebrated my 60th birthday last year with my first tattoos. . .a St. Louis Cardinal on my right ankle and my husband's name on my left flank. They're beautiful and I love 'em and I doubt if I'll change my mind for at least 20–30 years!

(My husband says if 60-year-old grandmas are getting tattoos, they've truly entered the mainstream.)

Janet Reuwer of OH Jul 30, 2008 06:54:23 AM

Body Piercing, Belly Button Ring

what is the risk involved with doing the piercing? my niece wants to do it.

anne carno of NY Jul 30, 2008 10:30:30 AM

Tattoo

Dear Dr. Healy:

I find the widespread use of tattoos to be objectionable and offensive.

The practice had its origin in Ancient Egypt, where prostitutes often tattooed their pelvic region with symbols of genitalia, presumably as advertising. Men took up the usage (of tattoos), and then tattoos became the symbol of oppression, persecution, exploitation, and slavery in Egypt, then Babylonia, Syria, Greece and Rome. The Catholic Church tried to stop the practice of tattoos but it arose again, in the Nazi Concentration Camps.

I see no reason why anyone would want to disfigure the beautiful bodies which are given to us.

I am sorry to hear that laser eradication is risky. That does not bother me in the case of voluntary tattoos, since they knew or should have known tattoos are risky.

However, in cases where the tattoos were acquired forcibly, I feel it is too bad that lasers are so dangerous. I would hope that in the case of German tattoos, the size of the tattoo would be such as to accommodate surgery as an option.

Thank you for an interesting and well-done article.

Has your opinion changed after reading the reader comments? Explain.

Answers will vary.

_____

_____

_____

Textbook

READING 2

1260L

Staying Healthy: *How Does a Healthy Lifestyle Help Us Control Stress?*

Use the SQ3R technique as you read this textbook reading.

Survey	Skim over the material. Read the title, subtitle, subheadings, first and last paragraphs, pictures, charts, and graphics. Note italics and bold print.
Question	Ask yourself questions before you read. What do you want to know? Turn headings and subheadings into questions and/or read questions if provided.
Read	Read the material in manageable chunks. This may be one or two paragraphs at a time or the material under one subheading.
Recite	Recite the answer to each question in your own words. This is a good time to write notes as you read each section. Repeat the question-read-recite cycle.
Review	Look over your notes at the end of the chapter, article, or material. Review what you learned and write a summary in your own words.

METHODS OF REDUCING STRESS

1   Scientists do not have a simple explanation for the common cold, much less cancer. But, they do have advice on how to reduce stress and stay healthy.

CALM DOWN

2   Stress may be part of your life, but there are proven ways to reduce the negative impact of stress on your body and your health. *Exercise* is one. Running, walking, biking, swimming, or whatever aerobic exercise you enjoy doing regularly lowers your resting heart rate and blood pressure, so that your body does not react as strongly to stress and recovers more quickly. Moreover, numerous studies show that people who exercise regularly and are physically fit have higher self-esteem than those who do not; are less likely to feel anxious, depressed, or irritable; and have fewer aches and pains, as well as fewer colds (Biddle, 2000; Sonstroem, 1997).

3   *Relaxation training* is another stress buster. A number of studies indicate that relaxation techniques lower stress (Pothier, 2002) and improve immune functioning (Andersen, Kiecolt-Glaser, & Glaser, 1994). Relaxation is more than flopping on the couch with the TV zapper, however. Healthful physical relaxation requires lying quietly and alternately tensing and relaxing every voluntary muscle in your body—from your head to your toes—in part to learn how to relax your body. Breathing exercises can have the same effect: if you are tense, deep, rhythmic breathing is difficult, but learning to do so relieves bodily tension.

REACH OUT

4   A strong network of friends and family who provide *social support* can help to maintain good health (Uchino, Cacioppo, & Kiecolt-Glaser, 1996). One review of the literature concluded that the positive relationship between social support and health is on a par with the negative relationship of health to such well-established risk factors as physical inactivity, smoking, and high blood pressure (House, Landis, & Umberson, 1988). Exactly why the presence of a strong social support system is related to health is not fully understood. Some researchers contend that social support may directly affect our responses to stress and health by producing physiological changes in endocrine, cardiac, and immune functioning (Uchino et al., 1996).

5   Whatever the underlying mechanism, most people can remember times when other people made a difference in their lives by giving them good advice (informational support), helping them to feel better about themselves (emotional support), providing assistance with chores and responsibilities or financial help (tangible support), or simply by "hanging out" with them (belonging support) (Uchino, Uno, & Holt-Lunstad, 1999; R. B. Williams et al., 1992). However, not all relationships are alike. Knowing a lot of people or having a partner may or may not be a stress buffer; what matters are the characteristics of one's friends and partners and the quality of

the relationships (Hartup & Stevens, 1999). For example, studies have found that married couples who argue in a hostile way—criticizing, belittling, and insulting one another—had suppressed immune function compared to couples who interacted in more constructive ways—listening to one another's points of view, seeking common ground and compromise, and using humor to break up tension (Hobfoll, Cameron, Chapman, & Gallagher, 1996; Kiecolt-Glaser, Malarkey, Chee, Newton, & Cacioppo, 1993; Kiecolt-Glaser, Bane, Glaser, & Malarkey, 2003).

RELIGION AND ALTRUISM

6   Health psychologists are also investigating the role religion may play in reducing stress and bolstering health (Rabin & Koenig, 2002; Siegel, Anderman, & Schrim-shaw, 2001; Smith, 2000). For example, research has found that elderly people who pray or attend religious services regularly enjoy better health and markedly lower rates of depression than those who do not (Koenig, 1997; Koenig et al., 1997). Other studies have shown that having a religious commitment may also help to moderate high blood pressure and hypertension (Levin & Vanderpool, 1989).

7   Exactly why there is an association between health and religion is unclear. One explanation however, holds that religion provides people with a system of social support that includes caring friends and opportunities for close personal interactions. As described above, a strong network of social support can reduce stress in a variety of ways, and in turn, reduced stress is associated with better health (Uchino et al., 1996, 1999). However, it is equally likely that people who enjoy good health are more likely to pray and attend religious services (Sloan, Bagiella, & Powell, 1999).

8   *Altruism*—reaching out and giving to others because this brings *you* plea-sure—is one of the more effective ways to reduce stress (Vaillant, 2000). Caring for others tends to take our minds off our own problems, to make us realize that we're involved in something larger than our own small slice of life (Folkman, Chesney, & Christopher-Richards, 1994). Interestingly, altruism is a component of most religions, suggesting that altruism and religious commitment may have something in common that helps to reduce stress. Altruism may also channel loss, grief, or anger into constructive action. An example is Mothers Against Drunk Driving (MADD), an organization founded by a mother whose son was killed by a drunken driver.

LEARN TO COPE EFFECTIVELY

9   How you appraise events in your environment—and how you appraise your ability to cope with potentially unsettling, unpredictable events—can minimize or maximize stress and its impact on health.

10   *Proactive coping* is the psychological term for anticipating stressful events and taking advance steps to avoid them or to minimize their impact

(Aspinwall & Taylor, 1997). Proactive coping does not mean "expect the worst"; constant vigilance actually increases stress and may damage health. Rather, proactive coping means (as in the Boy Scout motto) "Be prepared." This may include accumulating resources (time, money, social support, and information), recognizing potential stress in advance, and making realistic plans. For example, a recent widower anticipates that his first Christmas without his late wife will be lonely and makes plans to spend the holidays with friends. A woman who is moving to a new city knows the transition may be stressful. She finds out as much as she can about her new location before she moves—whether her friends have friends there, where she can participate in activities she enjoys (such as taking classes in drawing or karate), places and groups or organizations where she might meet people who share her interests (a house of worship, the best jazz clubs, the local animal shelter), and so on.

11   In many cases you cannot change or escape stressful circumstances, but you can change the way you think about things. *Positive reappraisal* helps people to make the best of a tense or painful situation. A low grade can be seen as a warning sign, not a catastrophe; a job you hate provides information on what you really want in your career; instead of brooding about a nasty remark from your sister, ask what does this tell you about *her?* Positive reappraisal does not require you to become a "Pollyanna" (the heroine of a novel who was optimistic to the point of being ridiculous). Rather it requires finding new meaning in a situation, a perspective or insight you had overlooked. After his partner died, one HIV caregiver told researchers, "What his death did was snap a certain value into my behavior, which is, 'Listen, you don't know how long you've got. You've just lost another one. Spend more time with the people who mean something to you'" (S. E. Taylor, Kemeny, Reed, Bower, & Gruenwald, 2000, p. 105).

12   One of the most effective, stress-relieving forms of reappraisal is *humor*. As Shakespeare so aptly put it in *The Winter's Tale*: "A merry heart goes all the day/Your sad tires in a mile" *(Act IV, Scene 3).* And journalist Norman Cousins (1981) attributed his recovery from a life-threatening disease to regular "doses" of laughter. Watching classic comic films, he believed, reduced both his pain and the inflammation in his tissues. He wrote:

> What was significant about the laughter . . . was not just the fact that it provides internal exercise for a person flat on his or her back—a form of jogging for the innards—but that it creates a mood in which the other positive emotions can be put to work, too. In short it helps make it possible for good things to happen. (pp. 145–146)

Health psychologists agree (e.g. Salovey, Rothman, Detweiler, & Steward, 2000; Vaillant, 2000): A healthy body and a sense of humor go hand-in-hand.

COPING WITH STRESS AT COLLEGE

13   It is two weeks before finals and you have two papers to write and four exams to study for. You are very worried. You are not alone. To help students cope with the pressures of finals week, and indeed, the stress that many students feel throughout the semester, many colleges and universities are offering stress-reduction workshops, aerobics classes, and counseling. At the University of California at Los Angeles, students are taught to visualize themselves calmly answering difficult test questions. Even if you do not attend a special program for reducing stress, you can teach yourself techniques to help cope with the pressures of college life.

1. Plan ahead. Do not procrastinate. Get things done well before deadlines. Start working on large projects well in advance.

2. Prioritize. Make a list of everything you have to do right down to doing the laundry, then start the highest priority tasks, the ones that really have to be done first (a looming deadline) or those things that will take a long time. Focus on the highest priority tasks, crossing them off as they are done, and adjust the priorities so that the most critical tasks are always starred.

3. Exercise. Do whatever activity you enjoy.

4. Listen to your favorite music, watch a TV show, or go to a movie as a study break.

5. Talk to other people.

6. Meditate or use other relaxation techniques. See the paperback *The Relaxation Response* (Benson & Klipper, 2000). ▪

Source: Morris, Charles G. and Albert A. Maisto. (2005). *Psychology: An Introduction,* 12th ed. Upper Saddle River, NJ: Pearson, pp. 469–472.

S—Source: (Who is the owner/author? Are they qualified/biased?)

Charles G. Morris and Albert A. Maisto, professors of psychology at the University of Michigan and the University of North Carolina, are the authors. They are very qualified because they have been studying and teaching psychology for years.

A—Argument: (What is the author's argument/point/opinion/attitude?)

There are a number of tools you can use to alleviate stress. The authors have a positive attitude toward these treatments and feel they will be effective deterrents to stress.

> **V—Validate: (What is the evidence? Is it in context/logical/truthful?)**
>
> The authors cited a number of research reports showing how each tool they include has been shown to be helpful to relieve stress. The evidence is logical, truthful and in context to relieving stress.
>
> **E—Evaluate: (How useful is this text to you? Will you SAVE it or toss it?)**
>
> This material is very useful because it supplies the reader with several confirmed tips to help relieve stress. It is also useful for supplying references that can be further researched for additional information. I will SAVE it.

Critical Thinking/Application

What ideas from the reading did you find helpful or useful for reducing or coping with your own stress? Do you disagree with any ideas? Why or why not? What other suggestions would you add to those mentioned in this reading that the author did not discuss?

Answers will vary.

_____

_____

_____

Literature

READING 3

Brain Surgeon: A Doctor's Inspiring Encounters with Mortality and Miracles

FROM THE BOOK JACKET

1   Welcome to tiger country: The treacherous territory where a single wrong move can devastate—or—end—a patient's life . . . *Brain Surgeon*

2   This is the terrain world-renowned neurosurgeon Keith Black, MD, enters every day to produce virtual medical miracles. Now, in this riveting book, Dr. Black invites readers to shadow his breathtaking journeys into the brain as he battles some of the deadliest and most feared tumors known to medical science. Along the way, he shares his unique insights about the inner workings of the brain, his unwavering optimism for the future of medicine, and the extraordinary stories of his patients—from ministers and rock stars to wealthy entrepreneurs and uninsured students—whom he celebrates as the *real* heroes.

Copyright © 2012 Pearson Education, Inc.

3   Offering a window into one man's remarkable mind, *Brain Surgeon* reveals the anatomy of the unflinching confidence of this master surgeon, whose personal journey brought him from life as a young African-American boy growing up in the civil rights-era South to the elite world of neurosurgery.

4   Through Dr. Black's white-knuckle descriptions of some of the most astonishing medical procedures performed today, he reveals the beauty and marvel of the human brain. He also celebrates the amazing strength and courage of his patients, who refuse to see themselves as victims. Ultimately, *Brain Surgeon* is an inspiring story of the struggle to overcome odds—whether as a man, a doctor, or a patient.

5   Keith Black, MD, serves as chairman of the department of neurosurgery and director of the Maxine Dunitz Neurological Institute at Cedars-Sinai Medical Center. Before joining Cedars-Sinai, Black served on the UCLA faculty for ten years, where he was a professor of neurosurgery. He was named the Ruth and Raymond Stotter chair in the department of surgery and was head of the UCLA Comprehensive Brain Tumor Program. Arnold Mann has been writing about medicine for twenty-five years. His cover stories for *Time* and *USA Weekend Magazine*, including his 1997 *Time* article on Dr. Black, have earned him recognition as one of the nation's leading medical journalists. He currently resides in Los Angeles, CA.

FROM CHAPTER 10: CELLULAR SIGNS

6   (from p. 187) "My patient's name is Tionne Watkins, and she is in the entertainment business. Sometimes called T-Boz, she first became known as one-third of the extremely successful R&B/hip-hop trio TLC. To date, the group has sold over 45 million recordings worldwide, and remains among the best-selling female singing groups of all time. Twice named to *People* magazine's annual list of most beautiful people, at this point in her life, Tionne was hoping to branch out into an on-camera television career. For her, any treatment option that carried a significant risk of loss of balance, loss of hearing, or loss of facial mobility would take away her livelihood."

7   [**Story Summary:** *Tionne came to Dr. Black after talking with several other doctors and doing her own research on her diagnosis. She explained to Dr. Black how complicated it can be to make a decision about a medical situation.*]

8   (from p. 192) "As a patient, you have to do the research yourself," she said. "I went on the Internet; I made phone calls. Takeo helped. I looked up the gamma knife; I looked up the surgery, and found all these different approaches. The more I researched, the more difference of opinion I found."

9   While looking into treatment options for her tumor, Tionne had discovered what many of my patients find: the Internet, while full of information, can also be full of **contradiction.** For vestibular schwannomas, the conflicting advice to patients on the Web mirrors what had been an active and at times heated

discussion in the professional literature among neurosurgeons, radiation oncologists, and otolaryngologists about the best way to treat this particular tumor . . .

10   *[Story Summary: Tionne and Dr. Black discussed the risks and decided to go through with the surgery. In the book, Dr. Black explains the vivid details of the surgery as if you were there with him. Tionne recovered from surgery so well, she did not have to go to the Intensive Care Unit. She was walking the hospital halls the day after surgery.]*

11   (from pp. 207–208) Several weeks later she was back in my examining room for her first post-op check-up, wearing her trademark running attire and sunglasses.

12   "How is your hearing?" I asked her.

13   "Great" she said, beaming. "I'm so happy."

14   "And the dizziness?"

15   "I'm still spinning, if I move quickly. But I can deal with that."

16   "Vestibular schwannomas start in the balance nerve," I said. "It's not uncommon for patients to be dizzy anywhere from a day to several weeks after surgery as the inner ear readjusts."

17   "It's going to get better, right?" she asked.

18   "Absolutely. You're doing excellent," I assured her. "You can go home to Atlanta whenever you want to."

19   "Like tomorrow?"

20   "Absolutely."

21   "That's the best news of all!" she exclaimed, overwhelming me with a hug. "Dr. Black, do you know what caused my tumor?" she asked intently.

22   "We cannot say for certain," I told her, "but some data shows that it might be related to cell phone use. There is nothing conclusive yet, but to be safe, I'm recommending that you use an earpiece to keep the cell away from the brain."

23   There is a great deal of discussion and indeed controversy about whether cell phones are a contributing cause of brain cancer. Cell phone manufacturers are clearly aware that there may be potential risk. Because microwave radiation diminishes with distance, cell phone owner manuals advise us to hold the phone a certain distance from our heads. Unfortunately, not many people follow these instructions.

24   At this point, the jury is still out. In addition to these Scandinavian studies that point definitively to a relationship, there are other studies that have concluded that no relationship exists. One of the difficulties is that some tumors—vestibular schwannomas among them—typically grow rather slowly. As a result, we may need more time to prove conclusively whether there is a link between cell phone utilization and brain tumors.

25   There has been a huge increase in cell phone usage over the past decade, both in terms of the number of users and in terms of the amount of time the average user spends on the phone. There is every expectation that this trend will

continue. A whole generation of young people uses cell phones exclusively—many in their twenties and early thirties have no landlines in their homes at all. Although research conclusions to date have been far from unanimous, we surely do not want to find out belatedly ten years from now—and millions of hours of cell phone usage later—that there is a correlation.

26   We certainly have enough evidence today to suggest that the prudent individual should take precautions. I am particularly concerned about the amount of time children today spend with cell phones glued to their ears. We know that because children's brains are still developing, they can be more susceptible than grown-ups to tumor formation. In the lab, it is significantly easier to induce a tumor in young rats than in adults.

27   I believe it is wise for parents to curtail cell phone usage in their children. Even adults, however, would be well advised to take one relatively simple step to decrease their exposure. Among my patients, I have noticed a correlation between the side of the head where the tumor appears, and the side of the head where the cell phone is generally held. The problem comes from holding the cell phone in contact with the ear, bringing the microwave radiation emitted by the device close to the brain. I use an earpiece, and I encourage my patients to do the same. As for Bluetooth devices, they are a source of some radiation themselves, and may not be as safe as a wire earpiece.

28   I'm often asked whether brain tumors are becoming more frequent. Unfortunately the answer is yes, even when one takes our improving ability to diagnose them into account. Tragically, many of the new victims are children: Brain cancer is now the leading cause of cancer death in people under the age of nineteen . . . ◼

Source: Black, Keith, M.D., with Arnold Mann (2009). *Brain Surgeon: A Doctor's Inspiring Encounters with Mortality and Miracles.* New York, NY: Wellness Central, book jacket, pp. 187, 192, 207–208.

Vocabulary

Study the word parts in ***contradiction.***

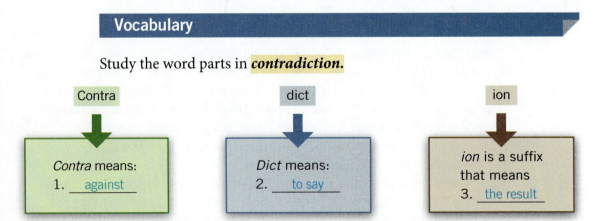

Contra	dict	ion
Contra means: 1. against	*Dict* means: 2. to say	*ion* is a suffix that means 3. the result

4. Using the word parts, what is the meaning of ***contradiction?***
the result of saying against

> "While looking into treatment options for her tumor, Tionne had discovered what many of my patients find: the Internet, while full of information, can also be full of ***contradiction.*** For vestibular schwannomas, the conflicting advice to patients on the Web mirrors what had been an active and at times heated discussion in the professional literature among neurosurgeons, radiation oncologists, and otolaryngologists about the best way to treat this particular tumor."

Contradiction is conflicting advice.	Heated discussion indicates there is disagreement.	There are different ideas about the best way to treat the disease.

5. Together, these facts let you infer that ***contradiction*** means
opposing opinions about the same subject

Dictionary definition: (look up ***contradiction*** in the dictionary).

6. What does ***contradiction*** mean?
direct opposition to things compared

Main Idea/Implied Main Idea

7. What is Dr. Black's main idea about how cell phone use is related to brain cancer?

a. Cell phones might cause brain cancer, so it is best to be cautious.

b. There is no conclusive evidence about cell phone use causing brain cancer.

c. Cell phones cause brain cancer, so it is best to not use them.

d. Nothing in the research is conclusive, so do not worry yet.

Supporting Details

8. What does Dr. Black say about children and cell phone use?

   a. There is no conclusive evidence about children and cell phones.

   b. There is no more risk to children than adults with cell phones.

   c. Children have thinner skulls, so there is more risk of damage from radiation.

   d. Radiation research is not conclusive regarding cell phones.

Patterns of Organization

9. What is the major pattern of organization in this reading selection?

   a. compare/contrast   c. definition

   b. cause/effect   d. simple listing

Facts and Opinions

Mark an **F** if the statement is a fact and **O** if the statement is an opinion, and **IO** for informed opinion based on expert opinion and training.

___O___ 10. "We cannot say for certain," I told her, "but some data shows that it might be related to cell phone use. There is nothing conclusive yet, but to be safe, I'm recommending that you use an earpiece to keep the cell away from the brain."

___F___ 11. We certainly have enough evidence today to suggest that the prudent individual should take precautions.

___O___ 12. I believe it is wise for parents to curtail cell phone usage in their children.

___F___ 13. Among my patients, I have noticed a correlation between the side of the head where the tumor appears, and the side of the head where the cell phone is generally held.

Inference

14–16. Based on the reading selection above, how do you believe Tionne will use her cell phone in the future? Support your answer with two specific reasons.

Answers will vary.

_____

_____

_____

Critical Thinking

17–20.

S—Source: (Who is the owner/author? Are they qualified/biased?)

Keith Black, M.D., and Arnold Mann are the authors. Dr. Black is chairman of the department of neurosurgery and director of the Maxine Dunitz Neurological Institute at Cedars-Sinai Medical Center. Arnold Mann has been writing about medicine for twenty-five years. They are qualified based on their years of experience in their respective fields. They are unbiased in their approach, but they are cautious on the side of the safe use of cell phones.

A—Argument: (What is the author's argument/point/opinion/attitude?)

Cell phones may be the cause for the rise in brain tumors seen in our country. As the use of cell phones has increased, so has the number of tumors. Safe precautions, like wired ear pieces, would be assurance against further radiation to the brain.

V—Validate: (What is the evidence? Is it in context/logical/truthful?)

The evidence is the number of brain surgeries that Dr. Black has performed and the information he has gathered from his patients about their normal daily activities. Tionne is just one example of his patients.

E—Evaluate: (How useful is this text to you? Will you SAVE it or toss it?)

This text is very useful. A doctor with years of experience with many brain operations performed in his career provides a solid case for the cause of brain tumors and how he came to this conclusion. I would SAVE this material.

Magazine/Periodical   **READING 4**

Smoker's Corpse, Diseased Lungs Appear on Cigarette Warning Labels

1   RICHMOND, Va. (AP) - In the most significant change to U.S. cigarette packs in 25 years, the Food and Drug Administration on Tuesday released nine new warning labels that depict in graphic detail the negative health effects of tobacco use.

2   Among the images to appear on cigarette packs are rotting and diseased teeth and gums and a man with a tracheotomy smoking.

3   Also included among the labels are: the corpse of a smoker, diseased lungs, a mother holding her baby with smoke swirling around them. They include phrases like "Smoking can kill you" and "Cigarettes cause cancer" and feature graphic images to convey the dangers of tobacco, which is responsible for about 443,000 deaths in the U.S. a year.

4   Each label includes a quit smoking hotline number.

5   The labels will take up the top half of a pack of cigarette packs. Warning labels also must appear in advertisements and constitute 20 percent of an ad. Cigarette makers have until the fall of 2012 to comply.

6   Mandates to introduce new graphic warning labels were part of a law passed in 2009 that, for the first time, gave the federal government authority to regulate tobacco, including setting guidelines for marketing and labeling, banning certain products and limiting nicotine.

7   The announcement follows reviews of scientific literature, public comments and results from an FDA-contracted study of 36 labels proposed last November.

8   In recent years, more than 30 countries or jurisdictions have introduced labels similar to those being introduced by the FDA. The U.S. first mandated the use of warning labels stating "Cigarettes may be hazardous to your health" in 1965. Current warning labels—a small box with black and white text—were put on cigarette packs in the mid-1980s.

9   The new labels come as the share of Americans who smoke has fallen dramatically since 1970, from nearly 40 percent to about 20 percent. The rate has stalled since about 2004. About 46 million adults in the U.S. smoke cigarettes.

10   It's unclear why declines in smoking have stalled. Some experts have cited tobacco company discount coupons on cigarettes or lack of funding for programs to discourage smoking or to help smokers quit.

11   While it is impossible to say how many people quit because of the labels, various studies suggest the labels do spur people to quit. The new labels offer the opportunity for a pack-a-day smoker to see graphic warnings on the dangers of cigarettes more than 7,000 times per year.

12   The World Health Organization said in a survey done in countries with graphic warning labels that a majority of smokers noticed the warnings and more than 25 percent said the warnings led them to consider quitting.

13   The legality of the new labels also is part of a pending federal lawsuit filed by Winston-Salem, N.C.-based Reynolds American Inc., parent company of America's second-largest cigarette maker, R.J. Reynolds, No. 3 cigarette maker Lorillard Inc. and others.

14   Tobacco makers in the lawsuit have argued the warnings would relegate the companies' brands to the bottom half of the cigarette packaging, making them "difficult, if not impossible, to see." ■

Source: Felberbaum, Michael. (June 22, 2011). Cigarette Packs to Bear Grisly Warnings. Associated Press. *Journal & Courier,* Lafayette, IN, p. C6.

 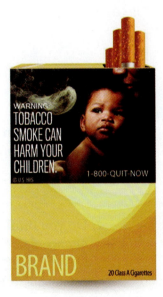

Directions: Imagine you are preparing for a discussion about this article in a college course.

On a separate sheet of paper, write at least 10 questions and answers about the information you learned in the article (i.e., main idea, supporting details, organizational patterns, purpose, tone, fact and opinions, inference, critical thinking).

Then, write at least 5 questions and answers about the vocabulary (context clues, word parts, figurative language).

Answers will vary.

Visual Image   **READING 5**

1. Is the woman in the picture biased one way or another toward chocolate? Explain your answer.

   Based on the expression on her face and the amount of chocolate she appears to be eating, she loves chocolate.

2. Do you think there is any reason for her to be eating such a large bar of chocolate?

   Possible answers include that this is just for an advertisement or for a dramatic effect.

Contrast the image of the woman eating chocolate above with the following reading about the health effects of chocolate.

"Dark Chocolate Is Healthy Chocolate"

Aug. 27, 2003—Got high blood pressure? Try a truffle. Worried about heart disease? Buy a bon-bon.

1   It's the best medical news in ages. Studies in two prestigious scientific journals say dark chocolate—but not white chocolate or milk chocolate—is good for you.

DARK CHOCOLATE LOWERS BLOOD PRESSURE

2   Dark chocolate—not white chocolate—lowers high blood pressure, say Dirk Taubert, MD, PhD, and colleagues at the University of Cologne, Germany. Their report appears in the Aug. 27 issue of *The Journal of the American Medical Association.*

3   But that's no license to go on a chocolate binge. Eating more dark chocolate can help lower blood pressure—if you've reached a certain age and have mild high blood pressure, say the researchers. But you have to balance the extra calories by eating less of other things.

ANTIOXIDANTS IN DARK CHOCOLATE

4   Dark chocolate—but not milk chocolate or dark chocolate eaten with milk—is a potent antioxidant, report Mauro Serafini, PhD, of Italy's National Institute for Food and Nutrition Research in Rome, and colleagues. Their report appears in the Aug. 28 issue of *Nature.* Antioxidants gobble up free radicals, destructive molecules that are implicated in heart disease and other ailments.

5   "Our findings indicate that milk may interfere with the absorption of antioxidants from chocolate . . . and may therefore negate the potential health benefits that can be derived from eating moderate amounts of dark chocolate."

6   Translation: Say "Dark, please," when ordering at the chocolate counter. Don't even think of washing it down with milk. And if health is your excuse for eating chocolate, remember the word "moderate" as you nibble.

THE STUDIES

7   Taubert's team signed up six men and seven women aged 55–64. All had just been diagnosed with mild high blood pressure—on average, systolic blood pressure (the top number) of 153 and diastolic blood pressure (the bottom number) of 84.

8   Every day for two weeks, they ate a 100-gram candy bar and were asked to balance its 480 calories by not eating other foods similar in nutrients and calories. Half the patients got dark chocolate and half got white chocolate.

9   Those who ate dark chocolate had a significant drop in blood pressure (by an average of 5 points for systolic and an average of 2 points for diastolic blood pressure). Those who ate white chocolate did not.

10   In the second study, Serafini's team signed up seven healthy women and five healthy men aged 25–35. On different days they each ate 100 grams of dark chocolate by itself, 100 grams of dark chocolate with a small glass of whole milk, or 200 grams of milk chocolate.

11   An hour later, those who ate dark chocolate alone had the most total antioxidants in their blood. And they had higher levels of epicatechin, a particularly healthy compound found in chocolate. The milk chocolate eaters had the lowest epicatechin levels of all.

CHOCOLATE FOR BLOOD PRESSURE: DARKER IS BETTER

12   What is it about dark chocolate? The answer is plant phenols—cocoa phenols, to be exact. These compounds are known to lower blood pressure.

13   Chocolates made in Europe are generally richer in cocoa phenols than those made in the U.S. So if you're going to try this at home, remember: Darker is better.

14   Just remember to balance the calories. A 100-gram serving of Hershey's Special Dark Chocolate Bar has 531 calories, according to the U.S. Department of Agriculture. If you ate that much raw apple you'd only take in 52 calories. But then, you'd miss out on the delicious blood pressure benefit.

15   A hint: Don't replace healthy foods with chocolate. Most people's diets have plenty of sweets. Switch those for some chocolate if you're going to try the truffle treatment. ■

Source: DeNoon, Daniel. *Dark Chocolate Has Health Benefits Not Seen in Other Varieties.* WebMD Health News.

S—Source: (Who is the owner/author? Are they qualified/biased?)

Daniel J. DeNoon is senior medical writer for WebMD, researching and reporting daily news stories and health features. He has been a medical writer since 1985. Based on his qualifications, he is a credible source.

A—Argument: (What is the author's argument/point/opinion/attitude?)

The author's argument is that dark chocolate without the added milk in the diet will provide a healthy serving of antioxidants that will lower your blood pressure.

V—Validate: (What is the evidence? Is it in context/logical/truthful?)

Studies by Dirk Taubert, MD, PhD, and colleagues at the University of Cologne, Germany showed that 100g of dark chocolate could significantly lower a person's blood pressure. Mauro Serafini, PhD, of Italy's National Institute for Food and Nutrition Research in Rome, and colleagues showed that only the dark chocolate without any milk present provided the most antioxidants in the blood in one hour after eating. The evidence is logical and in the context of a research study.

E—Evaluate: (How useful is this text to you? Will you SAVE it or toss it?)

This text provided good information backed by research to show the benefits of dark chocolate. I would SAVE the article.

3. After reading the article, what advice would you give to the woman in the picture regarding consuming the chocolate bar?

Answers will vary.

Additional Recommended Readings

Galeaz, K., & the editors of *Prevention*. (2008). *4 Weeks to Maximum Immunity: Disease-Proof Your Body*. New York, NY: Rodale Inc.

Klein, S. (2006). *The Secret Pulse of Time: Making Sense of Life's Scarcest Commodity*. New York, NY: Marlowe & Company.

Lance Armstrong Foundation. (2005). *Live Strong: Inspirational Stories from Cancer Survivors— From Diagnosis to Treatment and Beyond*. New York, NY: Broadway Books.

Schimmel, R. (2008). *Cancer on $5 a Day (Chemo Not Included): How Humor Got Me Through the Toughest Journey of My Life*. Cambridge, MA: DeCapo Press.

Theobald, D. E., Dugan, W. M. Jr., Burnett, J., Marmion, A. A., & Edgerton, S. (2002). *The Strength to Fight Cancer: A Family Guide*. Ripon, WI: The Quality of Life Foundation.

myreadinglab

For support in meeting this chapter's objectives, log on to www.myreadinglab.com and select Critical Thinking.

Appendix A
Reading Math Problems

- Have you ever been frustrated in math class?
- Do you think if you just knew what the problem was asking, you could figure it out?
- Do the words **math test** make you sweat?

If you answered "yes" to any of these questions, then this section is for you.

General Tips

- Think about how much math you do in your daily life. You probably already use it more than you realize. Knowing you already can successfully do math in many ways will build your confidence.

  Examples of everyday math: shopping and figuring out sales markdowns, calculating miles per gallon in your car, buying a car and making a car payment, tracking travel expenses, paying mortgage or rent, arranging the furniture in your apartment, investing/saving, choosing the best cell phone package, going out to eat and paying a tip.

- If you get stressed out on math tests, remember that the questions on your tests are the same type of problems that you've done before on your homework assignments. The difference with tests is that the problems have different numbers or letters. The more you practice on homework, the more confident you will be when you see the same form of the problem on the tests!

Reading Directions

- Don't hurry and start working the problem before *reading the entire question*, especially when multiple tasks are required.

  For example: The problem asks you to calculate coordinates for points on a graph from an equation, and then plot the coordinates on the graph. Be sure to calculate the coordinates, but *don't forget to plot them on the graph, too.*

- Make sure you read the entire problem! Many times the problem will ask you to set up the equation. If you read the question carefully, you might save yourself a lot of time and trouble if you don't actually need to solve it.

  Here are some problems from a college math textbook.
  Write a numerical expression for each phrase.

  a. *The product of 4 and –7, added to –12*
  When you answer this problem, look at the directions. They say to "*Write a numerical expression.*" You DO NOT need to solve the problem. Simply set it up. So,

  Write it as –12 added to the product of 4 and –7.

  . . . –12 <u>added to</u> . . . means <u>plus</u> and . . . <u>product</u> . . . means <u>times</u>

  So the answer is –12 (plus) 4 (times) (–7)

  Or, –12 + 4(–7)

  b. *The product of 12 and the difference between 9 and –8*
  Again, when you answer this problem, look at the directions. They say to "*Write a numerical expression.*" You DO NOT need to solve the problem. Simply set it up. So,

  The <u>product of</u> 12 <u>and</u> . . . means to <u>multiply</u> 12 <u>times</u> . . . .

  The <u>difference between</u> 9 and –8 means... 9 <u>minus</u> (–8)

So the answer is 12 (times) 9 (minus) (–8)

Or, 12[9 – (–8)]

Source: Lial, M., Hornsby, J., McGinnis, T., Salzman, S. A., &
Hestwood, D. L. (2010). *Developmental Mathematics: Basic Mathematics and
Algebra,* 2nd ed. New York, NY: Pearson, p. 667.

- When the problem tells you what <u>is</u> available and the question asks you what <u>isn't</u> there, don't forget to take the difference from the total.

  For example: The problem says there is a total number of viewers who watch television on a particular night. Then the problem gives the number of people who watched a certain program. The problem explains the procedure for how to calculate the percentage of viewers who watched that certain program. The question asks you what percentage of viewers <u>didn't</u> watch the program.

Knowing and Using Previous Concepts

- Make sure you study every concept you learned before a test because questions may assume you understand a basic concept taught in an earlier chapter. You may need to apply the concept you learned earlier to correctly answer the present problem.

  For example: The question uses adding polynomials (the new concept) in an application for finding all the angles of a triangle (which is the old concept—the three angles of a triangle equal 180 degrees). So, the question expects you to remember that all of the polynomials together equal 180 degrees.

Knowing Important Terms in a Word Problem

- When reading a question with multiple math operations, it is very important to determine the proper order of the operations.

  Remember the acronym **PEMDAS: P**arenthesis, **E**xponents, **M**ultiply/**D**ivide, **A**dd/**S**ubtract

- If you are someone who can successfully solve problems when given the equation, but struggle with word problems, it might be helpful to learn to recognize the important key terms or clues in the word problem.

For example: Following are words that indicate which mathematical operation you are going to perform:

- Words that mean addition: *sum, and, total, plus, in addition (to)*
- Words that mean subtraction: *difference, deduction, subtracted from, less, off*
- Words that mean multiplication: *product, times, per, multiplied by*
- Words that mean division: *difference, quotient, into, divided by*

For example: There are two ways to write a subtraction problem using the same numbers, but they will result in two different answers:

1. 25 minus 10. This is $25 - 10 = 15$

2. 25 subtracted from 10. Be careful not to write 25 minus 10 instead of the correct answer: 10 minus 25, which is (-15)

For example: Here is a problem from a college math textbook.

In the 2007 regular baseball season, the Boston Red Sox <u>won 36 less than twice as many games as they lost</u>. They played 162 regular season games. How many wins and losses did the team have? (Source: www.mlb.com)

Source: Lial, M., Hornsby, J., McGinnis, T., Salzman, S. A., & Hestwood, D. L. (2010). *Developmental Mathematics: Basic Mathematics and Algebra,* 2nd ed. New York, NY: Pearson, p. 732.

The key phrase in this word problem is that the team <u>won 36 less than twice as many games as they lost.</u> Let's pull this apart.

Wins equal 36 less than 2 times their losses.

Let's call losses L and wins W

$W = [(2 \times L) - 36]$

So, if Wins + Losses = 162 games then we need to substitute what we know.

If

W + L = 162 games total,

Then $[(2 \times L) - 36] + L = 162$ games total

Now solve the equation:

$2L - 36 + L = 162$

$3L - 36 = 162$

$\underline{+36 = +36}$

$3L + 0 = 198$

Divide by 3, then L = 66

So, if L (losses) = 66,

then W = 2L − 36

W = 2(66) − 36 = 96 so W (wins) = 96

- If the problem involves a fraction, don't develop a mental barrier. It is no harder than using whole numbers when you have to perform the same operation.

For example: Look at the following two equations:

1. $5 \times 2 = \dfrac{5 \times 5}{1 \times 1} = \dfrac{10}{1} = 10$

2. $\dfrac{5}{2} \times 2 = \dfrac{5}{2} \times \dfrac{2}{1} = \dfrac{10}{2} = 5$

Here are examples from a college math textbook. (p. 245) Directions: Solve the application problem. Write answer in lowest terms.

The Koats for Kids committee members completed 5/8 of their Web-page design in the morning and 3/8 in the afternoon. How much less did they complete in the afternoon than in the morning?

Completed 5/8 in the morning and 3/8 in the afternoon.

How much less did they complete in the afternoon than in the morning?

First we need to make an equation.

Morning completion minus afternoon completion equals?

$\dfrac{5}{8} - \dfrac{3}{8} = ?$

$\dfrac{5}{8} - \dfrac{3}{8} = \dfrac{2}{8} = \dfrac{1}{4}$ So, they completed ¼ less in the afternoon than in the morning.

(p. 333) Three brands of cornflakes are available. Brand G is priced at $2.39 for 10 ounces. Brand K is $3.99 for 20.3 ounces and Brand P is $3.39 for 16.5 ounces. You have a coupon for 50 cents off Brand P and a coupon for 60 cents off Brand G. Which cereal is the best buy based on cost per unit?

Brand G is $2.39 for 10 ounces	Brand K is $3.99 for 20.3 ounces	Brand P is $3.39 for 16.5 ounces
= $2.39 / 10 oz.	= $3.99 / 20.3 oz.	= $3.39 / 16.5 oz.
(−$0.60 coupon)		(−$0.50 coupon)
= $1.79/10 oz.		= $2.89/16.5 oz.
= $0 .179/oz.	= $0.197/oz.	= $0.175/oz.

Answer: Brand P with the 50 cents coupon is the best buy. ($3.39 – $0.50 = $2.89; $2.89 divided by 16.5 ounces is approx. $0.175 per ounce)

(p. 436) The owners of Baily and Daughters Excavating purchased four earth movers at a cost of $485,000 each. If they borrowed 80% of the total purchase price for 2½ years at 10½% interest, find the total amount due.

I = PRT
Interest = Principal × Rate × Time
They only borrowed 80% of the purchase price so $485,000 × 4 = $1,940,000 × 80% = $1,552,000
Interest = (P) $1,552,000 × (R) 10.5% × (T) 2.5 years = (I) $407,400
(P) $1,552,000 + (I) $407,400 = (Total amount due) $1,959,400

(p. 733) The world's most populous countries are China and India. As of mid-2005, the combined population of these two countries was estimated at 2.4 billion. If there were about 4/5 as many people living in India as China, what was the population of each country, to the nearest tenth of a billion? (*Source:* U.S. Census Bureau.)

To figure out this answer we first need to understand what is being given and what is being asked.

The combined population of China and India is 2.4 billion.

So, China population plus India population equals 2.4 billion.

Let's call China population = C and India population = I

So C + I = 2.4 billion

4/5 as many people living in India as China means

4/5 times the people in China = the people in India

4/5 C = I

So if C + I = 2.4 (billion).

Then C + 4/5C = 2.4 (billion).

1C + 4/5C =1 4/5C

1 4/5C = 2.4 (billion)

Divide 2.4 (billion) by 1 4/5 (or 1.8).

C = 1.3

Plug in 1.3 for C in the original equation.

1.3 + I = 2.4

2.4 – 1.3 = 1.1

Answer: China 1.3 billion; India 1.1 billion

Source: Lial, M., Hornsby, J., McGinnis, T., Salzman, S. A., & Hestwood, D. L. (2010). *Developmental Mathematics: Basic Mathematics and Algebra*, 2nd ed. New York, NY: Pearson, p. 245.

Understanding Charts and Graphs

- Be careful to not plot the standard form of an equation on a graph. You must convert the standard form to the line form.

    For example: Standard Form: $2y - 4x = 10$

    Convert: $2y - 4x = 10$

    $$\underline{ +4x = +4x}$$
    $$2y + 0 = 4x + 10$$

    Divide equation by 2

    Line Form: $y = 2x + 5$

    (Now you can put in a number for x and easily calculate the number for y)

    Don't just look at the first equation and draw the line at 10 on the y-axis with a slope of (-4) when the line actually starts at 5 on the y-axis and has a slope of $+2$.

- If the problem gives you information in a table that could be used to make a graph, the problem assumes that you can convert the data into the coordinates of x and y for the points on the graph.

The number of twin births in the United States has increased steadily in recent years. The annual number of twin births from 2000 through 2005 can be closely approximated by the linear equation

Number of twin births ⟶   ⟵ Year

$$y = 3.074x - 6029.7,$$

which relates x, the year, and y, the number of twin births in thousands. (*Source: National Vital Statistics Reports*, Vol. 56, No. 6, December 5, 2007.)

(a) Complete the table of values for the given linear equation.

x (Year)	y (Number of Twin Births, in thousands)
2000	
2002	
2005	

To find y when $x = 2000$, substitute into the equation.

$$y = 3.074x - 6029.7$$

$$y = 3.074\,(\textbf{2000}) - 6029.7 \qquad \text{Let } x = 2000.$$

$$y \approx 118 \qquad\qquad\qquad\quad \text{Use a calculator.}$$

> $\approx$ means "is approximately equal to."

This means that in 2000, there were about 118 thousand (or 118,000) twin births in the United States.

Including the results from Problem 9 at the side gives the completed table that follows.

x (Year)	y (Number of Twin Births, in thousands)
2000	118
2002	124
2005	134

We can write the results from the table of values as ordered pairs (x, y). Each year x is paired with its number of twin births y (in thousands):

$$(2000, 118), \quad (2002, 124), \quad \text{and} \quad (2005, 134).$$

(b) Graph the ordered pairs found in part (a).

The ordered pairs (2000, 118), (2002, 124), and (2005, 134) are graphed in Figure 7. This graph of ordered pairs of data is called a **scatter diagram.** Notice how the axes are labeled: x represents the year, and y represents the number of twin births in thousands. Different scales are used on the two axes. Here, each square represents one unit in the horizontal direction and 5 units in the vertical direction. Because the numbers in the first ordered pair are large, we show a break in the axes near the origin.

x (Year)	y (Number of Twin Births, in thousands)
2000	118
2002	124
2005	134

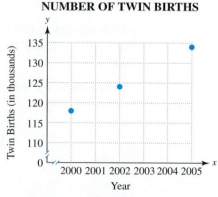

NUMBER OF TWIN BIRTHS

Figure 7

A scatter diagram enables us to tell whether two quantities are related to each other. In Figure 7, the plotted points could be connected to closely approximate a straight *line,* so the variables *x* (year) and *y* (number of twin births) have a *line*ar relationship. The increase in the number of twin births is also reflected.

Source: Lial, M., Hornsby, J., McGinnis, T., Salzman, S. A., & Hestwood, D. L. (2010). *Developmental Mathematics: Basic Mathematics and Algebra,* 2nd ed. New York, NY: Pearson, pp. 779–780.

Using Equations

- It will help you with understanding word problems in math if you take time to visualize the situation—in other words, use the written description and imagine the situation in your mind and then draw it on paper. This is especially useful with shapes.

  For example: A 70-inch board needs to be cut into three pieces—one short, one medium, and one long piece. The <u>long piece is twice the size of the medium piece</u> and the <u>short piece is 10 inches shorter than the medium piece</u>. Find the length of all the pieces.

  ** *Draw the board and the pieces as you imagine them in the space below.*

  You need to convert the short, medium, and large pieces into variations of the medium piece (*m*). The conversions would be *2m* for the long piece, *m* for the medium piece, and *m – 10* for the short piece.

  (not drawn to scale)

  Long piece = twice the   Medium piece = *m*   Short is medium less
  medium (*m*) piece = 2*m*   10 = *m* – 10

  So if the original board is 70 inches. The three pieces (short, medium and long) must equal 70 inches when added together.

Then the equation you set up is 70 inches = long + medium + short pieces

Or . . .

So . . .

$$70 \text{ inches} = 2m + m + (m - 10)$$

$$70 = 3m + (m - 10) \text{ OR } 4m - 10$$

$$\begin{array}{r} +10 \qquad\qquad\qquad +10 \\ \hline 80 \qquad = 4m \end{array}$$

Divide by 4: $20 = m$

Long piece $= 2m = 2(20) = 40$ inches
Medium piece $= m = 20$ inches
Short piece $= m - 10 = 20 - 10 = 10$ inches

- It is important to remember what the symbols mean in the equation.

  For example: The equation to find the slope of the line between two points is:

  $$m = \frac{Y_2 - Y_1}{X_2 - X_1}$$

  When the question states the two points to use in the equation [usually given as ordered pairs of (x, y)], you must remember which number is the "x" and which number is the "y" for the points. HINT: "x" always comes before "y" in the alphabet so "x" is always first in the ordered pair! ☺

Practical Practice

Have you ever asked your math instructor, "When am I ever going to use this?!"

Here is practical practice to help you apply some of the basic math principles such as adding, subtracting, multiplying, dividing, computing percentages, and using decimals.

Scenario:
You work at the local supermarket. You are currently living in a one bedroom apartment but want to move into a bigger place. Right now you work 40 hours a week at $10 per hour. Calculate if you will be able to afford a bigger place.

To calculate (or figure out) the year's income you multiply the $10 per (for every) hour times 40 hours a (for every) week. So $10 times 40 hours is $10 \times 40 = $ _$400_ every week.

Then multiply $400 every week times 50 weeks in the year. This is $400 × 50 = ___$20,000___

Divide the $20,000 by 12 months and you get $1667 per month.

Net Income
From this income, these are the percentages of taxes that are taken out:

Federal Income Taxes	10%
State and Local Income Taxes	5%
Social Security	7.5%
Unemployment/Medicare/Medicaid	2.5%
Total deductions equal	= 25%

**Calculate the taxes taken out for your salary.

Your income is ___$1667___ times 25% = ___$416.75___ = your taxes

Your income ___$1667.00___ – your taxes ___$416.75___ = net income ___$1250.25___ per month.

This is your net income.

Monthly Expenses
This is the current monthly budget. Here is a list of the categories and their monthly limits:

Rent	$450.00
Utilities	$100.00
Cell Phone	$ 40.00
Gas & Auto Repair	$150.00
Food, essentials/pets	$300.00
Savings	$ 50.00
Entertainment	$100.00

**Calculate your monthly expected expenses.

Add all the payment categories together such as Rent ($450) plus (+) Utilities ($100) plus (+), etc. List the **total of all expenses** here. _____

Answer ___$1190.00___ expenses per month

** Now calculate the monthly disposable income left after accounting for all items in the budget.

First we need to know what "disposable" income means. This means to take the **net income** and subtract or deduct (–) the **total of all expenses** (in the budget listed above). This is the income left over for you after you pay all your bills! But be careful. The net income is for the whole year (an annual income); however, the expenses are monthly.

Net monthly income _____$1250.00_____

(–) Total of all monthly expenses _____$1190.00_____

(=) Disposable monthly income _____$60.25_____

Do you have enough extra money to make a change to a bigger place to live? What other things should you consider that might affect whether or not you can afford (or should) move to a bigger location?

Many students will say that they do not have enough money to move to a bigger place. Other factors that you should consider are whether you should take in a roommate and if adjustments in your present budget would be adequate to make a move.

What variables might be considered in this equation of your decision?

For example:

- utility costs of the new place?
- transportation costs from the new place (can you take public transportation?)
- whether or not you have one or more roommates?
- whether or not you could get a higher paying job?
- get a student loan, apply for grants and scholarships

Now think about your personal finances. Change the budget above to your income and your expenses.

- Do you have a roommate to share the expenses?
- A student loan or grant to help with income?
- A higher or lower paying job to change the income?
- A different number of hours per week?
- Medical insurance?
- A car payment?
- Car insurance?
- A different cell phone bill?
- Any other difference?
- Use this scenario to help you calculate your budget.

Appendix B
Understanding Visual Rhetoric: Funny and Factual Practice

There are different types of visual rhetoric you will use as you read. In this appendix we will practice using:

- Tables
- Charts
- Line Graphs
- Bar Charts
- Maps
- Flow Charts
- Pie Charts
- Venn Diagrams

Table 1.

Population by Sex and Selected Age Groups: 2000 and 2010

(For information on confidentiality protection, nonsampling error, and definitions, see *www.census.gov/prod/cen2010/doc/sf1.pdf*)

Sex and selected age groups	2000		2010		Change, 2000 to 2010	
	Number	Percent	Number	Percent	Number	Percent
Total population	**281,421,906**	**100.0**	**308,745,538**	**100.0**	**27,323,632**	**9.7**
SEX						
Male.	138,053,563	49.1	151,781,326	49.2	13,727,763	9.9
Female.	143,368,343	50.9	156,964,212	50.8	13,595,869	9.5
SELECTED AGE GROUPS						
Under 18 years	72,293,812	25.7	74,181,467	24.0	1,887,655	2.6
Under 5 years	19,175,798	6.8	20,201,362	6.5	1,025,564	5.3
5 to 17 years	53,118,014	18.9	53,980,105	17.5	862,091	1.6
18 to 44 years	112,183,705	39.9	112,806,642	36.5	622,937	0.6
18 to 24 years	27,143,454	9.6	30,672,088	9.9	3,528,634	13.0
25 to 44 years	85,040,251	30.2	82,134,554	26.6	−2,905,697	−3.4
45 to 64 years	61,952,636	22.0	81,489,445	26.4	19,536,809	31.5
65 years and over	34,991,753	12.4	40,267,984	13.0	5,276,231	15.1
16 years and over	217,149,127	77.2	243,275,505	78.8	26,126,378	12.0
18 years and over	209,128,094	74.3	234,564,071	76.0	25,435,977	12.2
21 years and over	196,899,193	70.0	220,958,853	71.6	24,059,660	12.2
62 years and over	41,256,029	14.7	49,972,181	16.2	8,716,152	21.1

Sources: U.S. Census Bureau, *Census 2000 Summary File 1* and *2010 Census Summary File 1*.

When reading a table, always read the title for an overview. Then read the headings of the columns and rows. Think about the categories the table includes. It may help to have a straight-edged ruler to hold under a line when you are reading across information in a table to ensure you are matching the information correctly.

Directions: Use the table above to answer the questions.

1. How has the population changed from 2000 to 2010? There has been an increase of 9.7 percent or about 27.3 million more people in the U.S.

2. Which age group had the largest increase in population from 2000 to 2010? 45 to 64 years

3. What percent did that group increase in population? 31.5

4. Which age group declined? 25 to 44 years

5. What percent did they decline? 3.4

Figure 2.
Population by Age and Sex: 2000 and 2010
(For information on confidentiality protection, nonsampling error, and definitions, see *www.census.gov/prod /cen2010/doc/sf1.pdf*)

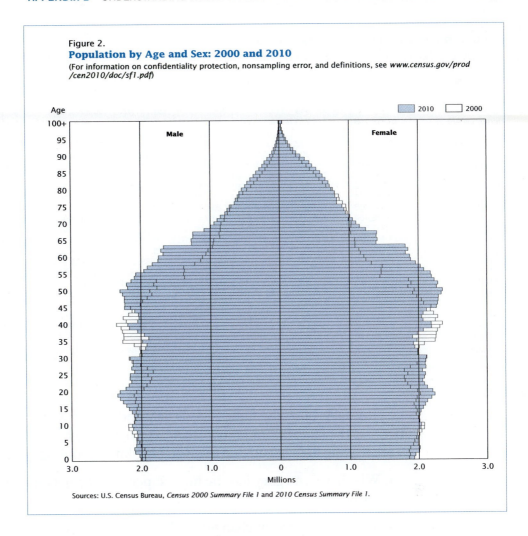

Sources: U.S. Census Bureau, *Census 2000 Summary File 1* and *2010 Census Summary File 1.*

This chart shows the number of men and women for every year rather than combining them in a group as in Table 1. The graph also allows the reader to look for trends in population by skimming the chart for wider and narrower years. Look at the legend of the map. This is the area that shows what each color means (2000 is light blue and 2010 is white). This helps the reader to see how the numbers changed in ten years.

1. How does this chart show the same information as the table?
   Answers will vary.

2. Describe trends or interesting facts you notice. Answers will vary.

Table 2.
Population by Age and Sex: 2000 and 2010
(For information on confidentiality protection, nonsampling error, and definitions, see *www.census.gov/prod/cen2010/doc/sf1.pdf*)

Age	2000			2010			Percent change, 2000 to 2010		
	Both sexes	Male	Female	Both sexes	Male	Female	Both sexes	Male	Female
All ages	**281,421,906**	**138,053,563**	**143,368,343**	**308,745,538**	**151,781,326**	**156,964,212**	**9.7**	**9.9**	**9.5**
Under 5 years	19,175,798	9,810,733	9,365,065	20,201,362	10,319,427	9,881,935	5.3	5.2	5.5
5 to 9 years	20,549,505	10,523,277	10,026,228	20,348,657	10,389,638	9,959,019	−1.0	−1.3	−0.7
10 to 14 years	20,528,072	10,520,197	10,007,875	20,677,194	10,579,862	10,097,332	0.7	0.6	0.9
15 to 19 years	20,219,890	10,391,004	9,828,886	22,040,343	11,303,666	10,736,677	9.0	8.8	9.2
20 to 24 years	18,964,001	9,687,814	9,276,187	21,585,999	11,014,176	10,571,823	13.8	13.7	14.0
25 to 29 years	19,381,336	9,798,760	9,582,576	21,101,849	10,635,591	10,466,258	8.9	8.5	9.2
30 to 34 years	20,510,388	10,321,769	10,188,619	19,962,099	9,996,500	9,965,599	−2.7	−3.2	−2.2
35 to 39 years	22,706,664	11,318,696	11,387,968	20,179,642	10,042,022	10,137,620	−11.1	−11.3	−11.0
40 to 44 years	22,441,863	11,129,102	11,312,761	20,890,964	10,393,977	10,496,987	−6.9	−6.6	−7.2
45 to 49 years	20,092,404	9,889,506	10,202,898	22,708,591	11,209,085	11,499,506	13.0	13.3	12.7
50 to 54 years	17,585,548	8,607,724	8,977,824	22,298,125	10,933,274	11,364,851	26.8	27.0	26.6
55 to 59 years	13,469,237	6,508,729	6,960,508	19,664,805	9,523,648	10,141,157	46.0	46.3	45.7
60 to 64 years	10,805,447	5,136,627	5,668,820	16,817,924	8,077,500	8,740,424	55.6	57.3	54.2
65 to 69 years	9,533,545	4,400,362	5,133,183	12,435,263	5,852,547	6,582,716	30.4	33.0	28.2
70 to 74 years	8,857,441	3,902,912	4,954,529	9,278,166	4,243,972	5,034,194	4.7	8.7	1.6
75 to 79 years	7,415,813	3,044,456	4,371,357	7,317,795	3,182,388	4,135,407	−1.3	4.5	−5.4
80 to 84 years	4,945,367	1,834,897	3,110,470	5,743,327	2,294,374	3,448,953	16.1	25.0	10.9
85 to 89 years	2,789,818	876,501	1,913,317	3,620,459	1,273,867	2,346,592	29.8	45.3	22.6
90 to 94 years	1,112,531	282,325	830,206	1,448,366	424,387	1,023,979	30.2	50.3	23.3
95 to 99 years	286,784	58,115	228,669	371,244	82,263	288,981	29.5	41.6	26.4
100 years and over ...	50,454	10,057	40,397	53,364	9,162	44,202	5.8	−8.9	9.4
Median age	35.3	34.0	36.5	37.2	35.8	38.5	(X)	(X)	(X)

(X) Not applicable

Sources: U.S. Census Bureau, *Census 2000 Summary File 1* and *2010 Census Summary File 1*.

This table takes the same Census data and groups it into five-year categories. Use the same technique of placing a straight-edged ruler under the line you are reading to help you find the matching information across that line.

1. Which age category has the highest percent change for males?
   60–64 years

2. What is the percent change? 57.3

3. Which age category has the highest percent change for females?
   60–64 years

4. What is the percent change? 54.2

5. How might knowing this information help you if you are in the field of advertising/marketing or health? Answers will vary. Some possible answers may include the age group of 60–64 may be retiring; have certain values based on their shared experiences such as the Vietnam War, Civil Rights movement, certain music, etc.; have certain medical needs other age groups do not have; may have extra time for grandchildren, etc. Also, this age group will continue to age so medical concerns and health care products may become more important.

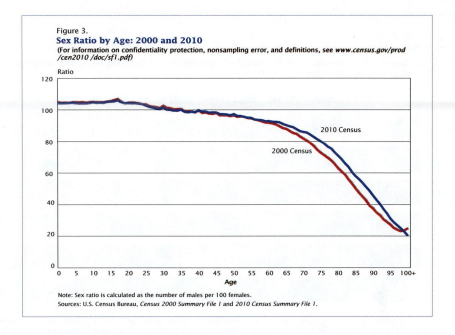

Figure 3.
Sex Ratio by Age: 2000 and 2010
(For information on confidentiality protection, nonsampling error, and definitions, see *www.census.gov/prod /cen2010 /doc/sf1.pdf*)

Note: Sex ratio is calculated as the number of males per 100 females.
Sources: U.S. Census Bureau, *Census 2000 Summary File 1* and *2010 Census Summary File 1.*

This is a line graph. When you read it, first think about the title and read any notes under the graph that give more details. Study the horizontal and vertical axis. The vertical axis shows the ratio of the number or males per 100 females. So the number 100 would mean there are the same number of males and females. If the number is greater than 100, then there are more males than females. The blue line shows numbers for the 2010 Census and the red line is for the 2000 Census.

1. What does the horizontal axis show? <u>Age</u>

2. At approximately what age is the ratio of males to females equal?
   <u>30–40 for both 2000 and 2010 Census</u>

3. What ages have more males than females? <u>Approximately 0–29</u>

4. What happens to the ratio after age 40? <u>The ratio of men per women</u>
   <u>declines and gets worse with age.</u>

5. When does the steepest decline start to happen? <u>Around age 65</u>

6. What could you infer about this trend in the population and how it might affect lifestyle choices such as living arrangements, travel and leisure? <u>Answers will vary. Possible answers include since there are fewer</u>
   <u>men, there are probably more widows. Women may choose to live more</u>
   <u>independent lives, travel, or engage in more social or volunteer activities</u>
   <u>with other women as they age.</u>

Figure 4.

Age Distribution and Median Age: 1960 to 2010

(In percent. For information on confidentiality protection, nonsampling error, and definitions, see *www.census.gov/prod/cen2010/doc/sf1.pdf*)

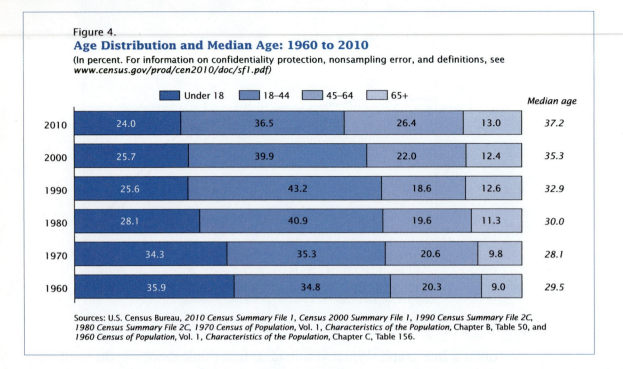

	Under 18	18–44	45–64	65+	Median age
2010	24.0	36.5	26.4	13.0	37.2
2000	25.7	39.9	22.0	12.4	35.3
1990	25.6	43.2	18.6	12.6	32.9
1980	28.1	40.9	19.6	11.3	30.0
1970	34.3	35.3	20.6	9.8	28.1
1960	35.9	34.8	20.3	9.0	29.5

Sources: U.S. Census Bureau, *2010 Census Summary File 1, Census 2000 Summary File 1, 1990 Census Summary File 2C, 1980 Census Summary File 2C, 1970 Census of Population*, Vol. 1, *Characteristics of the Population*, Chapter B, Table 50, and *1960 Census of Population*, Vol. 1, *Characteristics of the Population*, Chapter C, Table 156.

When reading a bar graph, read the title and study the legend and side bars or axis. This bar graph has four different colors stacked horizontally. The legend shows colors for different age categories. The left side of the graph shows decades and the right side of the graph shows the median age for each decade.

1. What happened with the "Under 18" category? The percent declined each decade—about 12% over 50 years.

2. What happened with the "18–44" category? The percent increased slightly each decade—about 2% over 50 years.

3. What happened with the "45–64" category? The percent increased— about 6% over 50 years.

4. What happened with the "65+" category? The percent increased— 4% over 50 years.

5. What happened to the median age for the population? It rose each decade—from 29.5 in 1960 to 37.2 in 2010.

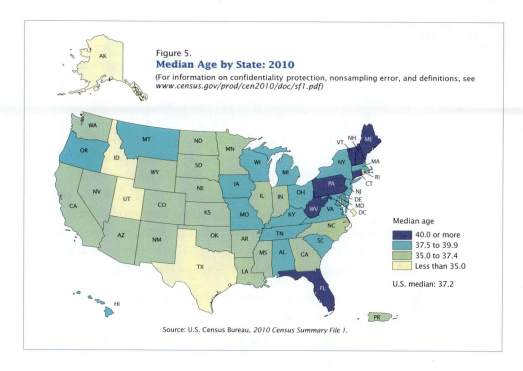

Figure 5.
Median Age by State: 2010
(For information on confidentiality protection, nonsampling error, and definitions, see
www.census.gov/prod/cen2010/doc/sf1.pdf)

Median age

- 40.0 or more
- 37.5 to 39.9
- 35.0 to 37.4
- Less than 35.0

U.S. median: 37.2

Source: U.S. Census Bureau, *2010 Census Summary File 1.*

To read a map, look at the title, the legend, and any other details. This map shows the median age by state from the 2010 Census. The legend shows different colors for age categories.

1. Which states have a median age under age 35? Alaska, Idaho, Texas, Utah, Washington D.C.

2. Which states are in categories with a median age older than the U.S. median? Alabama, Connecticut, Delaware, Florida, Hawaii, Iowa, Kentucky, Maine, Maryland, Michigan, Missouri, Montana, New Hampshire, New Jersey, New York, Ohio, Oregon, Pennsylvania, Rhode Island, South Carolina, Tennessee, Vermont, Virginia, West Virginia, Wisconsin

3. Find the state on the map where you live. What is the median age of that state? Answers will vary.

Flow Chart (funny)

Flow charts help us follow the logic of a system, concept or procedure. Before you try to comprehend the flow chart below, find the song *If I Had a Hammer* on You-tube (or a record album or CD). Use your auditory skills and listen to the lyrics. This song is a folk song by the artists, *Peter, Paul and Mary*. The song was recorded in the 1960's when many people were fighting the war in Viet Nam, battling civil rights issues, and working towards peace and unity as a nation. For years, my family often sat together around campfires and kitchen tables with our guitars and sang folk songs like this from the 1960's. My grandfathers and great uncles were WWI veterans and European immigrants escaping czars and poverty from their home countries. My father and uncles were WWII veterans fighting for democracy. My brother-in-law was a veteran from the Korean War, and my oldest brother served in the Air Force in the 1960's.

As you listen to the song and then read the flow chart below, think about the message.

What message is the writer of the flow chart trying to convey about the song? Answers will vary. _____

_____

Flow Chart of the song lyrics *If I Had a Hammer*

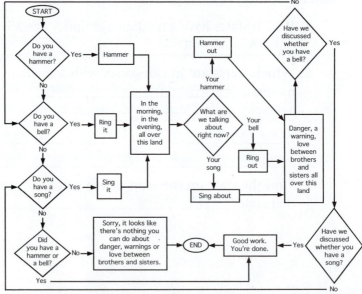

Source: Retrieved from http://www.huffingtonpost.com/2009/11/09/bonnie-tyler-rick-astley_n_350746.html?slidenumber=IZAy86hOyWw%3D&slideshow#slide_image)

Bar Charts (factual)

Education pays ...

Education pays in higher earnings and lower unemployment rates

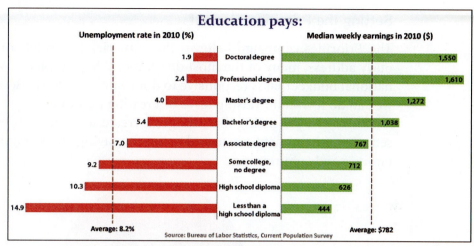

Source: U.S. Bureau of Labor Statistics. Retrieved from http://www.bls.gov/emp/
ep_chart_001.htm *Note:* Data are 2010 annual averages for persons age 25 and
over. Earnings are for full-time wage and salary workers.

The Bureau of Labor Statistics has some data on the employment status of the civilian noninstitutional population 25 years and over by educational attainment, sex, race, and Hispanic origin online. The Bureau of the Census also has some data on the educational attainment online.

The bar chart above depicts the unemployment rates and the income rates of people with different levels of education.

What can you infer from these bar charts? Answers will vary.

Some possible answers are the more education a person has on average, the less likely they will be unemployed. Another inference is the more education someone has, the higher his or her monthly income on average.

Pie Charts (funny)

The following pie chart uses satire to get the point across. Consider what point this graph is trying to make.

Setting the Priorities Straight

The Priorities campaign believes that America can solve, or start to seriously address, many of the most difficult problems we face. We can create a national budget that is responsive to domestic and international needs. And we can do it without raising taxes or creating new ones.

How? By insisting that Congress create sensible budget priorities. By reducing government waste and using the savings to strengthen American families and communities.

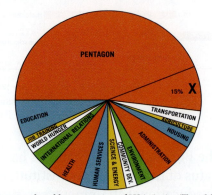

Figure reproduced by permission of USA Action/True Majority.

The pie chart above shows the federal budget divided into various amounts for purposes such as education, job training, world hunger, etc.

1. What stands out as extraordinary about the pie chart? The Pentagon budget is the largest category, using over half the money. Also, there is a large, unexplained 15% of the budget marked with an X.

2. What are the smallest pieces of the pie? Job training and Agriculture are the smallest pieces.

3. What point is this graph trying to make? Answers will vary: Over half of the budget is being spent on the military. There is 15% that is a mystery (noted by the X). The other issue being made is that the rest of the non-military concerns in the country share less than half of the federal budget. Each department gets a very small percent or piece of the overall spending.

Venn Diagram (funny)

The Venn diagram is a way of showing how two or more concepts overlap. The overlapping circles represent the things that concepts have in common.

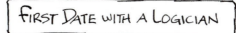

CartoonStock.com

What is the joke portrayed above? Answers will vary. _____

Draw your own Venn diagram showing what two people on a first date might include if they are trying to get to know each other.
Answers will vary.
_____

Text Credits

Chapter 1

Clark, Kim. From "For Many Jobless, It's Back to School: Reversing Course: Learn how to get in—and pay for—a good retraining program" by Kim Clark, *U.S. News & World Report* Mar 1, 2010. Vol. 147, Iss. 3, p. 66. Reproduced by permission.

Dictionary.com. Definitions of "formidable," "prestidigitation," prerequisite," "spectator," and "incredible." Reproduced by permission of Dictionary.com.

Marshall, Joseph M. "Perseverance—Wowacintanka," from *The Lakota Way* by Joseph M. Marshall, copyright © 2001 by Joseph M. Marshall III. Used by permission of Viking Penguin, a division of Penguin Group (USA) Inc.

See, Patti. "Outside In: The Life of a Commuter Student" from *Higher Learning Reading and Writing about College,* 3rd edition by Patti See. (2012), Pearson: Upper Saddle River, New Jersey. Reproduced by permission.

Chapter 2

Chapman, Gary D. *The Five Love Languages: The Secret to Love That Lasts* by Gary D. Chapman, © 1992, 1995, 2004, 2010. http://www.5lovelanguages.com/learn-the-languages/the-five-love-languages/. Reproduced by permission.

Maciones, John J. Excerpt on "McDonaldization," from *Society: The Basics*, 7th, © 2004. Printed and Electronically reproduced by permission of Pearson Education, Inc., Upper Saddle River, New Jersey.

Olds, Dori. From *With Help from a Friend*. Reproduced by permission.

Sills, Judith. (Nov/Dec 2006). "Work: When Personalities Clash." Reprinted with permission from *Psychology Today Magazine*. (Copyright © 2006 Sussex Publishers, LLC.)

Chapter 3

Baldwin, Amy. "Managing Your Time and Stress" from *The Community College Experience Plus,* 2nd, © 2010. Printed and Electronically reproduced by permission of Pearson Education, Inc., Upper Saddle River, New Jersey.

"Beat the Clock." Special Permission granted by Weekly Reader, published and copyrighted by Weekly Reader Corporation. All rights reserved.

FlyLady and Company. "Declutter 15 Minutes a Day—5 Great Tools That Make It Easy!" Reproduced by permission of FlyLady and Company, Inc.

Rowh, Mark. (Nov/Dec 2006). "Beat the Clock." *Career World,* Vol. 35, Issue 3, pp. 24–25. Special Permission granted by *Weekly Reader,* published and copyrighted by Weekly Reader Corporation. All rights reserved.

Pausch, Randy. From the book *The Last Lecture* by Randy Pausch with Jeffrey Zaslow. Copyright © 2008 Randy Pausch. Reprinted by permission of Hyperion. All Rights Reserved.

Chapter 4

Batstone, David. "How did this thing start?" and excerpt from the Thailand Project page. Reproduced by permission of Not For Sale Campaign.

CARE.org. List of items provided for people in crisis, excerpt from "Communities in Crisis," "Somalia Famine," and excerpt about violence against women. Reproduced by permission of CARE.org.

Compassion International. Statistics on child mortality rates; "Innocent Survival" from *Rock the Cradle* brochure. Copyright © 2010 by Compassion International. All rights reserved worldwide. Used by permission.

Equal Exchange. "Tragedy during trip to Uganda." Reproduced by permission of Equal Exchange, www.small-farmersbigchange.coop.

Evangelical Covenant Church. "Hindustani Church Reaching Out to Prostitutes." Reprinted by permission of the Evangelical Covenant Church.

Exodus World Service. *Current Situation in Sudan and Description of Exodus World Service Efforts in Sudan.* Reproduced with permission from Exodus World Service.

Heifer International. "From Goats to Mushrooms to a Better Life," "Reporter's Notebook: The View from Jaltenango," and "Lambs and Lemons Provide Education in Peru." Reprinted with permission from Heifer International—www.heifer.org.

Kristof, Nicholas D., and Sheryl WuDunn. *Half the Sky: Turning Oppression into Opportunity for Women Worldwide.* Copyright © 2009 by Nicholas D. Kristof and Sheryl WuDunn. Used by permission of Alfred A. Knopf, a division of Random House, Inc.

Maciones, John J., "The Extent of Poverty" from *Society: The Basics,* 7th, © 2004. Printed and Electronically reproduced by permission of Pearson Education, Inc., Upper Saddle River, New Jersey.

Not for Sale Campaign. From David Batstone: How did this thing start? and excerpts from Thailand Project page. Reproduced by permission of Not for Sale Campaign.

Peters, Marianne. From "Secondary Uses". *The Covenant Companion* April 2010. Reproduced by permission of the Evangelical Covenant Church.

Voices for Creative Nonviolence. "A Weaver's Welcome." Reproduced by permission of Voices for Creative Nonviolence.

Zydek, Heather. "Kenya by the Numbers" and "An Interview with Jenna Lee Nardella." Taken from *Relevant Nation,* edited by Heather Zydek (©, 2006, Relevant Books). Used with permission. www.relevantmediagroup.com

Chapter 5

Baldwin, Amy. Excerpts on "Pell Grants," "Work Study," and "Winning a Scholarship" from *The Community College Experience Plus,* 2nd, © 2010. Printed and Electronically reproduced by permission of Pearson Education, Inc., Upper Saddle River, New Jersey.

Ebert, Ronald J., Griffin, Ricky W., and Van Slyke, Barbara. Excerpts on "Financial Planning," "The Time Value of Money," and "The Rule of 72" from *Business Essentials,* 6th, © 2007. Printed and Electronically reproduced by permission of Pearson Education, Inc., Upper Saddle River, New Jersey.

Kirchheimer, Sid. "The FAFSA Factor" and "Don't Pay to Get Money." In *Scam-Proof Your Life: 377 Smart Ways to Protect You & Your Family from Ripoffs, Bogus Deals & Other Consumer Headaches.* © 2006 Sterling Publishing Co., Inc.

Lavine, Alan, & Liberman, Gail. From *Rags to Riches: Motivating Stories of How Ordinary People Achieved Extraordinary Wealth!* by Alan Lavine and Gail Liberman. © 2010 iUniverse.

Ulrich, Carmen Wong. "Creating and Sticking to a Master Plan" from *Generation Debt* by Carmen Wong Ulrich. Copyright © 2006 by Carmen R. Wong. By permission of Grand Central Publishing.

Weston, Elizabeth. "5 Lessons the Rich Can Teach You." Reproduced by permission of Elizabeth Weston.

Chapter 6

Chatzky, Jean. "Introduction" and "Step 5: Find the Money" from *Pay It Down! From Debt to Wealth on $10 a Day* by Jean Chatzky, copyright © 2004 by Jean Chatzky. Used by permission of Portfolio, an imprint of Penguin Group (USA) Inc.

Ebert, Ronald J., Griffin, Ricky W., & Van Slyke, Barbara. Excerpts on "Conserving Money by Controlling It," "Compounding Money Over Time," and "Making Better Use of Your Time Value" from *Business Essentials,* 6th, © 2007. Printed and Electronically reproduced by permission of Pearson Education, Inc., Upper Saddle River, New Jersey.

Ulrich, Carmen Wong. Excerpt on "Health Insurance" from *Generation Debt* by Carmen Wong Ulrich. Copyright © 2006 by Carmen R. Wong. By permission of Grand Central Publishing.

Chapter 7

Dunn, Collin. "Reduce Your Carbon Footprint by Half in Three Steps" posted on PlanetGreen.com on July 7, 2009. Courtesy of Discovery Communications, LLC.

Chapter 8

Chapter 9

Chapter 10

American Documentary Inc. Synopsis of *Food, Inc.* and user review of *Food, Inc.* Reproduced by permission of American Documentary, Inc.

Black, Keith. From *Brain Surgeon* by Keith Black, MD, with Arnold Mann. Copyright © 2009 by Keith Black, MD, and Arnold J. Mann. By permission of Grand Central Publishing.

Felberbaum, Michael. " Smoker's Corpse, Diseased Lungs Appear on Cigarette Warning Labels." Associated Press, June 21, 2011.

Gieringer, Dale. Review of Human Studies on Medical Use of Marijuana. Reproduced by permission of Dale Gieringer.

Healy, Bernadine. From "The Dangerous Art of the Tattoo" by Bernadine Healy, *U.S. News & World Report* 8/4/2008, Vol. 145, Issue 3. Reproduced by permission.

Lial, Margaret L., Hornsby, John, McGinnis, Terry, Saltzman, Stanley A., & Hestwood, Diana L., *Developmental Mathematics: Basic Mathematics and Algebra,* 2nd © 2010. Printed and Electronically reproduced by permission of Pearson Education, Inc., Upper Saddle River, New Jersey.

Morris, Charles G., & Maisto, Albert A., *Psychology: An Introduction,* 12th, © 2005. Printed and Electronically reproduced by permission of Pearson Education, Inc., Upper Saddle River, New Jersey.

Maciones, John J. Excerpt on "Being a Grown Up" from *Society: The Basics,* 7th, © 2004. Printed and Electronically reproduced by permission of Pearson Education, Inc., Upper Saddle River, New Jersey.

Nesson, Charles. *Health Concerns: What Are the Medical Dangers of Marijuana Use?* Reproduced by permission of Professor Charles Nesson, Harvard Law School.

WebMD. "Dark Chocolate Has Health Benefits Not Seen in Other Varieties." © 2003 WebMD, Inc. All rights reserved. Reproduced by permission.

Appendix A

Lial, Margaret L., Hornsby, John, McGinnis, Terry, Saltzman, Stanley A., & Hestwood, Diana L., *Developmental Mathematics: Basic Mathematics and Algebra,* 2nd (C) 2010. Printed and electronically reproduced by permission of Pearson Education, Inc., Upper Saddle River, New Jersey.

Photo Credits

Index